# Science Fiction Culture

**Feminist Cultural Studies, the Media, and Political Culture**
Series Editors

Mary Ellen Brown
Andrea Press

A complete list of books in the series
is available from the publisher.

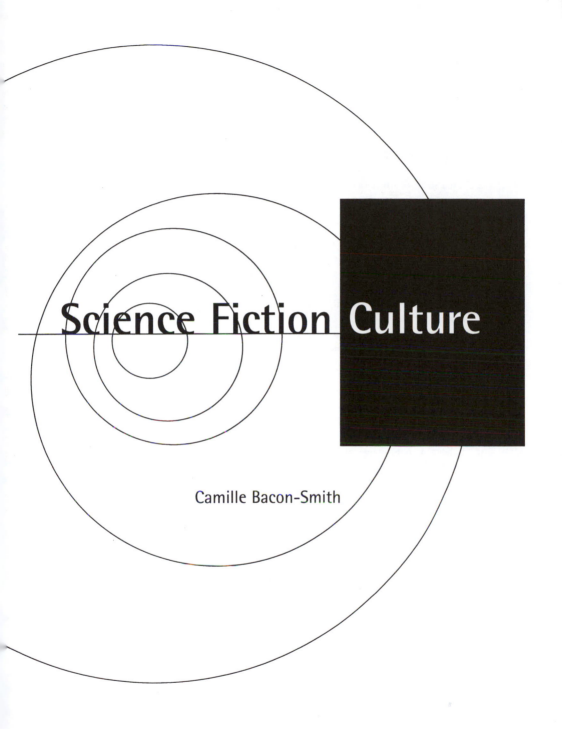

# Science Fiction Culture

Camille Bacon-Smith

University of Pennsylvania Press
Philadelphia

10 9 8 7 6 5 4 3 2 1

Published by
University of Pennsylvania Press
Philadelphia, Pennsylvania 19104-4011

Library of Congress Cataloging-in-Publication Data
Bacon-Smith, Camille.
    Science fiction culture / Camille Bacon-Smith.
        p.      cm. — (Feminist cultural studies, the media, and
    political culture)
    Includes bibliographical references and index.
    ISBN 0-8122-3223-2 (cloth : alk. paper). —
    ISBN 0-8122-1530-3 (pbk. : alk. paper)
        1. Science fiction—History and criticism.    2. Science fiction—
    Societies, etc.    3. Science fiction—Appreciation.    4. Literature
    and society.    5. Science fiction fans.    I. Title.    II. Series.
    PN3433.5.B33    1999
    809.388762—dc21                                              99-44730
                                                                    CIP

# Contents

# Introduction 1

A journalist who wants to know what the future will look like usually asks a science fiction writer. Hard science fiction, as the industry calls the subgenre most grounded in the physical sciences, looks at present science, extrapolates scientific development into the future, and then speculates on how society will reconfigure itself to cope (or not cope) with the technology that science has created. In the process, the genre often finds itself chasing its own extrapolations as they become the present reality.

C. J. Cherryh confronts the ethical issues of human cloning decades before the bioethicists and theologians of 1997 face the issue with a sheep called Dolly. William Gibson's *Neuromancer* creates the down and dirty universe of futuristic hackers in a crumbling postindustrial Japan, giving the computer-mediated communications industry a metaphor and an image. The computer nerd becomes the romantic, leather-clad hacker cowboy determined to bring the virtual world into existence. No matter how hard politicians try to rename the Internet the "Information Superhighway," they will never succeed, because science fiction writers like Gibson and Bruce Sterling don't think about it that way (no straight routes from here to there on the Net) and don't write about it that way. And it's the science fiction community that creates and popularizes the language with which we name the future.

So when the ethnographer asks the question, "What does postmodern culture look like?" the obvious place to find the answer is the science fiction community. The very name proclaims the postmodern fact of that community's existence: it is inextricable in both name and identity from the publishing industry that produces the science fiction and the audience that refuses to be passive but shapes a way of life around the celebration of a mass market commodity of the culture industry. The society of the spectacle has come home to roost, the simulacrum firmly placed at its center. In the hands of these postmodernist fiction purveyors, the simulacrum has an uncanny knack of becoming the "real" that other people must ultimately assimilate without the advance preparation the community affords its own members.[1]

There is no secret to why science fiction as a literary commodity has sustained its own postmodern culture for more than seventy-five years. From its beginning, both the fans and producers of science fiction (and its cogenres fantasy and, to some extent, horror) have placed the fiction, including fictional forms of print and visual media, at the center of a conscious effort to create the culture of the future around the *ideal* of the fiction as shared capital. Producers of the mass media live cheek by jowl with the consumers in open negotiation of community and the genre. Power shifts from position to position based on the goals and perspectives of the partici-pants and their perceptions of what the field of cultural production truly is.[2]

The community has experienced a number of dramatic upheavals that have challenged the very nature of both the community and its art forms—first in the late 1960s, when the New Wave, feminism, television science fiction, and a real-life moon landing brought whole new audiences to science fiction, and then in the mid-'80s, when groups such as women and gays, who had participated on suf-ferance, demanded equal voices. In the '90s, a new generation of young fans, propelled by conspiracy theory, cyberpunk, vampires, and computers, challenged the positivism of their elders in battles over the context of the fiction and the community itself. Each new wave of participants demanding entrance bring with them a will to change the community around their own ideas of social discourse, along with a demand for power to write the literature in accordance with the sensibilities they bring with them, and to find in the genre and in the social sphere reflections of themselves for purchase or participation.

As the class and gender and social style of participants have changed over time, so have the modes of social intercourse. The science fiction community expanded into computer-mediated social formation as early as the ARPAnet; as communities dedicated to a growing variety of genre and media interests grew up in the model of the science fiction convention, the science fiction convention was moving online, creating models that existed before the World Wide Web, even before commercial online service became available to the population at large. For a community that sustained its social connections through its own publications, fanzines, in publicly distributed texts as described in Chapter 2, the pre-Web online world created no cognitive disjuncture, but a much appreciated improvement in the speed with which the exchange of print communication could take place.

The science fiction community, including the industry that spawned and is a part of it, therefore offers a convenient laboratory for the examination of a con-stantly changing, constantly expanding, and constantly renewing social matrix taking place via increasingly complex modes of communication. Cultural capital—power—is not limited to the field of production, which must share pride of place with the field of information for the excercise of power. The established commu-nity of fans and producers must likewise come to terms with the desire of the powerless for the power, or appearance of power, that before the 1960s was held close to the patriarchal chest.

Whether or not the model described in this book becomes the way of life for the rest of us is still an open question. Not much of one, however: America Online has more than fifteen million subscribers, and, while it may be the largest service, it is by no means the only one. The number of ISPs—Internet service providers—is increasing daily, and ever-increasing millions of netizens are spending their time in the virtual reality that Gibson created in the pages of his books; many take that virtual reality to face-to-face social interaction much as the earliest science fiction community did. Clearly, however, science fiction culture, the commodity marketplace of the culture of the new, has found a way for the consumer and the consumed to create not merely a symbiotic relationship, but a fully integrated one.

Participants in the science fiction community regularly move from position to position, acting sometimes as consumer, sometimes as producer, sometimes as critic, and sometimes as community builder in the literary world that explodes the boundaries that scholars have put on roles or position-taking.[3] That is, the convention organizer may also write commercially published science fiction or fantasy books. The editor who buys the book for the science fiction division of a major press may tomorrow write for a fanzine, or write his own book, or participate in a lively online debate about the history of fan culture in the '50s. It becomes impossible to say who is immutably powerful, or in what position, in a constantly changing field of cultural production.

This book shows how power is negotiated in the postmodern society that includes the producers and consumers both of the popular culture products on which the society is based and a geographically realizable landscape for playing out its social matrix. It includes the consumers of both the industry products and the social world, as well as the successive generations of industry professionals and consumers acculturated here and often raised from childhood on its conceptual landscape. It does so by examining many facets of the community, establishing for each its position in the structure of the community and its relationship to the community in terms of the negotiation of power, and the perception of power as the observer shifts from position to position in the field.

In Part I we examine the way members of the community have recreated many common mainstream institutions, borrowing liberally from the tradition of associations and the press, business organization and the aesthetics of art, music, ritual, and theater to create a sense of place—a *conceptual* landscape—that core members carry within themselves and the community recreates—a mobile geography—on the *real* landscape somewhere in the world every weekend of the year. We will look first at the institutional practices that have structured the daily "home" life of the science fiction fan community, how it operates to create the concrete landscape of the lived community at the weekend convention, and how it has changed over time. We will examine the World Science Fiction Convention, the center of both the fan and the industry year, to see how aesthetic practices protect and reinforce the sense of a geographically concrete locus of culture and how those practices work to enculturate new members, including adults and children, fans and industry professionals. And we will look at the Internet and the changes online communication has made in the playing out of community in virtual space.

In Part II we look at certain specific changes in the demographic composition of the community and how previously marginalized special interest groups such as women, lesbian, bisexual, and gay fans and professionals and the new cybergothic young have struggled to gain their own voices in the community and the industry—that cultural capital, recognition, which Pierre Bourdieu defines as power in the culture industry.[4] In the process of gaining a voice in the community, the new special interest groups have reshaped the culture in their own image and have even created venues where their particular vision can be worked out, and where members can take shelter from the storm of controversy that surrounds any change in this community. More important for the larger culture in which the core science fiction and fantasy community resides, changes in the demographic makeup of the group have found their reflection in the changing literature, in which one will today find more women characters engaged in active, heroic roles, more characters of color, and more gay, lesbian, or transgender characters than ever before. Changes in the literature in turn influence—exert power within—the wider sphere of cultural production. Since this is a book about culture based on the creation of fiction, from time to time the content and the use the community make of that fiction becomes central to issues of the social. In those instances, the book will provide brief analyses of the fiction in question, as well as of the significance the work holds in the culture.

Finally, in Part III, we look at the institutions of production themselves, to understand how the changes in the community of the consumers have been reflected both in the process of production and in the cultural product itself. We will see how those changes reflect shifting power relations within and without the community, and how changes created by the shifting demographic makeup of the core audience, from which both authorial and publishing voices arise, have influenced the marketplace. Just as important for our purposes, we will see the effects on the genres and the community of powerful forces outside the community—including the increasing conglomeration of the publishing industry and the shift of control of that industry to Germany and England.

It is important here also to state what this book does not attempt to do. This work should not be seen as the final word on the genre community, but as the first word. I've omitted whole categories of activities, because the limitations of time and space made it impossible to include them. Role playing and other forms of gaming merit complete studies themselves, and Gary Alan Fine's *Shared Fantasies: Role Playing Games as Social Worlds*[5] still stands as the book all other such works must measure up to. The reader looking for information on media fandom is invited to look at my *Enterprising Women* for an introduction into that fan culture. Here, too, however, we are sorely in need of a new study that picks up the explosive growth of science fiction in electronic media and its impact on the community and the industry.[6] Filksinging—science fiction folksinging—and science fiction fanzines—part travelogue, part personal essay, part conversation—deserve more space than I could give them here, and I hope other scholars take up the challenge to correct these oversights with new studies that expand our knowledge of contemporary community formation.

Because this is an overview, I have likewise looked only at gross distinctions where other experts can parse much finer ones. I invite those with quibbles to take up the pen and add to our knowledge with these finer-grained studies. This is meant to be a basic text, not the great or final one. Likewise, I have not discussed method, which the reader may find in the the Methodology appendix of *Enterprising Women*.[7] That same method was followed here except in one significant area: as indicated in the notes throughout, many participants who gave interviews for this book chose to do some editing of their words for clarity and to update their positions or information. This gives the quoted material more of a written feel than such excerpts would normally have. None of the informants quoted here chose to delete any material; in fact, many added important additional information. Except within the normal standard of eliminating repetitive or irrelevant material by the use of ellipses, I did not myself alter any of the interview material.

Finally I would like to address in advance a concern I expect to hear from those outside the community under study. Many scholars have noted that the fan community is not unique but like many other communities formed around interest-based associations and therefore does not warrant a study. Science Fiction Culture may prove similar to other interest-based communities in many of its forms of contact, organization, and relationship to consumer culture. As one of the oldest, however, science fiction culture is where the forms began. The prototype for the generation-X fanzine is here, for the media e-mail list, for the mystery weekend, for the romance convention.

But science fiction culture can teach us about more than the formation of consumer cultures. When we look at the relationship between consumer and producer, between the product and its inspiration, we find that success in culture production is more likely to arise in the living rooms of dreamers than in the monoliths of urban power. And looking at the social lives of the artists and producers of science fiction, fantasy, and horror, we must abandon the romantic theory of the solitary writer bashing away at the lonely word processor in the middle of the woods. Literature is formed by consensus, not least of those who create it and who now and always share lively social connections, through which they debate the norms of their literary forms in a wide variety of forums, including the literature itself.

Most important, if our ultimate goal is to understand American culture at the millennium, we must look to what is similar among us, not only to what is different about us. It is only in the connections that we can understand the significance of the differences.

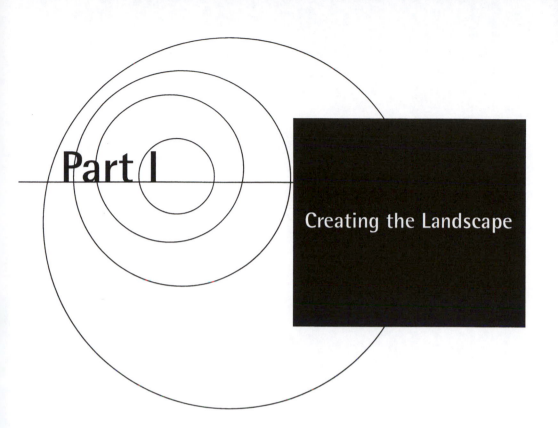

# Part I

**Creating the Landscape**

## Gernsback and Scientifiction

In 1926, when Hugo Gernsback founded *Amazing Stories*, the pulp magazine,[1] his goals included the tangible ones of profiting from the pulp explosion that was fragmenting contemporary romance fiction in the tradition of Dumas's Three Musketeers and Johnston McCulley's Zorro into various subcategories. Pulp magazine publishers divided fiction into separate publications for detective fiction, westerns (into which the McCulley Zorro stories moved after their early start in *All Story Weekly*), what is today known as romance fiction, and the fantastic.[2] Fantastic literature became "weird" literature, horrorlike fantasy as written by authors such as H. P. Lovecraft, heroic fantasy, and scientific fantasy that used technology to explain its effects, as in the galactic adventure stories of E. E. "Doc" Smith, which later came to be called science fiction. Influenced by the "cult of the engineer" prevalent in some intellectual circles at the time,[3] Gernsback turned to scientific fantasy to attract the young male readers of magazines like *Popular Mechanics*. He knew he could draw these readers to *Amazing* with reprints of the fiction of Jules Verne, H. G. Wells, and Edgar Rice Burroughs, who were writing "scientific fantasy" at the end of the nineteenth century and in the early decades of the twentieth. The science-based stories likewise served his secondary goal of promoting the study of engineering among young male readers attracted to pulp fiction. While he succeeded in drawing his target market, he missed the mark on the outcome. Gernsback's readers didn't, for the most part, want to become engineers. They wanted to be writers of the fiction published in his magazine and in those magazines that published "weird" fantastic literature.[4]

## Readers in the New Genre Ghetto

Members initially drawn to the creation of a new techno-literary community in the 1920s and '30s included in large numbers young men, and a few young women, of the falling middle class who could not meet their own expectations for success and power in the crashing economy of the '30s. The ghettoization of their genre resonated in the minds of these readers, many of whom felt a similar sense of isolation in their lives. Social reality began, for this small band of readers, to shape itself to the structure of the new pulp marketplace.

## The Inmates Take Over

In the 1930s, and more decisively in the '40s, the young people Hugo Gernsback had inspired began to fulfill the destiny of the genres of fantastic literature, most importantly science fiction. Fans such as Damon Knight, Donald Wollheim, Fred Pohl, and Virginia Kidd moved into the low-paying field of genre publishing as writers, editors, and publishers. They knew and loved the genres as no outsiders could, and they fought and struggled and supported their genre as professionals without ever giving up their ties to the fan community that had set them on their path. As fans, they shared with readers the perception of their literature as "ghettoized," and they worked to create not only a literature, but a cultural niche for themselves in which they could wield a power of their own as the creators, the apologists, of the fiction and, ultimately, as the realizers of the social universe in which the taste community of readers and producers came together. In this context, the fans who bought the books and created a face-to-face and print communication culture could exercise as much power in their milieu as the industry, which was itself made of community members.

In the following chapters, we will see how fans and industry professionals together created a shared world of the science fiction universe. While some scholars, and even some fans, would place the power in this section solely on the shoulders of the fans, we will see that the community could not have survived and thrived without the participation and active community building of the industry professionals, both as the providers of the core material around which the community has grown and as fans themselves, who work on committees and socialize using all the modes of social intercourse available to them. In the following chapters we will see how the physical landscape of the community plays out in the mobile geography of the convention calendar. We will see how new fans and new generations are socialized through personal contact, structured interactions, and ritual-like events. And we will see how the science fiction community in the age of computer-mediated communication has taken this model for communal life, developed over seventy-five years, and copied it whole as a template for online living.

# The Secret Masters of Fandom

This chapter is dedicated to Clint Bigglestone, who passed away during the early stages of this study. Clint's insights, and those of his wife and life partner Sarah Goodman, helped me to understand the complexity of putting on a Worldcon.

## The Cognitive Landscape of Conceptual Spaces

In the beginning, fans organized localized spaces—small clubs and group living arrangements—and purely conceptual space—the communication ties created through the letters to the editor pages of the science fiction magazines and through publication and dissemination of fanzines.[1] Clubs, individuals, or informal groups issued fanzines, the cheaply reproduced amateur publications containing the occasional piece of fiction but mostly gossip and chat. Editors of fanzines would critique or respond to the fanzines of other editors that they received in trade, and would likewise fill their own pages with letters from their readers responding to the comments they had published. While clubs and group houses or apartments tied fans into geographically proximate communities, science fiction fandom owes its social reality as a worldwide movement in the 1930s to the fanzines, which connected small local groups in loops of fanzine trading and open discussion carried on in the pages of the amateur publications.

Over time the best fanzines and their writers or editors developed followings as dedicated as those attached to some of the professional science fiction writers. At the World Science Fiction Convention (Worldcon) in 1992, for example, organizers honored Walt Willis, fan guest of honor from Ireland, with the Walt Willis Enchanted Duplicator[2] Miniature Golf Course, constructed in the fan display area of the main convention hall.

The course took its name from both the fan guest of honor and a hugely famous (to insiders) fan story, written by Willis and Bob Shaw, in which the naive young Jophan (Joe Fan) sets off on a Swiftian journey to find the Enchanted Duplicator that will produce the perfect fanzine. Jophan passes through the Forest of Stupidity on his way to the Mountains of Inertia, where he almost falls prey to the Letterpress Railroad (which pulls up its tracks after it to make the next forward move). He stops to talk in the Circle of Lassitude, but moves on until, after many such adventures, he arrives at the top of the Tower of Trufandom where he discovers that "THE MAGIC MIMEOGRAPH IS THE ONE WITH A TRUE FAN AT THE HANDLE."[3]

The Enchanted Duplicator is an allegory of the fan's progress through discovery of fan culture and entrance into the core of fans who participate actively in its creation via the cultural subset of fanzines. Fanzines may represent the beginning of the postmodern culture: a display of fanzines at the 1992 Worldcon began with the 1930s, but gave special emphasis to the 1950s, the period, most fans agree, when the form reached its height in importance in the community. The fanzines created a conceptual landscape out of the products of a popular culture industry to which the fans could hitch their own boundary markers. Few fanzines actually took the subject matter of science fiction, or the discussion of the books, as their own, preferring to use their publications for socializing in this new community. By 1936 fans were traveling from one city to another to gather and gossip and chat, to meet friends made in the fanzines, and to talk about the stories in the pulp magazines. The science fiction convention was born[4] and, along with it, a new form of fanzine writing: the convention report.

Over time the community has grown exponentially. In 1968, a report in the fanzine Amra complained that, at 1,000 attendees, Worldcons had become too big.[5] That number peaked at around 8,000, and has stabilized at about 5,000. The Internet has drawn millions into a world of science fiction correspondence that once numbered in the hundreds.[6] But the roots of a community whose geography exists primarily in the minds of its members were planted deep when the job was more simply done. The foundation of the science fiction community remains the relationships made through long-distance communication and the local informal groups and clubs, and conventions, described below.

## Conceptual Identity in Real Space

### Science Fiction Clubs

In 1936, a New York science fiction club decided to visit the science fiction club in Philadelphia, and those fans have since called their meeting in Philadelphia the first Worldcon. Like the fanzines, conventions bring fans and the industry together from around the world or around a region. Until the age of the internet, however, conventions always began with a local fan organization. Fan culture reflects regional distinctions that are often based on the amount, strength, and durability of the activity of the region's local organizations. Those distinctions, created within the core of the active fan community, are passed on to the wider fan community through conventions produced in each region. The convention circuit in the Northeast—Boskone in Boston, Lunacon in New York, Philcon in Philadelphia, Balticon in Baltimore, and Disclave in Washington, D.C.—is the most established in the United States. Local clubs in each of these cities have sponsored at least thirty annual conventions; Philadelphia and New York each have sponsored more than fifty.

The circuit itself developed out of a club culture that grew from a collection of small anarchic bands of would-be professionals. Those young men, raised to expectations of employment and status that the worldwide Great Depression took away,[7] created in their clubs and organizations the complexly structured hierarchical forms of the corporate middle class to which they aspired. Organizations like the Lunarians in New York and the Philadelphia Science Fiction Society in Philadelphia, both founded in the 1930s, continue to harbor a highly competitive corporate culture that today reflects the growing prosperity of the members, who are often professionals in nonliterary fields like law, accounting, marketing, or various branches of science. To an outsider, even one who works with the club members as closely as I did as an ethnographer, there sometimes seems little difference between the business and professional worlds the club members navigate during the day and their science fiction fan community.

In a series of interviews conducted in 1993, Ben Yalow, well-known fan and convention organizer, explained the activity schedule of the New England Science Fiction Association (NESFA), which sponsors Boskone each year in February:

> **Ben Yalow:**   Once a month there is a business meeting at which the club formally votes on things and discusses things and debates motions and authorizes expenditures and the committees report. And that is held on a Sunday at the beginning of the month. On a Sunday at the end of the month is . . . essentially a social get-together at somebody's house as opposed to the business meeting which is typically at the clubhouse . . . on the Wednesday after the business meeting or the other (social) meeting . . . the secretary has to get an issue of Instant Message [the club newsletter] out reporting what took place at that meeting. . . . And since we mail out 450 or 500 copies or something like that, then everybody gets together to collate and mail. So that in essence, there are structured NESFA meetings for four weeks [each month]. Of these meetings, only one is formal and businesslike, and NESFA may be unusual in the number of regularly scheduled meetings it holds. But many clubs that sponsor conventions hold at least two meetings per month, one for the general membership and one for the various convention planners to meet and discuss issues related to the annual convention.

Like its meeting schedule, the membership criteria at NESFA are complex to the point of arcane:

> **Yalow:**   NESFA has different membership classes. There are regular members who are voting members . . . full rights and privileges, etc., etc. There are inactive members who were people who were regular members, but who didn't attend enough meetings . . . to stay regular (two in any six-month period). . . . General members who show sufficient talent and interest and willingness to work and to participate in the activities of NESFA will eventually become regular. . . . And obviously some people . . . decide that they don't have the time to devote as much effort to NESFA as regular members would put in . . .

My next two questions, however, demonstrated the control that club structure exerts in the Northeast:

**Ethnographer:**    Do people ever get denied regular membership?

**Yalow:**    [hesitates] I would say that this is—I would say that this is rare. You know, I won't say that everybody will always. . . . Because it's a group with its own social dynamic and things like that, and if you're not interested in that social dynamic, then you're not going to be denied it, you're just going to decide that it's not worth banging your head against the wall, and go off and play with some other group that more suits your needs. Which makes perfect sense.

**Ethnographer:**    I've seen people who . . . really felt that if they came into this or that group and took over, things would be much better. Do you ever have that kind of problem?

**Yalow:**    Oh, every club does. Generally, if a club is well enough established with its own committed membership and things like that, then this is not a problem because a club outnumbers a person. And eventually the person will say, I really can't remake "bumpety-bump" into my own image, and go away. And generally most clubs, . . . the well-established ones with their own culture, their own dynamics, are far more tolerant of that because nobody's going to come in and turn the club.[8]

Well-established clubs show many of the characteristics of the mature corporation, outgrowing the flexibility of the entrepreneurial period and moving into rigid structures with many hierarchical levels of gates to negotiate. The mover and changer who survives the process has, in the course of acquiring power in the institution, also absorbed its traditions, rules, and bylaws, synchronizing with the organizational inertia that makes drastic change impossible. While this inertia may be frustrating to new members in times of fast change in the world and the science fiction community, it does provide a base of continuity that transcends the memory of the individual and passes the traditions from generation to generation of incoming fans. But trying to maintain that stability in the face of change can take a dramatic toll on committee members struggling to meet today's problems with yesterday's tools.

## Informal Science Fiction Communities

In the 1950s and '60s, as fan culture spread throughout the country, it carried the idea of fanzines, conventions, and fan artistic creation with it but left much of the hierarchical corporate structure of the clubs behind. Longer distances between cities, less dense populations of fans, and a less formal lifestyle led to the creation of informal science fiction communities: groups of friends who might gather on a regular basis but who did not organize along typical corporate lines for their socializing. Distances in particular led to the breakdown of the rigidly defined science fiction convention year that marked the passage, season by season, from one mid-sized Northeast convention/city to another to another. In its place, the West, Midwest, and South developed a convention year marked by fewer conventions and a more localized participation pattern. In the Northwest and South, a number of cities have smaller standing conventions; at least one regional-sized convention moves from city to city in the region each year, creating a circuit that plays out over several years.

Sarah Goodman, West Coast fan and convention organizer, discussed fandom in San Francisco:

> **Sarah Goodman:** The Bay Area fandom doesn't have a clubhouse. We don't have a central location. . . . There's a lot more independence . . . a Baycon [convention committee] needs to have a mind like a steel trap, because nobody ever puts anything in writing.[9]

In fandom on the East Coast, the corporate structure of clubs shapes the social life of a nucleus of fans involved in many different interests, including convention organizing. Many communities, however, socialize informally in organizations separate from the responsibilities of conventions. West Coast fandom has produced the Elves, Gnomes and Little Men's Science Fiction, Chowder and Marching Society, which has remained steadfastly unorganized since 1949, and Bay Area names including Marion Zimmer Bradley formed the Society for Creative Anachronism in the 1960s. SCA now has an extensive national network of local organizations divided into fiefs, baronetcies, and nations, according to historical preference and the size of the local group. SCA also holds the annual Pennsic, a two-week gathering in western Pennsylvania, where members dress in medieval garb, camp out, joust, and otherwise create a twentieth-century version of the medieval and early modern period.

The Midwest, like the Northwest, offers fans a less structured fan experience than that of the Northeast. Well-known short story writer Martha Soukup described her experience as a fan in Chicago:

> **Martha Soukup:** I pretty much started a science fiction club at my high school. And so we had our own little grassroots fandom there, with my best friend, with some other girls. We could never get any boys to join the club. . . . I subscribed to *Locus*, which at that time was a mimeographed newszine. I read about conventions, and the Worldcon was coming up in Kansas City in 1976, which was about a year away . . . so we went. And I met lots of fans. . . . And a group of fans called General Technics who are still around, and I am still kind of a General Technics hanger-on. . . . And I never was particularly good at electronics and other toys like that, but I like the techies . . . Until I moved out here [San Francisco], every New Year's . . . I went to Kalamazoo, Michigan, where Julio Pronie [lived], who still sells toy rayguns and stuff that he makes himself on his lathe in his basement for Isher Enterprises, based on, you know, named after the Ben Bova books. And [I] went to his New Year's party, which we called Ishercon, a weekend party, where people were actually sleeping in sleeping bags all over the floor.

At college in Chicago, Soukup joined the Moebius Theatre and gathered with other fans at the Thursday Night Meetings, which were structurally very different from the rules-of-order meetings of clubs like NESFA:

**Soukup:**   We had a weekly gathering called the Thursday Night Meeting, which we'd just meet at somebody's house. We called it a meeting. There were no motions. The only motion was, nearing the end of the meeting somebody would say where's Thursday next week, and somebody would say, I'll take it. And we were always, in Chicago, it was a rational thing to say, "Where is Thursday . . ."[10]

Informal organizations give fan communities greater flexibility to meet the changing needs of their participants than their club-based counterparts, but in the northeast, where much of middle-class life remains more formally structured by institutions, club culture remains strong. Even so, when it comes to convention organization, changes in the demographics of fandom and the composition of fan interests have demanded changes that the clubs have not always been able to accommodate. Out of this conflict, new venues and styles of organizing have sprung up to challenge the dominance of the club-organized convention circuit.

## The Convention: Mobile Geography on the Conceptual Landscape

### The Committee and the Hotel Industry

From a purely technical standpoint, a science fiction convention requires that a group of volunteers enter into a public commercial sphere of hotels, convention centers, printers, suppliers, and other service industries to carve out of contracts and budget a private space where the community of fandom can template its conceptual geography in real time and space. The volunteers are helped in this respect by the conformity of hospitality industry chains, which provide a physical setting that varies little from hotel to hotel, from city to city. They are often impeded in their efforts by a complete lack of comprehension on the part of the service industry about what is really going on in their space.

According to organizer Ben Yalow, part of the skill of a negotiator is recognizing and conveying to the hotel where it can expect its return. Fans, unlike other conventioneers, eat often, in unusual configurations, but drink relatively little alcohol. As Yalow explained, a savvy hotel can use this to its advantage:

I can tell them things like, . . . we have weird patterns in your coffee shops which, if you're sensitive to them, will make you a lot of money. . . . Three people sit down at a table for four. A friend joins them. Two people leave, at various times, each asking for a separate check. There are two empty seats there, two more people sit down, and then a fifth person comes in and drags a chair over and sits on the corner. . . . If the waitstaff is sensitive to that, it means it can get more business done, because you can sell empty seats at tables without waiting for the entire table to pick up and leave. It's good for them, it's more revenue, but they have to be sensitive. And I don't just talk to the sales staff, but then I go down and talk to the restaurant manager.

When Yalow talks about sensitivity here, he means that the waitstaff and management should be willing to give separate checks even at large tables, and to notice when a new customer has replaced the one who was sitting in the same chair, with the same group, just minutes before. Though facilities providers may resent it when organizers ask them to change such basic aspects of their operation as how they wait on tables, Yalow reports that those who follow the advice of the hotel liaison report satisfaction with the results after the fact.[11]

But a science fiction convention requires that a facility adapt more than just its coffee shop. As Teresa Patterson, organizer for Galaxy Fair in the Dallas–Fort Worth area, explained:

> You have to find a hotel that understands that people dress in geeky clothes and wear costumes . . . that knows their expensive restaurant is not going to be frequented except by the pros, that understands that there will be people awake and functioning and doing things all night as well as all day, because they [hotel management] are used to things that close down at night. . . . This is an extreme challenge.[12]

The science fiction community brings to the hospitality industry a set of cultural norms very different from those of an academic conference or traditional trade show. Ideas of personal space are different, and the casual shifting of eating partners in the coffee shop as described by Yalow easily translates itself to sharing hotel rooms with large numbers of friends and strangers, an ethic of personal hospitality common to many subcultures but seldom otherwise practiced at the Omni, Sheraton, or Hyatt. But hotels seem to have the most difficulty with the fan culture's concept of time. Most fans seem to rise later in the morning, eat later at night, and stay active and noisy well into the early morning. The staff at hotels unprepared for this pattern find they have a flood of complaints when food is not available at midnight while their security staff vie with the still active fans for possession of the public spaces well into the night.

### The Boskone Example: Controlling the Territory

By the early 1980s, the Worldcon population had stabilized at around 8,000 participants, but that same decade saw an explosive growth in some regional conventions. The less formal organizational structures seem to have flourished with this expanding membership base, but the changing demographics, with their changing interests and service requirements, taxed the capacity of many clubs to effectively control their events. While not the only convention to crash and burn under the pressure of changing times,[13] Boskone does demonstrate the effect that too much change in the culture can have on a group that is too rigidly structured to adapt quickly.

Since 1968, the year fandom experienced its first explosive growth, NESFA has organized Boskone, the longest-running annual convention in the Boston area. Coming into the 1980s, Boskone had a reputation for being a well-run, fun convention. By 1987, the year it crashed, Boskone was the largest regional convention in the country. At 4,500 attendees, the growing regional event threatened to overtake the stable numbers of the Worldcon, a goal some NESFA members had pursued with almost manic glee. In an interview conducted at the vastly reduced Boskone of 1993, with about 800 participants, committee member Monty Wells explained that some NESFA members had felt it was becoming the "Winter

Worldcon," and must accordingly do something for all the fan groups.[14] But Elisabeth Carey, also a Boskone committee member, pointed out that, although NESFA was trying, essentially, to put on a Worldcon-sized show every year, it was doing so without Worldcon resources or recovery time between conventions.

A Worldcon, as we shall see, draws from a worldwide pool of organizing talent. NESFA had only itself, and well before 1987 some volunteers on the convention committee were showing the strain. They complained that the convention had grown too big and was catering to too many disparate groups for them to manage.[15] The committee had added an expanded film program, even showing video programming on closed-circuit television in the hotel, and had added rooms for gamers. Most committee members saw these activities not as contributions to the primary purpose of the convention, but as "people sinks," to keep the crowds out of corridors. Many of the new participants were young and attracted to the convention for what Boskone considered its ancillary activities: video, gaming, costuming, and the like. In particular, video and gaming became the catch-22 of the convention. The committee increased the number of these events because they drew large numbers of participants out of the hallways and into the meeting rooms with a minimal staff requirement. But the presence of those activities in turn drew more attendees.

While the convention continued to grow, the rigid hierarchy of the club's organization made it difficult for new volunteers to establish themselves or make themselves known. This left the original staff and committee to handle a vastly expanded event with no additional help from the new attendees. And the new fans, generally younger, had no understanding of the etiquette of conventions or of hotels. According to Carey, most people would be accommodating when con committee members asked them to move to clear doorways and such, but they wouldn't think to do those things on their own. And the convention simply did not have enough volunteers to tell them all.

Some members were trying to put a cap on the number of people who could attend the convention, but the plan "melted down" before its proponents swayed a majority of voting members to their position. In the meantime, the growing size and changing nature of the convention made it increasingly difficult for the committee to negotiate for facilities. According to Wells, Boskone brought in about 1,500 guest rooms over the Presidents' Day weekend, a slow time of year for hotels. The fan community filled the rooms, but in a very labor-intensive way. As we have seen, very large conventions run twenty-four hours a day, and therefore require more staff at night for security, cleaning, and setup, with little expected return on extras like the bar that make a hotel profitable. As hotels developed more possibilities for filling their rooms, fan events grew less acceptable, and the task of finding any space at all became more difficult. Ben Yalow explained what happened next.

> **Yalow:**  The reason Boskone moved out of downtown Boston is very simple.
> We were thrown out. Boskone had exploded. The Boskone from hell, as we
> tend to refer to it, had between 4,000 and 4,500 warm bodies there, of
> whom, oh, maybe half knew anything or cared about science fiction in any of
> its aspects. . . . The convention was loud, noisy, caused difficulties for the

hotel, was unmanageable, and basically the hotels threw us out, . . . not only Boskone, but they threw out the Worldcon which was also scheduled to be held in Boston in that same facility. And after a great deal of negotiation, the hotel took back the Worldcon, but the hotels in downtown Boston are still fairly reluctant to take us or, for that matter, any science fiction convention. Arisia is in the Park Plaza,[16] but even so there is a great reluctance by many of the Boston properties to allow us back in. And by us, I don't just mean Boskone, I mean science fiction conventions in general.

What actually did cause the Boskone crash of 1987? For one thing, attendance exceeded the capacity of the hotel facilities by more than 1,000 participants, most of whom functioned in a state of celebratory hysteria caused by overcrowding, lack of regularly scheduled food or sleep, and an overdose of caffeine, sugar, and alcohol. At the same time, the staff and committee had not grown or changed hands in the years of Boskone's explosive growth, leaving the event with an insufficient number of people in control of overwhelming numbers. Bands of underage drinkers with open beer cans ran through the halls. Somebody turned on the fire hose in a hallway, destroying the carpeting. Pillow fights broke out in the rooms and the escaping feathers set off the fire alarms, which had to be checked by security. The convention was invited not to return the following year.

At this point, with no hotel and its committee exhausted, NESFA seriously questioned whether Boskone would survive. The club decided to cut back dramatically on the kind of activities it would support at the convention, and found a hotel in the Boston suburbs. The club discontinued its usual publicity and issued a letter to fandom explaining its new policies. Costuming was discouraged, and the convention no longer supported activities like gaming and electronic media science fiction, which appealed to the young newcomers.

Laurie Mann, 1988 convention cochair, explained that the committee had little choice in changing the convention:

> If we did not change the audience of Boskone rapidly, we would never be able to find a hotel to let us in. . . . We tried very hard to recreate Boskone as more of a convention for readers . . . we wanted to make Boskone appeal to people who saw it as more than an excuse to get drunk, trash the hotel and sit in front of a video screen for twelve hours without moving.[17]

Fandom in general took the letter announcing the convention's new limits to indicate that Boskone had developed an elitist attitude. Even young members of NESFA who were clearly part of the community took the restrictions to mean that they were no longer welcome, something the committee never intended. Looking back on the experience, Elisabeth Carey explained that discussing the changes was

> essentially a discussion between the color-blind and the tone-deaf. Some of the fans who felt excluded by our changes very often simply could not step back and get enough perspective on what many hall costumes look like to the outsiders [both hotel staff and mundane hotel guests] who are sharing the hotel with us. . . . They couldn't see why the paramilitary costume and the Trek costume got different reactions. That's the color-blind part. The

"tone-deaf" part is that many members of NESFA read that letter that was sent out announcing the changes, studied the language, tweaked it for clarity and information value—and thought it sounded just fine. . . . We were *very surprised* that not everyone understood what we meant, that we'd offended a lot of people whom we valued. It took anywhere from months to years for individual members to be able to read that letter and see what was wrong with the tone of it . . . I think the tone-deafness was a product of the trauma of "The Boskone From Hell" and getting thrown out of Boston, but . . . we caused ourselves a lot of additional trouble.[18]

Some members of NESFA and other unaffiliated convention fans in the Boston area formed Arisia, a new convention to provide a younger, fan-friendly venue that also welcomed costumers, gamers, and other groups shut out of Boskone by its new policies. Boskone's numbers dropped more dramatically than expected, and when I attended in 1993 it appeared to be a business convention, more important to New York publishing insiders than to fans.[19] According to Carey, this emphasis on the business of science fiction publishing has continued, and NESFA has become, in addition to an active fan organization, an aggressive small press devoted in particular to returning the classics of the genre to print.[20]

### The Significance of Boskone 1987

Boskone was the first convention in the Northeast to self-destruct in such a major way, but it hasn't been the last, and some clubs have protected themselves by limiting the growth of their conventions in a variety of ways. But the Lunarians in New York have lost members, and moving Lunacon to the suburbs to avoid problems with younger fans such as those experienced by Boskone has resulted in a stable but aging convention population. Philcon, at a hotel nearer to the convention's parent city than the conventions of either Boston or New York, has continued to support gaming and costume, but provides only minimal support to electronic media or written fantasy. All these conventions have discouraged to some extent the attendance of young fans in the gothic or cyberpunk subcultures, while clubs in the Baltimore and D.C. area have struggled to accommodate the growth of new and younger fan groups at their conventions.[21]

All these organizations suffer from a club hierarchy that imposes a corporate structure onto the core organizing segment of the community. Power and prestige accrue to those who come into positions in the hierarchy after they have been vetted by club members and enculturated into the hierarchical club culture. This is, of course, typical of most traditional clubs and associations, and it serves the purpose of providing its most active members with prestige in exchange for work. For club members who come to the science fiction community from positions of economic success in the mainstream, this model offers a structure and system of rewards that replicates the outside, but places them at a higher level on the ladder of prestige than they can hope to experience elsewhere. For club members who experience less success on the outside, the club hierarchy may provide the only prestige they have.

Unfortunately, this structure doesn't work well in a period of rapid change, particularly when that change is away from displays of prestige and upward mobility. Young fans coming to the Rotary-style science fiction club often feel out of place and unwelcome. In an ethos born in an age of downsizing and loss of status, they may spurn the entire value system that rewards work with prestige and access to the industry professionals who represent greater prestige still. And, unsure of their welcome, they often wait in vain to be asked to offer the help they would freely give in exchange for that show of acceptance.

Conventions like Arisia in Massachusetts, by contrast, have their own committees and organization separate from club culture, although many members of the Arisia committee are also NESFA members. Working outside the club structure gives the key organizers on the committee far more control over the convention than they would have if they were limited to the requirements of votes and majority rule. Arisia is like a number of the newer conventions springing up in the 1980s to accommodate the new fan sensibility and the new fan interests. In a telephone interview, Ed Kramer, who heads the organization of Atlanta's Dragon Con, the largest science fiction convention in the country,[22] explained how his organization operates:

> **Ed Kramer:** When we started the convention, the only thing that a lot of the people who worked with the convention were familiar with in Atlanta was a convention then twenty-two years ago, called the Atlanta Fantasy Fair. . . .
>
> There were seven of us, all who are still actively involved in the convention, and four of us make up the actual corporate board of directors. . . . We don't go over corporate material, like for instance, budgets and things . . . [with the fifty-four area directors]. That is basically a four-person board that handles that. . . . Our area directors are basically responsible for running the convention. And a lot of the more mundane elements are really something that they're not interested in.[23]

Kramer and his colleagues had seen the decision-making on major issues of convention policy taken out of the hands of Fantasy Fair's founders by members of the committee who were able to sway a voting base. They voted their founders out and ultimately, year by year, saw the convention diminish until it was no more. When they came together to put on Dragon Con, they knew they wanted to keep those decisions locked organizationally in their hands. Since the structure Kramer designed did not require a voting majority for most decisions, area directors were likewise given more autonomy to run their departments.

> **Kramer:** At our area directors' meetings, I don't think we've ever taken a vote. I mean, if it's dealing with things like pricing, the corporate board determines what the price is. The area director who is running security, for example, has no business determining what the at-the-door rate is. That's not their area of responsibility or expertise. The person who handles our finances is Pat Henry, who owns five stores in Atlanta. He has an MBA, and does an incredible job of accounting and finances. . . . He'll never let me spend money to the point where we don't go in the black.

Kramer reduces the likelihood of burnout in his committee by limiting the scope of the area director's responsibilities (they do not vote outside their areas). At the same time he broadens their authority within their area—(they do not have to submit their plan for approval to the other area directors, who might have more opinions than expertise. What we see in Kramer's organization is not a turning away from a business model of corporate structure, but a more modern '90s model that allows for streamlined decision-making and greater autonomy within divisional boundaries.

While a convention that has been a mainstay of the new fan community for almost ten years might seem to be a well-established institution, Ben Yalow reminds us that conventions such as Arisia and Dragon Con have not yet met the test of science fiction fandom time as have conventions with thirty to fifty years of history behind them. Will they survive the loss of their mobilizing personalities through age, infirmity, or a decline in enthusiasm? Or will the ways fans and the industry organize their face-to-face community continue to change as the long-distance community has done in its move from fanzines to the Net? So far, these conventions seem healthy and strong, but, as Yalow points out, they have not yet passed the most hazardous test: the move from counterculture to culture, from charismatic leader to institution able to go on without that leader.

### The (Nonexistent) Permanent Floating Worldcon Committee

Unlike most regional or local conventions, Worldcons redefine time, space, and the personal identity of participants for an entire convention center, while bringing millions of dollars into both the local economy of the convention city and its own mobile economy. Ben Yalow supplied a few numbers on MagiCon, the 1992 Worldcon in Orlando, Florida:

> Hotel rooms are about three-quarters of a million dollars. We used up over 10,000 room nights. . . . Total food/drink typically averages about $100 for the weekend per person, so add another $600,000. The airfare . . . is probably also in the $6–800,000 [range]. So you are looking at a total of about $2 million, plus what the con spends—our total budget was about a half a million or so—so a total of $2.5 million is a good low estimate.

Yalow calls this a low estimate because some participants, particularly publishing professionals, may spend a great deal more than the estimated $100 on entertainment, food, and drink over the weekend. The numbers likewise do not include the community's own industries that buy and sell everything from jewelry to chain mail to rare books in the dealers' room, nor do they include spending and income generated through the sale of art in the art show and auction. These latter two categories, while significant to the specific economies that support them, do not necessarily leave a financial impact on the community in which the convention is held.

But fan culture requires more than outside resources to produce a convention: it requires a large pool of experienced volunteer organizers. At MagiCon, for example, Philadelphian Darrell Schweitzer greeted conventioneers at the door of "Meet the Pros." Schweitzer, long-time fan and science fiction editor, reviewer, and writer, regularly cochairs the programming committee for Philcon. Laurie Mann, from Boston, handled Press Relations, and Ben Yalow, from New York, negotiated the contracts for the facilities. While chair Joe Siclari and convention vice-chair Becky Thompson lived in Florida, only Thompson lived near the convention city of Orlando, and Tom Veal, third cochair during the bid, lived in Washington, D.C. Melanie Herz, Dave Ratti, Tony Parker, and Judy Beamis from the Boca Raton area also participated in the local bid for MagiCon.[24]

Most of the above people, and a good many more, belong to the "totally apocryphal, nonexistent permanent floating Worldcon committee." This group, whose unstated membership is nonetheless fairly well known to its members, comprises what has been dubbed the SMOFs, the ironic, if sometimes bitterly applied, term "Secret Masters of Fandom." According to Laurie Mann, the term originated with fanzine fans. But, as Ben Yalow explained:

> As with so much of fanspeak, the term SMOF has transmuted many, many times. The term SMOF used to carry heavy ironic overtones, and was never taken seriously. Nowadays . . . people who came in not familiar with the history started taking it seriously and now it's . . . lost all its ironic overtones. It's now taken very seriously. . . . One of the key elements of it was that when it was taken seriously, it was always bestowed, it was never self-proclaimed. Again, that isn't true anymore. So the term has undergone that kind of change also, and at some level now means anybody who works on a convention, just about, will proclaim, "Hi, I'm a SMOF now."[25]

SMOFs may start in any of the fan activities available in the community. Peggy Rae Pavlat, a second-generation SMOF, attended her first convention in 1956 with her parents, well-known Philadelphia fans of the 1940s and '50s. Although Peggy worked at conventions in Philadelphia during the '60s and '70s, she divided her time between convention activity, fanzine activity, and attending the filksinging. She says in an electronic interview, "For the last ten years or so, however, I've been fascinated with the mosaic of creating a science fiction convention from the resources within fandom."

Like many SMOFs, Peggy developed her expertise helping out at local conventions and as a volunteer at major venues:

> **Peggy Rae Pavlat:** My experience working on conventions began with Philcons back in the 1950s when I would help with registration or whatever for several hours during any convention. When I went to my first Worldcon, Pittcon in 1960, it was natural to help in the art show.[26]

She moved to positions of greater responsibility as time, experience, and the needs of the convention dictated.

To augment the on-the-job experience they gain at conventions, today's SMOFs even have their own convention. SMOFcon meets once or twice a year to discuss the latest developments in tax law, contract negotiation, and other subjects more generally associated with professional rather than social organizations.

Commonly, as this excerpt from a group interview at Balticon in 1985 shows, each SMOF will develop a particular expertise that he or she will offer to the conventions in their circuit.

**Voice 1:**   There are certain people who have specialized in certain areas where they have become experts at them. And in effect, can do their work in almost any situation because they have become so good at it they are just dealing with the new environment, not actually functioning differently. The dealer's room is my specialty.

**Voice 2:**   Operations is my specialty, although this year I'm going with programming.

**Voice 3:**   And Marty's masquerade.[27]

Some convention organizers develop their specialization out of personal interest or at the need of their committees, but others see a lack where others do not and move to fill it. Samanda Jeude is such a fan, and Electrical Eggs is her contribution to fan culture.

## Electrical Eggs: A SMOF's Story

As an infant, Samanda Jeude suffered a severe case of polio that led to years of surgery and "working through the pain" to achieve her goal of independence. Jeude says:

> When I was seven . . . I overheard my parents talking with the doctor . . . this was in 1959 . . . and the doctor said, well, let's be realistic. No man is going to want to marry her, her body is twisted, it's distorted, it's ugly. She will never reach thirty, she will probably be on a body board by the time she would be in high school.[28]

Jeude fought hard to prove her doctor wrong, but he was not the last obstacle in her struggle for independence.

> When I hit my teens, we moved to a town where they had a tendency to lock away anyone who had any kind of disability. . . . So, until I got into fandom, I was accustomed to anyone coming up to me and saying, "I've heard of you," and spit in my face.

Things began looking up in college. She was reading science fiction—by the bale, she says—and fandom found her.

> [S]omebody said, why don't you come to a con with us. OK, fine, I'll go to a con with you. What's to lose? This was back in the good old days when you could get in for five bucks. . . . I think there were fifteen of us in the room. We walked into what was Rivercon I.
>
> My favorite author was Thomas Burnett Swann . . . I almost literally bumped into Swann. And being very intelligent, and very articulate, I immediately said, "Mr. Swann, ummn, uhh, umm, ur." And he said, "How nice to meet you. Oh, I see your name is Samanda, what a pretty name." Sat me down and talked with me for half an hour. This was my first convention. And this guy, at the time, was dying of skin cancer. I didn't know that; he did. He

was very gentle, he was very kind. He made me feel as though *he* had had his day made better by my presence.

Jeude continued to attend conventions and found, to her surprise, that people remembered her, and liked her for who she was rather than feared her disabilities. And through fandom she proved that long-ago doctor wrong on all counts: Jeude married Donald Cook and moved to Atlanta, where the couple worked on the four-year process of bidding for and holding the Atlanta Worldcon of 1986.

But her physical condition had begun to deteriorate. In 1984, at a symposium of doctors treating polio survivors, she discovered that her condition was not unique, and even had a name: post-polio syndrome. Still, Jeude refused to let her disability stop her:

> I got thrown into a [motorized] three-wheeler. And three weeks later we went to Rivercon . . . and everybody who saw me said, "Oh, we are glad to see you, you look great." A couple of total strangers came up to me and said, "Gee, you are as gorgeous as everybody told me." Total bullshit. And it suddenly began to sink in on me that this was a good thing. I wouldn't be able to walk at conventions anymore, but I could go to them again. . . .
>
> And about that time I met Esther Breslau. And Esther is also a polio survivor, but at this point she doesn't have the syndrome. And we both were really ticked off that Baltimore [Constellation, the 1983 Worldcon] was trying their best and it was impossible to get around. So we started thinking about it [services for the handicapped at conventions] in '84. . . . In '85 . . . we did up some guidelines and Esther tried out the guidelines at Chilicon, which was the NASFIC.[29] . . . We tested it at Confederation [Worldcon 1986] . . . and they gave us money to start up Electrical Eggs. And the name came because I was trying to tell somebody about my new electric legs, and I had the hiccups. Don said, "Great." Eggs are one of the strongest structures in nature, and yet it is very fragile. Perfect name for the organization.

Electrical Eggs, which began to provide services for the handicapped at Worldcons, later expanded to provide those services at some regional conventions as well. According to Marcia McCoy, Electrical Eggs member and coordinator of handicapped services for the MagiCon convention committee, those services include sensitizing committees to simple requirements of courtesy as well as meeting more concrete needs:

> A large number of visually impaired people have some residual vision and if you can put them very close to the stage they can really appreciate more of the program. . . . A lot of the hearing impaired are very good speech readers, and we try to put them where they can see the people who talk on stage at the con.

For MagiCon, matters of consideration included arrangements for the blind to "braille" the costumes at the masquerade, and for people in wheelchairs or three-wheeled carts to use service elevators so that they did not have to wait in large crowds for overtaxed general elevators. According to McCoy, Electrical Eggs also provides special services, including wheelchairs and three-wheeled motorized carts, program books in Braille and large print for the visually impaired, and American Sign Language interpreters for the hearing-impaired.

Handicapped access is just one way that community members see a need and meet it to take care of each other. As Jeude explained:

> A long time ago, when I was writing, I told Gordy Dickson I wanted to pay him back for all the enjoyment I'd had from his books, and Gordy's response was, "Never pay back in fandom, pay forward. Don't thank me, thank the people who are going to come into your life you're going to like . . . " So I figured, Eggs was my way of paying forward.

In the process of paying forward, a woman whose life doctors wrote off when she was seven has achieved status and prestige in her science fiction community. In doing so, she has made life better for that community.

## Confrancisco: The Style Wars

According to Ben Yalow, a Worldcon requires the work and expertise of about two-thirds of all the dedicated convention organizers in the country, a statement supported by the lists of hundreds of convention workers supplied in each Worldcon program book. While they scoff to a certain extent at the terms like "Secret Masters of Fandom" and the "Permanent Floating Worldcon Committee," these organizers do represent a pool of experience in putting together a Worldcon. Many of them come out of the hierarchical structures of the science fiction clubs of the northeast and Los Angeles.

MagiCon provides an example of a convention in which the participation of the national organizers came together to provide a well-run convention. ConFrancisco, the Worldcon that succeeded MagiCon, gives us a case study in what happens when regional organizational styles and the dominant East Coast hierarchy model of the Permanent Floating Worldcon Committee collide.

It is important to point out here that ConFrancisco was a successful Worldcon. Although all committees may not have functioned as smoothly as some participants might have liked, the convention drew the usual number of members for a convention held within the continental United States; it offered the usual number of panels and panelists, events, and standing displays. For the convention organizers, both local and national, however, ConFrancisco became a battleground of misunderstandings, hurt feelings, and pride gone awry in a power struggle that was at times subtle and at other times blatant.

As we saw above, the San Francisco fan community does not maintain a standing convention organizing structure, but depends instead on its chair to know the traditions and direct the show. Because of this informal way of doing things, they had not worked with the SMOF community on any regular basis and had no well-seasoned SMOFs on their committee. In addition to these drawbacks, extraordinary difficulties beset the ConFrancisco bid committee from its beginning. According to committee members Sarah Goodman and Clint Bigglestone, the original chair of the bid withdrew when she realized other commitments made it impossible for her to serve effectively. She appointed a successor who quickly left the bid, a casualty of personality clashes within the organization. Susan Stone, who followed, led the bid until her untimely death. Sarah Goodman describes what happened:

> I got a call saying Sue just died. . . . She had some kind of an aneurysm, I believe. And, she had a headache and she went into the Kaiser and she was in the emergency room waiting and she put her head down on her husband's shoulder and she never woke up again.
>
> We appointed . . . Terry Biffel. . . . He had been secretary, and he changed his title to secretary general so that Sue would remain the [titular] chair of the winning bid.

While the local ConFrancisco committee rocked under the loss of three bid chairs, one from sudden death, the "Permanent Floating Worldcon Committee" worried and waited to be asked for their help. Their concern reached a peak when they discovered that the bid had lost one of the two anchor hotels but had not reported that loss in its literature to the voting Worldcon members. A group of Permanent Floating organizers established a write-in bid for Hawaii, assuming that either the bid would issue a wake-up call to the bidding cities, or it would win, in which case they had the expertise actually to put together a reasonable convention without a local committee. For the San Francisco bid committee, the write-in came uncomfortably close to actually winning the bid.[30]

Unfortunately, while national convention organizers used the ploy of a write-in campaign to call attention to the skills going begging, the ConFrancisco committee read the write-in as an effort to take the bid, rather than as a bid for attention:

> **Goodman:**  These SMOFs, so defined . . . thought, oh, my God, the thing is really going down, and we'll wind up with no Worldcon. They came up with the Hawaii bid. The stated intent of the Hawaii bid, that was told to us by three different people who were involved in it, was either we'll give one of these big committees a kick in the pants and they'll get off their ass and get together, or we will at least have some kind of default plan in place. I honestly believe that this was the intention . . . [but] this was not helped by Ben Yalow saying something which was misinterpreted. . . . Somebody said . . . how will you run a Hawaii bid with nobody out there, and he [Yalow] said something that translated out to "It's easy. The same people who always run it. We just won't be bothered by the local yokels."
>
> What he meant, and again, I believe Ben when he tells me this kind of thing, was, "We always pull people together from all around to run it . . . and at least we won't have to deal with . . . the nonfans who have been invading more and more conventions. However, when you are accused of being a local yokel, you don't usually go back to the source and find out.

This explanation seems a bit ingenuous, of course. Whether one accepts the definition of "nonfan" that Yalow uses, it is clear that those convention-goers were not part of any organizing committee for the 1993 Worldcon. So it is not surprising that regional organizers took the comments amiss. As committee member Clint Bigglestone explained, "Some things were said which were . . . not intended in this light, but in many cases were read 'Hi, I'm a major SMOF. You may kiss my ring.' "[31]

While it appears on the surface to be a clash with the arrogance that gave the term Secret Masters of Fandom its acid bite in the first place, what we actually see is two very different styles of fan organization meeting and the resulting breakdown of communication:

> **Goodman:**   There was also a cultural difference. In Northern California local fandom, the way you get on a committee . . . is you come to people and you say, "I'd like to do such and such."

> **Bigglestone:**   There was no comprehension on the part of the people from the rest of the country that this is how things were done locally, and . . . there was not a whole lot of comprehension on the part of the people here that this would be looked at askance by people in other parts of the country.

> **Goodman:**   So there were people [local organizers] here who were going, "Well, those snobs, they're not interested in working on our convention," and . . . the next phone call [from a national organizer] was, "Well, you don't want me!"

A few highly expert con organizers, like Peggy Rae Pavlat from Boston and Bobbie Armbruster from Los Angeles, volunteered their services. But most of the national teams waited with growing impatience and rancor for the ConFrancisco committee to ask them to help, while the committee waited with growing resentment for the assistance of the experts who, it seemed, stood aloof only to tear down the hard work of the committee. The Permanent Floating organizers, accustomed to competing during the bidding period and working together afterward, believed the committee would ask for their help when they won the bid. But the committee was rocked again by tragedy:

> **Goodman:**   He [Terry Biffel] had come back from the Hague [site of Con-Fiction, the 1990 Worldcon, where ConFrancisco won the Worldcon bid] with what sounded like a very bad sore throat which never went away. Turned out that he had lung and throat cancer. . . . So we lost him about eight months . . . into the con [preparation period].

With the loss of yet another key leader, and still hurt and insulted by what they saw as unfair denigration of their efforts, the committee did their best with the help of fewer SMOFs in generally lower positions than those worthies were accustomed to filling.

Nor were the conflicts ended when Permanent Floating organizers did join the committee. Again, the regional cultural differences described earlier led to misunderstandings.

> **Goodman:**   Many of the groups that run Worldcons are club-based and there's a corporate culture and it varies from bid to bid. . . . [I]f some percentage, and I'm not sure what the magic number is, but 60 or 70 percent of your people already do it the NESFA way or the SciFi[32] way . . . then as people

come in you stand a half chance of enculturating them and finding them on the same wavelength you are . . . [but] there really isn't a ConFrancisco way of doing things. We do not really have an overriding corporate culture. We do not, did not come out of a club. As a group we have *not* done a lot of things together before this.

So, along with the hurt feelings that lingered from the bidding process and the devastating loss of their convention chair, committee members found themselves competing for the organizational model on which the convention would be fashioned. ConFrancisco never really cohered as a satisfying or pleasing experience for the convention organizers. Some activities may have suffered from the miscommunication brought about by the divergent organizing styles. As noted above, however, for the most part the paying customers—the majority of attendees who pay their membership fee and treat the convention as a combination of spectacle and gathering place for friends—saw little difference between ConFrancisco and any other Worldcon held in the continental United States.[33]

## Conclusion

In this chapter we have looked at the different ways that fans construct a sense of place in which to enact community. We have seen that how they construct that community life depends on the definition of fandom each uses to define the limits of the community. For some fans, such as Ben Yalow, fandom is based primarily in the books, the clubs, and the fanzines and rests on the complementarity of professional and amateur interests.[34] For others, among them Atlanta convention organizer Ed Kramer, fandom encompasses more:

> **Ed Kramer:** [Y]ou have to include all facets of science fiction and fantasy. You also have to include all the modalities in which you see them, which is not only in books, but you also see them in graphic novels, which are pronounced "comix" by people, you see them in computer games, you see them in movies. There's a whole category for the Hugos, for dramatic presentation.[35]

Even among members of the community who agree on its boundaries, differences in organizing styles lead to different concepts of community, which in times of rapid and sweeping change can lead to the kind of miscommunication that creates a poorly realized cognitive landscape of the community's mobile geography. Here we have looked primarily at the organizers and their organizations. In the chapter that follows we will look at their product—the convention itself—and how it socializes participants who bring to the experience widely divergent ideas of the community and the meaning of the convention.

# Worldcon: Mobile Geography in Real Time

3

Since their growth in the 1960s, science fiction conventions have held pride of place in the construction of the science fiction community for a variety of reasons. Conventions establish a concrete space on the template of the conceptual landscape of the community—the mobile geography in which, over a series of long weekends, community life plays out in real time. Industry professionals—writers, editors, and publishing executives—come back to nurture their roots or to find their place in a newly won social stratum. Fans and amateurs come back to celebrate not just the art of the genre, but the art of appreciation as well. And in its rituals they remind themselves that they are all one small town in which the local boy or girl from the fan side of the tracks can make good—write the books, receive the accolades, and help shape the reality that is the business and the metaphor that is the future.

At the same time, the convention space serves as a contemporary version of the Renaissance memory theater,[1] from which participants take away the renewed lived reality of the community as a memory to shape their participation over time and space in a community that is growing increasingly dispersed geographically as it encompasses more powerful distance communication systems.

Fans grow up to be organizers, amateur creators, and industry professionals. They raise their children here to continue in the tradition. Outsiders come here to learn the trade, or just to share in their love of the books that others produce. Movements in the literature are sanctioned or dismissed; the industry returns home with its mission reified and its direction clarified.

For the convention to succeed as a concrete realization of the conceptual space of the community, it needs to protect itself from attacks on the altered reality it creates. The world outside the conceptual community can impinge on the real space of the convention, destroying the *sense* of the real carefully nurtured inside it. To create that sense of the real together, convention-goers must establish and maintain powerful boundaries between their own centers of activity and the regular business of the hotel and surrounds.

At the same time, the boundaries must be sufficiently permeable that new members, drawn to the convention through friends, the commercial publications, or local human interest stories on the news, can reach the loci of enculturation within the convention space. And within the space the convention boundaries protect, the community must establish and reaffirm its corporate identity and community life through a series of events and rituals that draw together the vying interests of the members and reify their common center. This chapter will look at the World Science Fiction Convention to analyze how three issues of convention geography—boundary maintenance, enculturation, and rituals of solidarity and identity—pull the disparate meanings of the convention together.

## The Organization of Meaning

Worldcons, with their particular organizational problems, highlight the fact that in one venue the science fiction convention functions with distinct and sometimes overlapping meanings. J. Steven and Chris York, longtime fans from the Northwest region and more recently involved in the science fiction industry as editors and writers, explained some of the conflicts intrinsic to the convention milieu:

> **J. Steven York:**   At most conventions there is a certain amount of business that goes on between pros . . . but they are also there really to hit the fans and promote the books and to talk with their audience and get some feedback. At the Worldcon, I would say 90, maybe 100 percent of the pros who are here really don't care much about that. They are here to do business: to go to the publishers' parties, to talk to the agents, talk to the publishers, make deals, strike up new relationships. They are here for business, and they are treating this like a business convention. Meanwhile there's this entire fan convention—this enormous fan convention—going on underneath this or on top of it or something, but it is a total stratification.[2]

At a Worldcon like MagiCon, with 8,000 attendees, 1,000 may be professionals and around 7,000 will be fans who are not involved in the industry. But the fan convention itself harbors at least two concepts of space. First, for core fan participants it is a mobile geography of community life in which social ties are renewed, weddings are scheduled, children are reared, and, in some cases a livelihood is earned. This group is divided into at least four factions, each with its own competing interests. Two of these are

• Those for whom convention work—organizing or selling at conventions—forms their primary social identity.

• Those who find their fannish identity in the support and maintenance of fandom as a source of history-based traditions.

These two groups overlap a great deal. Ironically, while they see themselves as at the center of fannish culture, their community activities seldom have anything to do with the actual literature around which their community is based. Two further subsets of "true fans" include:

• Those who form their primary fan identity around a particular science fiction activity or product, such as costuming or filksinging or television science fiction, and who see the Worldcon as a convenient place to gather and share their own part of the science fiction continuum.

- Those who wish to change their identity from fan to science fiction professional, and who see the Worldcon as a place to learn from the masters of the craft.

These two groups find their solidarity based on the products of the science fiction industry. But even taking these four divisions of core fans into consideration, we still have less than a majority of the participants at a Worldcon. For many of the second group, those "paying customers," with a hobbyist's interest in the literature and other media of science fiction, but only a peripheral interest, if any, in the community as a source of identity, it is a place of amusement.

The meaning the convention holds for any participant is likely to change several times over a lifetime, from place of amusement to location of community as a fan, to organizer or professional, which brings its own special conflicts, as Chris York and her husband explained.

> **Chris York:**  As fans, you move in a different circle than you do once you're really moving into the industry. . . . You don't like to give up your friends, but . . . sometimes there's conflict of interest. What's best for the convention is not necessarily best for the pros . . . and oftentimes what would be the best thing for the convention to do is not necessarily what is advantageous for you as an individual. So you do find yourself in conflict.[3]

Conflicts range from the allotment of premium space and budget for the benefit of panels and courtesy to the professional writers who come to the convention for no more than a free membership, to decisions about what kind of events the conventions should sponsor.

But most convention organizers, while recognizing to some extent the needs of the professional group and the convention's need for the noncommunity fans to support an active convention, go to this great effort and expense because they are members of the nonprofessional fan community, working to create a place for their community life to flourish. To do that they must mark out a territory that represents the mobile geography of the community, and they must rely on both organizational and semiotic means to defend their boundaries.

## Defending Territory

Territory is a complex factor in the construction of the reality that plays out at the convention. In the convention, space does not operate binarily, in "front" or public space and "back" or private space.[4] Rather, there are a multiplicity of conceptually differentiated spaces within the convention venue, each of which is treated differently in the community, but each of which must be *defended* from the outside.

The alternate social reality created here requires defense in inverse proportion to the space the convention can command by force of numbers. If the convention takes all the available space so that intrusion by outsiders is unlikely, participants need not defend their space so demonstrably. A world convention like MagiCon, with up to 8,000 participants in attendance, can command several hotels and a convention center with little fear of confrontation with the outside, but it represents many diverse interests that make it more difficult for the individual to find and share community with like-minded participants. So a large convention like Magi-

Con requires that special-interest groups carve out their own space and defend their separate boundaries inside the larger community, but with far less vigor than would be needed against complete outsiders.

A convention sharing space with outsiders must defend the boundaries of its realities more rigorously, particularly if the group sharing the space seems likely to present a hostile presence. But participants are less likely to need identifying marks to establish space for their special interest because participants at the smaller convention are more likely to know one another by sight or reputation. Regardless of numbers, however, all conventions must provide a defended space for the playing out of events and the safe practice of community. The first line of defense, clothing, reflects the specific communal enterprise of science fiction.

### Strategies of Inclusion and Exclusion: The Dress Code
Clothing functions internally for the community itself to establish a visible marker of group inclusion/exclusion, and to allow for the expression of individual identity within the allowable parameters of the community.[5] At the same time, it creates a visible boundary that shuts out the mainstream culture that surrounds it and may even share space with it in the hotel. Clothing at the science fiction convention falls into two distinct categories: fashion, a fairly uniform style of casual dress that members of the community may wear in the outside world without drawing comment, and costume. Of course, not all participants choose to dress according to the fashion code of the community. During the convention, however, all fans wear badges with their names, nicknames, or alter-ego names (printed in large type so that long-distance friends can find each other) to show that they are participants and therefore belong inside the barrier.

### Fashion Code and Fan Culture
Like fashion in the outside world, science fiction fashion has changed over time. In its formative years, fans had no need of a fashion code. Relatively little science fiction was published until the mid-1960s, so an avid reader could absorb it all, and the group of fans itself was so small that the subsequent divisions into interest groups had not become the complex matter it is today. Of course, clubs and rivalries, both interpersonal and interclub, existed in the '30s, '40s, '50s, but the participants were sufficiently well known to one another that they did not require a fashion code to identify the combatants.[6]

Science fiction fashion[7] as we know it today developed in the 1960s, and marks the influx of the '60s counterculture that doubled the size of the Worldcon almost overnight. The style is similar to that described in *Enterprising Women*.[8] At its most basic it includes a tee shirt and a pair of jeans or fatigues, although women may wear a long dirndl skirt, either plain or in an ethnic or tie-dyed print. Accessories such as buttons and tote bags complete the "dress code." The tee or button provides a highly visible surface on which to inscribe the participant's interest with simple lettered messages or screen-printed art.[9] Although nothing in this style of dress would cause a passerby to pause on the street, the concentration of people wearing it in a space usually marked for more formal business attire creates a dissonance between the space and its use that begins to establish the boundaries the community requires.

In addition to fannish dress and accessories, many fans add a detail or two from a variety of costumelike options to signify the wearer's particular interest. Fans of Anne McCaffrey's Pern series, for instance, often wear a small dragon crafted of ribbon or padded fabric.

Science fiction fashion thus displays denotative signs of the specific interest of the wearer—hard science fiction or fantasy, a particular television series or movie—and invites comment from others who may be carrying the same signs on their persons. At the same time, the participant who wears science fiction fashion rather than a full costume seems to be expressing primary identification with the group rather than with a personalized vision of a character.

## Fashion Code and Status

Science fiction fashion, like fashion in the "real" world, can demonstrate role and status distinctions inside the community even as it functions as a barrier to outsiders. While some, like fantasy writer Steven Brust, may dress in a manner indistinguishable from the fans around them, industry professionals who appear as panelists at conventions generally dress more formally, placing themselves at some remove from the solidarity of the "masses" but still with a distinctiveness that marks them to community members as their own. Maureen McHugh, best known for her novel *China Mountain Zhang*, explains:

> I do have a style of clothing I wear almost only in my incarnation as a pro-in-public that includes my ear clip. It is noticeably enough different that my family calls it my uniform. I do it to establish a persona for myself since I am not convinced that I am interesting enough in person to be a writer.[10]

Martha Soukup, short story writer, adds:

> I almost only wear nice dresses when I'm at cons, especially for awards ceremonies. Neil Gaiman told me a while ago that he thinks writers should be "cartoons," by which he meant they should have a simple, recognizable physical presentation.[11]

Soukup prefers not to present herself as a "cartoon," but she does see its value: "Finding a cartoon and sticking to it gives you one (very big) less thing to worry about. Then you can go on and do whatever you want."

Nor are women the only professionals with a decided style in the science fiction community. David Hartwell, consulting editor at Tor Books, is known for his terrible ties, and cyberpunk authors affect a "hip" style. Steven Brust signals his interest in works of swashbuckling romance, like those of Alexandre Dumas, with a plumed cavalier's hat in the style of the Musketeers. As a science fiction professional and musician, Brust is not constrained to present any other corporate face, so he wears his hat wherever he goes, as a part of his regular style of dress.[12]

## Costume Function and Meaning

Costume marks the territory of the convention as more clearly "other" than science fiction fashion because in most cases costume would not pass unnoticed anywhere. And unlike science fiction fashion, a style that signifies a corporate identification with the community, costumes appear in a wide variety of styles and carry a range of potential meanings that cannot be decoded simply by reading the clothing. To understand costume, we must look at both the coding on the body and the intention of the costumer, which may remain hidden.

The costume itself will always provide a visual referent, sometimes to a specific character or situation, but almost always to a specific genre, subgenre, or special interest. Costumers walk the convention site like the living books in Truffaut's version of Bradbury's *Fahrenheit 451* walked their wood, their bodies the visual representations of the books, and movies, games, and television shows on which the community is based. This body-as-simulacrum often repels the outsider while it gathers to itself those who likewise find the source of new myths in the products of popular culture.

For many conventioneers, particularly newcomers who have not yet been completely enculturated into their own social networks, the boundary that costumers defend holds them safely inside—safely because their growing ability to read the costumes demonstrates their growing enculturation. Making this easier, costume has engendered a variety of classification systems, including, most importantly, genre.

## Genre Classification System

Fantasy, science fiction, and historical are the three main costume categories in this classification system,[13] but within each of these categories community members recognize a wide variety of subcategories and modes of expression.

*Science fiction* costumes draw from the forms of the genre that rely on the extrapolation of rational, scientific explanations for their actions. Most science fiction uses the future to explain the use of science we do not have, but some makes use of the idea of alternate universes, in which worlds contemporary with our present or past have developed technology based on different scientific discoveries. Space suits are easily identified as science fiction, but other costumes may give no outward clue to their futuristic meaning.

*Fantasy* costumes usually draw their inspiration from books or movies, comic books, or personal creations derived from mythology, folklore, or history. Fantasy has traditionally looked back into a romanticized or mythic past in which magic and magical beings abound, and the costuming reflects this tradition. Monster costumes can represent either fantasy or science fiction motifs. Monsters are often created by young men; the psychology of this has been discussed briefly elsewhere.[14]

*Historical* costumers, like fantasy costumers, look back to a romanticized past, but historical recreation fans focus on a period in documented history. The costumers often try to use materials and techniques as close to the original as possible. French, English, and Scots costume of the fourteenth through the nineteenth centuries is popular, and there is a heavy crossover population between the science fiction community and the "renaissance faires" that have grown in popularity over the past fifteen years.

For the person who creates and wears the costume, the purpose and meaning can be varied and complex. Participants may costume as an artistic endeavor, as play, or as an expression of a commitment to a special interest or a personal perception of the past or the future. At the same time, like science fiction fashion, costume is a declaration of solidarity with others who share the fantasy and its presence in great numbers in the convention site creates a visual boundary for the frame of the event.[15]

## The Cybergothic Code

In recent years, however, a new style of dress that blurs this distinction between fashion and costume has grown in popularity for the young. This group, influenced by gothic music, a lifestyle of carefully nurtured disaffection, and the cyberpunk fiction typified by William Gibson's *Neuromancer*, dresses in a pastiche of the punk style of the 1970s and the leather look of the contemporary biker and bondage communities, with a liberal addition of lace and velvet and gothic makeup à la Anne Rice's vampires: white face, with black or very dark red lipstick and highly defined eyes. Studded leather clothing and dog-collar jewelry are common among this group, as is pierced jewelry and hair in bright colors like purple or orange. As a group, the young gothic fans smoke much more than do their elders and attend fewer formal convention activities.

The new gothic fan is problematic for the science fiction community on many levels that play out symbolically through differences in fashion. The new fans come in with a different sense of science fiction history written in their dress—for many, the genre begins not with Robert Heinlein, Arthur C. Clarke, or Isaac Asimov, but with Anne Rice, William Gibson, or Neil Gaiman. The clothing remains ambiguous, however. If the fashion is costume, playing out the literature as other costumes do, does it signal vampires or the cyberspace revolution? It can mean either or both. If the clothing acts as fashion, then, like the rest of fan fashion, it carries with it a sign value ascribed in the outside world. In this case, however, the referents are not middle class leisure but the underground subcultures of bikers and the sadomasochistic community, Versace haute couture, and the ultra-hip neoromantic subculture of gothic music and postmodern despair.

Because this style of dress is practiced primarily by the young, the age group itself has become inscribed with sign value: young fans who do not dress in the traditional fan style are generally perceived to have a primary allegiance to gaming, or simply to the convention as a gathering place, and not to the science fiction literature that has the highest value in the community. In part this perception arises because fans who dress in the gothic-leather style do not attend panel discussions to any great extent, and because this group has selected gathering places where gaming is also popular. Traditional fans deny that the attitude is generational, and in fact they welcome young fans who dress in traditional fashion and evidence traditional fan interest in panels and writers. It is not youth that is unwelcome, apparently, but rebellious youth.

Of course, in the 1960s, when the science fiction fashion code developed, jeans, tee shirts, and ethnic dress were likewise referents to an underground culture, but that meaning has been subverted as the group that the clothing represented has moved from rebellion to institutionalization, taking its clothing with it.

I expected to see a growing contingent of gothic-style fans at MagiCon, but in fact I saw very few there, or at ConFrancisco in San Francisco the next year. It seems that the new young fans are valorizing their own gathering places, such as Dragon Con in Atlanta, mentioned earlier, separate from the traditional group.[16]

## The Function of Functions: Spaces and Enculturation

Within the defined boundaries of the convention, space is defended differentially, in accordance with the degree to which the activities practiced in it can be described as private or public. Enculturation occurs as new attendees learn to transit the space from the most public to the most private, and as they learn, in the process, to interpret what they see, experience, and do as a part of community life. In the most public space, the standing exhibits and dealers' rooms, new participants mingle with the professional and core members of the community but without any formal interchange. The outsider may be overwhelmed with the amount and variety of materials on display, but the basic template—the marketplace and the museum—provides a connection to outsider experience. At the same time, the newcomer has the opportunity to observe those around her, and to participate in a sort of parallel play where she can start to match behaviors with little fear of revealing her untutored status to others. But even a newcomer can't spend the entire convention in the huckster room and the display area.

### Programming

Convention programming serves a variety of purposes, not least of which is enculturation. Because it looks superficially like the programming at any major industrial show or conference, outsiders feel that they are having a familiar experience. So, it performs a valuable function as an interface between real-world expectations and those of science fiction culture.

Programming usually consists of several "tracks," and a typical convention will offer one or two written sf tracks, a track of video programming, and one or two special-interest tracks. A Worldcon, by definition, offers programming at its most global, and MagiCon is no exception. A typical peak-hour program, Friday at 1 p.m., offers sixteen different activities, including a panel discussion about the Sci-Fi Channel soon to go into operation and a science panel about contemporary antitechnology sentiments; three panels on science fiction/fantasy art; six on fan-centered interests like costuming and filking, including one panel titled "Sex, Fandom and AIDS"[17]; a video showing of *War of the Worlds* and a film showing of Hugo Award-nominated film *The Rocketeer*; seven panels on prose fiction, including topics such as "Failure of SF to Predict the Fall of Communism" and "What Does It Mean to Be a Hero?" At the same time, a variety of readings and autograph signings and kaffeeklatsches take place. Children's programming begins at 1:30 in the meeting space at the Clarion Hotel, with activities for the four-to-eight-year-olds and separate programming for eight-to-twelve-year-olds.[18] And the permanent exhibit area offers a filk performance on a small stage so that neophytes can sample more esoteric interests.

An academic may take away from this brief description a model that looks more or less like the typical academic conference. With the actual experience of the convention panel, however, that comparison breaks down. For MagiCon, I was scheduled for four panels and a slide presentation of *Enterprising Women*. When first discussing my participation, I offered a variety of topics on which I felt comfortable talking. Except for the slide presentation, however, I did not know until a week or two before the convention which topics I had been scheduled to discuss.[19]

Panels are scheduled for an hour each, and may include from three to six or even more participants and a moderator. Panelists do not give formal addresses. The moderator may ask the panel questions, or may present an idea for discussion related to the panel title to start the interaction among panelists, who may agree or disagree, who may share the floor on an equal basis, or who may monopolize the discussion. At some point during the hour, however, the moderator starts taking questions from the audience.

This is why many fans come to conventions: panel discussions give them a chance to see their favorite authors in person, to hear them speak on topics of interest in the genre, and to engage the author in an exchange of questions and answers. Many fans take from the panel a sense that they understand the inner workings of the creative process a little better. Others look to the discussion for models they can incorporate into their own creative lives as writers trying to get published, while others hope to extend this engagement out of the panel into one-on-one conversation, and ultimately to strike up a friendship with their favorite novelist or short-story writer, or with the fan sitting next to them who asked a question or agreed with their own query. In this way scheduled programming operates at many levels more deeply to enculturate a wide variety of fans. As fans make these connections, they tend to attend fewer panel presentations and draw more of their social interaction from the individual encounters they plan or that happen by chance.

Aware of the power of programming to enculturate new members, conventions like MagiCon provide panels on the history and practice of fandom as well as on the industry products, and they even provide speakers on the etiquette of conventions. At MagiCon Mary Kay Kare, a fannish "Miss Manners," talked to me about a panel she was doing at this and other conventions called "Miss Manners Goes to a Con":

> **Kare:**  [We] give tips to people who aren't real experienced at convention going on how they can fit in, how they can have a good time, what to do, what not to do. For instance, I've been going to conventions for sixteen years and I know a lot of people. So when I see them I hug them and I kiss them and we all stand around and rub each other's backs and stuff like that. And some people get the mistaken idea that you can do this whenever and however you want. . . . And so you sort of gently point out to them that, well, usually it's nice if you know these people first, and you know it's okay if you hug them and kiss them and they want a backrub before you start manhandling them. . . . And some practical things like wear your name badge where people can see it because they may remember your face but not your name or vice versa, and it's not cute to have it pinned down on your knee where no one can see it. . . .
>
> Most fans are very friendly and are very open to meeting new people,

and it's easy to just sort of stand around and watch what happens. And if people are not obviously having a quiet, closed conversation, most people are very open to having someone, you know, sort of join their circle and listen and stick in their two cents. Don't, however, attempt to take over and dominate the conversation. And it's okay to go up and introduce yourself to the writers and the pros and the artists. Don't interrupt them at lunch or dinner or important conversations with their publishers, but it's perfectly all right to go up and introduce yourself and talk to them. I asked Gordy Dickson [author of the Dorsai novels] if he ever got tired of people coming up and shaking his hand and saying, "Gee, I really like your books," and he said, "No." They're human beings like the rest of us.

. . . don't drink too much, and if you drink too much go to your room, be quietly sick there, not in the hall.

When I asked Kare whether she offered dating advice, she said that she did not, because convention etiquette for dating varied widely from region to region.[20] She did tell me the one piece of advice she gives on the subject: "to simply treat someone as you would like to be treated, which sort of forms the basis for most etiquette."[21]

While such basic instruction on etiquette may seem extreme, experienced convention organizers know that socialization is often a problem for new members in the fan community. Neophytes may have experienced difficulties interacting with neighbors in their geographic hometown for any number of reasons, not least of which might be their interest in science fiction. They come to this new community with a lot of hope, an equal fear of rejection, and, often, few developed social skills. Successful Worldcons make the integration of these newcomers part of their responsibility, and panel discussions, where fans can ask questions and receive answers, serve this purpose in a vital way.

## Enculturating the Industry

For the panelists, the hour serves both professional and personal goals. Most writers and artists will say that on panels they reach out to the fans, who in turn buy more books. At the same time, they will readily admit that attending conventions is not a cost-efficient way of reaching a buying public. At local conventions, most of the professional guests receive a membership but must pay for their own transportation, room, and meals. At World Conventions, everyone but the three or four guests of honor pays some admission charge in addition to his or her own expenses.[22] But panels do offer a place for people whose work is both solitary and exhibitionist to perform before an audience and to make contact with other people in their profession. Panels are a place for new writers to meet the revered masters of the field, and to demonstrate a degree of expertise in a topic of intellectual interest to the audience. Thus, for a professional, serving on a panel furthers enculturation in the part of the convention that serves the interests of the industry.

At MagiCon I had an opportunity to further my own enculturation as a professional in the study of science fiction. I participated on a panel on fairy tales with a number of women fantasy writers, including Andre Norton, an acknowledged influence on fantasy writing for more than forty years and the spiritual grandmother to women in the field. All the fantasy writers on the panel use fairy tales as the basis for some of their work. Some of the panelists hold advanced degrees from prestigious institutions. As the only one with an advanced degree in *folklore*, however, I was aware that the explanations these panelists gave of the folklore process were more important for the understanding they offer of the way the writers make meaning in their work than my technical discussion of folkloristic theory could be. Part of enculturation is realizing that a little-known academic does not, under any circumstances, tell an audience of fantasy fans that their childhood idol is wrong.

## Convention Suite

Organizations such as the Science Fiction and Fantasy Writers of America each have a hospitality suite for their members at worldcon, and MagiCon was no exception. The convention itself also organizes a hospitality suite, called the con suite, which is generally situated as far as possible from the main events of the convention and marks the boundary of the convention inclusive of all spaces in which the community is enacted.

The purpose a con suite serves depends on the nature of the convention and its participants. At a small convention where most of the participants are well socialized and known to each other, the con suite may stand almost empty most of the convention. Participants may use it as a place to gather before going on to an event held elsewhere, or as a place to obtain a quick free beverage between events. Other small conventions may use the con suite as the center of interaction, a place where convention-goers come to meet old friends and stay to socialize. The use patterns for con suites in these two instances are usually determined by the food on offer. A pass-through suite will offer pretzels, chips, and a few finger vegetables and dip, while a con suite designed as the major socializing locus will provide more substantial food, so that convention-goers can eat lunch or even dinner there.

For a large convention, the con suite generally serves the first purpose: as a meeting place. For neophytes, however, it also serves the important function of giving newcomers a place to rest or meet other new members during breaks in the activities. Here the new member can begin to make contacts around a bowl of dip or while digging a soda out of a bathtub full of ice. The con suite gives newcomers a first taste of party behavior as they watch the older hands meet and chat before going on to their next activity. Here, they may first hear about the parties that will dominate nighttime activity at the convention.

## Parties

As organizers have explained earlier, a large convention like a Worldcon is a twenty-four-hour-a-day proposition. For most fans, the day is devoted to the massive display and huckster room in the main hall, and to the panels, readings, and kaffeeklatsches in the smaller meeting rooms scattered around the periphery of the convention center. When the main hall closes for the night and the major programming events are over, fans and professionals alike turn to the parties, which often do not start until ten or eleven at night and may either end at a designated time or go on until the sun comes up or security shuts them down.

All parties are private in the sense that they are open only to members of the convention. Within that context, parties may be public, in that anyone attending the convention is welcome, or private, in that only particular groups are invited. Special-interest groups such as anime fans may give private parties so that their own members may gather and indulge their special interest, or they may give public parties to attract new fans to their interest. Clubs and organizations may give public parties to garner support for a convention or attract new members while giving their participants a place to gather with their friends. And publishers frequently hold private parties, open to professionals in general or to their own writers and employees.

At the same time, individual participants hold impromptu gatherings in their hotel rooms, some of which become parties by default. Hotel security regularly patrols the halls, trying to corral the official parties within their designated spaces and often closing down the impromptu parties for noise. Like clocks unwinding slowly after the day, convention attendees spend much of the night moving from party to party in a restless quest for people to talk to and for drinks and snacks. For newcomers, the party circuit can prove difficult. First they have to find the parties; then they must decide whether to introduce themselves to other partiers or just observe and move on, as many others in the party rooms are doing. To escape the pressure to socialize, however, the new fan still has some options open.

For the less party-inclined, night is the time for bad science fiction films like *Attack of the Killer Tomatoes*, or for filking. The singing and songwriting about science fiction, or about the convention itself, a traditional late-night activity, go on till dawn.

## Enculturating the Young

Adolescents from the outside continue to seek out fandom as a haven for lives that lack the strong sense of community they crave, and they are in turn enculturated by other adolescents in fandom, or in the same way adults find their place in the community. Conventions are expensive, of course, and advertised only in the community's own publications or locations, so they can be difficult for the uninitiated to learn about or travel to without a car. This relative difficulty in making the first contact limits the number of adolescent first-generation fans in attendance at any convention. Since most conventions require that an adult accompany children under the age of sixteen or seventeen, the very young and early adolescent children are, of necessity, second-generation fans, introduced to the community by a parent or other adult who must take responsibility for their behavior. Most new members who require enculturation are therefore adults or late adolescents.

Fannish families in the 1990s, however, are raising a second and even a third and fourth generation of participants. Many leading figures in science fiction today grew up reading science fiction and attending conventions from the time they were very young, often with their parents or other family members. Betsey Wollheim, co-owner and coeditor of DAW Books, grew up at her father's side at science fiction conventions, and she was not alone. Karen Anderson, a fanziner and sometime-collaborator with her husband, science fiction and fantasy writer Poul Anderson, raised their daughter Astrid in the science fiction community. The Andersons have been active in fandom since the 1950s and were a part of the founding of the SCA. According to Karen Anderson, Astrid fit right into the pattern of the avid fan from the start:

> **Karen Anderson:** At Christmas, when we opened our presents in the morning, we did a version of the Lucia ritual. . . . Before that she was allowed to open any one present. Certainly after she learned to read, that one present was the book.

Like many of the children raised in fandom, Astrid made her primary social relationships within fandom, then went through a period of separation from the culture in early adulthood:

> **Anderson:** She had, more or less, been involved with Greg Bear when they were teenagers. They both thought that they were too young to decide that they were in love.

During the intervening years, Astrid married outside the community, and Greg Bear, who discovered the community as a fan in his teens, developed into a well-respected science fiction writer. Then, returning to a convention, Astrid met Greg Bear again.

> **Anderson:** Then they encountered each other again at a convention. . . . And there it was . . . [she] married Greg. . . . Now they have their children. And she's definitely back into science fiction again.

For children raised in fandom, this period of separation seems a necessary part of the process of gaining autonomy. The young adults who leave the community can stay away, or they can return under their own conditions for participation. While it is not entirely clear, it would seem that the most self-assured and confident of the second- and third-generation fans do have this period of separation in their histories as well as a continuing interest in the genre. The Anderson family shows that, when presented with examples who are both social and readers, children who grow up in fandom can have a broad and exciting social life as adults:

> **Karen Anderson:** Greg [Bear] knows a lot of people at Microsoft. A couple of months ago, one of the Microsoft guys gave a party at a restaurant, several tables' worth of dinner party. He invited his boss, Bill Gates, and he invited other Microsoft people. And interesting people. No spouses. But Astrid was. Greg and Astrid both. And what's more, they were placed at the table with the guest of honor, Stephen Hawking.[23]

Kathy and Leo Sands show us the early part of that journey: raising young children in science fiction. Former owners of Tales of the White Hart, the Baltimore science fiction bookstore, the Sandses spent almost every weekend selling their books from a large display in the huckster rooms of conventions up and down the East Coast and at the Worldcons.[24] They traveled with their children, Kara and Matt, on the huckster circuit.

Over breakfast during Lunacon in March of 1993, we discussed raising young children in science fiction.[25] One meal the family tries to do together is breakfast because, as Leo explains, "it's the only time we can get together—as hucksters." One of the adults had to stay with the temporary store in the huckster room at all times while the room was open, usually from about ten in the morning to seven or even nine at night, so family meals were generally impossible once the day had fully begun. The ritual of sitting down together in the quiet of the morning gave the family a set time to focus attention on the children, who entered the conversation at will. While we discussed ways that families can reduce the stress of a wildly different weekend lifestyle, mom Kathy Sands mentioned the importance of food:

> **Kathy Sands:**   well, one thing about the idea of bringing a fair amount of food [with you]—friends of ours . . . never bring anything really, to conventions. And there have been times when . . . their kid was screaming his head off . . . waiting in line to order at the restaurant . . . you just don't set yourself up for that.

The ability to feed the children when they are hungry, not just when the restaurant can seat them, is one example of planning to reduce the stress on children that such a dramatic shift in their daily routine can produce.

When I talk to children like Matt and Kara Sands, who have grown up at conventions, however, baby-sitting is the one constant bone of contention, an inescapable part of convention life for the young in the 1990s:

> **Matt:**   One time they had a whole gaming floor in a hotel. Unfortunately, I could never get there because I'd go down to the babysitting, where I'd take one glance into the room to see what was going on, and they'd say, "You, in here, get out of the hallway!" [although] I was signed up so I could leave. A couple kids actually made a break-out attempt. [We laughed]. . . . Actually, I should have just gotten out of babysitting, checked out of there, and run up the stairs.[26]

As adults, we must sympathize with the baby-sitters into whose care the children are placed. The policy at Lunacon, where I interviewed the Sands, is typical:

> All children must be accompanied by an adult in order to purchase a membership, and all children must be registered with the Convention. . . . [T]he children must, at all times, be under the supervision of an adult or in Lunacon Child Care area.[27]

Baby-sitters are responsible to the convention for carrying out the policy that places unattended children in their care, as they are for the safety of the children. But even the baby-sitters who have been through the process themselves admit that they do no better:

> **Female Teenager:**   They didn't want to be there. They didn't, like, play with you or anything, so I did baby-sitting one year, and it was just, like—now I know why they were so atrocious. And I became those baby-sitters . . . every once in a while, if they are feeling, like, in a really good mood, they'll, like, read you a story or something. It's, like, . . . "Shut up, sit down, build a fort or something. All little kids love forts!"

**Male Teenager:** I can remember two or three conventions in my life that I went to baby-sitting and stuff, and you did things like make little paper dragons . . . make little science fiction things. Science fiction fantasy things.[28]

Some regional conventions, including Boskone in Boston and Balticon in Baltimore, offer a variety of activities for mid-range children. At Boskone, children six or older have their own activities in an area called "The Dragon's Lair," as Kathy Sands described:

**Kathy Sand:** This is the first year that she [Kara] was eligible, officially, for Dragon's Lair at Boskone. And she's been saying all weekend that Dragon's Lair is much more interesting. . . . There's . . . activities for older children that don't need that much supervision; they set something up, get it going, and . . . they don't have too much by way of adults wandering around. . . . They occasionally will have an arts and crafts project, where the adult will show them what to do. But . . . the kids are mostly on their own . . . and there's usually three or four different things that they can choose from at one time. It's sort of like their own little convention.

Baby-sitting services provided by the convention, in convention space, provide an invaluable service for parents who need a few hours each day to pursue their own interests with the assurance that their children are receiving care from the community they trust. And some conventions, like Boskone, do try to offer a positive experience of special programs and activities. But for both the baby-sitters who are paying their communal dues as a volunteer and the children they baby-sit, the lure of activity outside the room calls strongly.

## Learning Fandom

Clearly the learning experience enculturating children in fan culture starts in baby-sitting and in the activities that parallel adult arts at a level suitable for children. As occurs in other cultures, however, parents and the community at large provide the greatest amount of training. All children who attend conventions accompany their parents to some events. Children perform onstage at the masquerade, go to parties, and visit the "permanent" exhibitions. One of Kara's favorite activities, next to parties, is the art show, and she shows her pictures on a back panel reserved for amateurs. Discussing a sculpture she saw in the art show at Lunacon, Kara expressed both interest and uneasiness. Her parents' responses illustrate some of this fan training:

**Kara Sands:** I wanted the machine.

**Kathy Sands:** The lady who was hooked to the machine? . . . I liked that. It was a very powerful . . . piece of sculpture . . . she was hooked, brain, body, everything was hooked into this machine.

**Kara:** What would it do to her?

The sculpture in the art show initially fascinated Kara, but she began to show some concern that the machines might be hurting the woman or doing something frightening to her. At this point, Kara's father, Leo Sands, took the lead, his tone of voice unchanged but his examples and diction targeted to the six-year-old's positive experience at home and at the convention:

**Leo Sands:**    If she [the woman in the sculpture] imagined she was a dragon, then she was a dragon. They almost can do that now, Kara. They put things in front of your eyes, and put things in gloves on your hands and you can go to a cartoon world.

**Kara Sands:**    Cartoon world? How do they do that? Inside the cartoon? In real life?

**Kathy Sands:**    Yes. That's called virtual reality.

**Kara Sands:**    Ooh. I want to do that. Can they do it to me, can they?

**Kathy Sands:**    Well, it would cost a lot of money right now.

**Leo Sands:**    . . . If people want it, they'll find ways of getting it to people. And eventually, things like that get more affordable, as you have more practice with it.

At this point, her parents have reassured the six-year-old Kara that the woman in the sculpture is having fun in a way Kara can understand, that no one is being hurt, and therefore she needn't be afraid or disturbed. They have normalized the experience by talking about virtual reality in the real world, making it clear that virtual reality is, in the norms of the community, desirable. And they have begun to explain a little about the complex subject of virtual reality itself. But as laypeople they do not have complete technical knowledge of the subject. Kathy Sands is open about admitting as much:

**Kara Sands:**    Mommy? How do they get into the cartoon world?

**Kathy Sands:**    Well, that I don't really know, honey.

Kara pushes by giving back a piece of information she knows from earlier in the conversation, and the question focuses her parents on the level of the answer she expects, much more doable than the technical answer that seemed out of reach a moment ago:

**Kara Sands:**    Maybe, do they hook you up to a machine?

**Kathy Sands:**    Yeah. Probably several different kinds of machines.

**Kara Sands:**    You're dreaming—

**Kathy Sands:**    Sort of like dreaming while you're awake, yeah. And focusing on the kinds of dreams you want to have.

**Matt Sands:**    Now that would be nice.

**Kathy Sands:**    Instead of just whatever happens in your head while you're asleep . . . with virtual reality, you could have whatever kind of dream you wanted.

**Leo Sands:**  Well, somebody could give you a dream.

At this point, Kara seems satisfied with the answer, that virtual reality is like a dream that you can choose as you would choose a cartoon on television. Reassured, Kara loses interest in the discussion. But during the conversation about the painting, Kathy and Leo Sands's reassurances and explanations were very much in tune with the community standard that values information and technological advancement. And Kara has learned from her parents about a concept that is becoming more popularized in children's media today.

Howard Gardner, early education specialist, has described the way children learn, and how education could best capitalize on the innate "intelligences" of each child. According to Gardner, our education system trains children in one or two primary intelligences, using a limited number of channels. The system reinforces the value we place on the accumulation of facts, but not integration of knowledge / understanding.

Gardner suggests apprentice programs to teach students how to integrate new learning into understanding, or museum-based education integrating book knowledge with hands-on experience. This integrated system would make use of five entries into learning—that is, five uses of multiple intelligences to teach a particular subject: narrative, logical-quantitative (analytical), foundational (a contextual model that looks at the language and philosophy in a structured way to get into the subject itself), aesthetic, and experiential (the hands-on apprentice type of learning). Gardner has determined that the more entry points you use, the better the final understanding will be and the more likely that you will hit the way the student preferentially learns.[29]

When we look at the way Kara and Matt have been raised in the science fiction fan community, we find that the convention experience fulfills many of the necessary steps to a more flexible understanding-based approach to knowledge. It provides children opportunities to learn by exploring the options available in the community at the level of their early competence in children's programming, and in the company of adults who practice skills valued by their culture. Fandom also provides learning through many entry points:

1. Narrational, through the literature itself and through personal narratives of members.

2. Logical-quantitative, through the panels and science slide shows and lectures.

3. Foundational, in the infinite arguments about categories, definitions, and criteria for inclusion at every level of activity.

4. Aesthetic, with the arts of filk music, dance, and costume.

5. Hands-on experiential, at every point, as gopher, baby-sitter, participant on panels and in masquerades and dances, songs, and skits.

Children as well as adult neophytes can participate with skilled adults at every level of entry, finding explanations as well as a place for a willing hand. Kara, at six, had her drawing in the art show; Matt, at ten, was an experienced gamer. Volunteers in a wide variety of necessary and valued tasks work side by side with experienced hands, learning new skills as well as the new culture, and becoming valued members themselves.

Providing such a multi-entry delivery system, the science fiction convention is a *very* powerful teaching/learning institution for adults as well as children—much more powerful than the traditional educational system. So it becomes pressingly important that we understand what it teaches. Obviously, it shows new members, both the children introduced to fandom by their parents and the adolescents who find the community on their own, how to be members of the community. It also trains its members to learn in the particular way that fandom teaches its members. That includes not only multiple entrance points but a lot of independence in the process of seeking out and selecting the kinds of experiences the young fan wants to have. This is probably why so many fan children find their school experience unsatisfying, and why their teachers often complain that they are precocious.

In an interview with two teens raised as second-generation fans, we can begin to see some of the downside as well as the advantages of growing up in such a rich part-time environment. The informants were a male, age fifteen, and a female, age fourteen. Both live in relatively exclusive suburbs but consider themselves members of both the '90s alternative/punk movement and the science fiction community. Their parents were not present at the interview.

> **Male Informant:**   I've been coming to science fiction conventions as long as I can remember, basically. We have pictures of me when I was infant age in like a backpack sort of thing . . .

> **Female Informant:**   As long as I can remember, but I don't really remember much, because . . . my dad did film, so I just . . . got to sit underneath the film projector.

> **Ethnographer:**   Did you like growing up at conventions?

> **Male Informant:**   Personally, I've loved . . . going to conventions, I've loved traveling, and I get a lot more sort of grown-up intellectual conversation— more than I would than if I had grown up anywhere else, and I got more exposure to more interesting people that I would rather talk to, like more interesting grownups.

> **Ethnographer:**   What kind of people?

> **Male Informant:**   . . . 99 percent of the people that I have associated with, in convention life, have been friends of my father, or have been introduced to me through my father or through friends of my father. And he basically only hangs with people who are smart and nice and cool and fun to be with. I mean, it's also sort of an edge to me because I get to meet lots and lots of famous writers and stuff like that. . . . People like my friends in high school have heard of. So, "You're lying. You didn't really eat dinner with the great

Benford and Roger Zelazny and hang out with Carl Edward Wagner." "Yes I did."[30]

Both informants confirmed that meeting famous and important people who had something to say in the genre represented a major advantage in the fan community, but when pressed on whether they actually read the works of those writers, they both said no:

> **Male Informant:**    I actually like horror a lot better than science fiction, and it's been sort of embarrassing . . .
>
> **Ethnographer:**    You didn't turn to elves and unicorns . . .
>
> **Female Informant:**    No. My mom is into that stuff and it just disgusts me. . . . Like Anne McCaffrey, I just cannot stand her stuff. It bothers me so much. . . . It's like, I don't care about the stupid dragons. Shut up about the stupid dragons.

Here we begin to see a tenuous break in the system. Raised within the science fiction community, these teens have absorbed the traits that mark science fiction kids: a precocity of language and vision brought about by constant association with adults, those who attend as fans and those who work in the genre. And they take away a certain expertise: both these informants work in the technical area of their local high school theater groups. But they experience only the most attenuated interest in the thing that drives most people to seek out the community in adulthood and their teen years. In a sense, they are not quite part of either culture—not held to science fiction culture by the work, and a bit outside the mainstream:

> **Female Informant:**    Some of the bad things are, like, I meet so many interesting people here, and the people in my high school are like, you are doing what this weekend?
>
> **Male Informant:**    Yeah, what? [indicating the confused response of friends at school] . . . [Returning from a convention is] sort of a letdown; a convention is more, it's a freer environment, and you have a lot more choice of what you want to do . . . you can go to the art show, you can go see different obscure films that you wouldn't otherwise be exposed to. You can go listen to an author discussion . . . Which is, I think it's good.

Both teens say that at conventions and at home they gravitate toward people who are older:

> **Male Informant:**    It's been better, I think, to have older friends. It's like, um, when you are learning an instrument, the best thing you can do is play with people who are better players than you, and I mean, I think that if you're younger, I think that one of the best things you can do is hang out with people who are older than you. Granted, sometimes it will be a burden on them because you're sort of a dork, but it comes out better for you, because I think you get a better sense of just, sort of maturity.

These informants manage, with some work, to balance a life within science fiction with a culturally recognizable affiliation in teen culture as "punks," musicians, and stagehands. But both have had difficulty with grades at school, a locus of education that engages far fewer of the channels they regularly employ in their weekend learning, and both find themselves more comfortable with the adults who teach by example around them in the science fiction milieu.

For some informants, the pull of fan enculturation is so strong that the move into the science fiction community in childhood defines their identity completely.

## Jailbait (JB)

I met Jailbait in 1981, when he was about thirteen years old. I was interviewing his mother for *Enterprising Women* at the time. JB, who had not yet received his fannish name, was part of the science fiction landscape even then. In February 1993, we sat down in the convention suite at Balticon to reminisce about the twelve years that we'd known each other, and to examine those years from the inside, as Jailbait, who is now called JB, sees them.[31]

> **Ethnographer:**   Tell me, how did you get started in science fiction convention—we've talked about this for so long.

> **JB:**   [I]n May, '78, we did a one-day Trek convention, the Mini Trek Con three, if I remember right. At the Hotel Taft in New York. Looking back, it was a pathetic example, but it was still an amazing, and enlightening, revelation. . . . [I was] ten at that time. As near as we can remember, looking back at it, Louise Rogow [daughter of filksinger, fanzine publisher/author, and professional novelist Roberta Rogow] and I met at that convention for the first time.

While starting with his mother in *Star Trek* fandom, JB found a home in literary rather than media fandom:

> **JB:**   There is this nice, neat delineation between when I determined myself to be on the "outside" versus the "inside." In January '83, at Philcon '82.1,[32] I finally got to really know and meet people I'd been seeing at cons for years before that . . . when I got named JB. And when I first really got to know the inside parts of fandom as opposed to sitting there on the outside watching. . . . [I]t's much more noticeable in retrospect than it was at the time. Because I'd been seeing the same people around for ages, but suddenly they knew me, I knew them, we all knew each other . . . I'd turned fifteen four months [before]

Like most science fiction fans, JB began reading the genre in childhood. His enthusiasm for reading grew out of an early sense of alienation: he was one of only a handful of Jewish children in a rural conservative and Christian—not Jewish—small town in upstate New York. I asked him how he coped:

> **JB:**   For the most part I didn't. Mom had taught seventh and eighth grade. . . . I grew up knowing all the teachers . . . which of course is an inherent

disadvantage when you're trying to be social as a kid. . . . I switched in sixth grade to Poughkeepsie Day School, Poughkeepsie, New York, twenty-five miles from home. My graduating class in 1985 was eight people.

For JB, other students at the Day School "never quite clicked" with his science fiction lifestyle, but they were a lot more accepting of difference than his local schoolmates would have been. In a situation with limited transportation and a great distance to travel to school every day, however, JB had understandable difficulty forming close relationships with schoolmates:

> **JB:**   So, I had friends there [the Day School]. Sometimes hung out on weekends with them. Sometimes weekend parties, sort of things. But a lot more, most of my relationships were with people at cons. First girlfriends, etc., were all convention-based. You know, I grew up knowing how to deal with a long distance relationship because it started out that's all I knew . . . even if I'd started relationships with people at the Day School, it would have been a long-distance relationship anyway—twenty-five miles, no car, is a nearly infinite distance. So, it was difficult, but it was what I knew. Cons made it a lot easier.

For JB, science fiction fandom presented an opportunity to experience a real sense of community. By 1983, when he was fifteen, JB was spending his convention time essentially on his own, socializing within his new circle, which, as in the case of the teen informants above, proved to be older than he:

> **JB:**   Older. All of them. Or almost, except for Louise. You know . . . most of them, it was probably a minimum of four years older, running up, starting in the early thirties.

JB's circle of friends formed at New York University, where they gathered socially and also created APA-NYU (also called Apa-Nu):

> **JB:**   That group, largely, was the APA-NYU and NYUSFS-NYU science fiction society—largely New York City fandom, not the Lunarians.

An APA is an Amateur Press Association publication, much like a science fiction fanzine, except that participation is by membership. Members of an APA will generally be required to contribute a certain number of pages a defined number of times during the year to maintain their active status, and to supply copies of those pages for each subscriber. A central collator, or editor, collates the contributions and mails a bundle to each subscriber. Dues to the APA pay for the postage. APAs often begin as, or come to be, a close, long-standing social unit:

> **JB:**   There was, it was a heavily filking group . . . meetings were Thursdays in Washington Square hangouts, social, and eat dinner afterwards sort of social group . . . every Thursday for the past fifteen years at least, probably. Apa-Nu has been going on for 280 some odd months.

When he graduated from high school, JB followed the lead of his social circle and attended NYU:

**JB:** I went to NYU because of fandom. This may not have been the best reason. I went to NYU because of the city. I love the city . . . I had fandom already. I started out, became a bit of a nucleus of my own social group there which was largely interrelated with fandom. One of my NYU roommates is here now. . . . So, I dragged them into fandom.[33]

As we have seen, and will see again, commercial science fiction publishing is heavily populated by fans who aspired to a career in the genre. Others, with interests outside publishing, are sometimes able to make careers inside their community as well. JB has been one of them:

**JB:** Well, I've kind of very carefully insulated myself, just a bit. For one thing, I found a job . . . My interview consisted of walking up to my future boss at Balticon . . . in '88. And [I] said, "Karl, I need a summer job." And he said, "Okay." And I went down to Maryland for the summer, and worked for him. . . . Balticon '89, I walked up to Karl and said, "Karl, I need another summer job." . . . I moved down for the summer and stayed for three years and ten months at this point. Nearly four years.

I asked whether all the employees at the small computer consulting company were fans:

**JB:** Not all. About 80–90 percent were fandom.

As one advantage of working for a fannish employer, the fan-employee does not have to compromise the personal style of presentation developed in the fan community since the 1960s and still adopted by many men in fandom today: beards and long hair.

**Ethnographer:** Why are beards so common?

**JB:** Well, a lot of us just hate shaving. . . . A lot of women like facial hair. . . . When you can get people walking up to you and just scritching, it feels good.

But part of working in a fannish company is a high degree of dependence on people who may also have their primary interest in fandom rather than in the company. In 1993, Karl's company was closing its doors:

**JB:** Karl put a lot of his resources into it, and you know, just never did layoffs and got people to leave when [the economy was bad]—a lot of us are of the opinion that Karl got bored. [Well-known fan and costumer] Marty Gear was his vice president. Marty left. . . . Since [Marty's wife] Bobbie was Karl's second grade teacher, they've known each other forever. . . . So, part of it's the economy, part of it's just he was tired of it.

**Ethnographer:** And now you are in this situation—

**JB:** —where I am job hunting.

**Ethnographer:** What are the possibilities of getting a job that is going to be hospitable to a fannish sensibility at work?

**JB:** Well, first of all, there's InterCon, the new fannish employer, [to] do networking software for Macintoshes. They're based out in Herndon Virginia. The president and his wife, the vice president, were here last night, will be here again today. . . . A lot of people I know work there. My resume is out there now.

JB did go to work for InterCon, and then:

They [InterCon] got bought out and I left. They've since been subsumed and no longer exist as InterCon. Did the independent contractor thing, went to work at AOL on another fannish lead, then moved to Boston to work for another small, largely fannish, consulting company. They've been bought out and are changing.[34]

For some reason, while community members take pride in those who live the science fiction life as writers, editors, or others in the business of creating science fiction, fans like JB often make them uneasy. The aesthetic of science fiction has always assumed the lived fiction that the genre presents a model for the world outside to follow. Panels at conventions enjoying piling up the scientific predictions made in the books that later have become technological realities. Similar panels ask their members what will be the next prediction made real in the world, and how did they miss this or that development. (The transistor, for example, left science fiction racing to catch up in a world of miniaturization it had never anticipated.)

For most fans, their community is a place to play and to absorb possibilities that they can take back into the world with them. Fans honor the creators of those possibilities, but the fiction of superiority becomes difficult to maintain in the presence of members who do not function well outside the narrow definition of the community. The majority of successful fans who work in the world as doctors, lawyers, accountants, engineers, scientists, and bank clerks, secretaries, and loading dock workers look like anyone else in their everyday lives, and are already smarting from the "get a life" attitude of outsiders.

The presence in this ethnography of fans with long unruly hair and equally long unruly beards, who wear their jeans and science fiction tee shirts or tie-dyed Deadhead wear in the outside world of work, force the members to face their own doubts in a more public way than they would like. Is fandom a safe, a healthy place, or is it a gathering of misfits and damaged goods? Fans joke about their difference and deny it at the same time, but underlying the jokes is the fear we all have of being different in a society that sometimes deals harshly with those who do not fit the established norm. In a culture where everyone is trying to pass for normal, no one wants to stand too close to the most visibly evident counterargument in the room.

Children like those described in this chapter growing up in the fan community clearly suffer some of the disadvantages of any children brought up outside the mainstream culture, as well as some advantages that may have questionable value outside their fannish culture. Among the latter are social skills tailored to an older peer group. Learning skills developed along a multichannel approach can leave the children feeling frustrated in a mainstream school system that has lower expectations of them and relies on only one or two learning channels. But many of these children grow up to be healthy and powerful contributors to the community in their own right. For others, the science fiction community provides the support structure that doesn't exist for them in the mainstream. It is the need for such a support structure even more than the attraction of the literature that continues to draw new young members to the community in adolescence and young adulthood.

For many people outside fandom, fan acculturation is disturbing for another reason that may not be so obvious to those of us already riding the wave of the postmodern era. In the 1830s, Alexis De Tocqueville called America a nation of associations. That remains so today, and those associations have grown less and less tied to geography in the intervening years. But until now we have looked at these associations as adjuncts to the geographic culture, points of concentration where the business of reinforcing the norms of society can proceed with a degree of intensity that day-to-day life prohibits. With fandom, we see an association becoming more powerful than the geographic culture, crossing national borders and bringing all the most sophisticated training systems to bear on teaching a culture that appears on the surface to be very different from the normative society.

Abetted by communication and transportation systems unimagined fifty years ago, individuals can have more immediate and consistent contact with more members of their association in more areas of the world than ever before. And the culture the association teaches therefore has greater impact on the participants. When we look at fans like JB—not isolated individuals living a life of anomie, but socially engaged people with contacts all over the world—we may be looking at the world we will all be living in fifty years from now. It has become possible, in a virtual sense, to choose one's neighbors, one's culture. Until now, cultures by association have grown up haphazardly, harboring utopian visions and pure expedience, wild experimentalism and stern conservativism side by side. In an age where the larger culture is recreating itself around us, we have not taken control of where it is going, but stand back, occasionally astonished and as often chagrinned to see where we have wound up. And "where" is the world fans have been building in their conventions and living rooms.

Fandom, we see, can provide not just deep personal relationships but also business connections that last a lifetime. This element is common among professionals in the industries that produce the media products, the books and television shows and comix and movies. But the spillover into the industries the media create is producing a whole new ethos in the business sectors we rely on for the most cutting-edge industries today. The new entrepreneur, guided by a worldview created in the science fiction community, balances the challenge of cutting-edge industries with a work mode that is more like play. Gamesmanship in business takes on a whole new meaning when the games in question have been Dungeons and Dragons or Magic: The Gathering instead of baseball, and when the geeky young man in the baggy shorts and scritchy beard could be earning a great deal more than the corporate club member in his suit and tie.

## Mass Events

Mass events,[35] which include opening ceremonies and guest of honor speeches as well as the Hugo Award ceremony and masquerade, all have several things in common. Unlike the majority of convention events, which take place amid a plethora of activities from which the individual convention-goer may choose, these events occur at prime times but with little or no competing programming. Participants who may prefer to remain outside the celebration of incorporation find themselves funneled into these events by default. And more than other activities at the convention, the major events seem to create the greatest distance between audience and performance. Members of the audience show their appreciation with applause and cheers, but they do not interact directly with the action on the stage. Some core members of the community, who perceive the convention as a locus for the active participation of the members in their community life, may see mass events as the least "fannish" and the most passive events at the convention. But this assumption is false on a number of levels. The very anonymity the event imposes strips away the sense of individuality with which the participant enters the auditorium. As the event captures the attention of the audience, the consumer waiting to be entertained, the responses of the individual merge with the responses of those around him. His laughter or tears or applause joins with that of the crowd to reify the values that the community espouses, producing *communitas*, the elevated sense of awareness of participating in something larger than the self.[36]

## Guest of Honor Speeches

By specific intent the major events ritualize community values, sometimes in direct and unadorned ways. When, in his guest of honor speech, Ray Bradbury reminisces about childhood, playing with clay models in the back yard with Ray Harryhausen, he makes his point clearly—do what you love with your life, and the money will come.[37] To Bradbury, a revered writer of the fantastic, and to Ray Harryhausen, moviemaker of the fantastic, this means science fiction and fantasy, and the speech is an invitation based on the shared love of the genre.

As a member of the community, the guest of honor represents the community to itself. As an industry professional, he sets a standard that other professionals aspire to meet, and that readers come to understand is likewise a standard they should demand in the literature they buy. As a fan, the guest of honor can talk about her love of the genre and the ways she has expressed that love both professionally and in relationship with the community. And by honoring the guest of honor with their attention and their applause, the members of the audience show that they share the feelings that they, perhaps, could not put into words as the professional wordsmith has done for them. Feelings have become corporate and tellable in the discourse the guest of honor shares with them in the speech. The guest of honor, in a sense, provides the structure of the personal experience narrative that creates a mode of expression that fans in the audience can take away to explain their own phenomenological experience of fandom.[38]

## Symbolic Rituals: The Hugo Awards and the Masquerade

While the guest of honor speech is a fairly straightforward expression of appreciation for the community and the industry, other events have symbolic functions that far exceed their obvious value. The remainder of this chapter will focus on two such main events: the masquerade and the Hugo Award ceremony.

## Masquerade

The masquerade brings together all the universes of science fiction in a performance that merges the "onstage" and the "off." The master of ceremonies may wear costume or formal attire; the judges and many members of the audience also participate in costume. The masquerade at many regional conventions, and particularly at Worldcons, currently draws the largest audience of any event, but as it has grown in importance it has increasingly come under fire by long-time fans. Resentment of the event arises out of the clash of meanings the masquerade presents to the participants and the difficulty diverse groups have in reconciling these meanings.

For fans who relate most strongly to the history of fandom as primarily a small, long-distance community of likeminded readers who created their own fanzines to keep in touch with one another, the masquerade is a waste of resources. It draws an audience that this group perceives as primarily passive receivers of a produced show rather than the active participants these core members value. These fans already have their sense of solidarity, shaped over years in local and long-distance social groups, including the clubs, that create the real space of the community, and they feel no need of the constructed communitas of the symbolic event. One could say that their preferred learning channel is one of action in the logico-rational realm, and so the aesthetic-symbolic presentation does not compute.

At the same time, members of the community for whom costuming provides the primary fan identity have to some extent added to the conflict. In 1985, science fiction costumers in Maryland formed the Costumers' Guild to support costumers and the growth of costuming. The Costumers' Guild, now international in scope, has systematized the performance and provided standards for judging the competitive aspect of the event, but it has also added to this sense of division in some ways. Some core organizers say that costumers have lost track of the "real" meaning of fandom: the written material of science fiction and the highly developed personal essay style of the fanzines. They point to CostumeCon, the annual convention of the International Costumers' Guild, where costumes need not conform to the conventions of aesthetics in the science fiction community. For this dedicated costumer, the masquerade is just one of many places to demonstrate both a technical skill and a creative energy that may turn toward the expression of those things identifiably of interest to science fiction and fantasy fans.

## Masquerade and Communitas

Detractors say that masquerade and costume in general are both the mutant over-development of a once-subsidiary interest in fandom and an opportunity for dedicated costumers to show off their skills. But for the vast majority of participants at the convention the masquerade is much more.

To understand what the masquerade does for the general convention-goer, we must look historically at when the event took shape. According to Don Sakers, the Worldcon masquerade had taken its present shape by 1974. Ben Yalow has also pointed out that the massive increases in the science fiction population at conventions began to level out to their present numbers at about this time. Between 1960 and 1974, however, participation at the Worldcon had increased from about 1,000 participants to more than 5,000. In terms of a conceptual geography, we have moved from a small town to a small city.

As long as the convention fandom remained a small and relatively homogeneous one, fans could expect to enter the community already in possession of many distinguishing characteristics of the fan group—most were male, white, middle class, relatively young, often technologically oriented. The newcomer to fandom might have been in communication with other fans through the fanzines before he attended a convention, and he'd been reading the convention reports. He knew what to expect, and he had friends waiting for him when he arrived.

Fans entered the convention world in the 1970s and '80s through a much wider selection of materials: books, film, television, and gaming. When they arrived, they faced a vastly larger and increasingly diverse population. As an event, the masquerade presented an opportunity to display in a series of artistic presentations the diversity that fandom now encompassed. For newcomers entering through games or television, the masquerade opened up the world of science fiction and fantasy books; for book fans, it illustrated the range of genre options beyond the print medium. For a community suffering the effects of sudden growth and the loss of homogeneity, the masquerade became a ritual of inclusion for socializing newcomers as well as a source of affirmation for many long-term participants. As entertainment it draws the largest and most diverse crowd at the Worldcon. As ritual of inclusion, it turns that crowd into fandom.

Costumers seem to understand instinctively the relationship between costume and ritual, and the presentation of masquerade costumes can be as important as the costume itself. Costumers properly move across the stage in highly structured poses as the characters their costumes represent, or offer a short skit as part of their presentation. Sally Fink, who has judged the masquerade at world conventions and numerous regional conventions, supported the statement with this example:

> **Sally Fink:**   At Tri-Con, there were two costumes that were normal D & D [Dungeons and Dragons role playing game] characters . . . and then they gave me the presentation. They did a nice bit of swordwork . . . and one guy fell on the stage and the other one killed him, and this head rolled across the stage. The whole con went "Hunh!" That sort of thing, which is very unexpected, is appreciated.[39]

Of course the community does appreciate craftsmanship, but the totality of the performance is required for full aesthetic effect. Within the ninety seconds or so allotted to each performance, the costumer must present not just a pretty piece of clothing but a fully developed concept represented by the costume. Worldcon "costumes" may include as many as twenty participants in one presentation.

## Ritual Performance: The MagiCon Masquerade

As a ritual of inclusion, the masquerade brings together the industry professionals, the fans, and the costume artists to celebrate on the body the products around which the community gathers. Presenters may come from any of the many branches of fan and professional life, and judges are chosen from among the most highly respected costumers, graphic artists, and industry literary professionals. Susan Shwartz, a longtime fan and science fiction writer, served as a judge at the MagiCon masquerade in 1992. Her experience carries a powerful sense of appreciation for the ritual aspect of the event:

> Marty Gear has long been a friend of mine. Note: He always does the masquerades in vampire regalia. This is Tradition. Anyhow, I was flattered that he asked me to help judge the masquerade. While people know I love clothes and I dress up, it's still an honor to be asked to judge, especially for a pro who is not a costumer. Being asked to judge at a Worldcon is like being on one of the big, big panels with a lot of Hugo winners. It's a credit to you.
>
> That morning, I had my hair done. Not that anyone was looking at me, but, like the Hugos, the masquerade is an important occasion. And, as a judge, I wanted to do it up properly. I had a long chiffon skirt, a black sequined camisole, and a beaded cardigan jacket. And glittery shoes, of course. Suitable.

To this point, Shwartz is describing her response to the invitation to judge the masquerade. Twice she makes reference to the Hugos, the awards for literature and art voted by Worldcon participants. While perhaps not as prestigious as many outside literary awards, the Hugos represent a lifelong goal for many professionals in the field who began their science fiction lives as fans. As a ceremonial event, the Hugos generally attract a smaller audience than the masquerade, but for the professional and fan writer the event can mean elevation in the eyes of their peers. By making this comparison, Shwartz relates the honor of judging the masquerade to the honor of receiving an award. Next, Shwartz describes costumes that particularly stayed in her mind:

> I remember the "Heroes" exhibit. The costumes were exact replicas of the Estevez drawings and the Whalen cover of the Dorsai things. I was blinking furiously: I _love_ the Dorsai books. And when the Lost Dorsai (I think it was), Michael de Sandoval, put his cap on the young Dorsai's head, I lost it. All around me, even the judges were losing it; and people were cheering.
>
> The Ice exhibit was truly masterly. It won the award it should have won—most beautiful. Lapplander/Sami costumes transmuted via the SNOW QUEEN, as it seemed to me, in pastels. The master-class costumers can be truly awesome—and this was a big, well-organized group. It also won my private vote for _fine_ competitors. Because when "Heroes," which really _did_ express what I felt about SF, won for "Best in Show," the Ice people flourished maces, scepters, and fists, and shouted YES!
>
> Now those are _fans_![40]

"Heroes" seems to have affected everyone present in the same way. As Shwartz says above, the tableau won "best in show." More important, given that it was not among the most elaborate or slick presentations, when asked what costume they remembered most, convention-goers who attended the masquerade mentioned it more often than any other presentation. Here is the voiceover text that accompanied the presentation of the costume tableau:

> (Entry number 27 in the Journeyman Division.) I did not come quickly to books. Life offered many other distractions. But slowly I discovered and, almost in spite of myself, from them I learned. Among others I discovered the Dorsai and from them I learned. From Amanda I learned perseverance and of

persuasion and of family and of home. . . . From Michael I learned of self, and of honor, and courage as he made the ultimate sacrifice. And from Ian, and from Hinton, and from all the others, I learned. And I rode into the future on the shoulders of heroes.[41]

**Master of Ceremonies:** That was "Heroes," a recreation from the works of Gordon R. Dickson by David Chalker and Kathryn and Duane Elms.

Pierre Pettinger, reporting in GEnie's Costumers' Category, described the presentation:

> Entry 27 Heroes (Journeyman Class) by Kathryn and Duane Elms with David Chalker.[42] The lights come up on a small boy sitting between two huge books featuring covers from two of the Dorsai novels by Gordon Dickson. To a narration about reading, learning lessons from books, first from Amanda (a Dorsai character); the boy opens the first book and Amanda steps out. Then the narration speaks of learning from Michael. He opens the second book and Michael steps out. All three come to center stage, as the narration speaks of riding into the future on the shoulders of Heroes. Very impressive, very emotional, and very appropriate for the 50th Worldcon. Awards given: Workmanship—Most Evocative Costumes and Props—CostumeApa Originality Award Presentation—Best in Show.

Julie Zetterberg added that " 'Heroes' . . . "had several of us crying our makeup off backstage," and another poster added, "'Heroes' made me cry too. Trust me, there weren't a lot of us in the audience who had dry eyes."

"Heroes" stayed in the mind not because it was the most complex or beautiful costume, but because it represented the things most science fiction fans hold closest to their hearts: the stuff, especially the literature, and the sense of themselves as readers, learning and becoming through the books they read. It focused the hearts of the community on the reasons they are fans and gave an emotional center to the practice of fandom to which participants may devote their lives without ever articulating what lies at the heart of their actions. It wasn't just the costume, movingly presented, that created that focus, that sense that something deep at the heart of the community had been articulated. Rather, it was the sharing, in the dark, of a vision of community, an emotional bond that tied the participants together because they felt the pull of a common memory of childhood. That memory, however different in content, is so identical in affect that for the ninety seconds of the presentation, the entire audience became that child on the stage.

## Why Costume

In spite of conflict with mainstream culture and some censure from within the community itself, costume continues to thrive because it fulfills so many needs of the community. Unlike events such as the Hugo awards or panel discussions, which can invoke meaning for both community members and outsiders, costume serves specific insider purposes that are generally misinterpreted by those sharing space with them.

Fans use dress and costume like ritual garb to establish space and time as particular to the social functioning of the group, to train new members in the conventions of the community, and to reinforce a sense of identity among the established members. Costume acts symbolically to represent and define the sometimes surprising limits of the genre as constructed by the living community rather than the market forces that establish bookshelf placement in the local Walden or B. Dalton. For a smaller group, costume also represents a highly developed art form reminiscent of Victorian tableaux.

The convention is a performative event, in which a conceptual community tied together by long-distance communication, mass market publications, and occasional face-to-face meetings is physically played out for the benefit of the players.[43] The ritual performance of costume appears most strikingly in the formal masquerade. In part, long-term fans resist costume because they do not need it: their initiation lies in the past. But fandom has simply grown too large to expect new participants to enter the community with anything like socialization to its norms. Neophytes need costume to learn, and longer-term fans need costume, especially the masquerade, to provide that inclusive sense of unity that draws the new member and long-time fan together in the same community.

Fans who look back to the history of fandom point to the Hugos or the guest of honor speeches to provide this unity, but the literature is no longer the definition of the genre it once was. Costume, which includes the fan as actor and as audience, spans the breach between the written and the visual modalities of the genre in a display that appeals to the aesthetic and the emotional commonalities among community members. Costumes that re-create the art and film characters from across the history of the form, costumes that depict mythological themes or other themes that may be used in science fiction or fantasy, may likewise reinforce the sense the audience takes away that they are all members of the same group.

## The Hugo Awards

The Hugo Award ceremony, by contrast, expresses for (and to) fandom its self-image, the face by which the community would like to be known in the wider world outside the genre. This is the event for which press releases are prepared, the event by which the convention hopes the public will know and understand them: as a literary society recognizing the best in the literature of the culture.

Attendees of the current and preceding Worldcon, both industry professionals and fans, are eligible to vote on the Hugo Awards, named after Hugo Gernsback, the titular father of science fiction. The convention gives Hugo Awards in a variety of categories, both professional and noncommercial, and these categories reify in a public way the significance of activities the community values. In noncommercial work, the community rewards service that sustains it in the form by which members want the outside world to know them—for work at conventions and in science fiction (not media) fanzines.[44] Here we find no recognition of costume or costumers, song or singers or songwriters. These latter practices have grown meaningful inside the community, but they arise out of a different struggle from that early striving to read, to publish, to make the printed word a home, out of which the Hugo Award ceremony arose in the 1950s.[45] Most important, community members see these activities as too easy for the outsider looking for spectacle to trivialize.

In commercial work, the community does recognize a dramatic presentation, a science fiction movie or a single episode of a science fiction television series. But again, most of the awards revolve around the world of print media and in particular science fiction rather than fantasy or horror, both of which are seen as adjuncts to the genre where "true" meaning is found: science fiction, the fantasy of the rational. Even the art awards generally go to science fiction cover art and cover artists.

To a critic looking in from the outside, the awards and the award ceremony may seem to represent the fetishization of the commodity, mass-marketed pulp fiction. A closer look, however, reveals something deeper—a demonstration of the power to shape the genre that the fan community shares with the industry. As master of ceremonies Spider Robinson, well-known writer of science fiction, explained before announcing the winners at MagiCon, the 1992 Worldcon in Orlando, Florida,

> **Spider Robinson:** Publishers do pay attention to the professionals, they do pay careful attention to who wins the Nebula Awards.[46] But the ones they really pay attention to are those who win the Hugo Awards. [It] can make the difference between driving a cab and writing science fiction for a living.

Publishers pay attention to the Hugo Awards because they understand through experience a fact that critics of fan culture dismiss: fandom does accurately represent the reading taste of the vast majority of readers who do not themselves wish to participate or have never heard of fandom. Ironically, few eligible particpants actually vote for the Hugo awards. Of the seven or eight thousand potential voters eligible to nominate for the Hugo awards, MagiCon received fewer than 500 valid ballots.[47] Final voting usually includes fewer than 1,000 ballots from eligible participants.[48] In spite of the limited number of voters, however, this small sampling of readers who vote on the Hugos[49] have an uncanny knack for picking the books with survival value. Most Hugo-winning novels remain in print, and many, like Alfred Bester's *Demolished Man*, the first Hugo awarded, in 1953, and Ursula K. Le Guin's *The Left Hand of Darkness*, the first Hugo awarded to a woman for a novel, in 1970, have become acknowledged classics outside the genre.

The award itself is a basic rocket ship, but each year the host worldcon chooses an artist who designs a new base. Robinson described the base and its special significance for science fiction fans in 1992:

> **Robinson:** As is only appropriate for the fiftieth world science fiction convention, we have particularly special Hugos this year. The bases of this year's Hugo trophies were constructed and designed by Phil Tortelluci. Each of these bases was hand-painted by him, and each includes a piece of the gantry from pad 26, the launch pad from which the first successful American satellite was launched, Explorer 1. The rockets themselves are gold-plated this year, to commemorate the fiftieth Worldcon.

The award, like the ceremony, takes us back into the world and shares a particularly strong belief held in the community: the literature fans value merits the attention they lavish on it, not merely as well-executed escapist literature but as a template for the future. The pieces of rocket gantry embedded in the award serve as evidence that the belief in science fiction as a roadmap to the future arises out of an empirically provable past. Science fiction, most fans will tell you, put a man on the moon. And science fiction put a computer in your living room. The degree to which this is true may be debatable, but the belief in it is not.

As part of fandom's presentation of self to the outside world, industry professionals who win the award take the opportunity to restate publicly their connection to the fan community. Many of them—writers, editors, and agents—started as fans. As part of the science fiction literary establishment, they may continue to change positions: writers become editors and vice versa, agents often start as editors, and professionals at all levels of the industry may write or edit for free in the APAs and fanzines with no loss of credibility.[50] Fandom therefore awards the Hugos to both fans and professionals with a proprietary pride, and the winners accept the awards in the same spirit, as Nancy Kress expressed in 1992 in her acceptance speech for best novella, "Beggars in Spain":[51]

> [My] first worldcon was in 1980, and I didn't know a single soul when I went to that convention. I had just discovered such a thing as fandom and world science fiction conventions existed. . . . I attended the Hugo awards. . . . And I sat way in the back, in the top tier of the gallery. . . .[52] One of the people who won that night was George R. R. Martin, for one of his short fictions. Jimmy Carter was president then, for a few more months, and there were a lot of jokes about "lusting in your heart" going around. When George R. R. Martin won, he came up to the podium, and he said that for years he had watched other people win Hugos, and he had lusted in his heart for one. Then he took his Hugo, and he held it up like this . . . up over his head and he said, "And now I've finally got it." And so, in memory of that night, when I didn't know a single soul or any of you or how good science fiction was going to be to me, now I've finally got it. And one more thing. If somewhere out there tonight, somebody else is out there for the first time or second time and doesn't know anybody, and is sitting in the back somewhere, and you are thinking the exact same thing, go for it![53]

Here, in her acceptance speech, Kress reaffirms one of the most closely held beliefs in the fan community: nothing stands between the fan and community building or the industry but the decision to turn the desire into action. Anyone in the community can wind up on the dais with a Hugo in her hand, because the genre, like the community, is their creation too.

Anyone who has ever written a book knows that wishing won't put the words on the page, but the core of this community is not about wishing; it's about doing. Every moment of enculturation, every ceremony and conversation is about doing something valued in the community. At the Hugo Awards ceremony, fandom offers to the outside world its vision of itself not as consumers, but as creators of the genre and the world that genre creates.

# The Cyberscape: GEnie and the Rise of the Internet

# 4

Of late, a plethora of books about the way computers are changing how we live and see ourselves have made their appearance on the bookshelves. Sherry Turkle, with two books on the subject, may be the most knowledgeable of the writers mining this new world,[1] but she has hardly been alone. Writers like Clifford Stoll[2] warn of the dangers of cyberspace directly while others, like Andrew Ross, conflate the technology with its own creation-myth fiction, walking a carefully enthusiastic line between postmodern critique and an eye for the potential for resistance and trans-formation of technoculture.[3] Others seem to conflate all contemporary counter-culture under the rubric of cyber-cognate-of-your-choice, taking the reader on a tour of the freak show that is *Cyberia* hitting *Escape Velocity*.[4] The term "cyber" has become a metaphor for disconnection, or for the frantic efforts of a null generation to make contact without sacrificing their intrinsic isolation, an isolation reinforced by the spiky fence of body piercing and tattoo.

Of course, there is no null generation, just the usual subsets of alienation among the many youth cultures of the moment, a part of which science fiction culture has always attracted. And "cyber" is already a metaphor for what is, in this community, a basic form of communication. In science fiction, "cyber" always includes as part of its paradigm the mutually dependent questions of what is human, and where does communication occur, at the interface with technology.

Certainly, the strange and scary is out there, and with increasingly complex browser search engine technology it is easier to find than ever. Some people even live out there on the fringes Mark Dery describes in *Escape Velocity*, and we will meet some of them in Chapters 8 and 9 of this book. But we tend to forget that the books we are reading have been written by people who, to some extent, likewise live there. Writers whose books present a fearful vision of cyberspace may be stepping away from the computer culture, or may never have truly understood it at all. Those who invite us to the phreak show, however, approach their subject not as novices learning the ins and outs of everyday Net life, but as somewhat jaded denizens looking beyond the norm for something interesting to examine in their community.

## Science Fiction Was Already Out There

Anyone who participates in either of the closely linked communities of science fiction and the Internet needs no persuasion that science fiction has been a part of computing since its beginning, and the conceptual landscape of science fiction culture has to a great extent shaped the cyberscape. The fact is so self-evident that, when describing the interests of hackers and phreaks, the *Hacker's Dictionary* doesn't even mention science fiction as a generic concept. Rather, it points to specific subsets of science fiction as the purlieu of the community that has created the world of Net communication. Hackers, Steele and Raymond inform us, include *Analog* magazine in their reading, Dungeons and Dragons among their hobbies. Neopaganism and the science fiction community's religious parodies such as the Church of the Subgenius fall within the religious interests of hackers, along with Zen and the Judeo-Christian traditions.[5]

According to Howard Rheingold, SF-Lovers appeared as the first large e-list on the ARPANET in the mid-1970s. At the time, the list included only ARPA researchers like Vint Cerf sharing a sense of science fiction community in the new virtual venue long before the concept of virtual reality existed.[6] By 1979, however, Saul Jaffe, current moderator of SF-Lovers, and then a student at Rutgers University, had found the group as a BBS (bulletin board system) operating out of MIT. After a brief hiatus, the list moved to Rutgers University in the early '80s, where it has remained and continues as the grandfather of virtual science fiction communities.[7]

### E-lists and BBS and Usenet

In the time before commercial services, computer enthusiasts who were also science fiction fans had a number of options by which they could foster their online community. Bulletin boards connected individual computers via telephone line to a host computer. A bulletin board fan wanted to contact a science fiction bulletin board in San Francisco dialed direct to the phone number of the machine in San Francisco. If the fan lived in New York or Brisbane, that made for a serious long-distance phone bill, but it did give home computer owners access to computer-mediated communication without an Internet account.

Usenet (see Appendix 1 for a discussion of the development of e-mail lists and Usenet) would seem like the best compromise between the small town of bulletin board culture and the wide world of the Internet. Rec.arts.sf. and its sub-hierarchies have carried heavy traffic since the beginning of the Usenet. But for many people it still had serious drawbacks. First, one needed access to a server that housed the Usenet, and until the mid-1980s that usually meant a university or research institution account. Second, as the Usenet went worldwide, the number of people participating grew into the millions.[8] While the number participating in a specific topic seldom grew to such an unmanageable size, many topics in rec.arts.sf became uncomfortably crowded, to the extent that community building grew difficult. And because so many of the early participants, particularly on recreational topics such as science fiction, were late adolescent male university students, the tone of conversation seldom reached the levels that would interest those who fell outside this demographic category.

Demographics aside, Usenet and e-mail lists had one other striking disadvantage for the many newly technophilic computer users who fueled the PC explosion in the mid-1980s. They both required an account with access to electronic mail and a host site for the Usenet topic groups. Users did not need this higher-level access for local bulletin boards, but their telephone bill limited their participation in the global party. Although no longer limited to government funded researchers, the Internet still drew most of its material and most of its participants from the university and government systems.

The fledgling cooperative and commercial systems coming into existence in the mid-1980s offered an alternative to the heated world of the Usenet. The Well, as documented by Howard Rheingold, is the best known of the cooperative services, while Compuserve and GEnie split the commercial business. Prodigy entered the market soon after with the idea of the future—a graphical interface that offered a frame of advertising around the communication screen—but users still "jumped" around the system using text commands, and few home machines had the speed or memory capacity to download the images efficiently. Latecomer America Online (AOL) swept the competition in the 1990s with a user-simple graphical interface of button-style menus.[9] But this time the market was ready: the computers of the '90s had the speed and the memory to handle the graphics, and the shift to color monitors was almost complete. For science fiction, however, the most important of these services turned out to be GEnie.

## GEnie! GEnie!

I first heard the GEnie chant during the Meet the Pros party at MagiCon, the World Science Fiction Convention in Orlando, Florida in 1992. Badges with the magic lamp logo appeared on the lapels of fans and professionals who were greeting each other like long-lost friends. Susan Shwartz and Josepha Sherman, science fiction and fantasy writers from New York, explained the service to me and told me I had to join if I wanted to understand where science fiction culture was heading in the '90s. So when I came home I signed up.

It was a nightmare. GEnie had no interface in the way we think of them today, just text-based directories of pay services with one category that took one into basic services—those materials available on GEnie for only the basic charges, and no special cost-per-use charge in addition to its standard connect time fee. That one link for basic services led to the bulletin boards—discussion groups in the BBS style—on topics as wide ranging as Military, Pets and Pet Owners, and Science Fiction and Fantasy. I'd finally found what I'd been looking for. But, here again I was faced with more lists: lists of categories and, inside categories, lists of topics.

After spending a month figuring out how to send basic in-system e-mail (to members of the same service, as opposed to Internet e-mail, which I never did master on GEnie) and how to find, at the end of a series of menus, the message boards, I called Jim Macdonald, sysop for the Science Fiction RoundTable (SFRT).

"Sysop" is short for system operator. At the time I read the title of sysop as denoting a technical position, and imagined white coats and platter-sized disks. But Jim explained the GEnie take on the term:

> **Jim Macdonald:**   I am an independent contractor. I've got a contract with GE. I'm supposed to make sure that people don't use obscene language . . . nobody violates copyright or trademark . . . that nothing happens that is against the business interests of General Electric. . . . I read every post, and make a judgment call.

To fulfill the contract, a sysop had a few more commands at his disposal than other users, including the ability to delete or move offensive posts or to move messages that have simply been posted to the incorrect place. But Macdonald saw his position in more proactive terms:

> I use the genial host model. I'm the guy who meets the guests at the door . . . introduces them to people . . . that's one model for what a sysop does. Another model is the gardener model, where the gardener comes out and prunes here, fertilizes there.

Macdonald had a long history in science fiction and with computers when he took the position of sysop. When he explained to me how GEnie came to be, I understood why the system was so cumbersome to use and why the science fiction community became problematic for it:

> There's a large central computer somewhere in Ohio. And on that computer there are a whole bunch of files that are connected to phone lines that are owned by General Electric. They [General Electric] noticed one day that they weren't using these computers and phone lines pretty much after business hours. . . . And so they opened this up to the public to call after working hours, because General Electric uses their net during the daytime. And they made some money off the excess capacity.

Unlike Prodigy, and well before AOL, both designed for the public small-user market, General Electric provided for a minimum level of low-cost participation in some home-use service on their business system at off hours, from six in the evening to eight in the morning, with the lowest cost after eleven at night. They provided traffic control software based on the system they used to archive GE's internal e-mail and a corps of private contractors to act as sysops to keep things running smoothly.

Science fiction fans coming to GEnie between the 1980s and the early '90s had a ready made cognitive landscape of long-distance community in the convention culture. GEnie offered a structural hierarchy in the software—those categories and topics I had discovered—that Jim Turner, the original GEnie SFRT sysop and long-time convention fan, used to recreate the convention structure online. Categories brought together clusters of topics of interest to particular subfandoms much as tracks of programming do at a convention, and topics became the virtual equivalent of panel discussions:

**Macdonald:** You can take the convention mode for what the SFRT is, I've been trying to run it as if it were a major convention . . . a convention of 3,000, people, 4,000 people. It's a pretty fair-sized regional.

To run a convention, however, one needs an attraction, and according to Macdonald the solution to that problem also came from Jim Turner:

> We attracted a whole lot of professionals early on, and this was Jim Turner's idea . . . to grant free flags to members of SFWA [Science Fiction and Fantasy Writers of America]. Now, [a] free flag allows you to post during the day [and] . . . hang out in the real time conference or download from the library without paying for them. . . . And we give them [SFWA members] also the private hidden areas where they can hang out. There's the SFWA lounge, for example. You've seen that hanging up there like a ghost. And there's a whole lot of prestige in being able to get into there and being able to talk with your buddies and sit on the floor and call a cat a bastard and all this good stuff.[10]

Macdonald puts this practice in context for us:

> When free flags were first granted, reading and writing to GEnie cost around $30/hour during the day. By granting the flags, the SFWA pros could come during the day and post their messages that would be waiting for the other customers at night, when the rates went down to about $10/hour. It was like a grocery store and the SF pros were restocking the shelves during the day. Here were people who would ordinarily be commanding ten cents a word or more, giving me the words for free, that GE would then resell to the customers. It was great.[11]

The science fiction professionals flocked to GEnie, drawn by the free flags and the perks, private areas, which included topic categories for judging panels for the major committee awards such as the Nebulas, and categories of topics where writers in shared worlds[12] could discuss their work and collaborate online.

Macdonald, a science fiction fan and professional writer himself, brought to the mix a convention sensibility that pervaded the science fiction and fantasy sections of the service. While members of other RoundTables would shy clear of the SFRT because of its well-earned reputation for the rough and tumble nature of its boards, Macdonald recognized this as science fiction culture replicating itself on the phosphor landscape and treated it with the panache of a longtime APA member:

> We are blazing new paths. And I think a large part of it is because science fiction fandom was already a discrete group. It's not like all Apple users, say. We are a very defined subculture, with all our conventions and everything, and there's a long tradition of APA-hacking, for example, I've been an APAnage since golly, '78 . . . [GEnie] it's got all the advantages of your 3 a.m. bull session, with none of the disadvantages.

It was in those virtual 3 a.m. bull sessions that GEnie management and the fan community clashed. The corporate management did not seem to understand that the online science fiction community, like its real-time counterpart, thrives late at night. Many of the early service users came out of, or still belonged to, university systems where computer time had always been available to them only in the wee hours. For its part, the science fiction culture fostered at conventions identified late-night hours as those set aside for social life, including pranks, and not sleep.

But GEnie was a major supplier of online services to major corporations, and in the beginning online service providers did not see themselves as communication suppliers; they perceived themselves as vendors of a variety of services that could be purchased from them and used online. These included access to newspaper archives and investment services and a wide variety of for-profit databases. And they served the corporate market, clients who did not object to paying $18 an hour for connect time and more for fee-based services. GEnie stood for "General Electric Network for Information Exchange," a title that established the model but did not openly state the purpose of the company: the sale of goods and services in excess of the basic connect fee to its client. Once a home user signed on to GEnie, the marketers would lure him to the games, financial, travel, shopping, and chat services that GEnie offered for additional fees. The model worked perfectly well with their business clients, but they hadn't reckoned on the fact that a large pre-existing long-distance community would latch on to their service as the place to make the leap into the twenty-first century. While their business clients were moving into an understanding of computer communication on a telex model but faster and cheaper, and looking to the online service for research tools such as the Dow Jones database, personal computer users rushed to exploit this new way to do community, with science fiction fans in the rowdy forefront.

GEnie had envisioned the RoundTables more on the order of the bulletin board at the local supermarket—pin up a short note, receive a short reply or perhaps contact through e-mail to make an appointment for a chat room—but science fiction fans had discovered a flaw in the money-making system. GEnie sysops monitored messages *after* they were posted, not before, as Prodigy did. If you ran live, or nearly so, the boards could almost function as real-time chat. And at midnight the rates were low even for the paying customers. Participants in the SFRT stayed online, sometimes for hours every night, leaping from topic to topic, maintaining multiple conversations and brewing pranks with the speed and complexity of a live convention. Since this was a writers' culture taking place in a printed medium, no one wanted to appear at a disadvantage; posts were often witty, eloquent, and long. And while the denizens of the SFRT were engaged in verbal dueling, the system slowed to a crawl, making it difficult and inconvenient for the customers who wanted to purchase the pay services that kept the system afloat.

### Pitching Tents in the SFRT: Flamewars and Topic Drift

While trouble was brewing at the home office, the GEnie SFRT was making virtual community at a rapid and unruly rate. When Jim Turner became the SFRT's first sysop, comics were a small subset with just a single category, but they had grown to four categories, with numerous topics in each, and split off to form their own RoundTable a year or so before I joined. Their parting reduced the pressure on the SFRT services for a little while, but the online community had grown so fast, and was posting so enthusiastically, that science fiction fans quickly consumed this small gain. When I talked to Jim Macdonald in late 1992, the SFRT had once again exceeded the capacity of the system to carry it, and he was preparing to split the board into three parts. Jim had the technical headache, but I went to Susan Shwartz, who had first urged me to sign up, when I needed to understand the SFRT community from the perspective of a participant:

> **Susan Shwartz:** It really is a community . . . when it works, it's good. When there's an emergency, it's marvelous. You know, we can locate people, we can reach out to people very very nicely. But it's like any other aspect of the fannish community. When it's bad, it's horrible, because it closes in, and it really becomes the whole world for a while, and you've got to watch for that or become a "get-a-life."[13]

That community, however, was socialized to the norms of the science fiction community, which can at times be harsh:

> We're perceived as kind of an intellectual biker gang with an addiction to topic drift and flamewars. SFRT is perceived by other boards as very arrogant, kind of crazy. Flamewars are when you get angry and you say so, immoderately. GEnie is a conceptual medium. Since the reaction is speed-of-light time, and you can't see body language, you're going to react to strongly worded posts, and very possibly you are going to react wrongly. Longer and harder. It can be a real mess.

Shwartz admits to having been a bit of a flamewar artist herself in the defense of GEnie and her own position on a given issue, while acknowledging that participation in a flamewar can have repercussions:

> I have to watch to protect what I think is the truth, that makes sense to me . . . and I upset people sometimes if I'm forcible, and it can be a source of extreme psychic pain if you diverge from the consensus over time, because they will bring pressure to bear. The consensus is a very powerful thing.

For a sysop, the issue of flamewars can provide an ethical dilemma of its own. To ban them seems to smack of censorship, which the science fiction community abhors. And the science fiction community has a history of feuding in the APAs and fanzines that goes back to the 1920s. As an APA veteran, however, sysop Jim Macdonald has his own solution for the problem of flamewars:

> **Macdonald:** I've got a couple of topics where I just move them, and I put them down there and let people who enjoy that kind of thing do it. . . . Its the Radioactive Materials category . . . it's where we search you on the way in; if you don't have a [virtual] knife or a gun we give you one so you start even. . . . There are also notorious "gunslingers," and you find people mostly steering clear of them, and then again you find people who go gunning for the gunslingers. . . . And down in the Dueling Modems you will find discussions of other flamewars on other boards being rated. They are currently rating the flamewar about whether or not President Reagan's face belongs on Mt. Rushmore. That's a flamewar currently going on in the Public Forum.[14]

Veterans of the science fiction fandom feuds gave fanciful ratings based on an Olympic scoring style, often with eloquently satirical analysis of the rhetoric of the flamers. Science fiction may not have invented the flamewar, but it certainly drew from a tradition of long-distance written-word feuding and personal attack that went as far back as the New York fan feuds of the 1920s and the New York–Philadelphia feuds of the '30s. Most fans were grateful that Macdonald found a way to allow the fan tradition of vituperation to continue while leaving the majority to enjoy themselves out of the line of fire.

Topic drift, however, brought the SFRT into conflict with the sale of GEnie's more lucrative Chat boards, and it often brought the science fiction boards into conflict with the sysops of other RoundTables. In the language of the bulletin boards and e-lists, topic drift is the development of tangential discussion or personal conversation that rightly belongs in another topic or category. On GEnie, this could also mean that the discussion should appear in a completely different Round-Table, like Pets or Politics:

> **Macdonald:**   I was taking a bit of flak from GEnie management—when people started talking about recipes, for example, the sysop of the Cooking RT would complain to my product manager. . . . So I'd get these notes saying, "Please explain how Apple Crumb Cake is science fiction." . . . Sysops were paid by the amount of traffic they generated, and the sysops of other RTs were jealous. . . . Eventually I had to show my product manager some paper APAs, showing regular APA members talking about non-SF movies, and recipes, and gardening, and what-may-have-you and saying, "This has been going on in SF fandom since the 1920s. This is what science fiction is all about."
>
> I had something I called "SFRT Cammie Netting" which involved putting deceptive titles on the topics. People just looking at the topic lists would have no idea what was going on, unless they were regular enough visitors to read the messages rather than just scanning category names and topic titles. So a topic about pets might have a title like "alien species" but all the regulars would know what it really was.[15]

Unrest among sysops of those other RoundTables created one problem for the service. More significantly from GEnie's perspective, much of topic drift did not belong in the "free" bulletin board section of the service at all. Discussion that did not bear specifically on the subject matter of a RoundTable belonged on the Chat boards for an extra fee. Unlike Real Time Chat (RTC), the Chat boards offered the same bulletin board system as the RoundTables, but "allowed" personal conversation to take place there in the posts. And unlike the loophole discussed above, where fans and pros could take advantage of the fact that GEnie did not filter posts to participate in almost-live give and take in the topics of the RoundTables themselves, GEnie had a specific rule against topic drift.

But topic drift is intrinsic to the rules of social discourse in science fiction, and has been since the earliest fanzines issued convention and travel reports, discussed music and stereo equipment, and turned the mundane details of life fannish by relating them in fanzines and APAs. Members of the online division of science fiction culture used the SFRT to talk about their cats and horses and to offer each other virtual chocolate on bad days. They insisted their conversations were intrinsic to science fiction: participants didn't care about the opinion of someone who had never read Heinlein or Haldeman or Cherryh. They cared about opinions formed in the same literary stew as their own. So members of the SFRT used their Round-Table with impunity, in full knowledge that they broke the rules, out of a culture entrenched in the "postmodern" notion that anyone gets a say for the price of a stamp, the model that had fueled the APAs and fanzines for decades. They could not be stopped. And, as Shwartz pointed out, that was the key to GEnie culture:

> [Topic drift] cements the community. You get a network of associations. It is more intricate than a linear discussion. Sometimes the drift drives people crazy, and it isn't productive, but sometimes it's really good . . . it [the SFRT] has a lot of pros and we wanted it this way. . . .
>
> When Merlin [Shwartz's cat] died, everybody was mourning for him in my topic, and then I wrote my story, "Critical Cat," . . . and people really loved that story, and everybody likes to talk about their animals.

Merlin's death created another crisis for the sysop:

> **Macdonald:**   One of the big battles behind the scenes was when Susan Shwartz's cat died, and people were expressing sympathy, and the sysop of the Pets RT came by, and decided that I was stealing Pets' traffic by failing to delete the sympathy messages and locking the topic.[16]

For Shwartz, expressions of mourning belonged within the science fiction community, however, and not shared among the strangers on the Pets RoundTable. In her topic, Shwartz championed topic drift in subjects that interested her as a woman and as a member of the science fiction community:

> **Shwartz:**   In many ways, talking about clothes is a liberation for women. Because you're not just talking about clothes . . . you're talking about what a woman will permit herself to have, you're talking how a woman feels about herself. . . . It is a healthy thing to convince her that she is worth it. Also it is important . . . for men to perceive, "No, we are not going to be abashed because we're talking about shopping. You come in and sit down and talk about sports and expect it to be respected, but you snicker when we talk about clothes. . . . Well, . . . Sit and listen a while."
>
> And with [designer] Willow, with jewelry . . . we exchange [discuss] jewelry as a sign of "I have this, you have that, this is beautiful, we all appreciate these things." Its a forming of consensus in the community.[17]

To accommodate the RoundTable's key attractions—the professionals in the field like Susan Shwartz who made GEnie their online home—former sysop Jim Macdonald and current sysop Nic Grabien agreed to allow conversation in those topics set up for each professional to range as freely as the topic-holder wished.

While most topic drift on GEnie occurred in the organic way that conversation mutates over time, occasionally topics erupted in storms of creative mayhem that could leave sysops tearing their hair and participants chatting in the fallout for months. The most infamous of these topic hijackings, the Great Cattle Raid, occurred shortly before I joined the service, but has lived on in GEnie lore. Sysop Jim Macdonald told me the story:

> One night there was a cattle raid throughout the authors' topics. It started off in one topic with just a few little ASCII pictures of cows. Then it moved on to another topic with more cows, with everybody who was involved in the cattle raid running through and posting things, "Yippee Kayee—onto category 8, topic 12, hoy-ooh!" and then more pictures of cows. And it eventually wound up down in Katherine Lawrence's topic, where they slaughtered all the cows and had a barbecue.

I asked Macdonald if he had not planned the cattle raid to keep people interested in the service, perhaps on a slow night, but he assured me he hadn't thought of the romp:

> This was just ordinary customers doing this. And it happened one night, about eleven o'clock one night. I believe it started in the Judy Tarr topic and eventually the cattle raid closed out [exceeded the 999-message capacity of a topic] at least one topic, so they started a new topic to continue the cattle raid.

Pro topics established a conceptual "owned" space in which the fertile creativity of the science fiction fans and professionals could run wild, and it did. The more usual form of organic topic drift helped this process along in two ways. First, the idea that the topic did not have to stay specifically on a prearranged and formal trajectory, but could range freely, opened up the participants to one another and to the possibilities of free association. Second, and perhaps most important, topic drift refers, on GEnie, not only to the drift of the conversation in the topic, but to the drift of the conversation from topic to topic. So one can take a conversation with ASCII cattle in one topic and move it to another and another, in an accelerated and playful form of topic drift, just as a given discussion, of a convention, or of a subtopic like "charactertorture" in writing, can drift from topic to topic as the participants move around the boards. Topic drift within a topic allows normal conversation to occur. Conversational drift from topic to topic tramples the artificial boundaries that inhibit community formation across specific associational lines.

Eventually, fans who developed a following for their conversation also had topics of their own. But topic drift remained a bone of contention at GEnie long after the service eliminated its premium dial-up rates. For the culture that grew there, however, topic drift was vital for the development of the customs and rituals that cemented the community.

## Customs and Rituals

No community can exist without its customs and rituals of inclusion and protection. Science fiction, like any other community, has long-established real-world rituals, like the masquerade and the Hugo awards, and the lived world of online science fiction culture likewise has its own forms established on GEnie. One of the more important is a recognition of the rite of passage from being an aspiring writer to being a commercially published writer, as Shwartz described:

Somebody makes their first sale, and the fun is that that person's topic is then created, and that person is duly installed in the topic, and this is a great compliment. You know, you are now a pro, you now have a topic. . . . [T]he person has sold a story. The person posts the "yeah, I did it!" either in the editor's topic after the editor has, or the person posts it in the topic of a friend who has a topic. And then a topic is duly started.

It is generally bad form for a new pro to start a topic for herself; a friend in the business will usually do this with some fanfare as a form of welcoming the newly published into the ranks of the community they are joining: that of the pros. But topics could go away again if there was no activity for thirty days. This did not present a problem when the topic holder could reach the computer, but travel or illness could mean that a sysop might eliminate a topic in the absence of those who conversed there. So GEnie-ites again devised a way to circumvent the rules:

**Shwartz:** Somebody is away for a couple days or couple weeks, their topic gets trashed. You don't know what's going to happen. They could have a caravan or a pirate ship or a cattle raid or something. And you could have a yard sale, you can have terrible gardening. You could have an infestation of virtual cats or a ten–foot plastic fluorescent flamingo. You don't know. Or you could have the Kzinti using it as a litterbox, or one of Dennis McKiernan's dragons have an accident. This has all happened to me. Trashing a topic is cool, rather like toilet-papering a house when I was in high school—and yes, I am aware of how juvenile this sounds. It's fun anyhow.

Obviously, a simple message like "Mary Sue isn't back yet," would have served the stated purpose: to keep the sysop from closing the space due to lack of activity. But trashing topics also served much the same purpose as tagging does on city streets. While holding the space open, it left multiple reminders of the presence of the community in the temporary absence of the topic's center, the writer or editor who usually held court there. Sometimes, however, a member would disappear forever.

## Lest We Forget

All communities must find ways to acknowledge the passing of friends by death or by departure, and GEnie faced both kinds of crises and formed its own rituals to cope. Death is by far the most serious, and one that needs to be communicated quickly as people sign on. Susan Shwartz explained the beginning of the GEnie custom of posting a single ASCII rose at the death of a subscriber:

**Shwartz:** Has anybody told you about Mary?[18] The eleventh was the anniversary of her suicide. Mary was a young woman who sold her first story, she went to Clarion. Mary had a lot of demons, I think. And she was going pro, she was happy about it, she had joined the Science Fiction Writers of America, and then, she hanged herself, and it came on the board, and they put a rose up . . . and everybody posted memories of Mary and they collected her posts in a topic. . . . And thereafter, whenever somebody important to the community died, the rose came back. And now, Asimov's dead, so the rose goes up. If somebody's shaky, the word goes out, "Don't die, we don't need another god-damned rose." To the extent that when one person on the board was using a rose as a sort of vanity signature, everybody went "argh" and the rose had to go.

**Ethnographer:**   Do you know why they picked a rose?

**Shwartz:**   The single rose? Mary was a young woman, 24–25 years old. GEnie is as sentimental as hell.

Discussion of Mary's death and the community's response to it stands in marked contrast to the suicide described in Howard Rheingold's *Virtual Community*.[19] In the Well community, the participant erased not only his life but also his posts, leaving a gap in the structure of the community, in the history of its conversations. Although GEnie subscribers have the command option to delete their posts, Mary did not do so. Her posts were gathered together so that participants could see them again, could comment on them, and could offer their memories surrounded by the reminders of Mary's participation. During my participation on GEnie, I observed the appearance of the virtual rose on a number of occasions, deaths of subscribers and deaths of nonsubscribers important to the larger community of science fiction. It remained an important symbol of mourning for fans and pros alike.

The death of a participant can deal an online community a harsh blow, but so can threats to the integrity of the system from service providers, perceived as outsiders by the community. GEnie underwent a number of such crises, and developed a ritual both for retaining the community knowledge and for saying goodbye. Damon Knight started the GEnie History topic after a series of blows to the community—division of the SFRT into three discrete parts and a new price structure that hit hardest those who spent most time online—had sent the science fiction fans scurrying for a cheaper place to pitch their virtual tents.

### Fan History

Fan history has always played an important part in community maintenance. In books such as Damon Knight's own *The Futurians*[20] and in oral narratives told at convention panels and collected by oral historians of the community, science fiction fandom carries its traditions from generation to generation. In the History topic, members carried this tradition forward, recreating the story of the GEnie online science fiction community from its beginning in 1985 to the perilous times in 1993 when the community seemed about to move on. Flamewars dominated much of the discussion; often the mere recounting of a flamewar that took place years in the past would drag to the surface those same feelings of righteous indignation and hurt that fueled the original flamewar. Ironically, this focus on the feuds of the online community parallels the recounts of such early feuds in *The Futurians* and other fan histories, as online participants Mitch Wagner and Patrick Nielsen Hayden pointed out:

**Mitch Wagner:**   To my thinking, any history of online interaction in general, or the SFRT in particular, that focuses on the flamewars, would be about as interesting as *This Immortal Storm*, by Sam Moskowitz, with its deathless snooz-a-rama sturm–und–drang prose about fandom in the 1930s and the catfights back then. Does anybody care today who was and wasn't talking to whom on the Futurians?[21]

**Patrick Nielsen Hayden:**   Well, *The Immortal Storm* (note correct title) is certainly badly written and overwrought (James Blish called it "the only history of the 1930s to which World War II comes as an anticlimax"), but far from not caring who wasn't speaking to whom in the Futurians, I regard it as a pretty interesting and significant part of the early history of SF. I mean, some of those Futurians not speaking to one another were fans like Fred Pohl, Donald Wollheim, etc. Are you, Mitch, trying to tell me their relationships to one another are of no conceivable interest, just because they were (avert, avert) grotty fans at the time?

I know, I know, you're trying to be High-Minded and rise above this petty world of flamewars, etc. Doesn't wash. A lot of history is made of exactly this sort of petty stuff, some of which has real consequences.[22]

Later, in personal e-mail, Wagner admitted,

I feel like my original characterization of *The Immortal Storm* was unfair, and I retract it, because I've never read the book. I think Patrick is right to a certain extent—obviously if one assumes that Frederik Pohl's work has literary importance (and I do think it does), then the biographical details of his life become important, and that includes discussion of people he might have disliked and how Pohl acted (and acts) on those dislikes. Still, I think it's possible to get TOO caught up in the details of flamewars, and attach too much importance to them.[23]

Almost as important to fandom as its feud, the History topic recorded its traditions: the ASCII rose for mourning, the salmon of correction (shown by the symbol  and meaning that someone has done something thoughtless or foolish online, and needs a smack in the face with an old salmon, making the "whap" sound), and some of its historic occasions, like the Great Cattle Raid described above.

## Naming Traditions

Important among the events described in the History category is naming, the choosing of screen names that participants use much as CB operators use handles. Unlike some online communities, where members mask identity and even gender with their screen names, the science fiction community prefers to interact with real names and identities online as well as in person. Members sometimes use screen names like nicknames, however, when their identity is already known, and the circumstances of the nick-naming can become part of the lore, as in this example of John C. Bunnell becoming Djonn:

[T]hat happened not long after the Desert Caravan episode in which I played a djinni. There were entirely too many John Bs (Barnes, Betancourt, Bunnell) online, and I decided I needed a new NAMe. I think, in fact, that Katie may have suggested "Djonn" in an RTC, after the aforementioned djinn, and it seemed to fit. . . . The Desert Caravan epic, though, was in Judy [Tarr]'s topic; Susan [Shwartz] coordinated it, but it was Judy's soundstage. (This was, I believe, while she was traveling in Germany.)

The djinn of the Caravan tale, though, was quite different from the Man from Corporate, who predates that set of adventures by a bit. What eventually turned into Corporate started out as a multiversal mail order, catering, and talent-agent service in an old-CAT 24 topic Lea Hernandez had started, called something like "Puma, Kzin, Monkeyboys, Love Slaves." I forget now exactly how the shtick leaked out to the author topics (it was probably partly Susan Shwartz's fault, she having been one of the early denizens of that topic), but leak it did. "Corporate," BTW [by the way], was not originally meant to be the name of the company; it just sort of got attached somewhere along the way.

Then the Borgia group showed up, and somehow—again, I forget precisely how it worked out that way, and I swear it wasn't deliberate— Corporate found itself playing a sort of Loyal Opposition in a whole batch of very clever melodramas and Gothics and Regency galas in various author topics. It was only after *that*, when I finally settled into my own topic, that things really got exotic, leading to the Great Chocolate Chip Cookie Chase and the recent Nicknaming-the-Sysop strangeness. (The former is entirely Kevin [O'Donnell, Jr.]'s fault, for following the trail of cookies in the first place.) And that's probably more than anyone ever wanted to know about the Secret History of Corporate.[24]

From this explanation of how John Bunnell became Djonn, Bunnell ranges across a variety of fiction-as-game-scenarios that interlock and cross topics, sweeping authors and fans into the mix and leaving the mark of their passing in the nicknames of participants and their lingering alter egos. While the spontaneous scenarios were almost always played out for their humor, the game itself served as an exercise for the braided novels and shared worlds in which many of the writers participate.

And in the games, we can see the practice of grafting as an organic process that gives the genre coherence. Writers carry their tropes with them and use them to address new themes and debates, just as Corporate clashed with the Borgias above and as Djonn took his name from a game of Desert Caravans that Katie remembered when Bunnell was looking for a new handle. GEnie became a powerful force in the genre in part because anyone with the price of admission could watch and participate in the writerly process—the creation of Barthes's constantly mutable writerly text—which functioned as a speeded up version of the life of the genre as it has been lived since the 1920s. The witty participant, fan or professional, could win approval in front of a knowledgeable audience. Most important for aspiring writers, GEnie provided a leveling forum in which they could participate in the life of the profession and gain the respect of the men and women they would join as peers.

## Leaving Genie[25]

In August 1996 I left Genie in what was the second, but not the last, exodus from the service. For Genie, the canary in the mineshaft was the Publishing category, and access to the Internet was the lure. From the start Del Rey Books went to the

Usenet, offering a newsletter and Ellen Key Harris's presence in rec.arts.sf written for its online presence rather than participating in Genie or other subscriber services. For Del Rey, the Internet provided a large base of self-selected users likely to read science fiction but not limited to a subscriber service.

The SFRTs's regular sign-on of about 5,000 participants and lurkers a night could not compete when compared to the millions of Net users worldwide. But publishers, like much of the commercial and private user world without research or education accounts, did not have access to brand-name identified points of presence on the Internet. ISPs—Internet service providers—supplied this lack for a growing post-education, computer-literate market more interested in direct connection to the Net than in purchasing the premium services that providers such as Genie used to attract subscribers. When Panix, self-described as "the oldest Public Access system in New York,"[26] opened for business, Tor editors followed Del Rey's lead, moving away from Genie to the Internet.

ISPs like Panix and Digex, a similar service that opened out of DC at about the same time, offered old technology to a new market. The ISPs gave their subscribers e-mail, which made the spread of e-mail discussion lists into the general population possible, and access to Usenet, both technologies almost as old as the Internet itself. In cases like Panix, ISPs offered their own Gopher sites as well as access to similar sites on research computing systems and on a small but growing number of ISPs. The Web's predecessor, Gopher, and its search engine, Archie, provided a worldwide database and search/retrieval system established on model of an Internet hierarchical tree of categories of information.

By late 1996, however, challenged by the ISPs and the Web and the easy-to-use AOL, Genie had yet to make the transition to simplified Internet access or a graphical interface. Rather, General Electric opted out of the consumer computer service business, selling Genie to Youvelle, a subsidiary of IDT. In mid-1998 I rejoined Genie, which remains a self-contained bulletin board and premium service supplier with a declining customer base. Many of Genie's earliest subscribers remain on the service for the specific long-term complex conversations they find there, while maintaining accounts on more technologically advanced ISPs for their Internet and Web access.[27] Others remain specifically because the limited text-based service they receive suits their older computers. Youvelle continues to promise a viable Web-based graphical user interface, but since 1996, when it took over Genie, it has not upgraded its service or modified its fee, which includes a $2.75 per hour connect charge with daytime surcharge and monthly fee.

## Discussion Lists and Usenet in the '90s

With the gradual move to ISPs between 1995 and 1997, more science fiction fans and professionals suddenly had access not only to *new* Internet technology, but to the *oldest*: discussion lists and the Usenet. Many ISPs now carry Usenet as a service to their customers, and Web browsers like Netscape give others access to Usenet servers through the Internet, an ironic twist given that the Usenet itself came into existence as an alternative for university systems outside the ARPANET. As access has broadened, the discussion has done likewise. Far more women participate in the Usenet sf hierarchy than did in the 1980s, as do fans of all ages. Professionals in the field, including authors Lawrence Watt-Evans, Mary Gentle, and Brenda Clough and editor Patrick Nielsen Hayden, likewise participate on the Usenet, adding their expertise and in some cases quashing rumors that abound in a fan community. (In some cases, of course, those rumors turn out to be true, a fact to which those involved can also attest.) Perhaps most important, because the Usenet is available to anyone with computer access to a server that carries the service, readers who have never heard about conventions or fandom are finding a way to participate in the virtual neighborhood of the science fiction community.[28]

While participation has grown, topic drift, a hallmark of Usenet from its beginning, continues unabated, and it sometimes seems that more threads refer to extraneous topics, like the ever-popular issue of gun control, than deal directly with science fiction. This is consistent with the philosophy of free speech that shaped the Net from its beginning, and also with the philosophy of science fiction community members in general, who don't care what people outside their community feel on given general issues.

Given the numbers of science fiction fans and professionals online, and the wide range of topics discussed in the rec.arts.sf hierarchy, one would imagine that the flow of traffic in Usenet would quickly become unmanageable. But here, as elsewhere in community building, pressure to have a voice in the wider world of fandom vies with the opposite pressure for more intimate encounters in smaller groups of people with more narrowly focused shared interests. Participants who first make contact through the Usenet may create or discover a private e-mail discussion list to engage a limited circle of acquaintances in greater depth.

Discussion lists did not originate with Usenet; SF-Lovers, the first not-for-research e-mail list that arose on ARPANET, continues as a moderated digest at SF-Lovers@sflovers.rutgers.edu. (Moderated means that each post is reviewed by the list manager for appropriateness to the topic, in this case science fiction, fantasy, and horror, in their literary and visual media forms.) Newer lists for serious science fiction enthusiasts have also appeared at the Library of Congress (sf-lit@loc.gov, also moderated) and as part of the Modern Language Association's section on Science Fiction, Utopias, and Fantasy (sfuf@csd.uwm.edu).

These lists, which may include anywhere from a few hundred to many thousand subscribers, all limit discussion to the topic of science fiction and its related genres, as do many lists devoted to specific authors or media products. Like other lists, they can provide the illusion of community for the science fiction fan who finds himself set apart from his local acquaintances because of his interest in science fiction. While providing a place to discuss science fiction and its related genres, these lists often lack the free-flowing topic drift on which computer-mediated community depends. They become much more like professional lists that keep members informed but do not promote intense personal attachment.

While Listserv software was designed to receive messages from a wide number of sources and send them out again to a wide number of receivers, some users have found in it a new communication tool for an old form: the newsletter/fanzine. Saul Jaffe refers to SF-Lovers Digest as a fanzine, but more formal Internet-based newsletters also operate on Listserv, both fan-produced and publisher-produced.[29] The subscribers do not interact with one another on the list, but receive the newsletter/fanzine based on the distribution schedule of the list manager. The Listserv format has certain advantages for distributing a newsletter, particularly a nonprofit fan newsletter that, in paper form, might expect a circulation of fifty to a few hundred. Economically, sending a newsletter via Internet e-mail is faster, easier, and much less expensive than printing and mailing copies to each subscriber, which makes possible fan newsletters like the *Babylon 5* fan newsletter, *Zocalo*, with a subscriber base of more than 7,400, which does not count the readers who view the newsletter at its website.[30] For a newsletter, Listerv offers advantages over Web publishing. While Listserv software will send just about any form of information, the standard is based on electronic mail protocols, which can be read by all machines with electronic mail access. As one of the earliest Net protocols, e-mail does not require the speed or power of a machine that reads Web-based documents, so fans who cannot afford to upgrade their computers every two to four years can still read the e-mail newsletter and participate in the Net-fandom. And unlike the discussion list, a newsletter does not require the daily attention to message administration that a large list entails.[31]

Fans who do develop their first sense of computer-mediated community through these lists and newsletters may find that their enthusiasm wanes as members gradually lose interest in the topic of the list—move their active participation to a new media product or subgenre list—or when a personal crisis uncovers the fact that the very adherence to topic that drew the fan limits the list's capacity to provide communal support. These fans, who need a more intense personal experience of computer-mediated community than the public lists and newsletters provide, may abandon the search for community on the Internet, or they may add one or more of the smaller, more personal lists, e-mail circles, IRCs, and chats that form around the larger, more formal list.

Some public lists, particularly those devoted to a particular author and his or her works, or a particular media character or program, may develop complex systems of computer-mediated communication, home gatherings, conventions, and hardcopy publications that connect participants with a degree of intensity that varies depending on the number of interactive experiences each individual wants and receives. With that growing degree of intensity, however, community members can find themselves embroiled in feuds as bitter as the original experience seemed positive.

## The Action-Fantasy Discussion List[32]

At Toronto Trek VIII in August 1994, fans of a contemporary action adventure television show (referred to here as *Action* to preserve the anonymity of the participants in the fan group) gathered at a party to share their enthusiasm. Unwilling to let go of new friendships, the group decided to start an e-mail discussion list to keep the conversation going. A fan at Penn State University had the mainframe access and the experience to create the list that, to preserve confidentiality, I will call ACTION-F.[33] A few months later I found a flyer for the list on the announcement table at a local convention. Since I had already decided it was time to learn about the Internet, I joined the new list.

When I joined, ACTION-F had an early membership of about forty, most of whom were women, established names of long standing in a variety of fandoms I had studied in *Enterprising Women*.[34] Some members were already watching the show together in small local viewing parties, and the list was planning its first major outing, to a celebrity hockey game in Boston.

This is a fairly common way for a list to begin: a small group of enthusiasts find each other and start an e-mail list to bridge the gap between more sporadic face-to-face communal activities. Over time, more fans discover the list and join the conversation, often coming together in person as well.[35] List administrators, like the rest of fandom, are usually volunteers who manage the list in their spare time for no pay. Lists are seldom created or financially supported by the publishers or production houses, but may attract members of the production who also participate as individuals and not for pay.

Because ACTION-F was small and most of the people on it knew each other by reputation, if not in person, interactions quickly took on the personality of the participants while the list continued to grow. Since many early members were fanzine veterans, technical discussion about the production of the zines soon flooded the list. To handle the load, the manager soon created a corollary list for fanzine discussion, which took on its own life as those who had begun the discussion drifted into new topics of conversation and those with a specific interest in fanzines found the list and moved it to new issues unrelated to the original fandom.

ACTION-F began to workshop fiction, sometimes serious efforts and sometimes humorous ones, interspersed with occasional spurts of erotic playfulness involving the characters in the show. Again, a new, related, list grew up to handle the fiction traffic. Such splits in the distribution of messages do not seriously impair the functioning of the group but do mark a change from a small to a medium-size list.

By mid-June 1995, the list manager had a problem. She had started a number of lists, some of which had grown to more than 500 participants. While still a relatively small list, traffic on ACTION-F was booming as members prepared—online—for the next big event, a minicon, a small specialized convention within the much larger Toronto Trek. The list manager had to reduce the load on both her time and the mainframe. I agreed to take on the administration of ACTION-F and its fiction list as part of my study of the Internet, while another member took on the fanzine list.

At the same time I became part of a small, informal e-mail circle of list participants, one of many operating behind the scenes of the list. This particular circle worked on a CD of information, art, writing, and memories about the show to present to the cast at the Toronto Trek Minicon. Posts on the list and in private e-mail circles swirled around the usual deconstruction of the show itself and around the upcoming convention; on some days ACTION-F received as many as 100 messages.

In August the list went to Toronto, to the minicon organized by the official fan club for the show. The club presidents did not belong to ACTION-F, but of the 400 who attended the minicon, roughly 200 belonged to the discussion list. Many list members also belonged to the club and freely passed information between the two. Also in attendance were the presidents of the fan club for one of the actors, and the organizers for yet another fan club. Editors of a number of fanzines brought their wares, and about fifteen members of the production, cast, and crew made an appearance at the minicon. After the minicon, the list itself grew to more than 300 participants. Fans continued to meet for group viewings and organized visits to plays, celebrity hockey games, and other special events. But already the seeds of dissent were starting to show, and pressures toward schism would soon appear.

## Net Power

As noted at length in *Enterprising Women*,[36] fan communities begin to experience structural stress when they approach about 500 deeply involved participants. The reasons for the schisms vary, but when membership is much below that number, priority is on the survival of the group. Above that number, pressure to reduce the size of a group takes precedence. When an open e-mail discussion list enters the mix, however, the number of participants needed to produce a schism tends to be lower as the number of interactions, real and virtual, are increased and apparent intimacy is intensified by that increase in number.

To some extent, and like the schism that affected *Blake* 7 fandom in the late 1980s,[37] the availability of face-to-face interaction with those involved in making the show in front of and behind the cameras fueled the schism that cracked ACTION-F. The amount of "inside" information the list offers depends on the access insider members may have to the production, and their willingness to participate as informants to the list. Like many small lists in what were still early days for public use of the Internet, ACTION-F did not at first have an inside source online. Over the next several years, however, many fans did gain access to the show's cast and crew and one minor cast member joined the list, again as an individual and not as a representative of the show. As access increased, members freely shared their information, even pooling resources for charity. This fandom followed the practice of asking the production for items to auction for charity at conventions. Tapes and scripts from the production are always highly prized for the secret knowledge they contain. In some fan groups, this translates into withholding the knowledge to hoard status, but as the politics of ACTION-F unfolded, members gained status by sharing information. Members pooled their resources and made them readily available to the group, which at this time includes a script library donated by fans and members of the production and copies of which may be purchased for charity.

ACTION-F might have established some equilibrium based on the way the group negotiated insider status. But *Action*, the pseudonymous television show that inspired the list, was still in production, so access to cast and the producer translated into information that had value not only for insider status, but also for the possibility of shifting the course of the product in the real world. Ironically, of course, this kind of power of persuasion has always been available to science fiction literature fans through the conventions and, later, online. As we have seen earlier, however, many formal discussion lists on literary topics have moderators who control, to some extent, the direction of the conversation. Discussion lists focused on the works of a particular author frequently have present the author or a representative, who sets the tone for the list much as he or she would at a convention or panel about his or her work. The Usenet has its own formalities of hierarchies within which free speech and topic drift occur freely, in the context of a seventy-five-year-old culture deeply rooted in vituperation as tradition.

Before the Internet, fans in large enough numbers could change television policy, as Bjo Trimble's experience with *Star Trek* showed. While mail campaigns failed in some recent and notable cases,[38] other fan favorite television shows continue to receive last-minute reprieves due to rescue efforts by fans.[39] The Internet gave the organizers of "save our show" campaigns faster access to a small army of volunteers ready to start the crusade at a moment's notice, but the basic concept of exerting pressure on the producer of the product has existed in the science fiction community since 1967.

## Power and Conflict

To this point, media fandom in the 1990s seems identical to what we've seen in the past, but in fact a major shift in the perception of media fan power was taking place, one with the potential both to encourage and to endanger the growth of community online. Unlike literary fandom, and with few exceptions (the most notable, *Babylon 5*, will be discussed later), media fandom developed with a strong ethic of privacy and with considerable distance between the product and the average fan. The distance between producer and fan becomes confused when Internet discussion lists come into play, as does the issue of privacy.

When a discussion list includes only acquaintances, participants can continue to treat interactions as private. But anyone with an e-mail account can join a discussion list, and the e-mail account will not necessarily give evidence to the subscriber's true identity. When a list exceeds the number of participants known by person or reputation to a majority of the list members, any lurker can be a network executive or member of the cast or crew. Privacy essentially disappears. At this point, and particularly, as with *Babylon 5*, when there is not direct and open participation by the producer, attitudes of fans may vary. Some may wish to retain the privacy of the early list. Others may value the possibility that list members have the ear of influential people at all levels of the production/presentation hierarchy. These fans hope that the explanations and the rationales that arise in discussion lists may be more persuasive to those in charge of modifying or renewing the product than a flood of pleading letters might be, but may encounter dissension in their own ranks about what direction they want the product to take. In all cases, however, the real causes of conflict may become obscured as posts come under scrutiny as *public* behavior.

## Controlling the Etiquette

For ACTION-F, all these potentials for conflict were present. The production itself experienced some turmoil and cast changes, and later came under cancellation pressure. Members of the growing fandom brought to the crises their own preferences regarding the direction of the storyline and the purpose of the list itself, and to a great extent they transferred the vigor of the disagreements about content to the struggle for control of the etiquette the group would adopt for what was, in effect, a private exchange carried out in a public forum.

The schism itself developed along several lines, but the one most significant to list life concerned the right to express negative opinions. Some members, drawn to the show because they liked the predecessor from which it grew or because they saw particular episodes as excelling in their preferred forms, felt compelled to express their dismay, sometimes vehemently and at length, when the show failed to meet their high standard. Participants who disagreed with the assessment of the naysayers, or with the vehemence with which they expressed themselves, chastised their more negative listmates, spurring the need to reassert the negative opinion. E-mail circles waged campaigns against list members who complained or who otherwise "hurt the feelings" of other members. An excess of covert access likewise fed the conflict, as various factions within the production had their positions played out via sources on the list. Since access meant status, the right to assert access/status became a contested field inflamed by factions within the production/distribution complex whose indirect spokespersons relayed their different truths.

In part my own position as list manager exacerbated the pressures on the discussion list. As a folklorist trained as a relativist, I avoided a real leadership role when I became list manager, while resisting the efforts of others to "buy" that leadership position with insider knowledge status. And I tended to let the flame-wars absorb hundreds of postings over weeks at a time rather than interfere until, driven by simple human frustration at the amount of work the noise level generated, I would wade in with my own less than diplomatic efforts to quiet things down. My intervention, to protect open expression of both sides, would seem arbitrary and contradictory. If I had it to do over again, I probably would not have taken on the responsibility, but I suspect the outcome would have been the same regardless. The seeds of the conflict existed in the nature of human beings behaving as they do, asserting claims for status and struggling to define the rules of behavior for a private discourse taking place before an unknown public.

The schism itself appeared as a naturally occurring event in a true communal situation, much as feuds develop in any small town, but accelerated by the intensity of Net interaction. It is difficult to tell, at this point, whether the conflict on this and other similar discussion venues for *Action* had an impact on the decision, but efforts to save the product from cancellation failed. At the end, *Action* fandom remained small by casting off a number of dissenting factions and limiting the options for participants, who could either leave the fandom entirely or select from its parts those least influenced by their opponents, tolerating the presence of those opponents where necessary.

## Some General Principles of Net Community

The ACTION-F example is significant for a number of reasons. The size of the fandom at its largest barely reached the pressure point for a schism, and had it not been for an Internet discussion list, any schism would likely have affected far fewer participants. But discussion lists, particularly those connected with concomitant e-mail circles, house visits, conventions, and other events, intensify any pressure that might exist in the group. You are looking less at a community, perhaps, and more at a metaphoric family, a term used in the positive sense by many participants on interpersonal lists and perhaps more obviously true when its members are fighting, privately or in public, than when they are happy with each other. Here, as with many lists that do not much exceed 500 participants, fans often discover that there just aren't enough of them to support a completely separate fan structure for every side of a schism. In fact, that is often why the fights are so intense. Ultimately, they have to find a way to survive as a group.

Larger fandoms, of course, can experience a number of complete divisions without losing the basic integrity of a group structure. In some cases, like the many fandoms of *Star Trek*, participants in one subgroup needn't make themselves aware of the other groups at all.

## The Web

I first heard of the Web during some tutoring sessions on Listserv discussion list administration. Our postmaster, Stan Horwitz, mentioned this great new Internet creation, the World Wide Web. I had seen the WWW on the mainframe menu when I entered my university mainframe account but I hadn't yet figured out how to penetrate its secrets, nor could I think of any reason to try. I could find the information I needed for scholarly purposes on Gopher, and there seemed to be nothing but empty architecture whenever I did find a "Web" site.

In my usual technologically astute way, I dismissed the Web as a "never happening" plaything out of CERN,[40] the folks who gave us Listserv, midwifed by baby programmers out of NSCA[41] and created for the techno-nerds who were filling my life as I learned to run discussion lists. I was accurate in my assessment of the available technology in early 1995. Lynx, a text-based Web browser, was at least as difficult to use as Archie and Gopher. Mosaic, the Netscape prototype, offered a graphical interface to the Web but was cumbersome and undependable on the terminal, and unusable on my 386 computer at home. The .com suffix was a joke on the Net: no one in their right mind would devote their marketing resources to anything as limited and complex as the Internet, particularly when few home computers possessed the power or speed to process graphical layouts economically and the search protocols were so difficult.[42] Then I met Netscape; within six months I had my own website. Netscape[43] became my god, and its avatar was Yahoo.[44] In 1996, seduced by the graphical side of the Net, I did the unthinkable: I bought a Mac.

I was not the only one in the science fiction world seduced by the Web. The lure of a worldwide market of techno-savvy users drew some publishers away from services like Genie and Compuserve during the pre-Web period when most Internet access was text-based and available primarily at Usenet, Gopher sites, and through e-mail. But a wider market awaited an attractive and more user-friendly Net. By late 1995, that alternative existed; the exodus that had begun with access to ISPs and the text-based Internet became more rapid and final as faster home machines made Web-based Internet presence viable. Change meant the slow strangulation of services like Genie and Compuserve and certainly the death of their importance to the publishing industry.[45] While some individual editors stayed on at Genie and served as representatives of their publishing houses, by 1997 most of the Publishing topics had shut down in the migration to the Web. Web-based newsletters at publishers' websites, like *Plug* at Ace/Boulevard books, substituted for the community bulletin board chat with an occasional CGI-based Web bulletin board, such as the Baen Books "Bar" page, to maintain the illusion of community.[46]

For writers and artists the Web offered direct access to the marketplace, where they could display their books and covers and even offer bits of text to draw in the websurfing genre fan. Fanzine editors could finally offer their publications in full layout, with art, cartoons, and typography, in an electronic form that had the potential to reach a much wider readership than they had ever enjoyed under the limitations of mimeograph and print, and the Web offered the unexpected benefit of making preserved texts more available than they had been in print media.

## Web Surfing in Science Fiction Culture

The impact of the World Wide Web on computer-mediated communication in the science fiction community cannot be overstated. While the many media and web-page software packages can exceed the cost of the home user's computer, HTML is free and the basics are easy to learn. Most ISPs today offer webpage storage as part of the service to subscribers. So the Web brings not only the representations of the producers of science fiction, fantasy, and horror media into the home of the web-surfer, it also gives the websurfer the opportunity to offer his or her own representations to the world.

A webpage, for the most part, however, is interactive only to the extent that the viewer can make choices about the items on display he or she wishes to view. Talking back is difficult and often impossible, and the apparent interactivity of the website can give the user a false sense of community, much as a voyeur may superimpose himself, in his imagination, on the social life he spies upon. The publisher sites we have mentioned and others, such as the Tor Books site, offer an attractive and newsy introduction to the books and authors they publish. Some-times, as in the case of Baen Books' Bar, the reader has the opportunity to talk back about the materials on the site. But critical discussion is limited, as is discussion of the works of other publishers.

## Doing What Fans Do Best: Organizing the Net

A recent search on the Web search engine AltaVista produced more than 100,000 hits, or matches, for the term "science fiction." Some matches duplicate others, of course, but when added to the Usenet, e-mail discussion lists both public and private, and online service topics or folders, the volume of information and discussion about science fiction, fantasy, and horror has become impenetrable. Commu-nity becomes lost in the sea of representations. Or so one might think, if one did not remember the obsessive quality science fiction fans bring to community building. Obviously, the seeker needs a guide. And fandom has responded to this need with a number of sites dedicated to providing both information and access to community. SF-Lovers, the earliest discussion list dedicated to science fiction, has provided a website that continues its tradition of community building while it preserves its own legacy and that of the wider fandom to which it belongs.

## http://sflovers.rutgers.edu/

Saul Jaffe, list manager of SF-Lovers, also maintains the website for the list. Jaffe, employed in the Network Services group of the Telecommunication Division of Rutgers University Computing Services, is himself a long-time science fiction fan and the website shows the fan's dedication to all things science fictional, both literary and media. In addition to an archival copy of each *SF-Lovers Digest* discus-sion list for the 1980s and '90s, the website offers the following hierarchies of data:

- List of all files in the archives
- List of all archive files added or changed within the last month
- Information on SF–Lovers Digest
- Answers to Frequently Asked Questions on various subjects
- Lists of the winners of various awards including the Hugos
- Various reference materials about authors and books
- Information from book publishers
- Information relating to SF films
- Information relating to SF on television including episode guides
- SF, fantasy, and horror artwork
- Information relating to fannish activities including conventions.[47]

Of these categories, the most important to our purposes is "Various reference materials," which opens into another list of sources of reference materials. First on the list, and the most important to fans searching for a source of community, is the Science Fiction Resource Guide (SFRG) maintained as a mirror site[48] on the SF-Lovers' server and continually updated by fan volunteer Chaz Boston Baden. The SFRA offers its own hierarchy of data, but key among them for fans looking for an interactive community are "Fandom: Societies, Clubs, etc.," "Mailing lists," and categories for conventions, gaming, media fandom, fan home pages, and fanzines. Each category provides descriptions and links. Fandom, for example, provides links to clubs and organizations as geographically diverse as Arthedain in Norway, Asociación Española de Fantasí y Ciencia Ficción in Spain, Central Arizona Speculative Fiction Society, Inc. (CASFS), and the Science Fiction Association, in Singapore, and special interests as diverse as media fandom, Christian fandom, Tolkien fandom, gay fandom, and the preservation of the history of fandom. The SFRG zine page includes lists of paper collections of zines available to the public, lists of websites that archive zines online, and an extensive list of zines available on or through online sources.

### http://www.fanac.org

Among the sources listed in the SFRG as both collecting zines and offering information about fannish activities, FANAC, the FanHistory Archive project, has stated its mission as:

> To compile a historical archive of fanzines, convention publications, photos and other materials to preserve them for their historic and literary interest. Access to this archive to be available for research, exhibits, and educational purposes.[49]

Last among the nine steps the project plans to take for the preservation and dissemination of fan ephemera is the following specific reference to the Web:

> 9. Put on the Nets via the World Wide Web or equivalent, so that information and material is available to review and to download.[50]

FANAC, Inc. originated to serve as the host organization for the 1992 World Science Fiction Convention, MagiCon, and among the pages of history the project offers the websurfer can find photographs and other materials from the convention as well as a listing of fanzines with their basic historical data and link if available online, and links to other websites of importance to fandom.

If we look at the Web as a singular technology, divorced from the world of users in which it is embedded, it clearly does not serve as a forum for the interactions necessary for the creation of real community. But as a community created in the mobile geography of the convention cycle and existing only in the conceptual space of the members' shared history, the fan community has latched on to each new upgrade in available technology for creating and disseminating itself through its wares: conventions, fanzines, and late-night talk over too much caffeine. The combination of fan historian and Web seems not only obvious but necessary. On the Web, the conceptual space that exists in the minds of community members finds a virtual space where community members can stop for a series of concrete loci for the recording of community life. For readers learning about fandom for the first time on the Web, sites like SF-Lovers and FANAC can provide the often difficult-to-come-by information about where real community is being waged within the newcomer's reach.

### Television on the Web

The marriage of television and the Web seems an obvious ploy to exploit the audience with a false sense of interactivity. A look at Sci-Fi Channel's *Dominion*[51] does little to change that opinion. *The Dominion* offers maximum interactivity, including chat, games, bulletin boards, an online convention, and grab files in sound, video, and graphic image, among other options for the user. Unquestionably, the site offers a great deal to entertain the websurfing fan and, unlike many fan club sites, requires no fee to participate in its activities. Ultimately, however, *Dominion* exists to excite interest in the cable channel's regular schedule of science fiction reruns and low-budget, youth-oriented made-for-television movies. Community, where it may exist here, does so under the terms of the corporate entity that sponsors it for the promotion of its products.

Fortunately, an active and assertive media fandom had invaded the Internet before the corporate sponsors began to recognize the Web as a source of revenue. In the case of *Babylon 5*, Internet support for the media product existed before the show went into production, and persisted in spite of resistance by the production company.

### When It All Comes Together: *Babylon 5*

I first heard about *Babylon 5* in 1992 from GEnie members who discussed the show with the familiar terms of an on-air product. J. Michael Straczynski, *Babylon 5* creator, had a topic that soon grew into a full Category with a number of topics in the media fandom area of GEnie. Although he did not share the details of the plots, he did discuss his concept and his ongoing battles with the forces of power and money in Hollywood.[52] When *Deep Space Nine* went into production, we also heard the anger and frustration of a man whose concept seemed to have been usurped by the power juggernaut of science fiction TV: the *Star Trek* franchise.[53] I found it rather odd that a television show that did not exist could already have a fandom, and I watched with wonder Straczynski's accounts of his travails as he struggled to sway production companies to his vision of what science fiction television could be if given the chance.

Straczynski was not the only producer drumming up support on the online services: George R. R. Martin, of *Beauty and the Beast* fame, was likewise attracting a following to an idea he believed in. Martin's effort was unsuccessful, but Straczynski managed to convince Warner Brothers' syndicated branch, Prime Time Entertainment Network (PTEN) to take a chance on *Babylon 5*. At this point, it is difficult to say that the fan support behind *Babylon 5* gave Straczynski the leverage he needed to persuade the Network on the difficult sell. On the other hand, a number of series funded for syndication at the time did bring with them a ready made audience: *Kung Fu: The Legend Continues*, also from PTEN, brought with it the fans of the original '70s series, and *Highlander* brought with it the fans of the movies. *Deep Space Nine* carried the cachet of *Trek's* reincarnation, and *Forever Knight* cashed in on the booming market in vampires, fueled by the Anne Rice books but without her price tag.

Straczynski had a harder sell than most. In the early 1990s television had not yet caught up with its audience, which had come to look for development in characters and storylines in weekly series. Fan groups worked hard at reconciling inconsistencies and creating timelines in the "lives" of characters; Straczynski had tapped into this way of looking at television when he created the concept of *Babylon 5*. While it is unclear to what extent Straczynski actually did have the entire five years of the series mapped out, online he always discussed *Babylon 5* as an ongoing connected storyline. While a few episodes may have seemed thrown into the pot at random, most seasons built one major overarching story in the universe Straczynski had created, and each season fit into a larger story of the fate of the station and its universe.

For syndication, a completely interlocked story provides quite a few marketing limitations. Stations looking for syndicated programming want flexibility. A season-long story demands a fairly rigid airing schedule, and the stations most inclined to pick up syndicated action adventure often replaced that programming periodically with sports and other local events. And television producers and stations still looked at their product as ephemeral and their viewers as idiots who would take in whatever was set before them, with no powers of discretion or taste. Fortunately, however, cable and the increase in the number of licensed local UHF stations created a demand for product so difficult to fill that stations were willing to air the show even given the scheduling demands. And Straczynski, a long-time fan himself, had a plan for "doing it right" and an unshakable belief that there were enough "real" science fiction fans out there to support a show that gave them real science fiction.

At the end of each season, however, came the renewal fight. The show needed more viewers, it needed more markets, but many potential viewers found the story moving too slowly in its first year. The show changed protagonists and picked up momentum in the second year, but the five-year storyline made it difficult for new fans to join the party. That is where the Internet became valuable to the series. Discussion on Usenet brought *Babylon 5* to the attention of a potential worldwide audience, and the FAQ gave lagging American audiences episode guides with plot summaries to bring them up to date with the storyline. Audiences in England and Germany were waiting when the show arrived in their countries, and quickly moved it to the top of the ratings for American shows.

Straczynski had done as he'd promised: given science fiction fans a television show with the depth and complexity of a good novel. The fans responded with fan community-building '90s style: with discussion lists and a segment on the Usenet hierarchy (rec.arts.sf.tv.babylon5), with fanclubs and newsletters and websites to bring it all together. *Zocalo*, the *Babylon 5* newsletter founded in 1995, had more than 7,800 e-mail subscribers when it ceased publishing in January 1999. Fans can still access back issues on the *Zocalo* website.[54] The *Babylon 5* fanclub, which advertises membership of more than 9,000, also manages a website that offers bulletin boards and live chat as well as an online store for tie-in paraphernalia. Both TNT, the cable superstation, and Warner Brothers, the production company, offer websites for *Babylon 5*, as they do for many of their series, but the most important website in the *Babylon 5* firmament is *The Lurker's Guide to Babylon 5*.[55] The *Lurker's Guide* has organized just about anything anyone would want to know about the series, its fandom, or its creator. Among its many treasures, *The Lurker's Guide* has assembled the posts of creator Straczynski from the first announcement in 1991 that *Babylon 5* was a go up to the present, from all Straczynski's online haunts, including GEnie, Compuserve, and the Usenet. (Posts are limited to those of Straczynski, however, and the discussion to which he responds is missing, which makes some of the arguments difficult to understand.) Ironically, perhaps, the completely fan-managed *Lurker's Guide* offers far more sophisticated access to the history and community sources of *Babylon 5* than either of the commercial sites for the series.[56]

The most interesting thing about the *Babylon 5* story is the way Straczynski himself used the available resources of the Internet from their earliest commercial incarnation at Compuserve, GEnie, and the Usenet, through cooperation with fan organizers of conventions, websites, and newsletters to drive home his message about his series and his vision of sf on the air. Having done so, he kept his show on the air when cancellation seemed imminent, and parlayed *Babylon 5* into its own mini-franchise, with the scheduling of a spinoff series.[57] He could not have done so, however, without the determined efforts of fans who recognized the consistently high quality of the product, based on community standards, and sincerely appreciated the effort, and worked hard to keep it on the air.

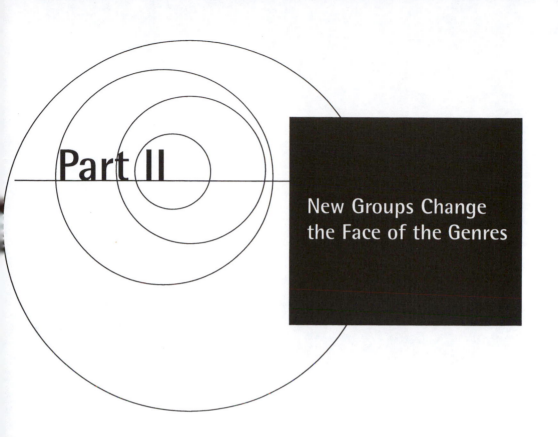

# Part II

**New Groups Change
the Face of the Genres**

Some of the best science fiction looks at the world around us with a certain ironic condescension. The Demolished Man fears not the death of his body for his crimes, but the death of the personality that underlies his criminal being.[1] Savvy advertisers convince the Marching Morons that a better life awaits them on Venus—they vie for the opportunity to fling themselves into space, unaware that their ships have no destination and are too flimsy to reach a destination if they had one.[2] The entire human population lines up to enter a giant box at the exhortation of one man who may or may not have been contacted by aliens who may or may not have their interest at heart and who may or may not be able to get them out of the box again if they should want to.[3]

As we have seen in the preceding chapter, the science fiction community has led the migration into the contemporary giant box—the computer—and rebuilt itself there. Few community members see the irony in their own community, that a group that comes together around the idea of the future and change, and absorbs technological change while it is still in the creation phase, should fight change so vehemently when it comes to expanding its own membership beyond its elite and mostly male company.

The reason for this seems clear: white men in positions of power have fought the incursion of those less powerful in all their institutions. The markers of power may differ from group to group. In the church, the minister has the right to guide a congregation as a priest or pastor. In the business world, power means money in the bank, a Cadillac in the two-car garage, and the authority to create in the marketplace of his business. In the science fiction community, members measure their power by their access to and understanding of technology, by their control over the creation of the communal geography, and, ultimately, by the creation and dissemination of the literature. The mostly male science fiction community through the early 1960s knew what most major institutions knew: a few exceptions from other groups who entered their ranks did not threaten their control or their power.

By the 1980s, however, demographic groups that included feminist women and lesbian, gay, and bisexual fans had settled in, bringing their own way of doing fandom with them, presenting a twofold threat. The numbers of strong writing women moving into science fiction and fantasy threatened to displace the dominant male forms of the literature, while the ways of doing fandom of these new groups threatened not only the positions of power, but the structures of power in the fan community. With the incursion of a new youth culture into the mix, the core of male community members who felt themselves still connected to the founding fathers of the fan community was seriously outnumbered, and many felt their own community had become alien to them.

Even at the end of the twentieth century, with some critics heralding the death of science fiction, the community still seethes with unrest as it redefines its geography, and its fiction, around generational as well as sexual politics. In the chapters that follow in this section, we will look primarily at three of the social changes that have overtaken the community, often in a tangle of conflict, suspicion, and even fear: the growing importance of women in both fan and publishing circles, the growing visibility of lesbian, gay, and bisexual fans and writers, and the changing youth culture.

# The Women Were Always Here: The Obligatory History Lesson

**5**

It seems possible, now, to look at women's struggle to gain a place in the science fiction community as nearly won, far more so than in the mainstream population. Women hold positions of power, authority, and creative prestige throughout the field of science fiction. Even First Fandom, those members who created the science fiction community in the 1930s, now makes its bow to the growing change in the demographics of the science fiction world. In Orlando, Florida, at the 1993 Worldcon, David Kyle explained why most of the winners of the First Fandom Award have been men:

> I want to mention that it seems to be masculine dominated, these old fan awards, but it was for a very good reason. That is, women were only entering the fields of science fiction fandom back there in the '20s and '30s and thank goodness things have equaled out since then.[1]

When I was researching *Enterprising Women* in the 1980s, I could not have imagined hearing a statement like that at a major awards event. Back in 1981, of course, men and women were nearing parity in their numbers at science fiction conventions, and a very few women were breaking through into the major prize categories given in the community. Many women writers, however, found their books still relegated to the feminist ghettos that kept the advances down and the distribution of women's books low in the 1970s.

## Women in Fandom: The '50s and Early '60s[2]

When I returned to the study of science fiction fandom, I did not question my original perception, that the presence of women was a relatively new phenomenon, in part because feminist criticism and analysis supported my on-site observation at the time: the 1970s mark the great divide in fandom. Before that time, the sf community belonged to men. During the 1970s and early '80s, women stormed the fortress, demanding a place in all aspects of science fiction life, and the men in place repelled the invaders with all the tools at their command. Writers like Joanna

Russ, Suzy McKee Charnas, and Ursula K. Le Guin regularly appear in the feminist criticism, but earlier science fiction was usually represented by the works of utopian rather than science fiction writers. Foremothers within the science fiction community such as Andre Norton, Marion Zimmer Bradley, and even C. L. Moore were often "disappeared" from the feminist record[3] or anachronistically criticized for their sensibilities.[4]

But, as Robin Roberts points out and my own research confirms, many of the feminist writers of the 1970s and '80s began as readers of the pulps, science fiction magazines of the '40s and '50s.[5] Like the examples in Roberts's book, Joanna Russ described to me her roots in the science fiction of the '50s:

> **Ethnographer:**    Why did you decide to go the science fiction route, rather than mainstream or another genre?
>
> **Joanna Russ:**    Why SF? I always loved it and read it omnivorously. I was also a finalist in the Westinghouse Science Talent Search getting out of high school (1953). One of the top ten, I recall, and the only female in the top ten. . . . Science had always fascinated my father, who made his own reflecting telescope at one point . . . and poetry had always fascinated my mother, who'd had one year of graduate school . . . and wrote it until she was thirty or so and I came along. They were my models, really.[6]

Russ's story, like those of so many women in the science fiction community, defies the common perception that women bring to the community a lesser history of identification with the genre than men. That perception crumbles farther when even a cursory survey of convention attendees in the '90s turns up numbers of women who participated in the community during the early '50s and '60s and who resent the way they have been written out of women's history of science fiction. These community members remind us that women did not suddenly appear with the rise of '70s feminism, and that, in fact, feminism has had many faces in the years since fandom began.

To understand the place of women in the science fiction community, however, we must first internalize the obvious: science fiction began as a subset of and reinforcement for the mainstream patriarchal culture of technological heroism during the 1930s, when the Great Depression had taken from most men their primary source of patriarchal power: their ability to create wealth. The men and women drawn to the science fiction community in the late '20s and early '30s found in the fiction a hope for a brighter future through technology. More important, they found in the world of pulp publishing a future that had the potential to return to them status and financial security that the Great Depression had shattered for most of the middle class.

More surprising, however, early poverty seems to be a common theme of fandom right through the early 1960s. While science fiction fandom still draws large numbers of young members with disposable incomes that are relatively small in relation to the cost of participation, the demographics since the late '60s has slowly shifted to a more upscale professional level in all areas of participation.

From the start, intelligent, active women were a part of this new world as professional and fan writers, as convention organizers, and as readers.[7] Women like Karen Anderson, who talks about her participation in fandom of the '50s, for example, likewise maintained a wide variety of activities and interests, including, in Anderson's example, little theater, Sherlock Holmes fandom, and the study of science and history. Until the 1970s, however, the number of women participating in the community never exceeded a small minority, as Anderson describes of her experience of fannish social life in the early '50s:

**Anderson:**  Now, at the WSFA [Washington Science Fiction Association D.C.] meeting, there were two women members when I joined, and two others joined shortly after me, and there were fifteen or twenty men members. So we would sit around make a stab at following Robert's Rules of Order, with new business and old business, and discussed whatever we had to discuss, and then a number of us would go to a bar. . . . So I'd have one bottle of beer and make it last . . . and then go home on the streetcar. And go to school the next morning. It was college by then.

In 1952, Anderson went to her first Worldcon, where she met Poul Anderson, already a successful author and soon to be her husband. Karen, a fanzine publisher in her own right, participated on the 1954 Worldcon committee with another science fiction couple, committee chairs Les and Es [Esther] Cole. When asked about the common assumption that science fiction was a male domain until the 1970s, Anderson bristles with indignation:

**Ethnographer:**  Not many women were involved in fandom in the '50s.

**Anderson:**  More than they think today.

**Ethnographer:**  This is what I'd like to talk about. [When I was looking at science fiction] fanzines,[8] a lot of women were involved. A small percentage, but more than I thought.

**Anderson:**  [A]n editorial entitled "The Women Science Fiction Doesn't See"[9] . . . was about the [professional] writers of the '60s, '50s, and '40s, who are ignored because scholars say it was Joanna Russ and Ursula Le Guin who opened science fiction to the female. . . . And there were an awful lot of women fans around. Many of them have dropped away. Many have died. And many of them you just don't realize they've been around that long. Let's see. Es Cole I'm sure hasn't been to a convention in years, but she was on the 1954 Worldcon committee, she and her husband. . . .[10] Nancy Share and Nan Gerding, they were well known in their time. Bjo Trimble, she was Bjo Wells when she went to her first Worldcon, which was the same as mine. She was one of the major fans of the early '50s, and never lost her prominence.[11]

In fact, Bjo Trimble was responsible for the write-in campaigns that kept *Star Trek* alive past its first season, as she is responsible for the successful campaign to name the prototype space shuttle after *Star Trek*'s *Enterprise*. She accomplished both feats because she knew the workings of the fan communications systems intimately from her work in the science fiction fanzines, and because she had at her command the address lists that she collected as a fanzine editor and fan organizer.[12]

There were, of course, always exceptions to the feminist generalization and my own early observations. As Anderson points out, some women were famous as fans in their own right—occasionally to the confusion of their male counterparts. Walt Willis wrote about his experience with '50s fanziner Lee Hoffman:

> In February, 1951, Lee Hoffman sent me a Valentine. *And I didn't realize.* . . . How can I have been so stupid? But I had such a clear picture of Lee as a tubby brown-eyed fellow that I just put the Valentine down to fannish eccentricity . . . I had to have a house fall on me. This happened—at least it felt like it—when she sent me her photograph.[13]

As professionals in the field, C. L. Moore, Leigh Brackett, Andre Norton, and Marion Zimmer Bradley had large readerships for their commercial science fiction and fantasy in the 1940s and '50s.[14] When we begin to analyze the responses of the women fans to their surroundings, however, and compare them to the comments of women who found fandom difficult in the period before the "great divide," we see an interesting pattern. Most of the women I have met who object to the historical depiction of fandom as a male domain were or are married, most often to men they met through science fiction or fandom itself. Anderson is the wife and sometime collaborator of Poul Anderson as well as being a fanziner in her own right. Sarah Goodman, long-time fan and programming chair at Confrancisco, likewise married within the community.[15] Karen Anderson's discussion of the way women felt accepted in science fiction fandom in the '50s is very telling in this regard:

**Ethnographer:**   As a woman in fandom, did the guys ever give you a hard time?

**Anderson:**   Oh, heavens no. They were so happy to have women they could talk to. Most women they knew, if they had a brain, they hid it. So, oh, read *The Female Man*, find out how women were supposed to conduct themselves, especially young women who wanted to get married. This has soured Joanna [Russ]'s whole life, being brought up that way.

The reference to *The Female Man* is telling. An excerpt exemplifies Anderson's point:

### A ROUND OF "HIS LITTLE GIRL"

SACCHARISSA:   I'm your little girl.

HOST (wheedling):   Are you really?

SACCHARISSA (complacently):   Yes, I am.

HOST:   Then you have to be stupid too.[16]

And another:

For fifteen years I fell in love with a different man every spring like a berserk cuckoo-clock. I love my body dearly and yet I would copulate with a rhinoceros if I could become not-a-woman. There is the vanity training, the obedience training, the deference training, the dependency training, the passivity training, the rivalry training, the stupidity training, the placating training.[17]

Like Joanna Russ in the 1970s, the women fans of the 1950s rebelled against the perceived need to present themselves as mindless children in the larger society. As Russ describes above, women who succeeded in fandom of the '50s entered into the search for compatible mates with as much enthusiasm as the men who pursued them—but generally with more success than the Joanna of *The Female Man*. These women did not feel that their role of "femmefans," as women in fandom were called, restricted their access to a voice in the community:

**Anderson:** I managed to escape it [the frustration of women's roles in the '50s], and one way I escaped was by finding men who were interested in my mind . . . there was no resistance to femmefans ever. And in Minneapolis, the Minneapolis fantasy society had about five men to each woman. Poul tells me that these women had their pick from the men, and the men were just so delighted to have women they could talk to, women who understood what they said . . . we had our pick.

**Ethnographer:** And you [women fans] actually talked to each other and weren't in competition?

**Anderson:** We were the only frogs in a world of fishes. And we male and female frogs were so glad to find each other. Well, I guess the men were sort of competing for the women's attention, but the women were by no means competing with each other, at least as far as I know.

If we see early fandom as organized around the patriarchal structures of the outside world, we find that it did have a place for women who identified themselves to a major extent with the male agenda. In 1958 in England, a woman who coedited a regularly published fanzine with her husband demonstrated this identification in an article about the gullibility of women. Using as her source of evidentiary support Vance Packard's *Hidden Persuaders*, she scorned women who, she claimed, could be convinced to buy anything offered by advertisers. According to this woman fanziner, women in general did not apply any critical or analytic thinking to the reading of advertising, unlike men, who could be influenced, but not completely persuaded by advertising. She concludes that women like herself were a breed apart, by implication sharing the male critical facility rather than the female gullibility.[18]

None of the women to whom I spoke about this topic during the fieldwork on this book ever made so sweeping a negative statement about their sex, but in some ways all made it clear that their participation in science fiction fandom was part of a difference they saw between those women around them who were socialized to the more passive roles of women, and those, including themselves, who were not. At the same time, it is also clear that the ability to synchronize their behavior to the expectations of men in the community accounts for much of their success. Women who wanted to be wives and mothers, who saw that role not as limiting but as opening new doors for them, could succeed in the world of fandom, in many cases matching or surpassing their husbands in the fan community. Few might have identified themselves as feminist during their early days in fandom, but all lived the maxim that they could compete in the male world on male terms and succeed without sacrificing their "basic female nature."

Still, no woman broke the guest of honor barrier at a Worldcon until 1964, when Leigh Brackett appeared as a writer guest of honor, a position no woman held again until 1975. And women who could not adapt to the male agenda or shape it to fit their own needs often felt oppressed by the community, which could exert as much pressure on its members to conform as the outside world did.

### Women's Discontent and the Fannish Explosion: The Late '60s and the '70s

Fandom may have seemed a hospitable place for the women who did make a home there in the 1950s and early '60s, but the record shows that, while those few women could work there, they did not have equal access to the honors accorded the male members of the community. A look at the number of women honored by World-cons or awarded Hugos, for example, will quickly dispel any notions the reader may have of a fair and equal fan community before the 1980s. Since 1964, only twelve women have appeared as guest of honor in any category. This may seem like a high percentage, but a typical Worldcon will have three or sometimes more guests of honor. Guest of honor categories include writers, artists, and fans. Juanita Coulson appears as fan guest of honor in 1972, but, like four other honorees, she received the honor as half of a couple, with her husband.

Ursula Le Guin appears as the writer guest of honor in 1975, one of only eight women so honored since 1939: the remaining seven are Brackett, (the first, mentioned above), Kate Wilhelm (honored with her husband, Damon Knight), C. L. Moore, Doris Lessing, Andre Norton, Anne McCaffrey, and C. J. Cherryh (the most recent, in 1998).[19] Worldcon organizers might object that the traditions guiding the selection of the guest of honor limit the number of eligible women. According to Ben Yalow:

> For American ones [Worldcons], at least, there is a strong set of traditional requirements that generally have been followed. Less so for non–American worldcons.[20] Generally, there's a feeling that your guest of honor should be somebody who has been in the field for a long time. Different committees differ on how long a long time is, the lowest number that I've heard has been about twenty years . . . to be significant in the field. To have produced a significant enough body of work that you won't be getting a "who's that?" No repeats. There've been a couple notable exceptions to that, but people grumbled. There's also generally a feeling that you don't pick your locals.[21]

The length and generativity of the guest of honor's career may seem like an obstacle to earlier, or more frequent, choice of women, but C. L. Moore, Golden Age writer and only the third woman to receive the kudo, did not appear as a guest of honor until 1981, where she was listed second, after Clifford D. Simak. Likewise,

Andre Norton did not receive this honor until 1989.[22] Other women, including Joanna Russ and Marion Zimmer Bradley, have never been honored, although their work often stands as the model for its type in the genre.

If the Worldcon committees have been slow to recognize the women in their midst, the fan voters of the Hugo Awards moved to recognize women's work somewhat more quickly, but, until the '80s, not frequently. Not surprisingly, the first Hugo presented to a woman was awarded to a husband–wife team, F. M. and Elinor Busby, along with coeditors Burnett Toskey and Wally Weber, for their fanzine, *Xero*. Cele Goldsmith received a Hugo for editing *Amazing* and *Fantastic* magazines in 1962. No woman won for best novel until 1970. Since 1970, women have won the prize for best novel eleven times, four between 1970 and 1979.[23]

## When It Changed

Clearly something happened to change attitudes in science fiction in the late 1960s and the '70s. When we investigate the period, however, we find that not just one thing but just about everything changed there. The great divide of the '70s does exist for most women in the genre, fans and professionals alike. In fact, science fiction and the fan community underwent more changes between 1966 and 1979 than at any other time in their history.

Some of these changes, like the growth of the mall bookstore chains and the development of better glues that made paperback books more attractive to the buying public, brought in more readers and expanded genre publishing in general. Others, like the space program, culminating with the moon landing and Neil Armstrong's famous walk, fired the national imagination with the possibilities of space exploration and colonization. Readers came to science fiction specifically to find that exploration spread before them in the pages of paperback books.

The two biggest changes to the community, however, resulted from the work of two men. Although written and released in England in the 1950s, J. R. R. Tolkien's *Lord of the Rings* hit the United States market in the mid-1960s and quickly became the cult favorite of a generation.[24] Out of Tolkien's work grew two stepchildren: a revitalized hunger for fantasy fiction with a concomitant explosion in the amount of fantasy published, and Dungeons and Dragons, the role playing game based loosely on the tropes Tolkien used in his books.

The second man, like the first, experienced a delayed reaction to his work. When Gene Roddenberry's *Star Trek* first hit television, it made scarcely a ripple in the mass audience that network television requires. While the loyal science fiction community supported and resurrected the show twice, spawning a write-in technique that has become a mainstay of ratings bottom-dwellers, the series could not compete with the real-life excitement of real men walking on our real moon. By the mid-1970s, however, a country exhausted emotionally and financially by the Viet Nam War rediscovered this paean to the ideal of American culture. Conventions organized around the *Star Trek* series attracted as many as 17,000 participants,[25] and a significant number of those *Trek* fans found their way to science fiction conventions, where they stayed and demanded a place.[26] Between 1939 and the mid-1960s, participation at the annual Worldcon increased from about 200 to about 800 for a convention in a major city in the continental United States. The

1965 Worldcon in Cleveland drew 850 participants, which tied for highest number of attendees to its time and marked the beginning of the expansion—only New York City had drawn so many participants in the past. In 1966, participation jumped to 1,500; by 1980 attendance had climbed to more than 5,000, and it has stayed between 5,000 and 7,500, based on the popularity and accessibility of the city, ever since. The new participants, women science fiction readers who found the convention culture through the more widely publicized *Star Trek* events[27] and primarily young male gamers attracted to venues where they could both meet other gamers and learn more about the mythological and genre-fictional origins of the games, arrived with their own set of priorities. Both groups stayed, demanding a part of the convention resources for activities and discussions focused on the special interests they brought to the convention.

## When It Changed II: Back at the Ranch House

Community members accustomed to sharing the Worldcon with just five or six hundred of their best friends and favorite industry personalities met this influx with understandable consternation and rejected assimilation of the new participants into the cognitive construction of their community. However, two changes moving at the very heart of the genre itself added their own cognitive stresses to the community. One, the New Wave, primarily a phenomenon of white male writers[28] coming out of literature and other humanities programs, accelerated the development of experimental themes and styles in science fiction.

Now, the New Wave, which hit its peak as a defined movement between about 1967 and 1969, did not invent literary science fiction. It did not even reinvent it. Writers like Alfred Bester in the '50s and J. G. Ballard in the early '60s were models that the New Wave could point to as forebears, and John Campbell, Jr. had begun moving the field into areas of speculation about the psychological and paranormal in the '40s. But, at the height of America's drive to explore space, the New Wave took the cutting edge of science fiction away from the hardware and engineering themes that had dominated the public perception of the genre from its inception. In the place of the stories of technological wonder, they offered works like Roger Zelazny's *Lord of Light*,[29] recasting a highly technological people in the personas of gods from the Hindu pantheon, and Samuel Delany's *Dhalgren*,[30] a massive stream-of-consciousness novel dense with a tortured sexuality set somewhere at the end of meaning.

As the New Wave took hold, women coming out of universities and backgrounds similar to those of the men who were creating the category of "literary" science fiction created their own subcategory of feminist utopian/dystopian fiction, asking, and answering, the question that follows Russ's list of "training" above:

> How am I to put this together with my human life, my intellectual life, my solitude, my transcendence, my brains, and my fearful, fearful ambition?[31]

The answer for a small but radical and very talented group of women was a vision of a separate future. Since it was impossible to envision equality for women in a society controlled by white men, the empowering future must banish them, the predatory male species—kill them off, or set them at a distance. Of course, like the men who were inventing the New Wave, feminists of the '70s did not invent the feminist utopia, which had its roots in the nineteenth century.[32] But both the New Wave and its subset, the Feminist Utopia/Dystopia, came into prominence during this period and marked a major shift in direction in the field.

### A Brief Digression to the Center: Sui Generis

Of all the writers of this period, Ursula Le Guin may stand as the towering exception to most of the generalities we will discuss. Closely identified with the New Wave, and in turn admonished and praised by the feminists, Le Guin described utopian futures that sought to transcend gender. Her most political fiction comments on feminist concerns from a position in which those issues can be seen as enmeshed within the larger question of what it meant to be a social being.

To science fiction Le Guin brought a childhood steeped both in science fiction[33] and in the worlds of her parents, anthropologist Alfred Kroeber, founder of the study of anthropology at Berkeley, and writer Theodora Kroeber.[34] From Theodora Kroeber's *Ishi in Two Worlds*, we learn that Le Guin's earliest exposure to anthropology came not from books, or from watching her father teach, but from the lived experience of the field, and the field come home in the form of Ishi, the "Last Wild Indian in North America," who stayed for a time at the Kroeber home.

To this early experience Le Guin brought her own studies in medieval French, a field consistent with the more literary-historical backgrounds of many of the New Wave writers, although the best of her work never moves far from the deeply felt ethnographic reflections of an adult mind trained to them from childhood.

Published in 1969, Le Guin's *Left Hand of Darkness* instantly received recognition for the powerful, complex, and subtle work that it is. It received the 1970 Hugo award for Best Novel, only the second in that category awarded to a woman, and has not been out of print since.

In the book, Genly Ai, sent to the planet Gethen as first contact by the space-spanning Ekumen, must pave the way for further contact between the worlds he represents and the sparsely populated winter planet he visits. Ai is himself male, and his perceptions of the Gethenians are distorted by their apparent lack of gender: the people of the planet Ai knows as Winter are essentially sexless until they enter kemmer, at which time they may take on the attributes of either male or female for the duration of the kemmer period or the pregnancy, if one occurs. Lacking this essential clue by which he is accustomed to judge behavior, Ai distrusts the "feminine" behavior of those closest to him, until he is drawn into true understanding of his mistakes in a deadly crossing of the Gethen ice sheet.

*Left Hand of Darkness* is powerful and moving and detailed in its depictions of the fatal mistakes a cultural explorer makes when he attributes his own meanings to the actions of the Other. The book's own layers of meaning unfold for the reader only with repeated readings; not surprisingly, it has become one of the few books written in the genre to reach the status of part of the literary canon.[35] In a recent computer network discussion among contemporary writers and editors in the field questioning what was the best book of the 1960s, Zelazny's *Lord of Light* was winning the tally until I suggested *Left Hand of Darkness*. When the question of the publication date was settled (some of the contributors to the conversation thought that it had been published in 1970), the vote had pretty much shifted to Le Guin.[36] Some readers contend that it is the best science fiction novel ever written.

Not surprisingly, feminists claimed the book as a utopian exploration of gender roles while New Wave proponents claimed it for its literary exploration of the issues of trust and friendship and the importance of stories, of folklore, for insight into culture.[37] Ironically, Le Guin herself did not see the novel as an exploration of gender when she wrote it, and she defended her position in the introduction to the 1976 edition of *Left Hand of Darkness* and in the 1976 article, "Is Gender Necessary?"[38] While Le Guin has since reconsidered her position in very strong terms in a revised introduction for the book and in the essay, "Is Gender Necessary, Redux,"[39] her early disclaimers set her own work at odds with her feminist intentions and firmly in the more male New Wave camp:

> The essay that confronts the whole matter directly is the one about my novel, *The Left Hand of Darkness*, called "Is Gender Necessary?" This 1976 piece has been quoted from a good deal, usually to my intense embarrassment. I came within a few years to disagree completely with some of the things I said in it, but there they were in print, and all I could do was writhe in deserved misery as the feminists told me off and the masculinists patted my head.[40]

If Le Guin had seen in her own book what other feminists saw in 1970, and if she had stated it as clearly then, would *Left Hand of Darkness* have won the Hugo? Would Le Guin have won again in 1975 for *The Dispossessed*? Would the Worldcon have honored her as the writer guest of honor that same year? In an alternate history, if Le Guin's later position on gender in *Left Hand of Darkness* had appeared from the start in the critical literature, the books would most likely have won the awards anyway—only a small fraction of the readers who vote for the best novel read the criticism written in the field. The question of guest of honor, however, is more open. In 1975, the Worldcon was hosted by Australian fans and held in Melbourne. If, in our alternate history, the 1975 Worldcon had occurred in the United States, it is certain that Le Guin, like many other women writers deserving of the honor, would not have been so named. She might have alienated the conservative core of fans who organize Worldcons, and even more certainly "tradition" would have dictated that her career had been too short. In fact, through 1994, only five women have been pro writer guest of honor at a Worldcon held inside the continental United States.[41]

### When It Changed III: Back at the Ranch House, Again

Le Guin is in most ways an exception to the rule for feminist women writing in the 1970s who did not receive equal treatment in the science fiction community. Joanna Russ, one of the most highly respected and best known of the feminist writers during this period, reports that she never received an advance more than $3,500 for any of her books, which likewise received poor distribution and marketing.[42] When I asked her, "Why science fiction (a field so hostile to women)?" she answered:

I had loved the stuff [horror and s.f.] but didn't try to write it until graduate school. I had written other fiction, "realistic" I guess you'd call it . . . and had been convinced through college—this was in the '50s—that my woman's experiences were not the stuff of fiction. I remember one class, which I detailed in *How to Suppress Women's Writing*, which was typical. Women couldn't write, all the stuff they wrote about was unimportant, &c.

The passage from *How to Suppress Women's Writing* describes how classmates dismiss her woman's experience:

[O]ne of the few women in a college writing class (at the time, I didn't wonder why there were so few of us), I submitted for class discussion part of a novel I was writing; it was about the comic sufferings of wallflowers at a high school dance. The class dismissed it: yes, it was funny but everyone knew about high school dances; they weren't important subjects. A male classmate's chapter of a novel drew, on the contrary, deep respect; here was writing that was raw, powerful, elemental and true. His piece about picking up a (totally mute) whore, a fight in a bar, and then (in the subplot) a husband of indeterminate character having painful intercourse on the kitchen floor with a wife, just out of the hospital for the excision of a coccyxal cyst, who stank. Terminal sentence: "That night their idiot child was conceived." Although my female friend and I went outside after class and laughed ourselves silly, I still began to wonder whether I had the proper kind of experience to be a writer. The class judgment had been clear in terms of content. Mine wouldn't do.[43]

For a woman of "fearful, fearful ambition," whose experience is deemed unworthy of expression, science fiction and fantasy held out both hope and an alternative: a woman could write about women's experience in a reality she constructs, in which women have the power to do that which has value to record. In a made-up world, she can be hero, assassin, and woman.

In a series of letters, Joanna Russ described what it was like to be a feminist and a woman science fiction writer:

**Ethnographer:** What kind of response did you get in the beginning for your work?

**Russ:** The second s.f. story I wrote I liked enough to send to *The Magazine of Fantasy and Science Fiction*. It was 1959. They bought it and sent me, I think, $50. I was thrilled. . . . In the beginning, I published about a story a year, and got little response. When I was 29 (1966) . . . Damon Knight . . . invited me to the Milford S.F. Conference in Pennsylvania . . . he had just found out I *wasn't* British, he said! . . . Anyway, he said he would have invited me before. If he'd known I was American.

This response was not uncommon for "literary" science fiction writers before the mass of the New Wave hit. Science fiction had never lost its ties to literary fiction in Britain, where no equivalent explosion in the pulp magazines shifted genre fiction into highly market-segregated consumer ghettos.[44] But it points out another issue that affected the early reception of Russ's work. My question, "Was writing sf a social act within the sf community then, or was the work and the social life directed outside the genre?" met with a ambivalent answer, which I put together as gleaned from several communications.

> I came to writing all by myself and then got to know writers like Laumer and McCaffrey and Sonya Dorman and Chip Delany &c,. &c., Kate Wilhelm, Damon Knight, a host of folks . . . at Milford long before I met fans. And I had no idea for *years* that fandom existed. I did go to some conventions from about the late '60s on and spoke at a few, but I didn't come to s.f. through fandom. I was quite pleased and surprised when I found that there was such a thing. . . . They helped keep me alive while I was teaching in small towns.[45]

From Russ, as from many women who were finding the fan community and the new books that addressed the issues of gender in the late '60s and early '70s, we hear the same wonder and joy that women expressed in finding media fandom in the '80s[46]:

> I remember many things about s.f. then: one, it was relatively easy to get a short story or novel published. . . . The field was so *small*—this was the pre-conglomerate days and people could barely make a living. There was a real feeling of being a besieged minority. And the pleasure of finding others as "weird" as oneself![47]

The ease with which a talented science fiction writer could publish changed dramatically when that writer tried to explore the issues of contemporary sexual politics outside the genre:

> I wrote *The Female Man* in 1971 and couldn't find a mainstream publisher for four years. Finally my agent sent it to Fred Pohl, who grabbed it for his Ace Specials, edited by the late Terry Carr, a fine editor and good writer. Then David Hartwell (another super editor, with a Ph.D. in medieval studies) bought other feminist s.f. of mine, and two feminist books by Suzy McKee Charnas, which make mine look a wee pale(!).

But Charnas reports that even women editors could make it difficult to publish feminist science fiction in the '70s.

> *Motherlines* was rejected by a female editor at a major SF house in 1977 with the words, and I remember them precisely, "It's a wonderful adventure story. If only the characters were all men, we'd buy it in a minute!"
>
> Got that? I didn't; she had to explain to me the prevailing mythology, which she either entirely bought into or presented as an unchallengeable party line, that a huge majority of SF readers were young men. I got the same line (rejecting the same book, but on the grounds that the story had elements that impressionable young—male—readers must not be exposed to) at about the same time from Judy-Lynn Del Rey at Ballantine, who had published my

first novel. But this may well have been her husband, Lester Del Rey, speaking through her.[48]

For many women entering the community in the 1970s, the fan community represented a contradictory forum. On the one hand, the highly literate "new" science fiction fed a hunger both for the humanities-educated writers and for their fans to meet and discuss the issues both literary and political: "I remember small conventions as immensely pleasant, very personal, a sort of combination party / free university,"[49] Joanna Russ reminds us. More women entered the community drawn by the mass appeal of the movies and television products like *Star Wars* on the big screen and *Star Trek* in syndicated reruns or simply found the community through these products after reading science fiction for many years. Between the two entry points, the numbers of men and women at science fiction gatherings in general began to approach parity.

On the other hand, the old guard of "femmefans" and core male members of the community drawn to the traditional science fiction of space ships and alien invasions continued to dominate the broader social context of the community as an elite bastion to be defended against the unread hordes and the feminists.

# Women in Science Fiction:    6
## The Backlash and Beyond

### Women in the '80s: The Backlash Years

In her letter remembering science fiction of the '70s, Joanna Russ made a telling point: "[W]e [women] cop (or used to) a very disproportionate share of the awards (we certainly did in the 1970s)." In fact, we can make some valid assumptions about the acceptance of women in the 1980s by looking at the pattern of guest of honor positions and Hugo awards given to women during the decade. Women appeared as guest of honor in one position or another in 1980 (Kate Wilhelm, professional writer, with her husband, Damon Knight), 1981 (C. L. Moore, as one of two professional writer guests of honor), and 1982 (Lee Hoffman, fan guest of honor). No women appeared as guest of honor in any position again until 1987 in the United Kingdom (Doris Lessing, one of several professional writer guests of honor, and Joyce Slater, with Ken Slater, as a fan guest of honor). 1989 marked the first time a woman appeared again as guest of honor at a Worldcon in the United States.

In a pattern too strikingly similar to be coincidence, women won Hugos for best novel in 1979 (Vonda McIntyre, *Dreamsnake*), 1981 (Joan D. Vinge, *The Snow Queen*), and 1982 (C. J. Cherryh, *Downbelow Station*), but did not win again until 1989, when C. J. Cherryh won for *Cyteen*. Joanna Russ picked up her last Hugo in 1983, for the novella "Souls," which appeared in the January 1982 issue of *Magazine of Fantasy and Science Fiction*. In a premonitory ending, the narrator challenges the alien visitor:

> I said, "Abbess, you said you would be revenged on Thorvald, but all you did was change him into a good man. That is no revenge!" . . .
>
> She said, "I did not change him. I lent him my eyes; that is all." Then she looked beyond me . . . at the great wide world with all its battles which I had used to think so grand, and the misery and greediness and fear and jealousy and hatred of folk one for the other. . . . She said, *"No revenge? Thinkest though thou so, boy?"* And then she said ". . . *Think again.*"[1]

The description of history through the eyes of this child narrator—hatred, greed, jealousy, fear, would seem to describe what Russ saw in fandom and the science fiction community around her. That backlash was clear in all its anger for the women in science fiction who saw with the abbess's clear vision.

Not coincidentally, this period marks the rise of the new and exclusionary science fiction form known as cyberpunk. Of the original cyberpunk authors, only one, Pat Cadigan, was a woman, although Lewis Shiner, a founding member, claims that Cadigan was not in fact one of the true members of the "movement" as he prefers to call it.[2] Those who were not a part of the Austin-based circle of *Cheap Truth* manifesto-wielding cyberbuddies were denied inclusion in the closed group; cyberpunk authors like Bill Gibson, working in the postmodern consciousness, defined their form so that women's writing need not apply—it was to be information-dense, but conforming to a male definition that excluded the "information" that is important to many women writers. Women who write a high-tech computer based fiction with a drugs-n-rock-n-roll sensibility that the readership recognized as cyberpunk were and still are often denied a voice on convention panels, excluded by the fractious boys' clubhouse atmosphere that prevailed wherever two cyberpunk "dudes" got together.[3]

The cyberpunk movement was just one manifestation of a concerted effort to force women out, and Lois McMaster Bujold commented on her response to the silencing of women in her own field of space opera:

> I tend to be a listener rather than a talker, except in milieus like this, where I have, so to speak, permission. So that doesn't really bother me. It takes a load off me . . . and I can, you know, listen, throw in an occasional leading question and fire them up again until they run down, which they almost never do. . . . It means that I'm learning more than they are. Once again, it's judo, you know. Those who listen rather than talk go away more enriched than those who talk rather than listen. So I end up knowing more, and knowledge is power. They're empowering me, and not learning anything that they can use. . . . As far as the boys' club goes, it's like, so what. There's a girls' club out there too. We've got C. J. Cherryh, lots of other women writers.[4]

Lois adds that she has taken a more assertive role on panels as the popularity of her work, particularly the characters in her Barrayar universe, has strengthened rather than diminished through the '90s. But, clearly, the backlash of the mid-1980s did not mark a withdrawal of women from the community. Rather, it signals a response by the voting core of fandom to the incursion into their community of women as a constituency of their own. This core continued to include women who identified with the community much as women in the '50s did, and there certainly remained a place at the heart of the group for those women who brought with them a traditional heterosexual attitude about the place of men and women in the community.

Ironically, the early '80s mark the exact time during which I first tried to write this book. In the introduction to *Enterprising Women* I discussed my failed efforts to engage members of the community in a dialogue that did *not* excoriate women for their disruptive presence. Kathy Sands, proprietor of Tales of the White Hart science fiction bookstore, objected to *Enterprising Women*'s depiction of women as embattled in the science fiction community of the early '80s. She explained that she had met no such difficulty as a woman science fiction fan. Sands met her husband, Leo, when he walked into her struggling science fiction bookstore:

**Kathy Sands:** He wandered into the store that day and I was high as a kite, you know, *Evening Magazine* was doing a thing on my store. We were going to have a party at my apartment, which was across the street from the shop . . . I was inviting everybody in the world. Well, anybody who came into my store that day, and he happened to. Hi! We're having a party, want to come? It was, well, fandom itself was a bit more informal than it is now. Everybody who found their way to . . . a very obscure science fiction bookstore was at least a potential fan. And, so, as far as he was concerned, this strange woman, who'd never met him before was inviting him to a party. . . . Anyway, when the friendship and eventually relationship and everything else developed, I also thought of the store as pretty much an ideal place to raise kids.[5]

For women who did not see their participation in fandom as potentially one-half of a heterosexual couple, or for the feminist writers of the '70s, however, the community could be more difficult. Suzy McKee Charnas points out:

*Motherlines* was published in 1978; *The Furies*, the volume that follows, not until 1994. There are many reasons for this, but one strong one was my distinct sense that if written, and if published (getting *Motherlines* published had been difficult enough), such a book would find no readers.

This was the period, after all, of younger women writers eagerly standing up at "Women in SF" panels and declaring in belligerent tones, "Well, *I'm* not a *feminist*" (as in "*I'm* not a *cannibal*"). They invariably went on to add: (a) "I *like* men"; and (b) "*I* write about whatever I want to." As if being "a feminist" meant hating men both as a class and as individuals, and only writing/thinking/speaking a predetermined party line.[6]

But there were two places newly developing to meet the needs of women fans: media fanzine fandom and the fandoms that rose up around the works of particular women writers.

## Media Fandom: A Disclaimer
In the wake of the uproar in the late 1970s and most of the '80s about fans drawn to the science fiction culture by movies and television, we sometimes forget that fans of those media were already there in the community. One of the first costumes presented at a convention recreated the futuristic costume from the movie *Things to Come*. Until *Star Trek*, however, movies and television played a supporting role to the primary community focus on the books. With *Star Trek* that changed.

Because scholarly attention, including my own, has focused so narrowly on the women's fanzine culture in media fandom, we sometimes forget that the whole *Star Trek* phenomenon took hold of the imaginations of both men and women, and in generally equal numbers.[7] During the first run of the show, *Trek* was just another sf product available to the general community. Bjo Trimble mounted her campaign to save *Trek* through her science fiction contacts, and even the first media zines had a more equal representation than developed later. At his home, Ben Yalow showed me a first edition copy of *Spockanalia*, produced by Lunarian Devra Langsam and signed by other club members who attended the collating party, including Yalow himself.

By the mid-1970s, however, *Star Trek* fandom was drawing a massive following through the endless reruns of the show. While *Star Trek* fans were likely to be science fiction readers as well, the media fans came to the community through their interest in television, perceived as an inferior source of science fiction. That perception of inferiority attached as well to the fans of the media. But men coming to the community through television had an advantage. Men had always been in the majority. The newcomer males, while annoying because they increased the numbers at the conventions beyond the level of comfortable intimacy, did not stand out as a cause.

Women, however, had always been a tiny minority in fandom. By the late '70s the presence of women in numbers approaching parity with the men threatened the sense of the elite that the small numbers in fandom had fostered.

During this period, and perhaps catalyzed by the equal number of women flooding into the community, media-related activities began to break down into gender-specific and non-gender-specific tasks. Non-gender-specific tasks included convention organizing, filksinging, and costuming. Male-specific tasks included amateur scriptwriting and skit writing, both for performance at conventions and for their home video cameras, and model building.[8] Of course, like media fanzine activity, male-specific tasks are sometimes performed by women as well, but in far fewer numbers than by men and seldom in leadership roles. By the '80s, these roles had fairly well solidified into a structure of their own, running side by side with sf fandom, sometimes at media conventions, and sometimes within the sf venues themselves.

For some reason, however—and I suspect this is the result of the feminist and literary interests in culture studies—scholarly focus has devolved on the specifically female task of fanzine publication in the area of television and movie fandom, often omitting the important information that fanzine culture has existed as a primarily male activity in the literary science fiction community since the '30s. And, as we have seen in Chapter 5, women have participated as a minority in science fiction fanzines both as editors and as columnists for much of that time.

But the fanzines the women produced in media fandom differ dramatically from the standard form that continues to exist beside it in the science fiction community at large. The traditional fanzines generally included trip reports and letters reviewing other fanzines, and perhaps books in the genre. One thing you almost never find in a science fiction fanzine is science fiction. Rather, science fiction zines are about fandom and fans as people. In the years when conventions occurred infrequently and at great distances from one another, fanzines were the social glue that created a community out of a worldwide scattering of readers. Today the zines preserve that unique blend of personal essay and travelogue, but in far fewer numbers than they did at their height.

Media fanzines, by contrast, fill the need of a mostly female audience for fictional narratives that expand the boundaries of the official source products offered on the television and movie screen. Copyright holders of these products, such as *Star Trek* in all its permutations, have seized on that part of the market for more product that has mass appeal. But corporate logic dictates that if the characters change in any significant way over the course of the book, they will no longer be available in their pristine form for the next writer. Likewise, they offer only one standard literary format—the novel—which is easier to contract than work for anthologies, and which sells better than other forms in the market.

To many viewers, particularly women, this left a product vacuum in several literary areas. Fan publications are often longer than a commercial novel, or much shorter. Vignettes, single scenes completed in one or two thousand words that shed light on some event or action in the aired series, appear in most anthology zines. Stories at all lengths between the two extremes also appear in the zines. The media fanziners break another market rule: they change the characters—even kill them—because the rules of reading fanzines are different than the rules of the larger market readership. Each story is perceived as that writer's take on the possible outcome of a given situation. Because they are not copyright holders, they do not consider their work "canon," and in fact fanziners hotly debate inclusion and exclusion in canon: what must be considered as given in their own fiction, and what they can discard. In the eyes of many traditional fans, however, the greatest transgression of the media fanzines is in the way they depict action—as centrally located around issues of emotion and trust and sex, re-visioning relationships in a feminine mode and re-creating the male characters, who are feminized to access a greater demonstration of feeling.

It was not until the 1980s, however, when the growing numbers of *Star Trek* and *Star Wars* fans began to assert themselves with a demand for convention resources to celebrate their interest, that backlash struck in earnest. And it struck at women most because they were the most visible, and because they represented an aesthetic of emotionalism that read as romantic for the traditional science fiction reader. Entering the fan community when they did, at a time when the presence of women as winners of the highest prizes in the science fiction community began to threaten the dominance of male hard science fiction and space opera writers, women in media fandom seem to have been the straw that broke the fannish back. Women stopped winning prizes, and participants at science fiction conventions used their positions on fan panels to damn the women of media fandom for all the ills that beset the growing sf community.

### The Politics of a Separate State of Fandom

While the backlash was "disappearing" women from the historical annals of the prize and guest of honor lists, it could not drive the women themselves out of the community. However, many women looking for a close and nurturing environment in the field did move into two areas, one of which continues to be media fanzines. Most of the women who sought out media fanzine fandom were and continue to be just that—fans, who express their interest in the source product by consuming or creating amateur materials related to the source product, and by organizing in the loose affiliations described in detail in *Enterprising Women*. But some women professionals in the science fiction field who were feeling the changes in the science fiction community in a personal and painful way likewise found in media fandom a place of comfort and renewal. Joanna Russ explained her own move to the media fanzine community:

> I only became acquainted with fanfic in my *forties* when a good friend (an old feminist colleague from the 1970s) called me and told me about it, then sent me a bundle and the Universal Translator. I went ape over K/S, wrote about it, wrote four stories or so under the pseudonym. . . . They were immense fun and woke me up personally, sexually, fictionally, every way. I had begun to feel that s.f. was dead-ended (I don't feel that now) and they got me into somehow writing s.f. and fantasy about stuff I really cared about. . . . They were, in a way, five-finger exercises. *It didn't matter* what I wrote or how unrespectable it was or how "unliterary."[9]

As described in *Enterprising Women*, the aesthetics of fan fiction in the women's writing community differ markedly from those imposed on canonical "good" literature, and the fact that the fiction did not value originality but rather made use of a standard set of characters and situations made the form even more suspect. Russ explained in an earlier letter why she felt obliged to write the article in *Magic Mamma's, Trembling Sisters, Puritans and Perverts* when she did: "I was following Audre Lorde's strategy (as she says at one point) to proclaim it publicly first before they can use it against you."[10] To an extent, this defensive strategy has been followed by most of the academics who have written about media fanzines out of their own experience. Each finds a need to defend herself or himself in the context of studies that valorize other popular culture ventures, as if to say, "My choice of hobby/identity is not inferior," an ironic position for scholars working in a subfield of a larger field, science fiction, which has itself been snubbed by academe.

While media fanwriting became a haven for some professional women writers, it became a training ground for others, to the extent that the phrase "filing the serial numbers off" has become common in the field. Lois McMaster Bujold describes her experience:

> My friend [name deleted], whom I talked about earlier . . . started writing fan stories again. And a couple of original novels—which started as a fan novels. You file the serial numbers off, and you keep rewriting it until it's not that any more, it's something of your own. And then she started making some short story sales.

A writer who takes a work created in the media fanzines and changes the character names, the description of space ships, etc., and then sells the work as an original piece of fiction as Bujold describes is said to be "filing the serial numbers off"—removing the identifying marks that establish its origins in the amateur publications.

Writers who create their own fictional contexts but make use of favorite characters or a particular character to guide their representation of their own heroes and villains are using what are often called "avatars." Those in the know often make a game of guessing who the avatar was, or what source product's serial number originally graced the original work. It is important to note that the writers are not plagiarizing the plots or other owned property of the media source products. However, some nervousness still exists in the industry about discussing too openly these "writers' aids," and therefore I am unable to provide the names of authors who have taken this route. A number of them have written both their fan fiction and their professional fiction under the same name, however, so a careful examination of the better zines over time is likely to produce a name or two that either cross back and forth from professional to fan fiction or develop their prose styles for the move to professional writing. The careful reader of the zines will likewise find not only the decidedly amateur efforts of writers whose talents would not take them farther, but also the professional-level work of writers who choose to remain in the amateur community that sustains and supports them.

## Women's Fictional Universes

Above I said that the media fanzine community provided one safe harbor for women entering the fan community in the 1980s. Communities based on the fictional universes of certain women writers created the second. As we proceed with the discussion of those universes, it is important to remember that they are not the separatist havens of women who hate men but, rather, defined spaces where men and women, though preponderantly women, can come together in a lived community structured according to women's ideas of what that means.

Marion Zimmer Bradley, a cofounder of the Society for Creative Anachronism and creator of the world Darkover, is one of the best known, but she is not the only woman writer whose fans settle in and live in her created universe. Jacqueline Lichtenberg created the Sime-Gen universe, based on body types, a sort of vampirism, and relationships to food as well as Judeo-Christian cabalism. Lichtenberg has had a committed following since she self-published her *Star Trek* fanzines in her Kraith universe in the 1960s; her Sime-Gen fans participate in fanzines and face-to-face discussion about her Sime-Gen novels and model community around their shared interest. In the '90s, the community has moved online as well. Katherine Kurtz's fans likewise meet and find spiritual and communal values in her Deryni saga, another multivolume series, and Anne McCaffrey's fans have created a huge, worldwide structure of Weyrs, or fan club / communities to share in their interest in her Pern universe, creating fanzines and letterzines and conventions and now, in the '90s, bringing their fandom online.

Nor is the phenomenon restricted completely to the works of women writers. I have heard that some fans of Roger Zelazny's Amber series likewise organize around an interest in his book. And fans of J. R. R. Tolkien and a select few other writers of the mythic gather in the Mythopoeic Society, and even hold their own scholarly meeting. But arguably none of these have created the widespread network of lived communities that have grown out of the shared interest in the works of the women mentioned above. Robert Silverberg, addressing this issue in Philadelphia in 1987, explained:

> There are eight or nine Amber books, there are God knows how many Darkover books. Those writers have produced an entire encyclopedia of work about their worlds. But of course you want to get the reader sufficiently involved so that he or she, and most of these cases I think are shes, will pick up the books and let them have a life of their own in the readers' minds.

Comparing this effect to his own books, Silverberg explained further:

> I don't think my work encourages that particularly, although I'd be happy if it did, because I tend to round it off and finish, and leave it in a finished state. . . . These [the series described above] are open-ended worlds. Their readership, the Darkover fans, I suppose the Amber fans, I know very little about them, but the Darkover fans—Anne McCaffrey fans—there's an element of feminism involved in those two cults that I can't hope to engender. The aspect of woman as goddess, woman as power figure. And of course it's taken on a life of its own—good for them. It's fascinating stuff, but it's not my stuff. It doesn't belong to me.

While the content and message of the books themselves create the impetus for a community that empowers women based in the fiction, Silverberg sees another contrast between himself and the women who demonstrably embody the meaning of the communities they foster:

> Anne McCaffrey is an extremely earthy, extroverted, outgoing woman, warm and boisterous. I'm not a particularly chilly person, but I'm very far from boisterous, and somewhat reclusive in my life. I'm busy doing my own things of great interest to me. Marion Zimmer Bradley lives at the heart of a bustling commune of I don't know how many people in Berkeley—she's sending six people through college who are children of her friends . . . I see her as far more plugged into a social framework than I prefer to be.[11]

### Darkover, Marion Zimmer Bradley, and the SCA[12]

Like Silverberg, Marion Zimmer Bradley participated in fandom in the 1950s. With science fiction and fantasy writer Poul Anderson, Diana L. Paxson, and others, she cofounded the Society for Creative Anachronism to foster the playful amateur study of medieval history. SCAdians, as they call themselves, organize in local groups that range from the smallest—a canton or college, through shires, baronies or provinces, to the largest, a kingdom. They gather for various activities that include a single group or many groups together, the most important being the annual Pennsic War—two weeks of jousting, costuming, and the creation of a Renaissance fair for the SCAdians themselves.[13]

Bradley began publishing the Darkover novels in the 1960s. In Darkover, one of the most popular series of books written about any imaginary landscape, Bradley combines her love of science fiction with her love of the sword and sorcery genre that gave birth to SCA. The series charts the cultural survival of a shipwrecked and isolated group of people on a planet with a hostile natural environment. On Darkover the shipwrecked humans make contact with the nearly extinct indigenous population and some individuals develop skill in the psychic power called *laran*. The society rises using psychic technology, and falls again into a feudal order after the misuse of this technology in war. Darkover is in this state of apparent feudal technology when it is contacted by the space-faring progeny of the world from which they have been separated for so long.

For Darkover fans, however, the basic story is not as important as the slow development of the culture and history of the fictional world as it plays out in scattered pieces across the series. In books such as *Heritage of Hastur* and *The Forbidden Tower*, Bradley explores the complex culture of Darkover. Readers come to the world in no specific chronological reading order, but do accumulate a level of understanding over a number of books until, after a certain critical mass of information has been absorbed, the world seems to take hold of the imagination as a lived experience. Bradley combines elements that are traditionally confined to fantasy—a feudal culture using telepathy and "magic" crystals in their technology—with a complex discussion of gender and sexual identity that finds a place and acceptance for both traditional and nontraditional roles for women in society. And in the very particular way that women in the genre tend to do, Bradley is a powerful voice using telepathy as a metaphor to examine the ideal of true communication with others. On Darkover, one could say, communication, through telepathy, is power.

### Why Darkover?

If one were looking for a feminist world to inhabit in science fiction, one would shudder and pass by Darkover without a second look. The feudal system keeps much of the female population in traditional positions of powerlessness as wives and mothers whose lives seem to be completely controlled by their husbands. Women who hold power, as defined by the psychic power exercised in the towers, must remain virgins as long as they continue to hold their positions as keepers. Women who chose a less ascetic life than that of a keeper but a more autonomous one than that of a wife may become Renunciates, who renounce marriage—though not necessarily men. However, this is a margin where lesbianism is explored as well as relationships with men that do not culminate in marriage and a lifetime of child-rearing. Renunciates themselves are circumscribed by Bradley's society—they work as midwives or as guides and bodyguards, and in the latter jobs they are even limited in the weapons they are allowed to use.

But our original question presupposes an error in purpose. One presumes that one is looking for an alternative world in which the problems of this one have been solved, from which the fan can draw answers. That is not what Darkover, or Pern, or any other of the powerful worlds created by women do. Rather, we can see that, similar to the function that the *Star Trek* genres had in distancing the writer from personal issues through complex levels of abstraction,[14] Darkover too set up a situation as problematic as that in which their fans live their real lives, while allowing the fans the safety of a number of levels of abstraction to distance themselves from the proximate identification with the very concerns that drive them to seek out a place to think and be heard. Among the most powerful of these distancing devices may be the way Bradley plays with time. The Darkover universe is situated in the future of space travel, but the culture of Darkover itself has fallen into a feudal culture reminiscent of the far past of the culture of the readers. Safe outside their own time—the events occur in a future, but they are saved from requiring answers to the ills of today by the decline of the space-faring culture into a past where issues of gender and sexuality and power were much more problematic for women—fans can explore both the difficulties of being a woman today and the options they can make for themselves in the world they live in. Darkover fandom establishes a space for the speaking of issues important to women, and a language, particularly the Renunciates and the metaphor of *laran*, to do so.

Ultimately, however, the answer to the question "why Darkover" must come down to the author herself. As Silverberg recounts above, Bradley situated herself, in person, at the center of the social matrix that her fiction creates. In Timonium, Maryland, every Thanksgiving weekend fans of Darkover hold a convention; Bradley herself attended for many years until health considerations made it impossible. For many Darkover enthusiasts, the convention is almost like coming home. Melissa Scott, historian and hard science fiction writer, explains how she came to Darkover through the SCA:

> That's sort of been a two-stage process. They recruited at Harvard, either my freshman or sophomore year, I forget which, early. And it was Carolingia, which at the time was a rather sexist bunch, and at the time I was also on the Harvard fencing team and was joining, interested in SCA so I could play some more with heavy weapons, and they were not amenable to this . . . it was years later when I started going to Darkover, it must have been six, seven years ago by now [June 1993]. And then I met people who were sort of normal and interesting and not sexist in the what is it, Atlantia. And there all the women do the fighting and the guys do the embroidery . . . (Well, that's an exaggeration! But women fighters were more than welcomed.)[15] Darkover is the only place where I do costume now, outside of the masquerades and the regencies. And that's because it's not a business con for me really, it's a working vacation, and mostly vacation. I see a lot of friends. . . . We [Melissa and her lifepartner, Lisa Barnett] move heaven and earth to get there. . . .
>
> Judy Gerjuoy is one of the better concom people. You know, she's your stereotypical femmefan, and yet she's so much more. She's such good people. She wants to be everybody's Jewish mother. This is her own statement. And she does a real good job of it. That's the convention at which I'm most fannish and most involved in fan stuff, It's such a relief. I guess what I really miss [as a professional in the field] is the chance just to sort of burble and be enthusiastic and not—to have fun with stuff without always having to think, okay, is there a deeper meaning, am I saying something that I will regret later.

In Darkover, Scott sees no contradiction in the seemingly paradoxical formulation of the nurturing, maternal concom and the unconventionally gendered activity of heavier weaponry for women who wish to take the more aggressive role in the medieval field of play, but it is this very synthesis of opposites or, rather, refusal to see the two in opposition, that draws some fans to Darkover.

Nor is it an accident that so many writers have contributed their vision to the world of Darkover. For a number of years, Bradley allowed her fans to participate in her universe, and she has gathered the best of their stories, along with the works of other women professionals with permission to write in the Darkover universe, in a number of volumes of an anthology series set there. Fantasist and writer of military science fiction Susan Shwartz describes her entrance into Darkover fandom, and the start Bradley gave her in her writing career:

[I]n '77 I graduated [Harvard again!], I got a tenure-track position at Ithaca College, I was dead broke. There wasn't any fun to be made up there. It was cold, it was snowy. At first I was sort of rewriting scenes from other people's work, which I realize now is fannish-type writing. And through an ad in DAW books for the friends of Darkover, I got in touch with the Darkover community, and through that, got in touch with some writers and some fans and started going to conventions.

Beginning in 1980, Shwartz has had several stories anthologized in the Friends of Darkover collections. Writers including Mercedes Lackey, herself the mistress of a fan culture centered around her world of Valdemar, have had their start under Bradley's wing.

Currently, Bradley has completely moved away from the Friends of Darkover, which has become inactive as an organization. The author now devotes her energies to the Sword and Sorceress anthologies and the publication of a professional magazine, *Marion Zimmer Bradley's Fantasy Magazine*, where new writers who aspire to professional careers may try their wings at their own fantasy universes next to the established figures in the genre. While Darkover fans continue to gather and share their appreciation of the fictional universe, Bradley has discouraged literary involvement within the remaining fan base.

But it would be a mistake to assume that all women entering the science fiction community in the 1980s found themselves drawn to the alternatives of media fandom and the fandoms surrounding the fully fleshed-out universes of a few women authors. S. N. Lewitt, a very different kind of writer and long-time member of the gothic community described in the next chapter, tells of a very different experience:

I went to cons to learn how to be a pro. My first con, I dressed up in costume, and played around and had a lot of fun, and, umm, went to Darkover parties and stuff. By my second con, I found that all very boring. I wasn't interested in being someone else's fan . . . because I already had my book, my world plotted and worked out, and I knew I was good enough to get it published, which in fact happened. . . . I think that what turned me off at the Boskone I went to, the very first con, one woman at the Darkover party came up to me and said, "What do you do?" And I said, "I'm a playwright." And she said, "Oh, do you write Darkover plays?" Right. Yeah. Yeah. I'm working on trying to analyze Jean-Claud Vanataly and Chekhov, and my own stuff, and this, and you're asking me if I write Darkover?

**Ethnographer:**    Logical question at a Darkover party.

**Lewitt:**    It might be, but, um, it was an assumption . . . I don't mind people asking me, but this woman, afterwards, after I said, "No, I don't write Dark-over plays," was sort of like, "Oh, well, who wants to talk to you? Who and what are you?" And like, oh, well, you want to deal with that, that's your problem, baby, it ain't mine.

For a new writer gaining security in her own skills but as yet untried in the marketplace, the fandom of another writer, particularly one whose work differs markedly in style, form, and intent, can be particularly hard on the fledgling ego. When the new writer truly shares the love of the material around which the fandom gathers, she can put aside those self-interests; when she finds herself placed there by default (it's where the women are . . . ) the results can be disheartening in the extreme. But with a woman writer at its center, and with the complex and rich culture of Darkover as its metaphoric language, many women in the '80s found that Bradley's hostile planet nurtured not just the goddess in women, but the writer in them as well.

## The End of the Backlash

Women in science fiction, both professional writers and fans, migrated to separate states in the '80s because they found acceptance there. They developed their own systems for mentoring writers and providing community life for women. For some, participation in a women's fan community has become a permanent identity; for others, it provided a place to wait out the backlash.

By 1990, the backlash had substantially disappeared, leaving only the residual stereotypes that mark the field's version of the wider culture's view of women. Of these, the idea that women write primarily fantasy and men write primarily science fiction seems to capture the mainstream version of "women feel, men use tools."[16] Fortunately, science fiction fans do not let their maxims get in the way of reality, as a look at the Hugo winners for the 1990s shows. Women won for best novel in the years 1991, 1992, 1993 (a co–win), and 1995. In 1992, of six novels nominated, four were by women; of five novellas, four were by women; of five novelettes, two were by women; and of seven short stories, two were by women. Of five editors nominated, two were women. Women won in two of the categories, novel and novella.

Connie Willis's *Doomsday Book* won a tie with Vernor Vinge's *A Fire Upon the Deep* in 1993.[17] But perhaps the most phenomenal example of the new acceptance of women in the mainstream of science fiction in the '90s has been Lois McMaster Bujold, winner of the Hugo for best novel in 1991 for *The Vor Game*, in 1992 for *Barrayar*, and in 1994 for *Mirror Dance*.

### Lois McMaster Bujold and Miles Vorkosigan

As did most of the women who give their histories in this book, Bujold came to science fiction early:

> **Lois McMaster Bujold:**   Well, I came by the taste honestly. My dad read science fiction. He was a professor of welding engineering at Ohio State University and an old Cal Tech man. . . . So, he would buy the science fiction magazines . . . or paperbacks to read on the plane, so this stuff was lying around. . . . I first started reading it . . . because it was there, there in my house . . . I got my first subscription to *Analog* when I was thirteen.

Again like many women in science fiction, Bujold found fandom just out of high school, and her experience in 1968 sounds remarkably similar to that of Karen Anderson in 1951:

[I] fell into conversation with a guy in front of the sf shelf, and he invited me to the local fan group meeting, which in 1968, when I walked in the door, was twenty-two guys and me. Today, I would know what to do with that situation. Back then, it was totally wasted on me . . . and I went to my first conventions. I was active in fandom for two or three years, up 'til, I suppose, early to mid-college. And so I got to go to a couple of Worldcons, and some other local conventions. Met a bunch of people through it, including my now ex-husband.

Elsewhere I have discussed[18] how women must often struggle for a much longer time than men to succeed at a writing career, and Bujold was no exception. Her reasons may give us considerable insight into this phenomenon:

I was listening to a biography of Joseph Campbell on TV, and he talked about a sort of latent period in his life, where he did nothing but read for five years. And at the end of it he came out, you know, ready to say something. So I think the period in my twenties when I read widely, but didn't try to write— that, and having children in my late twenties, was a part of my life when I was growing a center to write out of. It was writing out of a whole new world-view which I didn't have until I grew it.

While growing her own center, Bujold also watched the career of her friend Lillian Carl, who had just published her own first novel. With Carl and Patricia Wrede, Bujold formed a "round robin" critiquing circle, in which each of the three women would circulate chapters of her own works and critique the works of the other two.

[S]o, I had this three-year period of training where I was basically getting my stuff critiqued by the other two, and having the experience of critiquing theirs, which also sharpened my skills, I think . . . I set myself the idea, okay, if I had gone back to school to get a degree in chemistry, which was my original lifeplan . . . I would spend four years. So, I would spend four years as an apprentice novelist, and it would cost less than going to college, by far. And if I didn't get a break in four years or three books, which is what it took Lillian, I would reconsider my options.

Out of the years of thinking and years working with Lillian Carl and Patricia Wrede came Bujold's new worldview, in the person of the son of Admiral Aral Vorkosigan. Miles Vorkosigan, frail, hyperactive, deeply ironic about himself and the world around him, struggled onto the bookshelves.

I wrote *Shards of Honor*, or what became *Shards of Honor*, and *The Warrior's Apprentice*. And started sending them out. They went out to an agent and came back, they went out to a publisher, and it took months each time, and I went ahead and worked on the next one.

*Shards of Honor*, which Bujold admits is "a gothic novel in science fiction drag," recounts the adventure of Cordelia Naismith, reluctant but efficient soldier, who meets and falls in love with Admiral Aral Vorkosigan, a leader in the enemy fleet, as they alternate taking each other prisoner and rescuing each other from various dangers, including the evil excesses of the admiral's own superior. *Warrior's Apprentice* takes up the story with their son, Miles Naismith Vorkosigan, one of the most unlikely heroes ever to turn a bad situation to his advantage. Bujold continues:

> And in the meantime, the books were going back and forth, creating tremendous hope which was tremendously crushed whenever one came back again. I talked continually to Pat and Lillian, what can I do differently, what can I do else, what can I try next? What are these people doing in New York? How do they pick these things? How can I assure that I will be chosen? It is all very mysterious, trying to figure out publishers, how you get an agent, how publishers pick books. All this unraveling of the mysteries of publishing was something I was going through at that time.
>
> But at any rate, we got to the fall of '85, and *Warrior's Apprentice* had been rejected by two or three places, and Lillian and Pat both said, well, why don't you try it on Betsy Mitchell at Baen Books next, because even if she rejects it she will probably give you a good reading and some feedback. So it got sent in to Baen. And the first reader read it, and Betsy read it, and Jim Baen read it, and reached page 125 and called me on the phone and bought all three books. And it was like, oh, wow. From nothing to everything in one phone call.

The reader's report for *Warrior's Apprentice* makes clear the difficulty in describing the particular charm of the Vorkosigan series when he justifies his recommendation to purchase the book based on the fact that it is impossible to put down rather than on the outline of the plot. Bujold understands the problem of that first reader:

> I write in the framework of space opera, and a description of the plots of my books sounds dumb because, while I am pushing the envelope, I am pushing it in the opposite direction. I am not pushing outward, I'm not distorting the form; I'm pushing inward, I'm creating depth of character, which is, supposedly, not done in space opera. But I'm doing it, because no genre policeman has ever knocked on my door and said, "You can't do that" . . . it makes my books very hard to describe, because on the underside they're a psychological novel and on the top side they're a space opera. And when you are trying to describe a book, you usually describe the top side. You describe the plot.

Bujold's plots do seem to be a jumble of every space-faring tall tale that has hit the space opera subgenre in its long history. Miles is the son of a count on a feudal backwater of a multiplanet space-faring universe that includes political intrigue, interstellar war, kidnappings, mercenary pirates, and evil twins. But the sardonic wit of her hero, the insight that each character brings to his or her situation, and the often surprising reversals of expectations create something exciting and new.[19]

Purists have complained that, for a variety of reasons, including the insufficiency of their science and their lack of originality at the plot level, the books do not deserve their three best novel Hugos. While admitting that the Vorkosigan novels don't have especially originally plots, and looking to their quality as character studies to merit the Hugo, Bujold rejects the complaint that her books contain insufficient science:

**Ethnographer:** I'm wondering, about the decision to make reproductive technology the technological focus of this sf book, and also the kind of, this is part of a larger question about women in hard science fiction and space opera stuff, and seeing it differently. How do you see this, a book like *Barrayar*, fitting into "science" fiction?

**Bujold:** . . . I worked seven years in a hospital, for crying out loud, I've had two children. I know all about biology. I've done it. . . . and it was a bit of technology that nobody else much was doing. You always look for what other people aren't doing and do that, because there's no point in trying to compete with them where they are strong. It's like judo. You go for their weak spots with your strong spots . . . but biology has come into its own as a science in the last twenty years.

And the other thing is, it's also a corrective. The idea of the uterine replicator was used in *Brave New World*, which was written in 1930. But I looked at it and I said, "No, Huxley did it wrong. If we had this technology, that's not what would happen, this is what would happen." So it really is hard science fiction. It is the extrapolation: if you have a new technology, what changes will it make in people's lives? That's what science fiction should be exploring. You know—"What are the consequences of a new technology?" It's not "What is the technology?" it's "What is the consequence?" That's what makes it a story.

In the opening of *Ethan of Athos*, I explained the design of the uterine replicator and how it would work. Because in this technology, all of a sudden, we were in my area of expertise. . . . You write to your strengths and you go around your weak areas. And the guys do this too, but they don't always see that they're doing it.

Reproductive technology is not new to science fiction, of course. It figures in C. J. Cherryh's 1982 Hugo winner, *Downbelow Station*, and again in her 1989 Hugo winner *Cyteen*. But if we compare the two uses of the technology, we see a striking difference. On the surface, Bujold's story considers artificial uterine technology an extension of motherhood. On the surface, Cherryh's stories represent the replicators as part of a system to mass-produce human beings in factories. Of course, the meaning of neither story resides exclusively in the surface, and in fact Cherryh uses the factory system, set against the actions of her characters, to question the meaning of the factory system itself. Many readers, however, continue to make the distinction that Cherryh questions, between fiction of the emotion and "nuts-and-bolts *science* fiction." To these readers, the factory system of Cherryh's reproductive technology is "hard science fiction," whereas the use of the same technology to assist a mother to bring her child to term is not.

Fans of Bujold, however, continue to inhale her books, to love the characters, and to vote Miles and his creator winners of the most prestigious prize awarded by fans, the Hugo.

## How Did the Backlash End?

It would be wrong to assume that everyone in the field now accepts the position of women as a force in science fiction and fantasy. To date, women have won few prizes in fantasy, and some male writers still silence women on speaker panels at conventions. Some members of SFWA, the Science Fiction and Fantasy Writers of America, recently made an abortive try at excluding media tie-in novels as eligible publications for consideration in qualifying for membership in the society. This may be seen as an effort at "cleansing" the genre. When we press for motives, however, we cannot overlook the association of the television fan with the influx of women into the fan community in the '70s. But in spite of the holdouts, clearly something has changed in the acceptance of the work and participation of women at all levels of the science fiction community. But what changed?

The first and most obvious answer is the effect of the growing parity of numbers at science fiction conventions since the 1970s. The men grew accustomed to the situation. Many young fans of today were not even alive when the community appeared to many to be an all-male society with a few token exceptions. Although some young men may resent the threat to their privilege that emancipated women represent, it would be a general resentment, specific neither to science fiction nor to the fan community. Older fans might continue to harbor their feelings of embattlement, but in the '90s they are outnumbered not only by the women, but by the men who accept if not welcome the women. Accordingly, they must voice their opinions more carefully if they want to remain a force in the community themselves. But many of the men who reacted so vociferously against the women in the '70s and '80s have simply gotten used to that presence. "Normal" is different now, and like all change, it may be resisted at first, but in time the change itself becomes the norm.

Another answer lies in the breakdown of barriers that, as Bujold points out, left the way clear for other women writers to follow:

> I am not in the position of being a pioneer. I have never had to break in anywhere. All the barriers have been bulldozed down before me by other people. You know, C. J. Cherryh proved that women could write hard science fiction and win Hugos for it. Ursula Le Guin proved that women could [win] Hugos, period, whatever they were writing. Anne McCaffrey proved that women could be bestsellers, and that was the biggest bulldozer of all. So, when I came along, publishers were ready to ask, "Could this be the next Anne McCaffrey? Could this be the next C. J. Cherryh?"[20]

Bujold points to the groundbreakers, many of whom were brought into the genre by male editors. Donald Wollheim, Terry Carr, David Hartwell all brought to science fiction some of the most dynamic writers of any time in the history of science fiction, and some of those stars were women. But as we look at the publishing practices in the '70s and early '80s, we see women still as the exception, the exceptional, in the field. To win the major prizes, as we can see from the history of women in the community in the '70s, one needs only the exceptional in print. But to win general acceptance takes more. A quick scan of the book spines in your local Walden Books or Borders today will reveal, by contrast to the '60s and '70s, growing parity in the shelf space devoted to women's science fiction and fantasy compared to men's.[21] Open the books, and you will discover what you may have already assumed: women no longer must demonstrate overwhelmingly superior skill and insight to win a book contract. In fact, women's science fiction and fantasy today demonstrates the same range of skill and accomplishment as that which men in the field have always enjoyed.

Clearly we are looking at a third answer to the end of the backlash: a shift in reading practices that *preceded* the acceptance of women by the community's core taste arbiters. Simply put, readers were buying and reading an increasing number of books by women even while they were reacting to the women's presence with indignation. This shift in reading practices began in the '70s and continued, as Bujold asserts, to pave the way for women of the '90s. But how did that happen? Why did editors start selecting more books by women? The answer, to a great extent, parallels the growing acceptance of women in the community at large. Women's writing in the genres began to receive wider publication and distribution because women began to command more positions at all levels of the publishing/editorial process. They were there, they had to be reckoned with, and ultimately, the became the norm.

## Women in Publishing

In an interview in Boston in February of 1993, Beth Meacham, Executive Editor at Tor books, described the acquisitions process:

> Editorial is a branch of publishing. People who have the word "editor" in their titles are people who work with text. Within that, you have a hierarchy within the acquisitions and working-with-authors part, which starts with editorial assistant, runs up through assistant editor, associate editor, editor, senior editor, executive editor, editor in chief, and editorial director. Those are the titles. . . .
>
> So. As you move up the editorial hierarchy, from editorial assistant to editorial director, it's one of those ascending pyramids of promotion. There are lots and lots of editorial assistants. There are fewer assistant editors, even fewer associate editors. There are even fewer editors, until you get up to the top of the line, which is your editor in chief and your editorial director, and a house will only have one of those. . . .
>
> The title of executive editor tends to be held—across the board—by people who have been editors in chief. It is a title you get kicked down to when you want to . . . go back to working on books. And I've known a lot of people who have just sort of pulsed back and forth between the two jobs.[22]

Since 1980, science fiction publishing has seen an increase in the number of women at all levels of this hierarchy. During an interview conducted in November 1993,[23] Laura Anne Gilman, former editor at Ace Books and current executive editor at Roc, confronted the issue of women "taking over" editing:

> [T]hat's always been true . . . at least on the mass market, or paperback, side. It's really been a female-dominated field. For a variety of reasons, one of

which is that it's a liberal arts field, if you will. It's also not an incredibly macho field. Editing requires working with people, it requires interaction, and while many men are very good at it, they don't want to go into it. And the pay has, of course, something to do with it. If you traditionally have to be the main breadwinner, you can't afford it.

Of course, male editors of science fiction and fantasy did consider their job "macho" in the context of the publishing arena—they were guiding the creation of a high-tech men's fiction—and the many male editors who remain in the field do not consider the work less masculine than they did in the 1970s and early '80s. While the science fiction histories indicate that the salaries were always low in genre publishing, as Gilman states, we must see that in the multiple and complex contexts which situates the genre. As Sheila Gilbert reminds us:

> [A] hundred years ago it [publishing] was kind of the gentlemen's profession. It's where the younger sons of wealthy families went and, you know, did something literary and [contributed] to the culture. And they could afford to do it because the family had all this money anyway.

At the beginning of the genre in the '30s, men entering the field carried with them both the enthusiasm for the new fiction of an optimistic future and often the tradition of noblesse oblige of status lost during the Depression. And as long as the readership remained as financially limited as the publishing staffs, neither side of the business—producer or market—experienced an economic dissonance when they interacted within the community. During the late '70s, however, an increasingly affluent and professionalized readership had outstripped the earning power of the lower end of the publishing field and an increasing number of women who had grown up around the genre entered the field willing to take the work at the entry-level pay scales. By the '80s, a major shift in the gendering of science fiction and fantasy publishing had taken place. Gilman herself entered publishing in 1989 as an editorial assistant, and she draws her perception of the field from her own experience at Ace:

> We've been called the henhouse by male writers. . . . [A]nd that is, in my mind, male insecurity: "A woman can't understand my writing. My God, what are they going to do to me, they are going to emasculate me." We've had that happen. I've also had a lot of male writers who felt incredibly comfortable with a woman editing them. I've had a lot of women writers who might have felt more comfortable with a male editor; I don't know. They haven't made a point of it.

Gilman could take for granted the presence of women in powerful positions throughout the publishing industry. Discussing the chain of command at Berkley in the mid-1990s, Gilman mentioned Chief Executive Officer Phyllis Grant, also Susan Allison in the multiple positions of vice president at Berkley, and executive editor and editor in chief at Ace, the Berkley science fiction and fantasy imprint. Ginjer Buchanan, the senior editor—now senior executive editor—rounded out the Ace publishing hierarchy. But when asked, in October 1993, for specific entry dates for women editors at Ace, Gilman's answer placed the feminization of science fiction editing clearly in the early '80s:

**Ethnographer:**   How long has Ginjer [Buchanan] been there?

**Gilman:**   She's coming up on ten years [now, more than fifteen]. . . . Susan [Allison] has been there. Well, since Susan started with ACE in its various incarnations, she's been there a long time. . . . As a matter of fact, Susan started out as Jim Baen's assistant. His secretary, actually—she's always quick to point that out—his secretary years and years and years ago.

During this same time period, the mid-1980s, Beth Meacham moved to Tor Books. Tor has become the publisher of choice for many science fiction and fantasy writers with aspirations to a high level of the art, but it did not always have this sterling reputation. When I mentioned that Tor had an enviable position in the marketplace, Meacham answered:

It makes me feel good to hear you say it, because when I joined Tor, at the beginning of 1984, it was a disaster area. . . . I used to talk about it: that, you know, I was coming in, and my job was to be a little tugboat to turn the Queen Mary.

**Ethnographer:**   You did.

**Meacham:**   Yeah, I did. But oh, God, it was hard. And it just makes me so happy that it worked.

Meacham is one of the most prominent figures in the world of science fiction editing today and has herself moved back and forth between the positions of editor in chief and chief executive officer at Tor:

**Meacham:**   I was editor in chief of Tor for about five years.

**Ethnographer:**   But you're still at Tor.

**Meacham:**   Mmm. Fired myself . . . I literally did. I looked around and I said, I'm not happy, I'm not productive, I'm not doing the work I'm best suited to do. . . . I talked to [publisher] Tom Doherty about it, and told him how I was feeling, and that I was burning out, and that I could probably be editor in chief for a couple more years, but then I'd be gone, dead, away. Or he could let me kick myself downstairs, out the door, move to Arizona, and go back to editing books for him, which is what he decided he wanted to do.

As the major player in the field, Tor Books has a number of innovative practices that add to its success, some of which will be discussed later, and it has a number of senior editors, both male and female. But the growth of the company's prestige list was guided by one of a growing number of women in positions of power in the editorial world of science fiction and fantasy in the '80s. While those editors may not have chosen women authors preferentially over men, they did come to the field without a bias against women purely on the basis of their gender. Their presence gave more women writers an equal hearing than ever before.

## DAW Books: The Little Family Dynasty That Could

Of the major commercial houses publishing science fiction and fantasy, only DAW Books is completely owned and run by women: Betsy Wollheim, daughter of founders Donald and Elsie Wollheim, and long time editor and copublisher Sheila Gilbert. During a discussion over breakfast in San Francisco at ConFrancisco, the 1993 World Science Fiction Convention, Wollheim and Gilbert talked in depth about their roots in science fiction and fantasy, and about the company they co-own, the company that Betsy Wollheim refers to as "The Little Engine That Could."[24]

> **Wollheim:**   You know, DAW's a very special company. We were the first company devoted exclusively to science fiction and fantasy, ever, in history. I think a lot of people don't realize that.
>
> **Gilbert:**   And also, we are just about the only family company in publishing, not just in science fiction.
>
> **Wollheim:**   And not only that, but we are the only company that is not owned in any way by any financier. Sheila and I now own this company, which was formerly owned only by Elsie and Don . . . and me. . . . [N]o corporation owns any part of us. We are a closely held family business. We have never taken a loan from a bank. No one has ever financed us. And we are the only company that exists that has ever been like that in science fiction and fantasy. . . . We have purity of artistic control.

When Donald A. Wollheim founded DAW Books with his wife Elsie in November 1971, he had already earned a place at the forefront not only of science fiction but of publishing in general. Wollheim came to science fiction as a fan, a member of the fractiously contentious Futurians, of whom many participants rose to positions of power in the creation of the genre of science fiction as we know it today.[25] Between 1945 and 1950 Donald Wollheim served as editor in chief at Avon Books, where he originated the first paperback line in publishing history. In 1951 he moved to Ace Books, where he founded their paperback line and where he stayed for the next nineteen years. Over the course of his career, Wollheim also wrote eighteen novels and more than fifty short stories, of which one, "Mimic," has recently been made into a major motion picture. Throughout his lifetime as fan, writer, editor, and publisher, however, Wollheim earned a reputation for his difficult, combative personality, to the extent that some combatants recently took the occasion of his wife Elsie's death in 1996 to continue the feud, even though Wollheim himself had died six years earlier.[26] While Wollheim's problematic personality certainly may have aggravated the situation, some of the accountability must fall to the poverty-level payments made by the industry in the 1950s, and to A. A. Wynn, publisher of Ace Books:

> **Betsy Wollheim:**   And at Ace he worked for A. A. Wynn, who was a very old-fashioned kind of boss. He was incredibly cheap, and authoritarian in his attitude: "I am the boss," end of story. . . . I think a lot of authors who were annoyed by Ace's small wages—of course we're talking about 1952, '53—

went somewhere else for sometimes no more than fifty dollars more, which aggravated my father. They didn't realize that my father also was making a poor salary and was practically running the whole company. . . .

My father was an aristocratic-seeming person who'd come from an upper-crust line, and so he always seemed like he was somebody who had money, but we actually never had money. We didn't have any more money than the authors did. . . . A. A. Wynn was somebody the authors never met, so my father really took the hit for his boss's stinginess, but he was a very, very loyal employee.

In 1971 Donald Wollheim left Ace to found DAW Books with his wife, Elsie Wollheim. DAW Books became the first privately owned publishing house devoted exclusively to the genre.[27]

But leaving Ace did not mean that the feuds were over. Wollheim's paradoxical personality cast a long shadow in which his daughter and successor would grow, but no one understood him better. Over that breakfast in San Francisco, Sheila Gilbert and Betsy Wollheim tried to explain this complex man who was father to one and long-time employer and friend to the other:

**Wollheim:** He was very intimidating—he put forth a very intimidating facade.

**Gilbert:** He was actually shy. People thought he was very aloof.

**Wollheim:** My father, oddly enough, presented this incredibly rigid, powerful, frightening, intimidating persona, but it was all a facade because he was extremely shy. He felt ugly; he had had polio in the 1918 epidemic, which had left him somewhat "wrong" physically—he had a heart murmur, his left leg was shorter than his right, he limped, his left hand could never quite respond in the same way neurologically as his right hand, so he could never play sports. His father was a doctor, a surgeon . . . and his father believed that if he didn't tell his son that he had had polio he wouldn't grow up with an "invalid mentality." This was common thinking in the first half of the century.

And so my father never found out why he was somewhat physically spastic until he was thirty-five years old, and went into his father's office and read his own medical file. He came home and said to my mother, "I had polio!" And so, all these memories that seemed to have no basis floated back for him, and he realized all those years when he thought something was "wrong" with him, it was because he had polio. But be that as it may, my father grew up feeling extremely insecure—

**Gilbert:** —very socially awkward.

**Wollheim:** I don't think he really had friends until the Futurians. . . . But my dad developed a very extreme and rigid personality for a lot of very sound psychological reasons. Extreme. And my grandparents' house, the house my father grew up in, was a very gothic environment.

And my father—my father was one of the most complex and difficult-to-understand people I've ever met in my life. Even having grown up with him, I still try to unravel the mysteries of why he did what he did and why he felt what he felt. And he was a difficult man to grow up with. I adored him, and he caused me great pain.

I wondered, as the reader may, how a man lacking in social ease could succeed in a business that depends so heavily on personal communication, but Betsy Wollheim and Sheila Gilbert both agree that Donald Wollheim showed a much more charming side in the office than in social settings.

> **Wollheim:**    You see, he really did better at the office than he did in a social environment. He was actually a lovely person to work with . . . he used to like to sit and schmooze with his assistants, his editorial assistants. . . . [H]e used to like to have coffee at three o'clock. He would insist that his assistants would sit with him and have coffee so that they could shoot the breeze for half an hour. And I'm friendly now with somebody who originally started in this industry as his assistant, who now is an independent publicist, who says she used to be very annoyed by this, because she would be interrupted from her work and she wouldn't want to sit with the boss for half an hour. . . . But I know I loved doing it; I worked with him for ten years, before he became too ill, and I used to really like coffee break time. We would just sit and shoot the breeze.
>
> But you know, it was so funny, because certain people, for example, Marion Zimmer Bradley and Carolyn [C. J.] Cherryh, developed extremely close friendships with him. I mean, Carolyn and Don were incredibly close. . . . And Marion considered my father her real father . . . I remember Marion; in my father's office, she used to pull a chair right up to the other side of his desk, and they would sit there across the desk from each other and she would say, "I want to do [blah, blah,]" and he'd say, "That's a bad idea." And she'd say, "Well, I want to do it anyway." He'd say, "Okay, okay." People were too intimidated by him. If they had not been intimidated, they would have realized that actually he was a much softer person than he would wanted people to believe. And so people who had courage got along with him.
>
> **Ethnographer:**    Well, that's why when you said Carolyn Cherryh, I could see her [getting along with Donald Wollheim], because I can't see Carolyn Cherryh being intimidated by anybody.
>
> **Wollheim:**    Well, Carolyn is also a very shy person. Carolyn and my father just clicked and my father adored Carolyn. Absolutely adored her. . . . I've known Carolyn since anybody knew Carolyn. From way back . . . I remember my parents redecorated my bedroom for Carolyn. They put a queen-sized brass bed in it for her. I remember I used to say to them, "Well, that's not mine, that's Carolyn's room."[28]

During a follow-up telephone conversation, Betsy Wollheim reiterated the importance of these relationships to the company's ongoing policy. Donald Wollheim, she said, always had a large female author population at DAW, and most of the company's biggest writers in the '70s and '80s were women. That was always the way with DAW: their biggest sellers and their authors who received the most awards and critical note were mostly women when her father ran the company, and most of their top authors today are women as well. While the company does not discriminate against male writers, and publishes quite a few, only Tad Williams among the men has received the kind of critical and financial success of women such as Marion Zimmer Bradley, C. J. Cherryh, Melanie Rawn, Mercedes Lackey, or Jennifer Roberson, just to name a few of the successful women DAW publishes.

## Passing the Torch

As second-generation science fiction fans in the second generation of fandom, Wollheim and Gilbert have watched the genre change and grow since childhood. For both women, the books and the community seem to have been kept fairly separate from fandom when they were young.

> **Gilbert:**  My father was an avid reader and he had all the magazines when he had his candy store. And so we grew up being exposed to science fiction. Books like the *Star Beast* were some of my early childhood reading . . . I read every color fairy book any number of times when I was little.

> **Wollheim:**  Uhuh. Every single Oz book. I read a lot of really obscure children's books, because my father had a massive library.

> **Gilbert:**  A lot of mythology books. . . . [O]ne of my favorite books when I was real young and reading at a kid's level was my father's Dragon book, a big book, a lot of things like that.

> **Wollheim:**  Well, I never discussed science fiction books until I was a later teenager . . . with anybody but my father. I used to talk to him a lot about books, because he used to give me the next book. I'd end up saying, "Oh yeah, this is good, it's like this, this, this." And he would go through the shelves, because I wasn't allowed to touch his library, so I had to ask. And he'd pull out all sorts of wonderful books for me, and it was very nice.

Reading was primarily a private event, but again, both women came to the community of science fiction as children:

> **Wollheim:**  I was brought to my first convention at age six, in 1958, and I always trailed around after my father. . . . [As a teenager] I voluntarily went to these things [conventions], for a brief period of time. And then when I went to Baycon, in the Claremont Hotel, in—what? Was it 68?—and I was 16, going on 17, I had such a wonderful peak experience it was the height of the Society of Creative Anachronism, I remember having a romantic encounter in the Eucalyptus Forest, behind the Claremont, lying on the hill. I had the shortest skirt there—very cool . . . it was all a very heightened experience. I went away from that thinking, well, I'll never go to a convention that will be as wonderful as that, so I've grown now, so this is the end. Of course, I did attend conventions after that, I didn't have a choice . . . I remember I had to leave St. Louis, where Sheila met Mike, her husband, that was the St. Louis worldcon where—

**Gilbert:**    No, that was the one where he decided to come looking for me because his mother told him he was going to meet somebody.

**Wollheim:**    So this was a peak experience for Sheila and Mike. I left in the middle of the convention to go to college for the first semester, so I was only there half the time. Then I went through a period of really really not wanting to have anything to do with fandom.

While many fans, particularly second generation ones, may leave the community at about college age, Wollheim had more reasons than most to distance herself from the community of her parents:

I had been frequently—increasingly—attacked as a later teenager, and in my early twenties . . . by people who had had problems with my father in the past. . . . And so I was put in the very awkward position of having to defend my father, just because he was family, on issues where I had absolutely no data. That began occurring when I was some tender age like eleven so that was very unpleasant for me. A lot of people, who would have attacked my father, attacked me instead, because they were too scared, too timid to attack my father, they were too cowardly to attack my father. And I was put in a very difficult position.

Sheila Gilbert entered fandom in the '60s, drawn to it by her sister:

And my sister Marsha, when she was up at City College, met Charlie Brown—there was a science fiction group there. And they got married, and so that's how I started going to conventions, because he was the one in the group who knew about these things. I was around thirteen when I went to my first convention. That's how old I was when they got married. Which was actually at Lunacon, in New York, and that's where I met your parents: I'm not sure if I met you there or not.

**Wollheim:**    I met Marsha many years before I met you, maybe three or four years before I met you. I was about eleven. She was engaged to Charlie at that time.

**Gilbert:**    She and Charlie were very involved in New York fandom . . . and they would have parties at their house. At that time there were actually a lot of authors around New York. And when I was like thirteen or fourteen, and shy, I would sit in on one of these parties reading a book, but listening to everything that went on, and being helpful, like refilling things and whatever. But eventually as a result I got to know a lot of people through them, and got very peripherally involved with their fanzine, because they started *Locus* together. But I was in college then, so I was very, very peripherally involved and I used to really enjoy going to these things; it was very exciting.

**Wollheim:**    It really was exciting.

Wollheim and Gilbert grew up in the heart of fandom and publishing—the New York science fiction community where the Futurians were giving way to a new generation of fans and professionals. Charlie Brown's *Locus* is now categorized for the purpose of Hugo competition as a semipro zine, which does little to convey its real importance as the newsmagazine for the industry. But, while Sheila Gilbert entered the field professionally to work for Ace books, Betsy Wollheim did not so much choose publishing as a career as she let it choose her, in the fall of 1975:

> I sort of drifted into the family business because I started working in photography, and I had a very unpleasant experience with a man who ripped my shirt open. Previously, I had been in Boston for two years working for two different printers—the printer for *Harvard Magazine* and the printer for the *New England Journal of Medicine*. It was enlightening about the printing industry, but it was a less than thrilling experience—and so I ended up working in the family business.

In 1985, when Donald Wollheim became critically ill, Betsy Wollheim and Sheila Gilbert took over the running of the company as a team.

> **Wollheim:** Sheila and I are very lucky. We are copublishers, and I think we are the only copublishers there are, and when Don died, there was no question that if I would be publisher, Sheila would be publisher. We had been running the company this way, and we continue to run the company this way.

In 1988, after Donald Wollheim's incapacitating stroke, ownership of the company passed to the second generation. In 1990, Donald Wollheim died. It seems curious that the end of the backlash coincided with the death of a man who had always given women writers an opportunity, who brought Marion Zimmer Bradley and Tanith Lee and C. J. Cherryh and others to the bookshelves of the world.

Control of the company had passed to his daughter and copublisher Sheila Gilbert five years earlier, at the very point where women were taking major strides into positions of power throughout publishing. But if we look at it differently, as a marker of a passing of a particular historical phase in the lifespans of the genres, we see a different truth.

> **Wollheim:** We've been around for three decades, but a lot of people don't know us because we are not horn tooters. We care about our company . . . we're not self-promoters. We're here to sell our authors and our books. Our company.

> **Gilbert:** Well, there's a lot of people who are very much newcomers compared to us, and they make a big splash and have all these popularity parties and things like that, and those people, suddenly those are the people who are on the Hugo ballots and they're everybody's darling, and what their contribution to the field is, a lot of times is very questionable.

> **Wollheim:** We probably have more information than a lot of people around. The two of us . . . there aren't that many of us. And this is what I was saying, I made an interesting observation. Now, [X] and my dad had some kind of falling out which was perceived in a more hostile manner by my father than by [X] and [X] never, apparently, had bad feelings about my father. My father

believed he did. And my father had bad feelings about [X]. . . . Now, this all happened when I was too young to be involved at all, and I never really had any connection with [X] whatever. And I would see [X] with his ex-wife, all the time, because it's a small field. You saw everyone all the time. But I never spoke to [X]. Never.

And in the last ten or so years, I've noticed that if there was a crowd, or a crowded room and [X] was in it, we would always have some communication. It was interesting, because I think people who've been around as long as Sheila and I, and [X]'s been around even longer, I think those of us who are still in this field, whether or not we knew each other back then, we feel a connection. And I now am beginning to become friendly with [X] and he acknowledged also that we were both there when, and it is a very special thing.

I mean, my father and Sam Moskowitz were arch-enemies. Sam Moskowitz red-baited my father—my father was a left-winger, politically— . . . yet Sam Moskowitz was one of the few people who came to visit my father when he was terribly ill after his stroke. And I think that time dissolves, has dissolved these old feuds, and now we feel like there's some inner network of the rest of us who were in that former world.

The new world includes major publishing houses and science fiction and fantasy lines run by women; it includes more fiction by women on the shelves, winning prizes, and finding acceptance in the social venues of the science fiction community. But the women who were there when science fiction came of age as a literature want us to remember that earlier time is our heritage too. Women have been a part of science fiction since its beginning, and the presence of those women growing up in the field, working as secretaries and editorial assistants and editors, made it possible for women today to exercise the power and influence that they do. And those pioneering women of science fiction didn't do it alone. They did it alongside those men in the field who valued them as fans and as professionals as well as women, and who also worked to break down the barriers for good science fiction and fantasy by women.

# Gay and Lesbian Presence in Science Fiction

7

Science fiction's early reputation for hardware-driven adventure stories for pre-pubescent boys would seem to preclude issues of sexuality. In fact, stories with adult themes that included sexuality had no easy time finding an outlet in the United States, where issues of man's relationships with technology were the norm as well as the stereotype until the New Wave of the 1960s expanded the sexual horizons of the genre. But ever since science fiction's inception as a literature of technological romance, a subset of writers and fans have grappled with the definitions of sexuality that the genre would embrace. Theodore Sturgeon wrote passionate stories with sexual themes as early as the '40s.[1] In 1953, when the science fiction fans awarded the first Hugos, Philip José Farmer won the "New SF Author or Artists category" for "The Lovers," a novella published in *Startling Stories*.[2] Sometimes lagging behind the general population, sometimes surging ahead of it, the debate continues into the twenty-first century.

Homosexuality as an issue has been a part of this science fiction debate since the beginning. Many fans and literary critics may be well acquainted with Samuel R. Delany's struggle to find and express his identity as a gay man and science fiction writer in the '60s and '70s.[3] Fewer may know that the debate in science fiction arose in the post-World War II period at the same time as the emergent rights movements in gay culture.[4] During a lunch interview at Lunacon in 1993 with then-officers of the Gaylactic Network Brian Hurley and Naomi Basner, Brian described an exchange at a meeting of First Fandom members discussing gay fandom.

> **Brian Hurley:** I'm thinking Noreascon III in '89. . . . There were a number of gay panels so someone brought it up in the First Fandom meeting, "Well, gee, what about all these gay panels and they are so crowded,"—you know, in terms of the rooms are crowded with people going in to listen—and someone said, "Well, right from the very beginning of fandom there has been a gay presence," because this is again a place that accepted people, you know. And maybe the political climate and even our own understanding of the gay and lesbian identity was different, but I think it's just become a little more formalized. We've always been there. I think that's sort of an important thing.[5]

Don Sakers, gay writer and the editor of the anthology *Carmen Miranda's Ghost Is Haunting Space Station Three*,[6] agrees, but also remembers hearing about less positive responses to gay presence in the community in the '40s:

**Don Sakers:**    There has been a long history of at least tolerance and moving toward acceptance in the science fiction community. I don't know if you've had any chance to talk to Forry Ackerman, but he was apparently writing stories for lesbian magazines back in the '30s, for fanzines. And I know from reading fan history that sometime in the late '30s or early '40s in Los Angeles there was some big scandal involving homosexuality in some way. And no one talks about it, so I don't even know what the outcome was.[7]

Informants who prefer to remain anonymous confirm Don Sakers's comments about the scandal, which involved a fanzine editor who was a member of the Los Angeles Science Fiction Association (LASFAS). This community member stirred up West Coast fan circles with his claims, in the mid-1940s, that LASFAS was full of gay members. The scandal often draws comparisons to the McCarthy-era red-baiting, and I have *never* heard the instigator discussed in approving terms.[8]

Forrest J [Forry] Ackerman, mentioned above, draws mixed feelings from long-time fans. Born in 1916, Ackerman participated in science fiction fandom from its inception, and wrote in the first fanzine in the genre.[9] A self-declared heterosexual editor-collector-fan known best for his writing in fanzines and the small press, Ackerman embodies many of the best and worst traits of fans. Some consider self-aggrandizement his greatest talent. He is gregarious and uncritical in his love of all things science fictional and horrific. He boasts the largest collection of monster movie memorabilia in the world, and he lays claim to having created the much-hated term "sci-fi," beloved of bookstores and those insufficiently in the know to use the fannishly preferred "sf."

For the gay and lesbian community in science fiction, however, Forry Ackerman holds an honored place as one of the first science fiction fans openly to support the gay and lesbian movement both within and without the science fiction community. In his guest of honor essay for the 1994 Gaylaxicon, Ackerman explained his early activism in lesbian politics, for which the convention honored him:

The Daughters of Bilitis—sapphic sisters of San Francisco—decided to come out of the closet and have a free-to-all conclave, inviting newspaper reporters, the Mayor, the Vice Squad, religious leaders, anybody and everybody concerned to learn more about what makes tribades tick. I had befriended "Lisa Ben" (the pioneering editor/publisher of *Vice Versa*, "America's Gayest Magazine") and, for the purpose of contributing to that publication, adopted the persona of "Laurajean Ermayne." This was in 1947, when lesbianism was a subject (quote) "spoken of only in whispers." . . . [I]n the December 1947 issue of *Vice Versa*, I contributed what (as far as I know) was the first lesbian SF story ever published, "Kiki." . . .

[B]ecause of my cooperation with Lisa Ben (aka Tigrina) and her periodical—and my support of the lesbianic publication *The Ladder*—the Daughters of Bilitis made me an SOB(Son of Bilitis!).[10]

As Ackerman explains on his webpage, his interest in the cause of lesbian acceptance grew out of his early friendship with Lisa Ben:

> During WW2, as a Staff Sergeant, I had befriended an intriguing young fantasy fanne. When we went to movies together, I would come out raving about Marlene Dietrich and she came out raving about . . . Marlene Dietrich, not Gary Cooper. Like me, she liked Betty Grable's legs, not Clark Gable's ears. It finally dawned on me—before she herself even realized her nature—that she must be (a word spoken only in whispers then) a . . . lesbian! I sort of nudged her out of the closet. In 1947 she went on to boldly create the legendary *Vice Versa*, America's first underground "Uranian magazine," a typewritten and carbon copied affair. She had so few contributors that I, as an empathetic writer, adopted the pseudonym Laurajean Ermayne and wrote reviews, poetry, and fiction.[11]

For Ackerman, the stand for the lesbian community meant also taking a position in fandom against those forces that saw homosexuals under every bed much as the McCarthyites saw communists. But when Forry attended a meeting to find out what lesbians were about, the idea of a gay and lesbian fandom demanding its place in the science fiction community was unthinkable. By the early 1960s, Marion Zimmer Bradley's Darkover series included a number of gay characters and a social structure to accommodate them. Since the '60s, a number of prominent women writers have included gay and lesbian characters in their works—often works thought to be targeted at girls and young women. Fewer men with reputations in the major science fiction publishing houses have written gay themes.

The appearance of gay characters in the literature did not necessarily signal an equal acceptance of an openly gay or lesbian presence in the literary community, however, as Joanna Russ showed in a letter dated May 10, 1994:

> I'm sure being an open lesbian has not been good for my career. Also doing all sorts of non-fiction feminist writing. I mean, put it together: book reviewer . . . feminist, lesbian highbrow—I've never made more than $3,500 advance for any novel. ANY. . . . Sexual orientation, by the way, is something one often doesn't know the effect of. When Delany finally came out in one of his Neveryon books in an unmistakable way, the big chains dropped all his books, his advances plummeted, and he is now teaching English at the U. of Massachusetts, in Amherst. . . . What would've happened if I hadn't come out, hadn't reviewed, hadn't been so loudly feminist—I really don't know.[12]

I would place the work in which Delany first expressed his sexual orientation much earlier, in *The Einstein Intersection*, published in 1967,[13] although it would, I suppose, be more possible to ignore or overlook in the earlier work. As Russ points out, however, Samuel Delany has been the major exception: a prominent, respected, literary writer of science fiction who is both gay and male, and who explores gay life in a dense and complex manner in his fiction and nonfiction work. And Russ is also correct that Delany's work, both his early, popularly accessible books and his more complex and challenging work, disappeared from the shelves shortly after the

Neveryon books debuted in the '80s. The reasons, however, are themselves neither simple nor straightforward.

To begin, we have to understand several basic components of science fiction culture as it plays out at the levels at which Samuel Delany is accorded membership. To the core of science fiction professionals and fans, Samuel Delany's is one of about half a dozen names that define the New Wave of the 1960s. To this group, Delany will never lose his place as a historical icon in the development of the form as a literary genre. However, few of the people in this group, which includes writers such as Norman Spinrad, Thomas Disch, and Roger Zelazny, maintained their hold on bookstore shelf space beyond the '70s, and of those who did, the caliber of the work generally fell well below that of the glory days of the New Wave. The movement caught the audience for the new and the sophisticated both inside and outside the science fiction readership, but the taste level of the common denominator had always been lower than the place where the New Wave was created.

Few enough writers created in the New Wave, and the overall expectations among booksellers for the size of the science-fiction-reading audience was sufficiently in synch with the numbers of books produced to put the books on the shelves and sell them in numbers large enough, for the time, to keep them there. But movements in literature don't stay new for long. Writers either fall behind as their form loses its relevance to audiences looking for the new, or they adapt to the new as it comes toward them in subsequent movements, or they seek out that common denominator and make a living doing the knowable. Since their very presence in the new movement would almost surely define that movement in terms of the old, it is by definition pretty nearly impossible for the hip star of one movement to be the hip star of the next. The occasional pragmatist does make it out of a dying movement with an income intact, catching the wave of the common denominator, but by the late '70s the construction even of that audience had changed. Stephen Pagel, former buyer for more than a thousand chain bookstores, claims that:

> The customer is really the one who has the power, because again the industry will publish what the customer wants. . . . [O]bviously not everybody sells like, we were talking about Eddings, McCaffrey, Card, some of those [today] . . . but when you've got millions buying up here, and then the others, you've got just thousands buying down here, that's a huge gap.[14]

During the '60s and early '70s, the New Wave and feminist science fiction movements attracted a new, hip college audience that had ignored science fiction and fantasy in its earlier forms. Some books did sell in the millions,[15] and the lower sales expectations for science fiction made it possible for the less accessible writers to survive in print. But Delany *was* popular at the time. According to the *Encyclopedia of Science Fiction*, even the impenetrable *Dhalgren*, published in 1975, sold a million copies, and the first Neveryon books also sold well.[16] But audiences are fickle. By the '80s, New Wave wasn't new anymore and the feminists were suffering backlash. Worse, good books are hard to write. There simply wasn't enough of the good stuff to hold the educated audience of the New Wave; the audience had been there, done that, and moved on in search of the new. So the bookstore chains found new fodder for their voracious appetites: the younger readers looking for space opera like Star Wars and much of the early science fiction, and fantasy like Dungeons and Dragons. The industry had always found the tastes of this audience easier to satisfy because more people could write it, faster and at least moderately well, and that meant the bookstores could sell more books.

## The Struggle for a Voice in the '80s

The later Neveryon books published in the mid-1980s grew more estranged from the taste culture of the common denominator even as the common denominator was itself dropping like a stone, The books didn't fit the style of the cyberpunk avant-garde, so sales dropped. As Russ says, part of that estrangement came from content that was more overtly defined by a particular gay male sensibility that the mainstream found offensive. But Delany had a bigger problem than dropping sales and a more public awareness of the fact that he was gay. According to an editor at his publishing house, Delany never turned in the second book in the Diptich that began with *Stars in My Pockets like Grains of Sand*. Delany seemed unwilling or unable to complete the contract in a manner acceptable to the publisher. To exert pressure, the publisher withdrew Delany's early, accessible, books from press until he fulfilled the contract for which he had been paid a significant advance.[17] Fortunately for fans of Delany's work, a publisher does not have a lock on books forever. If the publisher refuses to reprint for a period specified in the author's contract, the rights revert to the author. The rights to a number of Delany's better known books have reverted to the author, including *Dhalgren*, *Trouble on Triton*, and the Neveryon books, which are now back in print, in trade paperback, through Wesleyan University Press. Unfortunately, their current format makes it unlikely that newer readers who don't look past the paperback shelves in their bookstore will find and enjoy Delany's work.

## Efforts to Organize

The New Wave and feminism brought a new audience into science fiction and opened up the form to sexual issues as never before. Gay and lesbian writers such as Delany and Russ were among the forefront of those changing the face of the genre. But even as late as the '80s, gay and lesbian fans and professionals had not won their right to present themselves as an interest group with a voice in the science fiction community. Few writers were out, and fans seemed welcome as long as they fit in to the essentially straight establishment. By 1980, however, gay professionals and fans were trying to change that.

In an interview at the 1993 Lunacon, Naomi Basner described her experience coming out during this first effort to organize gay fandom:

> Interestingly enough, the stirrings of gay fandom . . .—a lot of people had been players for the past decade or so—really dovetailed with my coming out. Worldcon '80, which was Noreascon II, and I refer to that [as] the summer I was peeking out, I wasn't coming out yet, but I was peeking out. . . .
>
> [N]ow there's different opinions as to whether there had actually been a gay science fiction panel before that. [Samuel] Chip Delany seems to remember one previously which seems to have been before my time, so it is very

possible that there was one and then they got it back under the carpet again. But then there were stirrings in '80, definitely, because Eric Garber and Lyn Paleo were starting to compile *Uranian Worlds* at that time. . . . I remember going there and they had about four pages of the bibliography—just recommended reading of gay interest that was part of their research that became *Uranian Worlds* later on—that was being handed out as a freebie.

And I was not—I don't know what I was but I was discontented [laughter] and I noticed that I was picking that up. I went to the panel that was the gay science fiction thing which I remember as being the first one in modern, this current generation of fans . . . so interestingly enough there I was, and I wasn't quite ready yet to find these people but later on when I was . . . and I had been fairly political for a while, and then there was really a group.[18]

Lambda award-winning writer Melissa Scott likewise remembered the Noreascon II meeting, but from a more central perspective:

That was at the Noreascon . . . Lisa [Barnett] and I had just gotten together at that point. I had been out maybe a year or so. And there was a meeting, of gay and lesbian fans and friends, up in one of those fan rooms. [I] walked in and there was Samuel R. Delany, who I had never seen before in my life. And Marion Zimmer Bradley, and those were the two that I really remember, and it was like, oh my God, look who's here.

And maybe twenty-five, thirty other people. And they were trying to get together an organization. . . . Everybody who was willing put their name on a mailing list, and Lisa, Don [Sakers], and I volunteered to run the newsletter. And we rented a post office box in Milton. And nobody ever sent us anything. We sent out at least one issue, we may have sent out a second issue, but it was Lisa, me, and Don. We asked for information, we asked is anybody doing anything . . . is anybody going to any conventions, anybody want to write a book review? And the three of us were all aspiring writers and discovered that we'd rather talk to each other, and let the whole thing die. Jerry Jacks was involved in that, out in California. I think he got more going out on the West Coast at that point, but not much happened on the East Coast.[19]

Efforts to organize seemed to disappear for a number of years, then, according to Brian Hurley, Frank Robinson presided at another attempt during ConFederation, the 1986 Worldcon in Atlanta. Once again the meeting demonstrated the degree to which underground networking of gay and lesbian fans was working, but the group seemed no closer to a functioning organization that could provide a visible presence in the structure of the Worldcon itself. In 1986, however, gay and lesbian fans were ready to become a "fandom," and John Dumont and one other person, in Boston, were ready to do the job.

## The Gaylaxians

While the writers in that room in 1980 certainly had the charisma to draw a crowd in spite of the risk that coming out in 1980 might have represented, they did not have the commitment to the fannish enterprise of creating an organization for gay fans that marked the Gaylaxians, who went away from Worldcon in 1986 not only with a mission, but with the fannish tools to succeed:

> **Melissa Scott:** The Gaylaxians . . . I would never say "no" to John Dumont if he kept talking at me. He's—they—were very organized, and they were fannish organizers. Neither Lisa nor Don nor I were terribly good at the fannish organizational style. . . . But those guys were able to put every waking hour into it. And they were extremely gregarious, and the key may have been that they were all in the same physical area. They were all in the Boston area, and . . . they pulled it together, and that's become a real good organization, I like them.

I first heard about gay and lesbian efforts to create a fan organization in November of 1986, at the media convention Boston Bash. Hindered by a leg in a plaster cast, I did not make that meeting, but over the years began to hear more and more about the organization as it established local chapters and created an annual convention, Gaylaxicon, as Naomi Basner, New York member, remembers:

> John Dumont in Boston . . . decided it was time that there be gay fandom . . . so they started a group in Boston and the idea kind of passed on. Various people independently started branches in different cities. So Boston did it first, and then a group started, Albany was second and then we were third, and then Philadelphia then Washington . . . we knew each other and started finding each other at cons and meeting together.[20]

Ironically, it was that very fannish enthusiasm that caused some of the authors to draw a bit apart from the more successful organization of the mid-1980s, as Melissa Scott pointed out:

> They are very good about preserving your privacy as a gay person. But it's more complicated too—I don't have a post office box, and they are not set up to keep an address and phone number secret for a writer. . . . And being a very fannish organization they've not been real good about that. Everybody is accessible to everybody else in fandom.

Club and Gaylactic Network organizers, who have themselves experienced the struggle to find and define a gay identity in a culture often hostile to their very existence, understand and respect the need for their members' privacy from the outside. But they are also fans, enculturated in the more gregarious forms of fandom, a part of which accords status for access to the producers of the science fiction. The writer, naturally enough, sees access as a personal thing, a right she may limit for privacy or for safety, but which is denied her by the organization's open exchange of information. While some might argue that every person whose name and address appears on the list takes the same risk, most of the names and addresses on the list the reader will identify as strangers. The presence of the writer in the public sphere, and the presence of her thoughts and words in the pages of the books, may give the reader a false sense of familiarity that, for the writer, can translate into strangers on her doorstep. And the issue of privacy became more important as the club grew to include more chapters.

While Scott does not participate in the Gaylaxians' meetings and club activities out of concern for her privacy, she and her companion, author and editor Lisa Barnett, like many other writers in the industry, do participate as guests at the Gaylaxicon. Any conflict between the early, thwarted, organizers and the newer generation seems limited to a bit of disappointment that this early chapter in gay activism in fandom seems forgotten by all except the few who were there.

A more important issue for the '80s, however, may be the establishment of an identity as a gay or lesbian fan or pro.

### Identity and the Gay Science Fiction Fan

The reader can only understand the problem of conflicting identity for gay and lesbian science fiction fans if he realizes that the term "science fiction community" is not a metaphor, not hyperbole. Core fans, like the rest of us, have multiple identities based on relationships or lack thereof to the world beyond their skin: son or daughter, next door neighbor, lawyer, Methodist, hermit. But the fan's repertoire also includes the category "fan" in its meaning as a socially connected member of a group called "fandom," rather than its more simple meaning as a description of a specific relationship to a pleasure. Out of the wealth of those outward relationships to the world each of us holds, we choose one that we feel fits us best—that most substantially reflects our inner reality back out to the world. Our actions within the paradigm of that relationship define our primary identity to ourselves and express that primary identity to those around us. The primary identity is where we invest the major commitment of our time and effort even when the gain we might receive from that commitment is not obvious to others. That is because, of course, the gain, the value, is in the strength of the web of relationships that support us in that identity. And only someone within the web, supporting and being supported by it, can see that as a gain.

Here is where the problem arises for gay and lesbian fans, particularly those who live in the major cities such as New York, Chicago, and Los Angeles. An active participant makes a major, if not primary, identification with the fan group, which includes an investment of time and effort to sustain relationships within the special interest group—gay and lesbian science fiction—and to fight, with other members of the SIG, to gain a place for the gay and lesbian voice to be heard in the larger science fiction community.

Many of the writers who have worked to organize a voice for gay and lesbian science fiction already have another major area of identification in the field. It is not so much that they want to make a living writing gay science fiction, as that the inner world they want to express finds its words and structures of expression in the metaphors of science fiction. One could say that, when they open their mouths, science fiction comes out. So, they *need* to have a voice in the world of science fiction, or they will be speaking in a vacuum, because only the world of science fiction will listen to the language of science fiction.

The answer to the question "What does the writer-activist gain from this identity?" is therefore clear: he gains a public forum in which to speak to science fiction readers about issues relevant to his identity. When we look at the gay or lesbian fan, however, the question becomes harder to answer both for the outsider looking in and for the fan, particularly the fan looking for a place in science fiction in the 1980s. Before this period, few actual gay characters appeared in the literature. In early science fiction, the alien existed for the most part to represent the enemy, something to be destroyed—as the fiction used its metaphors of the alien to represent World War II and the Korean War—or just difference, equally to be destroyed for the preservation of a homogeneous "melting pot" society. Women represented home and hearth, the goal of the male quest to prove his masculinity, first with the challenge of some sort of battle, then with whatever men did when they saved the girl. The sources of power in the fiction were all male, white, and heterosexual, one supposed, although the books never did actually explain what the hero did with the girl he had won with his valorous deeds.

Of course, there were always exceptions, such as Theodore Sturgeon. And even the most concrete of the hard science fiction writers, like Arthur C. Clarke, could touch the heart with mystery in stories like "The Sentinel" or "The Nine Billion Names of God." But to find the positive representations of any difference at all in science fiction, the woman or gay man wandering through a bookstore had to weed through an awful lot of material where the position of identification said "white straight male" and the characters left for the rest of the population were "target" or "prize."

By the time of the New Wave, this was changing. The Viet Nam War created controversy about the alien and the need for war. Science fiction writers, coming out of literary as well as science programs at the universities, reflected both a more literary approach to the genre and a more complex approach to the idea of alien. The feminist movement brought both gay and straight women into the field, admitting they'd been identifying all these years with the guy in the captain's chair, not the bimbo on his arm, and demanding their turn at the laser canon. In 1975, Marion Zimmer Bradley's *Heritage of Hastur* told the story of Regis Hastur, a young gay nobleman of Darkover coming to terms with his sexuality and his telepathic gifts. Bradley followed with a number of Darkover books in which figure the Renunciates, a guild of women who choose not to marry, some of whom take women partners and some of whom choose nonbinding relationships with men.[21]

Like mainstream American culture, science fiction fought the changes that swept it. Fandom retaliated against the women who had won a place in the '70s and the fiction itself fractured into even more subcategories. Some houses clung to the simplicity of an earlier logical positive technoculturalism to which cyberpunk, the assertion of straight white male supremacy of the '80s, gave renewed literary credibility. Others responded with greater enthusiasm to more issue-oriented fiction.

Out of the chaos, the stage would have seemed ready for the next voice, gay and lesbian identities, to take their place in the literature. In 1987, Ellen Kushner's *Swordspoint*, a fantasy adventure of the swordsman and his student-scholar lover, appeared and became a cult hit among gay readers and among media fans of slash[22] fiction who also read science fiction and fantasy.[23] The Gaylaxians held their first convention in 1988,[24] and in 1989, Bradley protegee Mercedes Lackey's *Magic's Pawn* introduced Vanyel, the gay student–mage, and the homoerotic love relationship that would shape his future through the three volumes of the Herald Mage trilogy.[25] But Vanyel's tribulations seemed more attuned to the fantasies of adolescent girls than those of the gay male; Vanyel's partner dies in an accident at the end of the first book, after which Vanyel pines for his lost love and bonds primarily with his horse until the two lovers are rejoined in death at the end of the last volume of the trilogy. *Magic's Pawn* seemed a throwback to the tragic romance. That is, gay characters, like the independent woman of an earlier romantic fiction, were acceptable in the mainstream of science fiction only as long as their behavior conformed to the norms of romanticism, where sexuality is a function of love and grief is its greatest expression. Lackey added to the mix a new consideration for gay and lesbian fans: the representation of the group by writers who mean well but do not share in a knowledge of the internal life of the gay male character.

## The Gay '90s

### The Gaylactic Network

In spite of ambiguous and conflicting messages in the fiction of the 1980s, many gay fans found a place to call home in the chapters of the Gaylaxians. Others had no local organizations to call on, or preferred a less intense involvement in the fan organization. So organizers created the Gaylactic Network to offer a source of contact and information about the gay science fiction world for interested individuals who are not affiliated with a local chapter. According to Naomi Basner, a member of the Gaylactic Network,[26] the group developed a charter at the second gay and lesbian science fiction convention, Gaylaxicon II, held in Tewkesbury, Massachusetts, in 1990:

> **Basner:**    And, [we] formed a board of representatives from each of the groups and their various officers and we had a speaker who was out of Detroit and we have an APA that we communicated between the reps . . . and it's a coordination thing that was done and it's also a communication thing. . . . And even though there is a charter or bylaws, it's still very—not free-form— it's not tight, not rigid.

While remaining informally open to the new, the Gaylactic Network still provides a structure for gay and lesbian fandom to use as a platform from which to demand its own voice in the politics of science fiction.

> **Basner:**    Then you start forming history, because now . . . we have a name, we have a presence, we are people; I can say "I'm on the Network board, I've done this and I was quoted in the *Advocate*." . . . I can say, "Oh yes, and when I was at such and such con, we did this and we did that." . . . Then we're getting to the point now where sometimes people [at conventions] would go, "Oh, I've been looking for you" and that sort of thing.

While the Gaylactic Network, with its presence on the Web and at conventions, serves as a powerful vehicle to draw gay and lesbian fans together, maintaining the club base of the organization has been difficult, particularly in the major cities. The Toronto group is not specifically affiliated with the Gaylaxians. New York City had a branch that disbanded, and Philadelphia, too, has had its struggles to maintain some cohesion as a club.

## The Philadelphia Area Gaylaxians (Phag)

By the 1990s, the New York City branch of the Gaylaxians had folded and the Philadelphia area branch comprised a small group meeting at the small West Philadelphia apartment of Jed Shumsky. In 1992 I attended a meeting of Phag in Jed Shumsky's living room.

I arrived at Jed's in time for the group viewing of *Star Trek: The Next Generation*. About twenty people were in attendance, some women, but a majority men. A wide range of sexual identities were represented, including gay, straight, bisexual, and transgender. While *Star Trek* played in the background, we munched on snacks and people talked in a desultory manner. There was none of the Robert's Rules of Order meeting style that I had seen at Philadelphia Science Fiction Society meetings, although two women at the meeting did complain that most of the work of maintaining the club and its newsletter fell to them.

I asked if there was much gay science fiction, and T. R., a club member, answered, "Yes. Want to see the book?" He handed me a hard cover copy of *Uranian Worlds: A Guide to Alternate Sexuality in Science Fiction, Fantasy and Horror*, by Eric Garber and Lyn Paleo, the book Garber and Paleo were researching back in 1980, when Naomi Basner first tiptoed out of the closet. The book made the rounds, and I asked what had brought the members to the club. As with most small cultural groups, the answers seemed to be shaped out of the shared aesthetic of need that creates the mainstream fandom and seems inextricable from the fiction itself. That is, when asked why they are a part of *this* particular group, members answer in terms of the literature as much as they do in terms of the group and its members. When they do talk about the club specifically, they use the same kind of judgments that we hear from many subculture groups, including other small-scale fan organizations and special interest lists on the internet:

> **T.R.:** [I've been] reading sf forever, like since I started reading, so forever. . . . Why do I like being in this club? . . . Well, because it's an insane group of people, which, of course, is not necessarily just inherent to this group of people as far as sf fen go. But, it's a fun, insane group of people, and because we all just happen to . . . share similar interests in more than just science fiction . . . science fiction of the gay and lesbian and feminist nature. And you don't get a lot of discussion that way in other science fiction clubs. So for that reason, that's why I came to my first meeting here, not knowing any of these nutcases.

Science fiction fans have traditionally prided themselves on their eccentricity—thus the propeller beanie that has long been the symbol of fandom—and here T.R. uses the language of other, non-gay-related science fiction organizations to which he has belonged, including the Lunarians, who put on the annual Lunacon in Rye, New York. To the tradition of science fiction interaction, he adds that of interest in the gay and lesbian and feminist science fiction. Jed Shumsky added his considerations:

> I like science fiction because it provides sparks for the imagination. It really is the only literary forum that I know of that is working out new ways to live

and new approaches to coping with our society, by talking about societies in different forms and turning our society on its ear. And in terms of this group, writing and reading about alternative sexualities and how cultures can exist that are open to the ideas of alternative sexualities are very encouraging and something to work for and something to live for. And I think that this group is sort of a community building experience in itself in terms of providing a place to discuss how to live one's life through what we read about and how we live.

Here the possibilities of using the literature as a template, and the club as a sheltered place to practice living a culture where participants rejoice in each other's sexual differences and learn to practice their own sexuality free of fear, come to the fore, but again, very much in the way that science fiction fans traditionally talk about the relationship between the genre and the lifestyle.

Diane brings in another favorite trope of science fiction fans, regardless of their sexual orientation:

> As a group, there's a very active intelligence. Sf readers in general—this group in particular—has attracted high caliber of people with intellect, perceptions that are interesting to hear about, not only in sf but in real life.

To this point, group members had discussed their participation in traditional fannish forms, calling up the self-image of the eccentric but highly intelligent and loving member of an alternative family structure that we see a great deal more in the informal social organization of fandom, including media fan circles and Internet fan lists, than we do in the formal structure of the large East Coast science fiction clubs (although those clubs, too, have their subgroups about whom members respond similarly). Soon, however, the group homes in on specifics:

> **Voice:**    I am working in artificial intelligence. I am in the process of trying to create what was sf ten years ago and make it real. So sf to me has another aspect to it; it's sort of like, okay, let's explore the ramifications of, well, what happens if I get this to work. . . . A perfect example comes out of David Brin's *Earth*. He discusses the concept and the ramification of a computer network with eight million people on it. I am working on trying to develop systems to deal with information overflow. The vocabulary for some of the things that I am going to try and create may come out of this book.

Here again, in the gay and lesbian science fiction community as in the broader science fiction community, we find members using the fiction to create the technologically real world that, in this case, had surpassed the fiction between the time of the interview and the publication of this book. Sociological speculation, as usual, takes longer:

> **Jed:**    Conversely, Elizabeth Lynn has created societies where the entire society is composed of bisexual people. And she talks about how that society functions without actually making that the main point of her story.

> **Diane:**    By dealing with these hypothetical societies that are in many ways either idealized or exaggerated, it takes the threat out of it, so that a lot of

people are a lot more able to read something like [Brin's] *Startide Rising*, where there is an innuendo of a sexual attraction between a dolphin and a human, and you can take that and apply it to, say, okay, well, here's this "abnormal sexuality" and you see it between the characters, and it develops, and you grow to want them to end up together because you like them as characters. Then you can say to yourself, well, what's so different about a dolphin and a human and a woman and a woman or a man and a man . . . it takes the fear out of it. It takes the fear out of saying, "I don't understand how this is" because you can understand it. It puts it back onto the "this is a living entity, this is a living being."

**Male Voice:** . . . [It's] not as simple as "books are less threatening." SF tends to force open those doors . . . and if you get less reaction, it's because the people who would read science fiction are basically more open-minded, because they want to explore new avenues, as opposed to the conservatively minded people who get upset about those kinds of things.

In the process of discussing alternative societies, Marion Zimmer Bradley's name, of course, appears in the conversation, reminding us again of her pivotal role in shaping a particular kind of gay inclusion in the written science fiction:

**Voice:** Bradley [has a] very strong following. A whole sort of stable that she has developed that has more or less taken her original themes of openness in sexuality, openness in ideas, being able to follow one's own path, particularly with the renunciates, which have gotten a lot more popular support. She has in turn encouraged people like Misty Lackey, and I think, Jennifer Roberson and several others who have shown up in her sword and sorcery anthologies in particular, to sort of get that ideal. And it is almost like they, as a group, through encountering her, have sort of taken her vision and added to it, and changed it, and helped it evolve. . . . I guess our ideal as a group is not necessarily to live what's in the books, but to take what we feel works in our reality, and in our group, and apply that.

In fact, some fans of Bradley have chosen to live in group homes they call guild-houses in the Renunciate form, and some even take Darkovan names. Others, as the club member explained, take from the books of Bradley and her followers the ideals of diversity and try to incorporate those ideals, not the actual practices of the books, in their real lives. For those who follow either path in their struggle to make a better, more understanding and understandable world, the effort to incorporate utopian ideals in everyday life ties them to a part of the culture of longing that has been a part of us all since the Pilgrims hit Plymouth Rock. That yearning, for a world that accepts them and nurtures them, wound throughout the discussion of the club as a family until it was time to head for the University of Pennsylvania's gay and lesbian dance.

In spite of the rhetoric, however, the club has moved, changed memberships, nearly died out, and been resurrected several times since this interview. Identity is never an easy concept, and the Philadelphia Phags met with a number of complications in navigating the shoals of self-definition. Drawn away by the demands of work and study, or by the pull of activities in the mainstream of gay culture, members seem to remain involved in their reading of the genre, but less involved in the active practice of gay and lesbian science fiction fandom in Philadelphia. Like the New York chapter, this small organization in a big city could compete only with great difficulty against the pull of conflicting obligations and negative perceptions. Clubs in such cities as Washington D.C., Boston, and St. Louis, however, seem as strong as ever.

## Gaylaxicon

Like other special interest groups in science fiction fandom, the Gaylaxians have a convention, Gaylaxicon, where writers and fans of science fiction and fantasy with gay and lesbian themes can come together to attend panels and meet other like-minded fans from around the world. The fledgling group in Boston held the first of what they hoped would become the biannual Gaylaxicon, in Provincetown, Massachusettes, in 1988, but by 1990, at the convention in Tewkesbury, where the Gaylactic Network itself reorganized, demand for an annual convention won out. By 1992, when I attended the Philadelphia Gaylaxicon as a guest, to discuss *Enterprising Women*, participation had grown from around 90 in 1988 to 360, and in D.C. the following year exceeded 400.

I met convention committee member Carl Cipra at that Philadelphia convention, but did not get a chance to interview him until the following convention, Gaylaxicon IV, in Rockville, Maryland. Cipra had participated in general West Coast fandom until moving East and discovering the Gaylaxians:

> I moved here from California about six years ago. Most of my experience in fandom is still California—Westercons, and things like that. And I found out about the Gaylaxians four or five years ago, at Boston Worldcon. And then soon after we formed a chapter down here in D.C.[27]

Discovering the Gaylaxians moved Cipra out of his less committed role as a convention and fandom participant and into club and convention organizer. At the time of this interview, he had helped to organize the D.C. chapter of the Gaylaxians, called Lambda Sci-Fi: D.C. Area Gaylaxians, and he had worked on the two Gaylaxicon committees mentioned here. When I asked him whether the traveling nature of the convention posed a problem to organizers, Cipra said it did:

> Continuity of committees, yes, a big problem. . . . It does not [have a permanent floating committee]. There is a separate entity every time. Now, the first three Gaylaxicons had pretty much a continuity in staff, because Boston ran it each time, but when the fourth one came up [in Philadelphia], we had some Boston people involved, but it was mostly Washington and Philadelphia that did it. And this time, in Rockville, it was just D.C. doing it.

This lack of continuity on committees from convention to convention left no one ready to pick up the pieces when the 1993 Gaylaxicon, scheduled for Chicago, fell through. I had been hearing about the problems with the Chicago organization since soon after the Philadelphia Gaylaxicon, as people waited to hear from the next convention committee about memberships and participation in programming. Finally, when it was too late for someone else to pick up the pieces for the convention, word leaked out that the convention chair was too ill to proceed. In the process of his illness, he had suffered some paranoia and had not delegated any of the responsibility for the convention to other committee members, so no one was in a position to take over for him.

> **Carl Cipra:** It's a special problem that the gay community has, of course. So many of the gay-run organizations have received crippling blows from AIDS. And it just hit us, finally, last year. . . . He was, in retrospect, I know he was very sick at Gaylaxicon in Philadelphia. We did not suspect *how* sick, because—[he] didn't talk about it. . . . He played it very close to his chest. That was [name deleted]. And we since that time discovered that he was only in the earliest stages of organization on that, and without his drive and push, it [the Chicago Gaylaxicon] collapsed when he died.

Of course the 1993 World Science Fiction Convention had also suffered losses of its chair—not once but twice. But that organization had a number of committee members involved in the details of preparations, so it was able to pull off the convention in spite of its losses. For Gaylaxicon, hindered by a smaller base of organizers and a disease that can produce secretiveness and paranoia in its sufferers, the loss of the chair created a disaster in 1993, and greatly hampered the efforts of the D.C. group to organize its convention in 1994.

> **Cipra:** Well, we quickly worked around it, and worked through [the World-con in] San Francisco, and they were very helpful, so that we could get the business of the convention going, even though there was no Gaylaxicon as such. And of course, San Francisco being the very gay-friendly city they are, we had people on the [Worldcon] con committee who were interested in having us there, participating.

Part of working around the loss of Chicago's chair, and the convention itself, meant coming together at the 1993 ConFrancisco. Part meant reestablishing the databases of names and addresses that normally pass from one committee to the next. Cipra assured me that the databases were once again in order for the next committee, the St. Louis-Toronto Gaylaxicon held in Niagara Falls, New York, in 1995.

This unlikely combination of chapters throwing a convention together high-lights a specific problem of small special interest groups in general:

> **Cipra:** St. Louis wanted to throw it [Gaylaxicon VI], but they didn't have the staff for it. The Canadians wanted to throw it, but they're not a part of the Gaylactic Network, and according to our charter, only the Gaylactic Net-work can throw a Gaylaxicon.

By working together for a common goal, organizers in Toronto and St. Louis put on the convention in Niagara Falls. With the two groups working together, both could participate as hosts while neither ran the risk of a situation such as Chicago, where the loss of just one person could derail the entire convention. As in Chapter 3, we see here that the absolute geography of convention location is not as impor-tant as the number of people willing to work on the event, wherever it is held. But the arrangement leaves one with the question, why has Toronto chosen not to align itself with the Gaylactic Network? There are, of course, the requisite personal disagreements, but substantively, the two groups divide on at least one issue specific to the gay and lesbian community:

> **Cipra:**  They [Toronto] have a different alcohol policy than the Network does. . . . They had alcohol in their parties. We do not. . . . [T]he gay community has always had an alcohol problem, and fandom has always had a reputation for alcohol, and the founders of the Network wanted to offer the Network as an alternate to the bar cultures. So that carried over into the Network and into Gaylaxicons, that there is no alcohol. It also gets away from liability problems, that sort of thing. So that is why we don't have alcohol at our parties.

When I pointed out that this is consistent with a convention policy standard in many parts of fandom, Cipra explained that the Gaylaxians carry the policy further than most committees, who are primarily interested in their own insurance and legal liabilities:

> But still, a lot of the room parties, and bid parties [at other conventions] are just loaded with alcohol. We frequently have people show up at our parties, when we throw parties at local conventions like Disclave, [and] they see that there's no alcohol, and they leave.

In fact, when I look around Gaylaxicon, I see a fandom on its best behavior—less raucous than most conventions I've attended, with very little costuming, and a general air of carefulness in general. I asked Cipra about this; he agreed that the observation was accurate and we tried to puzzle through to reasons:

> **Cipra:**  I think it's because gay fandom hasn't really caught on. I mean, we've had a hell of a time promoting costuming at all. You really don't see hall costumes here . . . you'd think a community full of faggots would have costumes everywhere, and it just has not caught on. It's the strangest thing.
>
> **Ethnographer:**  Here, I can see people being a little more hesitant because we're sharing the immediate area with so many diverse groups. But in Philadelphia, I don't think there was anybody else in the hotel.
>
> **Cipra:**  Well, . . . now we're guessing, because we have theorized and wondered about this ourselves—the fact that those who are really seriously into drag are not into science fiction. And on the whole, the gay community at large views the science fiction gay community the same way the world at large views science fiction fandom: "Oh, them. Those Trekkies."

Ironically, many of the fans at this convention do costume when they attend the larger general interest science fiction conventions. And little of the costume and other fannish display would be particularly out of place in the gay community if it were not attached to science fiction. There seems to be a sense, however, that unlike the gay and lesbian community, which has its geographic safe places in the cities, the gay science fiction fandom is breaking new ground against prejudice on two fronts, and doing it all alone. The conservatism of the behavior one sees at Gaylaxicons seems to say to the straight world in which the convention takes place, "See, we are not ravening hordes with no sense of good manners. You can trust us not to have sex in the hallways or steal your children." The message to the gay community seems to be, "We are not ravening hordes of Spock-eared nerds developmentally frozen at age thirteen. You can trust us not to wear propeller beanies when testifying in front of Congress."

## Perceptions of Fandom in the Gay Community

At this very moment when the underground gay movement in science fiction was ready to demand its place in the science fiction community, its members found themselves facing stunning disapproval at home. Many gay and lesbian fans have said that they found it much more difficult to admit to reading science fiction in the gay community than to tell people they were gay in the science fiction community. The disapproval of the gay and lesbian community has troubled both fans and professionals in science fiction. The mainstream of gay culture seems to object to science fiction, as a literary genre and as a community, for a number of reasons:

1. The reputation of the genre. Many discriminating readers saw science fiction only in terms of its lowest common denominator audience, straight white adolescent males with a taste for games and explosions. They thought of science fiction in terms of the logical positivism of its early years and scorned the underlying message of the fiction of that time: that any social ill can be solved with a sufficiently costly and energy-consuming construct of quasi-scientific engineering. The idea that a fiction of technocultural ideology might be useful for the expression of their own interests did not compute.

2. The backlash against women. Organizers for a gay and lesbian voice in science fiction in the '80s were trying to expand the possibilities of the genre at the very time that male community members were reacting with outrage to the presence of women at the conventions and on the bookshelves. While the industry may have begun to open up to the possibilities of a more diverse reading audience, the community itself was functioning under a siege mentality.

3. AIDS. If a disease as devastating as this can be said to have had one positive effect on a community it has otherwise savaged, the need to do something about AIDS did draw a huge number of gay people out of their isolation and into an active community of support. Particularly in the major cities, the '80s saw a proliferation of social and activist organizations in the gay community, and an increasing number of people coming out of the closet to participate.

Men and women in the gay community looked at the reputation of science fiction, and wondered why someone would willingly adopt a genre that excluded them and their concerns so unequivocally. Critics looked at the backlash against women in fandom, and wondered why a lesbian would want to go there. And as the gay and lesbian community grew in strength to fight its own battles for care and attention in the face of inconceivable loss, any movement away from the specific needs and activities of the gay and lesbian community could be, and often were, read as a denial of the gay community.

In essence, members of the gay community recognized in science fiction a greater threat when it was open to gay and lesbian participation than when it was not. Both the gay and science fiction communities have structured interactions realized in subcultures, and each is a powerful force for its members' self-definition. When science fiction culture did not allow for the expression of gay needs and culture, potential members had a clear choice: to self-identify primarily as gay and participate as a full member primarily in that community, or to submerge the gay identity in the identification with the science fiction community.

I do not, of course, mean submerge the gay identity in the Freudian sense of repression or suppression of homosexual desires. Rather, the core science fiction fan who was also gay in pre-1980s fandom chose a primary identity unrelated to his or her life of sexual desire. The life of gay sexual desire continued actively or not as the participant acted out that part of his or her life, but the orientation of sexual desire was a factor in the creation of a secondary rather than a primary identity. People for whom their sexual nature was not a function of their primary identity were not likely to participate in any useful way in the gay community, so their loss was not felt.

With the stirrings of gay activism in science fiction, fandom suddenly gave the mainstream gay community competition for active members. Now the fan torn between her sexual identity and her fan identity could find a place where she could reconcile the conflict and merge the competing identities into one: the gay science fiction fan. The mainstream gay community needed active participants to raise money and awareness, not only about disease but also about the basic rights being denied gay people in the mainstream world of work and home. They needed more members out and participating in the fun and social life of the community to forge the communal bonds that keep a community strong when they have a common crisis and a common goal—and that give it a focus for existing when the need is purely social rather than materially critical. Influenced by the reputation of the genre, gay community members found the activism of science fiction fans for a voice in the fiction and the fan community shallow and insignificant. The effort to make a place for gay and lesbian fans in the science fiction community smacked of accommodationism, a strategy that the mainstream gay community had tried and rejected as unworkable in the 1950s.

## Gay and Lesbian Fandom and the Industry

An active gay and lesbian fandom serves the purposes of its constituency in two ways: it furthers the interests of gay and lesbian readers in the communal activities of the culture and it makes the group's presence felt as an audience to be courted in the product that the industry creates. By the late 1990s the effort of fan organizations and writers and fans seems to be succeeding. WisCon, the convention for feminist science fiction, has always been open to and accepting of lesbian fiction and ideas. Gaylaxicon has been joined by Diversicon, a Midwest convention celebrating diversity of all kinds in science fiction.[28] And perhaps more conclusive for the growing importance of the gay and lesbian audience, the science fiction publishing industry now takes notice:

> **Cipra:** Del Rey Books contacted us [the Gaylaxicon committee] and said, "Well, gee, we would like to have input from your fans. Will you provide us with a listing of your membership?" To which we answered, "No, we will

not . . . our chapter does not provide our membership roster to anyone." Even the [Gaylactic] Network. . . . It's a world that is still not—you don't want to pass around people's sexual orientation to the wide world. So we told Del Rey, "No, I'm sorry, the Network makes a rule that we don't provide them. Del Rey said, "Oh, well then, can we send you paperwork, and you can have people send back to us their address if they want to?" We said, "No problem, yes." I don't think they ever sent that. But at the same time they said to us, "How would you like a load of free books?" You'll notice they're all gone now.

They also provided us with Nicola Griffith's *Ammonite*, which won both the Lammy, for science fiction/fantasy, last year, and this year it won the James Tiptree Award for promoting sexual diversity. It was the first time we had that.

We were also contacted by the Baltimore Worldcon committee, who asked, "Well, how about if we throw a party in your con suite. We'll provide you with all the food and drinks and stuff like that, and we will shamelessly promote Baltimore Worldcon." . . . They were supporting some of the goods that go into the con suite, stuff like that. They were there last night.

In the '90s in science fiction, both the industry and the convention-organizations seem to be recognizing that gay and lesbian readers represent an important target audience that at least some science fiction publishers, including Del Rey and Tor, now seem ready to satisfy. Nicola Griffith, winner of the Lammy and Tiptree award for *Ammonite,* won the 1996 Nebula, awarded by the Science Fiction and Fantasy Writers of America (SFWA) for her novel *Slow River*, which also received a 1995 Lammy, as co-winner with Melissa Scott's *Shadow Man*.

But there remains a singularly difficult barrier to breach for the gay and lesbian special interest group: the absence of prominent male writers who are openly gay and participating in gay science fiction. High-profile lesbian writers such as Ellen Kushner, Tanya Huff, Melissa Scott, and Nicola Griffith have made both a critical and popular success in science fiction. Among the men who still made up the majority of science fiction writers and fans, however, only Samuel Delany, discussed above, actively used his position as a major science fiction star to support gay participation in the community. But Delany's books were even then moving out of the popular mass-market category into the realms of the university press. The Lammy awards have even eliminated their category for men's science fiction or fantasy, because the award went consistently to women writing about gay men rather than to gay men.

There seem to be a number of reasons why men have been less sanguine than women to announce themselves as gay. Some of these reasons arise in the culture at large, some in the industry itself. For one thing, gay men have more to lose than gay women. While they remain in the closet, gay men share the status of men who are otherwise in the same demographic categories. In science fiction, that has traditionally meant white middle class heterosexual males, who still hold the majority of highly paid jobs and write the majority of the science fiction and fantasy books published. If they make their sexual orientation known, these men run the risk of losing not just status but also income if their publisher declines to buy their books or if their audience turns away from new gay content. Women never had the status to lose, so the cost even of exclusion adds little to the cost of being female in the first place.

Gay men are perceived as more threatening than gay women to the mainstream. While the obvious reason is the fear that straight men may have of sexual attack, a greater fear may be the loss of status that can befall a man for his sexual orientation. For the man who, consciously or unconsciously, values his privileges not least because they are unquestioned, the fear of losing that status is emasculating in a very literal sense. To lose the high status of his sex means he becomes like women. The very fear itself makes him more like a woman, because freedom from the fear that women and minorities experience is one of the most unquestioned of the perks of being a white male. While the gay white man really may not have the luxury of living without this fear, the pretense of it makes up part of the protective strategy that defends those privileges he does hold onto.

Women, by contrast, did not have the status to lose, but they did have the feminist movement, where straight and gay women worked together to win greater rights as women to a voice in the community. The utopian tradition that feminist science fiction continued always included an exploration of single-sex female communities, so straight and gay women reading and writing in the feminist tradition had a common ground of same-sex bonding ready-made in the literature. Perhaps more important, however, as we have seen in Chapters 4 and 5, even as a part of the male core of the reading community reacted in backlash against the women in science fiction, those women had become increasingly visible in position of importance in the industry. A lesbian woman, therefore, could expect to find at her publishing house another woman to work with. For the lesbian writer this common bond of gender could make entrance into the field more comfortable, if not easier. The gay man, however, still had the fear that his public identity would be censured and rejected by the male editor, while acceptance by the female editor might represent a feminization of the work in direct violation of the norms of the masculinization of contemporary gay culture.

In the 1990s, a new cadre of men, both straight and gay, writing gay characters, has appeared, most notably in the collection *Bending the Landscape*, edited by Stephen Pagel and Nicola Griffith. This short-story anthology, currently available in the general readership science fiction section, offers a wide variety of stories about gay characters by both men and women, straight and gay. Even here, however, few of the men writing make open statements about their sexual orientation in their biographies, and all are in the early stages of their careers. Women have proven that a gay writer can take on issues of gender and win respect and standing in the science fiction community. And gay men have worked long and hard to help create a gay and lesbian fandom for writers and fans alike to have a home. Lesbians and gays will never have an equal place in the genre, however, until gay men in the field realize that they owe their community the visible proof that gay men can write science fiction, fantasy, and horror as well as their straight and lesbian counterparts. Until that happens, the mainstream of gay culture is right in questioning the devotion of gay men to a culture in which their best do not even accept themselves.

# Youth Culture                                                    8

## Beating at the Gates

Gay and lesbian fandom has met with little resistance in the 1990s for a number of reasons. The relaxation of the '80s backlash seems to have encompassed lesbian as well as straight women. Then, gay and lesbian fans fought for their voice in the community with the tools the community recognized and understood: formal organizations, at least on the outside—conventions, committees, and the literature itself. Media fandom, with its battles over homoerotic fiction in the '80s, had already set a precedent for the appreciation of gay-oriented fiction by straight women as well as gays.

But none of those very logical reasons might have made a difference if a new youth phenomenon hadn't been hitting the science fiction community at the same time. This new group, most identifiable by their black leather clothing, drew fire away from the gay and lesbian community. The new battle, based on age and style, has created a generational schism so profound that old-line fans in the '90s have found themselves in a strange state of publicly declared denial. At most conventions today, you will find panels with some topic that denotes the aging of the community or asks, "Where are the young science fiction fans?"[1] At the same time, the same social groups asking the questions denounce the new wave of young fans as a scourge on the face of the community.[2] During our interview detailed at length in chapter 3, I asked Jailbait (JB) about this group. I wondered how the young raised to traditional science fiction culture viewed the incursion.

> **JB:** The kids in black leather . . . very often severe makeup? Yes, the goth community is what they're usually called around here. [sigh] I know a lot of them. . . . They started out all severe, it's become a cultural lifestyle for them, and they've actually, in their own gothic way, mellowed out a lot. . . . I knew Amelia G. when she was still at Wesleyan in Middletown, Connecticut, had a good Jewish last name. . . .

> **Ethnographer:** So they are not really alien to this place.

**JB:**    Not to me. Then again, at Disclave, two Disclaves ago . . . there was this big debate on the steps, I think it was Red Steve fighting against Joe [a fan in his fifties]. . . . "Why are you here . . . " It is the same sort of alienation thing that got most everyone into fandom in the first place. . . . [F]or some people it's turned into dress in black leather, look dangerous, wear ammunition around my neck. . . . [I]t is the same alienation that got Joe into fandom lo these many years ago, only it's more modern and he's doing generation gap things. One of the biggest problems, they're noticeable, they're visible, and hotels don't like them, which is always a problem. . . . They smoke a lot.[3]

As we have seen in Chapter 2, hotels always present some difficulty for science fiction conventions. Fans run on a time schedule very different from that of traditional business meetings; they dress differently, have a different eating schedule, and hotels may be hostile to changing their routines to suit the customers who spend a lot in the coffee shop, but very little in the expensive restaurant, and not much more in the bar.

Goths add several inconveniences for hotels already unhappy about changing their routines: while fans in general look strange to them, most hotel staff find goths terrifying. The goths wear leather and chains and black jeans. They often sport hair dyed bright unnatural colors like acid green or purple, and display tattoos and some piercing. The goths of science fiction, sometimes called cyberpunks, travel in groups and settle in the bar or lobby, where their style of dress is variously read as violent and destructive in the sense of motorcycle gangs, or sexually deviant in the sense of sadomasochism.

Valerie Steele, in her study on fetish clothing, points briefly to the goths, punks, and cyberpunks as fashion cultures that borrow the clothing of the fetishist as fashion.[4] The use of fetish clothing as fashion does not necessarily indicate a fetishistic attachment to that fashion, nor does it necessarily indicate an adherence to the sexual practices, such as sadomasochism and bondage and domination, that make use of fetishistic clothing as part of sexual practice.

The actual practice of fetish clothing by goths and cyberpunks is ambiguously threatening to traditional science fiction fans and to the personnel in the hotels that serve the convention circuits. When I first saw the goths appear in numbers at conventions, they scared me as much as they scared everyone else. They would appear, en masse, dressed in leather and chains—chains on boots and jackets, as jewelry, including the occasional chain linking pierced hoops in lips, noses, ears, or eyebrows—long hair, black tee shirts touting death bands on the men, leather bustiers on the women, tattoos, and in-your-face jewelry of religious inversion. They would land somewhere in the lobby, mix little, greet tentative approaches with suspicion, and generally spread a smoke-sharp pall of the apocalypse on the event. Clearly an alien culture had come to roost, but what culture was it? In 1993, at Balticon in Cockeysville, Maryland, I had the chance to find out, in a context that came close to matching the Boskone meltdown of 1987.

## Balticon 1993

While Balticon's expansion was neither as precipitatous nor as great as Boskone's, in 1993 the convention did reach the self-destruct point, and the goth science fiction community came in for much of the blame. Unlike Boskone, Balticon had always seemed a convention more friendly to gamers and media fans than most traditional conventions in the Northeast. For costumers, Balticon was the center of activity on the Eastern seaboard. When I began attending Balticons, they were held in downtown Baltimore, but in 1993 they were back at the Hunt Valley Inn, in Cockeysville, a popular hotel used by many media conventions as well as Balticon. Shore Leave, which attracted about 800 participants when I attended them in the '80s, fit comfortably into the hotel, and the staff seemed to cope well with the fans and their schedules.

But Balticon, with a membership of 2,000, was a very different story, one that tracks the downfall of Boskone in significant details. Sleeping rooms were divided between two main hotels, but all the programming and sanctioned parties, such as bid parties, occurred at the Hunt Valley, which did not have sufficient space to hold the people. Science fiction writer S. N. Lewitt, a member of the goth community in Washington, D.C., had explained that the goth community in the area was quite large as a "scene." So, I was not surprised when Friday night the goths took over the bar in numbers that effectively shut out both the science fiction professionals and their fans for the duration of the convention.

Later Friday evening we met Red Steve in the con suite. Lewitt introduced us, and I asked what books he liked to read. Not surprisingly, Bill Gibson was high on his list. More surprising, C. J. Cherryh was also on his list. In fact, his favorites might grace the shelf of any science fiction fan. Red Steve, as mentioned above, had cocreated The Zone, a live action role playing game based on a cyberpunk universe for enacting at conventions. He had a game planned for Saturday night at Balticon as part of the convention activities.

The connection of goths to horror and vampire fiction seemed axiomatic, but I had known in a general way for quite some time about the attraction of cyberpunk for the goths. I did not understand it, but couldn't help noticing that the numbers of goth fans at conventions seemed to pace the growing popularity of the subgenre. Gibson's cyberpunk universe reflects the dark outlook of the goths, and features hackers in leather, an amalgam of symbolic worlds I had recognized but thought strange until I talked to Amelia G. and Forrest Black during a group interview that included S. N. Lewitt and another housemember, Sarah, at Hollowpoint.[5] Forrest Black and Amelia G. both worked in the computer industry. Black did LAN contracting for major federal projects, and as part of his job he configured their networks and worked on the system architecture. Amelia G. was a freelance computer graphics contractor who also worked on government and private contracts.[6] I asked Black and Amelia G. about the crossover between hacker culture and vampires:

**Ethnographer:** Back up. The hacker vampire crowd?

**Amelia G.:**    I think it's just an age thing . . . people who are more likely to have been hackers when they were twelve couldn't have done it until there were, like, home computers. So it's partly like a generational thing.

**Ethnographer:**    That explains the computers, but where did the vampire thing come in?

**Amelia G.:**    The vampire thing, I think, is partly, it's something that cycles, as far as, like, interest in that type of mythology, and I think it's just been on an upswing that's coincided with people who are about the right age to have been hackers at some point, or who, just, perhaps, are still hackers. Although, almost no one you will talk to will actually say that they are a hacker now. . . .

**Black:**    I think there might actually be some kind of . . . reason behind a crossover between a hacker culture and a more gothic culture. Because generally speaking, hacker-type people, well, they're antisocial because they spend a lot of time at home with their computer, and . . . they have a personality type, in my opinion, that would gravitate toward a more gothic kind of, like, black, whatever, person. . . .

**Amelia G.:**    I know that I spend an awful lot of time home on my computer. And what I do all day at work is I like, sit around with a mouse in my hand, and I come home, and what I do is with a mouse in my hand. And every once in a while we go out, and I have to say I have a pretty, like, black outlook on it.

**Black:**    Yeah, it might actually be something to do with just a biochemical, like, reaction to the fact that, well, gee, I stay up all night, I hide in my basement, and I don't come out very often. Ergo. . . .

So hackers and the goth sensibility seemed to come together in a vaguely dark and romantic vision of vampire lovers and the fantasy, or memory, of the excitement Bill Gibson evokes about moving through other people's computer systems. The fiction resonates with the sense of dark futility of the goth sensibility and has given the new generation of smart kids and computer nerds an image to copy that projected the sense of romance:

**Ethnographer:**    How did hackers find style?

**Black:**    I think, they looked around and they said, well, who's got a date and who doesn't? The ones that were smart . . . that look around, they go, who looks cool? And they find their little examples of . . . that, you know, industrial gothic guy or whatever is like all cool or whatever.

**Amelia G.:**    He's getting all those babes with the leather bras on. "I could take some of that."

**Black:**    Seriously. Absolutely. And you look around, you don't find too many other examples . . . your normal attractive, sportsmany kind of guy is not going to be there, because it's just a different culture, so they're gonna look around, they're gonna say, well, these cool people are, they're able to get dates or whatever, so perhaps I should emulate their style. And it is a style that works very well for hackers because they don't get a lot of sun. And so—and they use a lot of stimulants to stay up all night, so . . . just works.

**Amelia G.:**   They look haggard?

**Ethnographer:**   Haggard and edge.

**Black:**   Exactly. So, they decided that maybe they should buy black jeans instead of blue jeans, and maybe they should wear like, whatever, and it just sort of develops into something where someone would be into a sort of a gothic vampiry look, and a hacker-type person. And also, vampires, theoretically, mythologically, or whatever, are fairly intelligent, and they like to be able to say, "I am intelligent and I have style."

Surprisingly, even though Goth music, a dirgelike rock with infusions from industrial and heavy metal, forms the basis for goth cultural in general, and even though they did enjoy the sound, among other types of music, none of the goths I talked to pointed to the music as the source of their look.

**Amelia G.:**   I guess I am counterculture. But to me some of the identifications on that are very—they're very fashion conscious, they're very, "what music did you listen to today?"—You know, well, are you a Goth Industrial wank boy or a metalhead, which are you? And I don't identify very strongly with one group. You know, it would be kind of cool if I did, but I don't. I think that's the reason why I am so aggressively alienated.

Though music did not seem to be the center of the gothic identity for these participants, all the sources for the look of Cambodia/Hollowpoint[7] can be found in the science fiction culture of horror fantasy and cutting-edge near-time science fiction and the mythology of darkness and intelligence that the horror and vampire fantasies project. This does not mean that the leather and chains have lost their cross-subcultural meaning as clothing of intimidation and sexuality, of course, and Amelia G. was publishing her own leather pornography magazine when I interviewed the group in June of 1993. But sexual preferences here are not specifically or necessarily coded according to the sadomasochistic subculture.

**Amelia G.:**   I like a lot of the weird leather sex and stuff; it was totally something when I was twelve, I was like hot for that. And I think it's something that totally grows out of, like, the kind of fiction I read as a kid. Because as a kid I read predominantly, like, either medieval-type-based fantasy stuff, fairy tales, and like, those stories about the one little boy who tames the wild stallion, but no one else can ride it. I think that definitely feeds into a lot of leather sex mentality. Because, I don't think it's a big stretch from like, knights in shining armor to, like, hot boys in black studded leather.

**Black:**   See, I'm in denial. I think a lot of this fetish stuff looks really cool, but it has absolutely nothing to do with sex. I think it just looks really cool.

At this point, Lewitt and housemember Sarah entered the discussion, challenging Black's assertion and adding their own interpretation:

**Lewitt:**   You *really* think it has nothing to do with sex?

**Black:**   Not nothing, but not as much.

**Amelia G.:**   Forrest thinks it looks attractive, but he is not as much into the activities as the look. And while I like the look better than the activities—

**Lewitt:**   Yeah, but the look is a fetish; the activities are something else.

**Sarah:**   I think part of the reason I like leather, and this is weird, is that, when I was a very little girl I spent most of my time at the stables, and, like, all the equipment was leather, and it makes me feel good to smell leather. It makes me feel like I'm a little kid again, it makes me happy. That's why I like leather, and I transfer feeling happy to everything, you know, anything that makes me happy is good. . . .

There is clearly a flirtation with sadomasochism and the bondage and discipline aspects of leather symbolism, which will be discussed at greater length in Chapter 9. But the style represents a youth-cultural construct created out of a wide variety of sources all using certain symbols in common for meanings both divergent from and tangential to each other. All the meanings seem to frighten the locals.

Balticon—its hotel filled well beyond its capacity, its most prominent and public gathering place appropriated by the group marked for difference by age, sensibility, dress, and public behavior, including heavy smoking indoors—was heading for disaster by Saturday night. Typical of anthropologists everywhere, I wanted to understand the impending doom, so I wandered through the bar to find out what these "foreigners" were doing in the territory they had seized. I found one group collating a zine, another group discussing the latest Bill Gibson, and another strategizing for the game later that night. Many were having private conversations, just as the traditional fans would do. But they all eyed me suspiciously as I wandered through. I complimented one young woman on her dress. It took her a moment to realize that I meant it, that I was not being hostile, but then she smiled and thanked me, and made a comment about its construction. In a sense, as Forrest Black and Amelia G. intimated, goth is guerrilla theater as lifestyle, and clothing is very much costume as well. It seemed, when I looked past my own fear of difference, that fandom was going on here much the same as it went on in more traditional fan groups. JB was right.

### Fire Alarms

Unfortunately the air circulation system of the hotel, its windows sealed as modern buildings often are, could not cope with the level of smoking in the vastly over-crowded hallways and public spaces. On Saturday, amid the chaos of overcrowding and late-night activities, the fire alarm went off twice. The first alarm was initially attributed to the goths, either as a malicious prank or as the inadvertent result of the smoke level, but was quickly determined to be an accident caused by a workman trying to repair the system. The second brought in the fire marshal, who closed down the public spaces of the convention because of the overcrowding in the lobbies, hallways, and bar. While the goths were no more at fault for the overcrowding than any other group meeting at the convention, they were blamed for setting off the fire alarms that drew the fire marshal and resulted in the shutdown on Saturday night. According to convention organizers there was considerable damage to one hall, and management told the convention that it could not return the next year.

In the aftermath, much of the science fiction community put the blame for the disasters on the goths, and indeed one thing should be stressed: this group, like many other young people today, smoke quite heavily. Much news media attention has focused on the rise in smoking among the young, the effects of advertising geared to the young, and the fact that smoking is suddenly hip again, and the goth community are certainly not immune to the effects. The smoke, on which many of the specific complaints focused, was indeed so dense that, when the fire alarm went off for the first time, it was difficult to determine if there was actually a fire in the building, if the smoke from the cigarettes had set off the alarms, or if someone had set off the alarms with malicious intent and the smoke had no bearing on the alarms. None of the above proved true, of course: a repairman had hit the wrong switch by accident. The second alarm went off in all five wings at midnight—too well timed to be anything less than a deliberate prank. The goths, different because of their age, their dress, and the defensiveness of some members of the group, became the obvious target for the blame. I suspected the goths might be wielding their aggressive look defensively, however, and I knew exactly the person to ask.

In 1986, when I'd first gotten to know S. N. Lewitt, she was a struggling new writer bursting with a well-founded confidence in her career, and I was working on *Enterprising Women*. I'd noticed her goth clothing style, and I'd seen her with the goths from time to time. In the fall of 1992 we began to discuss Cambodia, the goth house with which she and a number of the core convention-going goths of the D.C. area were associated. This discussion continued via e-mail for about six months—ironically, during the period that Cambodia was breaking up and becoming something new.

> **Lewitt:** For the first year, the living room of Cambodia was truly, really, the coolest place in the D.C. area. . . . Any night you could count on seven to ten people there playing games, reading, listening to music, trying to figure out what to do to offend general society. . . . Within the first few months Johnny made the first bullet necklaces. They are still a symbol of being Cambodian. Anyone who claims to be Cambodian who does not have a necklace is not. . . .
>
> Anyway, the second year the projects started. Amelia and I began *BLT* [*Black Leather Times*, a zine about the doings of the house group]. Red Steve began the Zone, a LARP [live action role playing game]. . . .
>
> Yeah, the whole crowd wears a lot of black and talks nasty, but a large number no longer quite are . . . this is no longer the active center of a community, but just another group house with a lot of people who have a lot of leather.[8]

At Balticon in March 1993, armed with this new information, I had already determined to approach the goth community myself. Little did I know that I would see, on a smaller scale, the same kind of meltdown that crashed Boskone six years earlier. A few months later, I had a chance to talk to some of the members of Cambodia, who had decamped to a large house in suburban Gaithersburg which they named Hollowpoint. In the following description of Balticon 1993 I shall combine my own observations, the comments posted on the GEnie online service by traditional science fiction participants after the convention, and comments by the members of the goth community at Hollowpoint against whom some of the worst allegations were made.

## Hollowpoint

In June 1993, two months after Balticon, S. N. Lewitt arranged a meeting for me with some of the goths I had met in passing at the convention. I wanted the view from the other side, and I wanted to know what these new young fans were about. Their large suburban house in Gaithersburg was so new that the yards were still a sea of mud and twigs that would someday be trees. The new house, named Hollowpoint after the ammunition, had wall-to-wall carpet, an inexpensive kitchen table and chairs, but little other furniture that I could see in the formal living room. Mail-order catalogues of computer accessories and leatherwear lay scattered on the table.

As one of my goals, I wanted to decode the clothing. As described above, leatherwear is a complex of multivalent symbol structures, and I wanted to know which meanings the group ascribed to their own use of the clothing. As we can see from the section above, the clothing reflects the literature to an extent, and Bill Gibson, author of *Neuromancer*, is generally credited with making the hacker a sex symbol in science fiction literature. For goth culture, the leather, lace, velvet, and dead white makeup all represent multivalently the apocalyptic worldview represented in the music. While goth culture is not itself a subset of the sadomasochistic subculture, there is a clear fascination with the ideas of domination and bondage, which may or may not be acted out in any way for sexual pleasure. In discussion, that element of representation and practice, as well as the nature of leather as fetish, did come up, and will be described in greater detail in Chapter 9.

More important to this chapter, I wanted to know about convention-going from the other side of the goth divide. How did the hostility affect these people, and why did they continue in the face of such rejection? The group I spoke with included a nineteen-year-old woman the group had taken in when she was an underage runaway, Sarah, Amelia G., Forrest Black, and another male housemate who joined the group late in the proceedings. The group said they attended about five conventions a year, but:

> **Amelia G:**   Maybe only two or three for the whole weekend, for me, but a lot of times like stopping in. You know, walking around, getting hassled by a bunch of people, and going, man, I hate this. Let's go. Do something else.

Amelia G.'s comment gave me the opening I had hoped for. I asked if they had experienced any trouble at Balticon.

> **Amelia G.:**   Well, I know that I personally was folding *BLT*s with a bunch of people. And we weren't being loud, and we weren't being rude, and we were

just, like, sitting in a corner, and like, "We are closing this whole section down." But for the most part I just felt pretty alienated from it.

**Black:**   But my personal little beef, and one of the reasons why I run into problems every freaking time I go to one of these conventions, is because I do not personally appreciate the split between the old school sort of swords and sorcery fantasy like furry creature people and the newer school technology science people . . . there are bad examples and good examples on both sides, of, like, appropriate and inappropriate behavior, but as far as like a split goes, it is not a healthy one, and it is feeding entirely too much animosity.

Black is not just speaking of the fantasy/science fiction distinction, which has been part of the community almost since its inception, but also a specifical contemporary split between the fans of traditional forms of far-future spaceship science fiction and the fans of the new near-future science fiction based on computer infrastructure. The distinction is not only fundamental to the aesthetics, but crucial to the worldview the form represents—the glowing positivistic optimism that fuels the notion of space flight, alien encounters, and Yankee Ingenuity versus the dark and inverted vision of a decaying society ruled by the technologically privileged while the technological underclass hacks at the bastions of that power with its security bypass software.

Of course, the underdog of cyberpunk is not the true underclass, which has no access to high technology or to the training that makes it possible to wield that technology. But the creators of cyberpunk brought to the form a sensibility out of the previous generation's rebellion—the drugs, sex, rock and roll Weathermen Underground set to the tune of a new technology. That creation captured the imaginations of the twelve-year-old hackers, girls like Amelia G. who still remember the boys who wouldn't let her join the computer club when she was thirteen, and boys like Forrest Black made wary of government by direct contact with its downside. Cyberpunk resonates with the frustration of the technologically privileged young oppressed by virtue of their age or appearance. Ironically, the community that created the form that expresses the needs and feelings of the cybergothic generation denies what it has created while it rejects the sensibilities of the group that responds to its message most keenly. And the rejection still hurts.

**Black:**   There's actually only so motivated to be around people I can get. And if I go somewhere, and a bunch of people say I'm a bad person and label me, like, outcast or whatever, I'll leave . . . they only have so much programming that actually appeals to me personally so it's not like I can just ignore the people in the hallway because I'm running from place to place. Generally I'm just hanging out with a bunch of people. Except I feel as though I am sort of looked down upon as not having the proper qualifications to associate with that group of people. It bothers me.

**Amelia G.:**   . . . I haven't done fandom stuff across the country, but the first convention I ever went to was Boskone back when it was cool. And I think that the Northeast cons have, sort of the tension, but it's much more between "I read books," "Well, I go to movies and I'm good looking," "Well I read books and I'm intelligent." And that's the split there, sort of, whereas, it's sort of, the mid-Atlantic, it's much more of like a fashion thing. It's like, I'm fat and I wear spandex so I'm intelligent. And I'm thin and I wear leather, so obviously I don't read, right? Well, fuck you, you know. It's more stylistic.

And we've been doing a few DeepSouthCons lately, which I had a lot of fun at mostly because none of our nasty little "friends" were there. . . . I'm sure there is probably some tension like that, but I didn't particularly see it. It seemed like it was a much more easygoing thing. I didn't feel that anybody was "you know, what's wrong with you, why aren't you like that?" But that may be just because most of the pros in that area are people who are more likely to run around with leather jackets but were also capable of using a computer, so they can relate to where I am at, so I just didn't feel alienated on account of how it was some other group, other than me, that was alienated there.

Much of the negative stereotyping in fandom centers around the issue of reading the genre fiction. Media fans, and many women fans in general during the 1980s, were stereotyped as nonreaders, present either to celebrate television science fiction or to pick up the more intelligent men. So I was not inclined to believe the same claim against the goths when I heard it a few short years later. I wanted to know, in their own words, what the goths really did read, and how far their tastes in the genre diverged from those of the more traditionally clad fan. The only difference I found at all was a continuing appreciation for cyberpunk, which had been declared dead by Hartwell and the originals at Boskone the same year.

**Amelia G.:**   I really really like cyberpunk, but I guess because they decided that it wasn't, I don't know, economically in vogue or whatever this year, there hasn't been anything that is any good.

**Black:**   I think it's because the powers that be are scared of it, personally.

**Amelia G.:**   . . . the whole cyberpunk thing attracted a lot of people into fandom that, like, some of the people who were really big in fandom would have really preferred stayed away from it. Um, like, I seem to have the strong ability to evoke strong feelings in other people.

Amelia G. had been interested in science fiction and fantasy as a child, but had lost interest until—

**Amelia G.:**   . . . the whole cyberpunk thing really pulled me back into the whole science fiction genre, which I had gotten really tired of. It was something new and vital and exciting that I could relate to. It was a view of the world that spoke to me. I absolutely adore William Gibson. His prose is so dense, there's so much in it, like, it's worth actually reading the whole paragraph and not skimming. I really like Effinger too.

**Black:**   Some of the cyberpunk stuff is about the only fiction I can bring myself to read. I really like nonfiction. When I was a kid, I was, I guess, theoretically classifiably disadvantaged or whatever. When I looked around, I saw a lot of my friends, like, smoking a lot of dope and just getting into a whole big fantasy thing. And I looked at their parents and they just weren't ever going to change. And I didn't want to end up like that. So . . . if I am reading something that's completely fiction, I'm like, wasting my time. Unless it's particularly good and has things like archetypes and something that I can learn like a structure and theory, or whatever. . . . But some of the cyberpunk stuff I can read because of the fact that I really like the whole network theory and stuff like that, because it's things that I can relate to and I can actually apply,

**Sarah:**   I read the Belgariad literally, like, twenty times . . . I was so into it. I really loved, but I got really tired of it after a while, and now every book I read that's fantasy, I'm like, "not this shit again." It's just the same. Right now, my most recent, you know, one of my favorite books is by Orson Scott Card— *Ender's Game*. I've read it like five times in six months.

So the goths at science fiction conventions do read science fiction and fantasy. And they play role playing games like The Zone, based on the cyberpunk science fiction genre. And they create zines and do all the other things that committed science fiction fans do. Still, and particularly in the conservative climate of the conventions created by the science fiction clubs started on the East Coast in the 1930s through the '50s, the group is stereotyped and rejected, blamed for disasters and generally disliked by other fans and even many professionals in the field, for whom alienating a reading population would seem a risky business. Accordingly, I asked the obvious question: Why do you go to conventions?

**Black:**   You're asking me? Uh, 'cause my friends like to go. Sometimes, I believe that being antisocial is a bad thing and that I ought to go out and try to make some little friends and converse with people with some more interests and whatever. And sometimes I forget that they are mean to me when I do that . . . some of the techie people are interesting to talk to, and they're hard to dig up if you're not actually in their face. There are a few resources there that are worthwhile, but for the most part every time I go, I remind myself that I have no reason to be there. So I'm not entirely sure what draws me there.

Of course, Black does have a good reason to be there, and the reason itself demands the response it receives.

Science fiction fandom reflects the larger culture's discomfort with the gothic-leather-punk manifestation of youth culture and its need to commodify the fetishist, to contain him. It is harder to contain the cyberpunk in science fiction because the number of youth flaunting the dark and dangerous leather look is sufficient to mark an overpowering presence rather than an occasional anomaly. The mainstream of fandom responds accordingly, with fear and even hatred, much as the generations of power have always feared youth cultures. Youth culture represents the Oedipal confrontation at its heart, the fear the old have at the peak of their powers that they will lose everything to age and decline as the usurpers displace them in the hard-won position to set the norms for the culture. Every generation passing into dominance recognizes the need to seduce the young to their point of view. If the young, in winning, overturn the values of the literary generation that went before, they deny that generation's bid for immortality in the pantheon of the arts.

The extremes of youth culture—the hippies of the '60s, the punks and the gothics and leather crowd of the '90s—express in their clothing and personal style the failure of the older generation to win the battle against age and a new sensibility. But more important, the Oedipal dance pivots around a focal symbol of power: sexuality. When it borrows from a wide variety of sexual subcultures that have long been deemed threatening by the mainstream, the leather crowd adopts the symbolic power to threaten that those subcultures have attached to the clothing. Science fiction has long prided itself on creating the future that we live in. With cyberpunk, that hubris has come home to roost. Writers, creating a cultural milieu of the computer out of the bits and pieces of the high and low tech, fetish and biker and militant power of leather, and perhaps more significantly borrowing from the body piercing of punk to sexualize the penetration of the body with the technology, have created their own Oedipal sons and daughters.

## Dragon Con

When I talked to youth culture fans, the Atlanta convention Dragon Con often came up as an example of a friendly convention. With a total number of attendees at more than 19,000 and growing, Dragon Con regularly exceeds in size the largest Worldcon, yet it seems to cope with the youth invasion without suffering the melt-down of some of the tradition-bound convention sites in the Northeast Corridor.

In spite of this success, many "SMOFs," organizers of regional and world conventions, spurn Dragon Con and speak scathingly of its organizer, Ed Kramer. In November 1994, to find out who Ed Kramer was and why half the people I spoke to thought he was the god of conventions for the youth culture while the other half considered him a charlatan, I called him on the telephone. I wanted to know what he was doing, and how he did it.

The first question, and a sensitive one, concerned the profit status of the convention. I had been told that Dragon Con did not conform to the fan practice of volunteerism, and that in fact Kramer ran his convention for profit. So I asked: Did Kramer actually earn his income from the convention? The answer was a resounding "No!" When we first talked, Kramer had a day job with a grant contractor in the health care field. He now holds a position writing grants and directing technology for a branch of the Georgia Department of Education.[9] He explained that Dragon Con, like the conventions with nonprofit status, relied on volunteers for its board and area directors:

> **Kramer:**  Our accountant at the time of our incorporation had never formed a nonprofit corporation. So, he incorporated us in the only way he knew how. I mean, he was an accountant and he only worked in for-profit. There are stockholders, which basically put money in to begin the conventions, and there were seven of us, all who are still actively involved in the convention, and four of us make up the actual corporate board of directors.

The convention does have an office and does employ an office manager, who answers the phones and maintains the organization's 67,000-person database,[10] but the work of actually putting on the convention is performed by volunteers. Their profit status, however, also gives the committee more leeway in what they can do, since they are not required to prove a specifically educational component to their programming.

When I pointed out that other conventions have suffered some serious burnout in their committees, Kramer explained that his fifty-four area directors have autonomy for their area of the convention, and that the committee places in directorships people with professional or avocational expertise in their area. The area directors can then recruit volunteers and make the best use of them. Dragon Con has more than 1,000 volunteers, more volunteers than most regional conventions have attendees. For many Dragon Con fans, however, this is their Worldcon, and organizers bring to it not only their years of experience, but an established reputation with the hotels and providers they work with every year.

Some fans had complained that Dragon Con was not really a science fiction convention but a comic book show. Ed Kramer vehemently insisted that Dragon Con is a science fiction convention, but admits that his definition may be more flexible than that of traditionalists:

> **Kramer:**  [I]f you look at what makes SFWA, the Science Fiction and Fantasy Writers Association, you have to include all facets of science fiction and fantasy. You also have to include all the modalities in which you see them, which is not only in books, but you also see them in graphic novels, which are pronounced "comics" by people, you see them in computer games, you see them in movies. There's a whole category for the Hugos, for dramatic presentation.[11]

True to his definition of the genre, Kramer's Dragon Con includes some 300 genre writers and artists, but also comics artists and writers and science fiction television and movie guests. The convention devotes one whole area of a hotel to gaming and also runs live action role playing games at the main hotel:

> **Kramer:**  We generally also have six live games, which can be seen as interactive literature. . . . And the people who participate in live role playing are not necessarily gamers. We started out using the Society for Interactive Literature in 1989, and that has expanded a great deal. And probably about 4,000 fans will participate in live gaming activities. . . . It doesn't occur at the gaming hotel because it is very foreign to the tradition of table-top gaming. . . . It's far more theatrical. . . . It involves a number of players who have been, I guess performers would be a better word, who develop incredible plotlines and performances and it is all really complex.

At Dragon Con, the live action participation fiction engages more participants than most conventions draw for all their events combined, and keeping the con-goers busy seems to be Kramer's motto for a successful convention:

> **Kramer:**  It's . . . a five-day convention as four days. . . . We actually begin live music and have open gaming and other areas of the convention begin Wednesday evening, and by noon of Thursday, the entire convention is in full swing . . . and the convention does not shut down until 5 P.M. on Sunday. We cram as much into the convention as we possibly can.[12]

Kramer defends Dragon Con's position in literary science fiction as well as in areas such as gaming and comics:

> There is as much science fiction programming as at a Worldcon: last year, over 550 hours' worth in eighteen program tracks. And, we strive to make the guest list the best we can each year. I mean, we bring in a wide, diverse group of guests. . . . And the thing is that people are multifaceted. There's so many science fiction fans who also play games, read comics, and watch movies. . . . For example, Neil Gaiman and Charles Vess, who won the World Fantasy literary award for a comic book story in *Sandman*, or Alan Moore won a Hugo Award for the graphic novel, *The Watchman*.

With the names of these graphic novelists on the table, I pointed out what I'd noticed, that the program book contained many more names in the comics area than in science fiction. Kramer explained:

> Many of the comic book guests . . . do not do programming. They are set up in an artists' alley, where they can be there and talk to people and meet people and sell their sketches. So, if you look at our programming at the conventions, it probably is almost 70 percent congruous with what would be at a more traditional SF convention.

Ultimately, of course, the interview came down to the big question: Why aren't the new generation of fans trashing your hotels if they are trashing Balticon's hotels and Boskone's hotels?

> **Kramer:**   We had 19,000 fans this past year [1998], with no hotel or facility damage. . . . And the reason why is because we provide for as wide an audience as possible. I try to bring in guests each year that are very diverse and basically meet the needs of the population that attends the convention.

Of course, Boskone had tried to do the same thing in the '80s, and by 1987 had gone into meltdown. It seemed reasonable to assume that Dragon Con would meet the same fate, but Kramer offered his response:

> How do we do this? We didn't start out with fifty-four directors we started out with a lot less. . . . As the convention expands, we basically split up directorships. My background is in management. As the convention is expanding, I can recognize when we need to expand the facilities. And we have not stopped doing that. We do not let size get in the way. We are planning for a larger convention each and every year. In 1997 we made our transition into the Atlanta Market Center, which is the fourth largest convention facility in the country, and that is where we'll stay until our next expansion in 2001. . . . What happens is that we have generally a 15 to 20 percent growth each and every year. So it happens gradually, and it gives us a better idea to know what we do for next year.

Unlike conventions that have planned future conventions based on past numbers, Dragon Con assumes an expanding population and increases its facilities accordingly. Activities are separated so that fans with an interest in only one part of the convention can experience their part of the event without crossing heavily into the territory of other interest groups. And they take care of their staff. When I asked how Dragon Con attracts so many volunteers, he answered:

> Because we treat them right. . . . A staff member over the course of the convention may work four four-hour shifts—sixteen hours. The rest they may do as they like. We comp their memberships. . . . [F]or any director that has an area that runs twenty-four hours a day, we provide them sleeping rooms. . . . Anyone where we tell them that they have to be on property, we provide a hotel room for them.

Kramer seemed to have a formula for a successful convention in terms of staffing and space, but he was working to attract the very fans that some conventions were trying to expel. I wondered how he managed it, and so the question came round again to why he succeeded where others had failed in providing for the new generation of fan:

> **Kramer:**  That's because you haven't provided them with something that they consider appropriate. For example, this year [1994], one of the artists we brought in was James O'Barr, who wrote *The Crow*. Who is basically seen, very often, in a leather jacket, and he is very open about a lot of things you described, and he loves to talk. And he, by his choice, was set up in a room ten hours a day doing autographs. He brought down an entire gallery of his artwork—ten years' retrospective of his artwork, original art. We gave him an entire room, a small room, and he basically set up and signed autographs every day. And then we had the music that he wrote performed by a band called Trust Obey, which was the actual original soundtrack to *The Crow* graphic novel. And they did a live concert. James O'Barr has returned to Dragon Con every year since.
>
> We actually have lots of live concerts at the convention. Aside from Trust Obey, other notables recording acts which have performed at Dragon Con include the Screaming Liederhosen, which is a jazz blues band that did all the background music for Ren and Stimpy; Loose Caboose from Boston, a reggae band, that performed with Mark Bode; Blue Oyster Cult's Eric Bloom that has performed with Michael Moorcock; the Flash Girls, with Emma Bull; live musical performances by John Shirley, John Skipp, Craig Spector, and Richard Christian Matheson; and such diverse bands as Edgar Winter, Godhead, Glass Hammer, Man or Astroman, Trio Nocturna, ODK, the Neil Norman Orchestra, the Misfits, the Changelings, the Bloodhound Gang, and GWAR. We also have disc jockeys that play dance music all night. We close our dances down at six o'clock in the morning.

Kramer insists that the alternative and goth fans are interested in programming, if the programming is appropriate.

> **Kramer:**  [G]oths tend to like horror programming. And we also have mainstream guests each year, like somebody like Eric Lustbader, from 1994, Clifford Stoll, Tom Clancy, Timothy Leary.

One thing Kramer seems to bring to Dragon Con is a level head and unflappable personality when it comes to the variety of fans who attend his convention.

> **Kramer:**   I remember a few years ago, the security that the hotel provides, which is six marshals, got very concerned because there were about a dozen skinheads that were in our ballroom, basically getting ready for the concert to begin. And I said, in my entire history and knowledge of conventions, there's never been a problem with skinheads at a convention. They're here because they're probably just fans. And they sat there and listened and watched the show . . . and it's like, nothing happened. They were fans.

Like Arisia, formed as an alternative to Boskone, Dragon Con actively courts the young alternative and leather crowd:

> **Kramer:**   We advertise on the alternative radio stations. When I say alternative, I mean that are playing what's considered alternative music . . . and we have things for them. . . . See, the thing is, there's another convention that is local to us called Chattacon, which is in January, which is a literary convention. Now, it's a fun literary convention. Southern conventions, I think, are a lot more fun than the northern ones are. There's just a different atmosphere to them. But in general, a vast majority of people who attend Chattacon also attend our convention. I guess what I'm trying to say is, people who are—and Chattacon is a good size, it's like 1,400 people—the people who go to a . . . specifically literary convention find just as much at Dragon Con as they do at any other convention.

When Black and Amelia G. talk about the friendlier conventions in the South, they include Chattacon and Dragon Con among them. The conventions are themselves younger and still flexible, forming their traditions around the new youth rather than the generations of the '40s and '50s and '60s. But they form around new definitions of what makes a science fiction convention as well. In this new order, the creative value of interactive literature is recognized along with the virtuoso performances in the literary genre; the music and the art of the alternative lifestyle become part and parcel of the science fiction-fantasy package that programs for cyberpunks and fans of dark fantasy and horror. In the simplest terms possible, they aren't mean to the sensitive kids and younger adults like Forrest Black, and acceptance meets appreciation in an expanding youth culture of science fiction in all its modalities.

## Gothic Display and the Future of Fandom

Ironically, of all the changes we have studied in science fiction culture, this is the only change in the community that could have been predicted based on the community's own history of generational change.

A predominately male youth culture, steeped in logical positivism and striving for professionalism, shaped the community in the '30s, and photographs of fans at conventions through the '50s show the men in suits and ties. In the '60s, the community faced major change as the countercultural young brought new ways of dressing, writing, and perceiving the world. The dress code we now recognize as the norm for science fiction conventions—jeans, tee shirts with science fiction mottos or pictures, or the ethnic dress style of some women—replaced the suit and tie of the '50s convention-goer, influenced by the same counterculture making itself felt in the generation at large. The writing, called the New Wave, reflected the countercultural interests in the humanities, in social consciousness, and in sexual freedom.

The science fiction community had always held itself out to be a refuge for those who felt themselves alienated because of their superior intellect and sensibility, and the youth cultures that shaped science fiction during these and other, less marked, turning points in the fan/literature community were equally radical and alienated. But thirty years later in the fan and publishing communities, the counterculture of the '60s has mutated into a status quo that fears the new generation of "interlopers" based on their style of dress and interaction. The genres and their community stand at a dangerous crossroad, with yet another alien group to absorb in its diversity, or risk becoming obsolete if it turns its back. Fandom will go on, in its new forms, in new places, but the generations that have gone before could be left behind, their numbers dwindling, to wonder where the new, young fans went.

They went to Dragon Con.

# Sexual Identity and Fandom

# 9

Sex has always been a part of the science fiction community, if not of its literature, as the parade of second- and third-generation fans through this book can attest. But for most of the community's history, even during those periods of greatest controversy and political activism about sexual orientation, discussion or display of identity related to sexual practice has remained limited to very small and private in-group interaction. To some extent, the rejection that the gothic cyberpunks experience is a direct result of their dress and style, which consciously and publicly refers to the transgressive sexuality of the sadomasochistic bondage community. Ironically, as we have seen, the multivalent dress code of black leather, tattooed skin, and general extremes of dark display does not always code for the sexual practices. At the same time, as we will discover below, the transgressive sexuality that seems frightening when worn as a sign on the body existed within the community long before the arrival of the cyberpunks.

## Hollowpoint Redux

When I talked to the goths at Hollowpoint, I found that the response to their look represented the barest tip of a deep iceberg of signification attached to the clothing, but that indeed sexuality was much at the heart of it. Unlike commodity fetishists or fashion followers, including many goths, the gothic-cyberpunks at Hollowpoint did have ties to the S&M community. Catalogues for fetish clothing lay scattered among the computer and gun catalogues on the kitchen table, and part of the conversation went beyond the explanation of clothing as fashion, to the reflections on personal sexuality that fashion choices might indicate. In this discussion the participants demonstrate a knowledge of the forms of the subculture, and continue to challenge the meaning these forms have for themselves and each other:

> **Voice 1:** John really wants leather jeans. . . . He does have a bit of a leather fetish, I guess.
>
> **Amelia:** Oh, oh, you think so?

**Voice 1:**    Well, you see, he's not sure that it is a fetish. To you it just seems completely normal and obvious. I tried to point out to him that he is, like, a little bit kinky, but he doesn't believe it. . . .

**Forrest:**    Isn't there a difference between just, liking something because it's cool and actually, like, calling it a fetish and saying that you get off on it? I think latex clothes are really cool, but I just think they're really cool.

**Amelia:**    I think that you'd be more motivated to fuck me wearing a latex dress than not. As a result, I think that can be classified as a fetish.

**Voice 1:**    yeah . . . I heard someone, I think it was Cecilia [Tan, publisher of Circlet Press], who said, if you find something that is not normally associated with the Christian right wing, associated with sex as sexually exciting or attractive, then it is in fact a fetish. And that seemed to make sense. That's when I figured out, I do have a fetish about hair and leather, and—

**Forrest:**    Technology

For Forrest, who begins by denying the fetishistic quality of his appreciation for the clothing, the symbolism of technology in the latex clothing combines with the sexual and the hacker fantasies of someone expert in the technological field. He and Amelia both work in computer fields, and as we talk, both leaf through computer catalogues, occasionally dropping an aside about the price of software or a piece of hardware into the conversation.

Technology may in fact be the postmodern sexual fetish practice of the cyberpunk. While some authors of the postmodern technoculture have described this fetishization in terms of disaffection with the real in favor of an onanistic fantasy practice with the machine,[1] others have seen the technology as a mediator more in the spirit of the term "mediation"—not replacing flesh and blood encounters but facilitating them in face-to-face, frequently nonsexual interactions.[2] Both images are true as far as they go, and both are wrong, in the sense that they miss a larger complexity of relating.

Forrest recognizes that he prospered in the corporate technology market represented as the enemy in the cyberpunk fiction while standing at an ironic distance from his own participation in the corporate economy. To make the irony complete, of course, Forrest is talking about both the corporate game and a real game, The Zone, which he and Red Steve worked on while at Cambodia (see Chapter 8), but which has metamorphosed in a brief time to exclude the criminal side of the game in favor of the play of capitalism:

**Forrest:**    I'm "wait, I get to play a corporately affiliated like, technologically advanced person, according to your rules?"

**Amelia:**    Forrest's exact comment to that was "I figured out a way to get paid for that."

When I suggested that perhaps playing a corporate character was more fun in a game or a book, Forrest answered, "See, I think it's exciting in day to day life. I get off, I think it's a trip."

Forrest played the game, and was paid very well for it, and the joke is on the people who paid the bill, because they were playing *his* game, and they didn't know it. Power is sexy in the culture of the rugged individual. Cyberpunk, with its metaphor of the cowboy, consciously structures its image on the quintessentially American symbol equation that combining ultimate freedom with high risk equals ultimate power. Ultimate power, of course, brings with it sexual opportunity in an almost Darwinian process of selection. Power is sexy, and today technology is power. No wonder that technology turns the cyberpunk on.

Amelia, in what seems at first to be a digression, shows us how early that connection between sex and machines can occur.

> **Amelia:** But I really do feel that there are all these guys there who are going, "Oh, but isn't it personality that counts," and look, it's not my personality you are looking at . . . to me the little anecdote that sort of, I don't know, sums up how I feel about a lot of it, is that when I was thirteen I really wanted to be in computer club . . . computers were pretty new. It was cool. And I got there and I was the only girl there, but I still wanted to do it. And the boys wouldn't let me, because they felt that I was a girl: "I don't want a girl, to touch me, period." And every time some like creepy computer geek guy is all like being a jerk to me at a con, I think about that, and I'm like, you guys should have been nice to me then.

> **Voice 2:** You mean every time a computer geek is coming on to you at a con.

> **Amelia:** Yeah, that. Because it's really obvious that they want to fuck me, but it obviously never crosses their minds that I'm intelligent. Actually, I have graduated from college. With honors, actually. Double major. You know, they—they don't even believe it. They think you are lying.

For Amelia, a computer graphics designer, sexually aggressive clothing flaunts her desirability and then withholds it as revenge against the fannish representatives of the group who rejected her for her sexual identity when she was thirteen. That sexual identity even at thirteen combined the longing for the cybernetic with the longing for acceptance as an intelligent female. The longing for the cyborg[3] had marked Amelia at puberty, and, fully gendered, the cyborg takes revenge on those who would have denied her the privilege of technology by denying them the privilege of sex. Of course, these cyberwomen make a distinction between men who can succeed at both relationships and technology—the cyberpunk—and those who still, as adults, have gained power neither in the real world of technology nor in the real world of relations. Dreading his own flesh and stung by the rejection that reinforces his own self-loathing, the computer "geek" functions in no world at all. In a sense, the cyberpunk recognizes the generative power of the machine and wields that generative power in the world. By turning his personal computer into a symbolic sex toy, the computer nerd expends that generative power on himself, abandoning the world and the flesh to create an illusion of power out of a technology that, ironically, could have given him all the things he hides from in his fantasies: the power to change the world and to attract sex partners.

Amelia and Forrest, of course, understand this dynamic perfectly—particularly the sex connection. In 1992 Amelia had just begun to publish *Blue Blood*, a magazine of hard rock, leather, vampires, and kinky sex. With Forrest, she continues to publish the magazine today, and the *Blue Blood* website offers back issues, an erotic leather photo gallery, and books of Amelia's collected or edited stories. The medium is the medium, not the message; its power lies in its capacity to communicate in the postmodern freedom of competing voices. With the same understanding, Amelia and Forrest no longer avoid convention panels, but instead serve as panelists themselves at a number of goth-friendly conventions, including Dragon Con.

## The Literature of Sex and Science Fiction

In rare cases through the 1950s, sexuality appeared as the overt topic in science fiction.[4] For the most part, however, sex did not exist until the New Wave, particularly as it was practiced in England, during the late '60s and early '70s. By the mid-1970s, however, science fiction had retained the *idea* of sexuality—an idea that women in the feminist sf ghetto pursued in particular—but the graphic depiction of sexual acts in science fiction and fantasy did not develop as a trend the way it did in romance or suspense fiction. One cannot say that the number of actual descriptions of sexual acts diminished during the later '70s and '80s, because the numbers of those descriptions were low in their nascent period as well. Rather, the promise of more openly adult material in science fiction hinted at in publications like *New Worlds* seemed to fizzle out in what Marleen Barr aptly described in the title to a mid-1980s article: "Permissive, Unspectacular, a Little Baffling: Sex and the Single Feminist Utopian Quasi-Tribesperson."[5]

In the '80s, that began to change, but it is important to keep in mind that sex has not at any point dominated the science fiction and fantasy genres. Most of the books remain accessible to the average young adult (early- to mid-teen) reader. Even science fiction and fantasy written with adult themes for adult readers may not count sexual acts among the specifically mature concepts the author tackles. But a sexual revolution did influence the genre, in part fueled by women who looked at the specifically erotic materials written by fans of *Star Trek* and other television and movie sources.

As these materials surfaced into the consciousness of the women in mainstream science fiction, they were first met with ridicule and horror, but gradually they desensitized the audience to the idea of some graphic sexual practice described in detail in the literature. Men who may have felt constrained to restrict the level of detail in sex scenes in their stories found freedom in the new permissiveness to write more explicitly, while other science fiction fans used the APAs and nets to distribute their own amateur sexual literature. Cecilia Tan, publisher of Circlet Press, explains how she got involved:

> I had an idea that there was a definite audience out there already. I read some computer bulletin boards and I read a newsgroup dedicated to bondage. And people can post all kinds of things there . . . and some people would post

fictional stories, most of which were awfully written . . . but a couple of which were very well written and had science fictional aspects in them. Either they had nonhumanoid characters, furry characters, or they took place in zero gravity . . . people were really exercising their imagination. And I thought, this is great. And I thought, well, maybe I'll write some. And I knew that there were people out there who liked to read it, I just didn't know if people would part with money for it. (The time frame of this was 1991.)[6]

Of course, the eroticization of science fiction did not occur in a vacuum fueled only by its amateur writers. This same period marked the rise of the "steamy" romance, which generally contains at least three explicit sex scenes, proving that romance readers would pay for sexually explicit literature in their preferred genre. The early '90s saw the appearance of slickly published erotic magazines for women, such as *Yellow Silk*, on the shelves of mainstream bookstores, as Tan pointed out:

There have been a couple of big mainstream anthologies out recently—there's one called *Slow Hand: Women Write Erotica*, and I think it was from one of the big New York houses that does literature [HarperPrism]. It's a short-story collection, it's all by women. And then there's the Herotica collection that Down There Press published the first volume and it was so successful that Viking Penguin bought the rights to the second volume. And now . . . [January 1999] the Herotica series is up to five volumes, with a sixth one on the way. Harper also published this year,[7] my own collection of erotic short stories. The trend of major publishers publishing erotica written by women continues. Linda Jaivin's *Eat Me* and Alina Reyes's *The Butcher* are two recent examples, and the Best American Erotica series, edited by Susie Bright, although not all written by women, tends to feature this new wave of erotic literature.

All these influences have led to a growing interest in sexual materials in science fiction and fantasy circles. What may be more surprising, however, is the degree to which antipornography feminist interpretation has influenced the discussion in sexual literature in science fiction. At Hollowpoint, house members discussed a panel at a science fiction convention they had attended that shows a clear coopting of feminist rhetoric in the style of antipornography activist Catherine MacKinnon by the panel members, and the rejection of same by the younger, more cynical fans.

**Amelia:** We went to this panel on porn and science fiction,

**Voice 2:** [A]nd all these obnoxious people were trying to explain how erotica and pornography were really two different things, and basically what they had to say was that erotica was what turned them on, but pornography was what turned other gross people on.

**Amelia:** No, some of them said that erotica was what turned women on and pornography was what turned men on.

**Forrest:**    Same thing.[general laughter]

**Voice 2:**    Those were all women who said that.

**Amelia:**    No, a couple of guys said that. They said they thought things aimed at men were just insensitive. They were sensitive: "Hey baby, want to give me a blow job?" [laugh] Well, they didn't say the blow job part during the panel, but it was implicit. They were really liberals. They think that more women will fuck them if they say that.

**Amelia:**    They were right. They were ugly.

**Forrest:**    So it was the same thing.

**Amelia:**    In an indirect sort of way, I suppose.

**Amelia:**    Well, I think the people on this panel could have gone on all day about how offended they were by pornography.

**Voice 2:**    This one woman was going on just endlessly about how it was really awful to her that she was into, like, fantasy role playing games, but you know, she would go into these stores and there were just, all of these women and they all had really big—

**Amelia:**    This woman was really flat-chested.

**Voice 2:**    And they all had really big breasts, and it was just very upsetting for her, because she was very visually oriented and she couldn't stand it for, like, longer than an hour and she would have to leave. And how long can it possibly take you to shop for rpg [role playing games] material?[8]

While placing Circlet Press firmly in the camp with science fiction porn fans (and creators) like Amelia and Forrest, Cecilia Tan described this distinction from more classic visions of erotica:

> I recently was talking with the editor of *Yellow Silk* magazine, which is the journal of erotic arts, and her definition of erotic is a very classical one. She says that the literal meaning of erotic is the opposite of thanotic. She says there is Eros and Thanatos. Thanatos is the deity of death and destruction and negative things and Eros is the deity of . . . life and light and wonderful things. . . . And she says, what's erotic is what celebrates life . . . birth and flowers blooming, law of nature . . . and so in her magazine you find a lot of natural imagery . . . and you don't find destructive relationships.

The rhetoric described above continues the argument that places erotica within the sphere of female—life-affirming, birth-motivated, "natural," and "good"—while the sexual sphere of the male is oriented toward sterility and the death of feeling as typified by the politically charged word "pornography." But it is the women creating the genre's porn businesses who argue against the "female" model, and who cynically ascribed sexually predatory motives to the men who championed the model in the public forum: "They think that more women will fuck them if they say that."

Tan offers an alternative definition that draws a distinction between the work she publishes and the rhetoric of both the eros–equals–life argument and the hydraulic model of traditional porn targeted for men:

> My definition isn't quite that strict. I am sort of interested in the dark side of things. I like cyberpunk, for example. But I don't think you need to have just one or the other. A tremendous amount of literature is death oriented or thanotic; it's destructive. Not just science fiction, I mean all Western literature. But science fiction does, I think, tend to get into . . . distopian futures and so forth, and I think that finding the erotic element within that can be challenging and fresh and new.

Tan uses Lauren Burka's story "Mate," set in a cyberpunk universe, to make her point. During the search for an industrial thief, employees are required to undergo a sort of lie detector test, where a machine is able to read their minds. The employee falls in love when the machine taps into the sexual fantasies of a man who enjoys, among other things, being tied up. The two establish a sexual relationship, which is explicitly described in the story, and which includes a cybernetic collar enabling the "mind-reader" to tap into the thoughts and fantasies of his lover at any time.

A story like "Mate" fulfills Tan's requirements on a number of levels. In the best tradition of science fiction, the technology in the story is integral not only to the plot but also to the relationship. At the same time, the relationship is "hot," the sexuality explicit, and the desires it inscribes, while not thanotic, owe little to the imagery of nature or birth. For Tan, speaking in 1992, cyberpunk offered a rich ground for exploring the erotic in science fiction:

> [C]yberpunk is one genre where there are all these dark undertones and the erotic aspect really isn't explored that much. It's sort of like, if sex happens in a cyberpunk book, usually . . . it's a rape scene or it's . . . some gang or something like that. Or it's like, in William Gibson's novel [*Neuromancer*], Molly was a prostitute, and . . . it's just sex. The real eroticism of it isn't really explored, and I felt that it should be.[9]

Tan sees this definition as distinct from the "thanotic" version of sex that much pornography presents. She uses the video industry as an example:

> [I]n a porn video there's never time to establish who the characters are, you know. All you really care about is that they get in bed . . . [in the catalogues] there's two sentence about each video . . . there'll be a one hour-video that has ten sex scenes in it, and there'll be a two-hour video that has only twelve. . . . Most people are going to go for the one that they have to watch less "junk" between, which is sad for me, because to me, especially for literature, to really be excited when the two characters get in bed together I have to know how did they get there, why are they there—I have to care about them. And in the same way, if you watched videos of total strangers getting killed, you would just be . . . disgusted, whereas you feel terrible when a character you like in a movie dies. That's when it means something to you. Sex is the same thing. You have to care what's going on.

The distinction here is not between sex as life or sex as death, but between sex as an act of hydraulic physics and sex as an act that engages the mind and the imagination and the senses. Sensual sex in text form requires, in this model, a context in which the sexual act takes place. The characters needn't know each other, but the reader must know them, or at least one character, well enough to build a basic identification. The context also requires a place, and a reason that the writer spells out as story. And, most important, sensuality, in this formulation, arises out of the imaginative play of lovers eroticizing the body and the mind and even the world around them. We are not talking about less explicit material—Tan's offerings can be quite shocking to readers who don't expect real pornographic detail—but about material that exploits the full range of writerly skills to heighten the sensual aspects of sexual engagement. By emphasizing the storytelling skills, they create a more concrete imaginary reality for the reader.

> **Cecilia Tan:**    I wanted to write something that had both the quality of what's to me good science fiction literature, you know, good characterization, plot, well written, so forth and so on, but had these sort of explicit aspects that you find usually only in really cheap, badly written porn. And then of course, people who were interested in publishing good science fiction literature usually aren't interested in seeing something so explicit, and people who are interested in seeing so explicit, they don't care if it's well written and if it's science fiction, it's too weird for them. Porn magazines don't want to have to read, you know they don't want to have to learn a new concept to get to the hot part.

Much of the work Circlet Press publishes has involved representations of sadomasochism. While Tan invites other kinds of literature, including less explicit literature, she and partner Corwin recognize that the new sexual openness in science fiction and fantasy has proven a double-edged sword. The greater acceptance of explicit literature in the genre mainstream means that their own publications can be sold and discussed openly. That very acceptance, however, makes it difficult for them as a small press to attract somewhat less explicit material that the author can publish in the larger mainstream science fiction and fantasy presses, and for considerably more money.

## Alt.Sex.Bondage [ASB]: The Party

Earlier in this chapter we talked about the sexualizing of the idea of technology as a tool for the generation of social power. But technology also operates as social mediator of the distances between people, bringing together those who share similar self-identities and not just accidents of geographical propinquity. For Cecilia Tan, the Internet has served not as sexual surrogate, but as source of community of sexual identity:

> Before I got on the computer net . . . I figured I was like the only kinky individual really in the world. . . . And so I figured that all my life I was just going to have to try and break the subject really gently to my boyfriends. It would be, like, by the way, would you mind, like, tying me up? You know,

and then I suddenly discovered there was this whole community out . . . there hundreds, thousands, millions of people out there who actually practiced these things to be able to do them right. It was like my eyes lit up. So now, I am firmly entrenched in the community . . . we sort of created our own subgroup within science fiction fandom.

While Tan recognized the existence of the national organizations of leather sado-masochistic players and activists, she preferred to contain her social identity within a group she cofounded with a few friends: NELF (New England Leather Fen):

The group coalesced out of this cross-section of science fiction fans, who all were interested in SM, all lived in Massachusetts, and who all had email. We tended to stick together when we went to events in the larger leather community because we were seen as geeks or a little weird.

Tan has since become director of a National Leather Association chapter[10]

To this point, we might view this story as the rise of techno-onanism described by Dery and Turkel. But here is where the story takes on its science fiction communal aspect.

**Tan:** At the time, alt.sex.bondage, the [Usenet] newsgroup, was about fifty messages a day and you could count on all of them being on the topic . . . this was in 1990 or so . . . There was a sense of online community in the group. So it happened that a bunch of us who were all somewhat younger (early twenties) and also into science fiction and fantasy . . . realized that that summer Gaylaxicon was going to be in Massachusetts and some of us were planning to go to it. And although we were all a little paranoid about trying to have total strangers from the Net come to our houses . . . we had few qualms about inviting them to a party at a hotel. . . . We never said it would be a play party . . . [but] not only did lots and lots of people play, we were up literally until dawn having fun.[11] It was funny, we had bought licorice whips, and they used them. It was very funny. It was like party crafts, and it was really fun, and we said, let's do this again.[12]

With Philcon we weren't quite sure what to expect but we went merrily ahead. I spray-painted fifty black clothespins and wrote on them with a silver marker "asb Philcon 91" to use as souvenirs for attendees. We had a sign-in sheet at the door where people had to read the rules before entering . . . we had closer to three hundred people go through, some just curious, of course, but many did come to finally meet people face to face that they knew through the newsgroup.[13]

And eventually some people did move into houses that were large enough that our local group started having parties by itself. And now, at cons, it's now taken off to the point that I don't even go to the parties anymore.[14]

## Finding Sexual Communities in Science Fiction

Fans who were once at the center of the sexual revolution in science fiction have moved away from the openly public Usenet alt.sex.bondage newsgroup and convention parties in favor of private e-mail lists and small, by-invitation-only gatherings at the same time that the convention parties have become more openly discussed and more disruptive. During an interview with JB described in earlier chapters, he discussed his own introduction into the ASB community, and his experience with the move to greater privacy.

> I start out in New York fandom. NYSFS, also doing the entire Bos-Wash corridor for conventions. There was a time period when I was one of the very very few people who knew the Boston fandom, who knew the New York fandom, and who knew the Washington fandom, and could introduce them to each other. And okay, it starts out there, it ends up I go to NYU because it's near NYSFS. So, at NYU I get on the Nets eventually, . . . got on a mailing list called Elbows, which is this great and lumping behemoth of a . . . mailing list that is almost exactly like Apanu. It is a mailing list for discussing anything you want to discuss. And . . . there is a strong overlap with the Boston ASB crowd. . . . And um, that was the first connection. I'd been reading it for a while, when it was first created, in fact, I seem to remember I was on the Nets and reading news when ASB was first created. . . .
>
> ASB (the Usenet newsgroup alt.sex.bondage, now replaced, more or less, by soc.subculture.bondage-bdsm) as a whole has gotten too large, and there is a Baltimore area, or Baltimore-Washington mailing list, called LMNOP, just referring to the alphabet soup that usually comes of these things when referring to it, and they're having a party, which also involves, you know, LMNOP and anyone who happens to know them, which is again . . . segments of the same large social group.

Reference to the same social group led me back to the original point of the interview. JB had entered into his fan community between the ages of twelve and fifteen, joining his fan community in geographic proximity for college. Given the open, apprentice-style environment of the science fiction community, I experienced my first twinge of real concern about the science fiction experience for young teens. I remembered seeing JB at around fifteen, with his New York friends at conventions, and he had seemed to elicit a high degree of protectiveness from these friends. Still, I had to ask:

**Ethnographer:**   When did you get involved in it? About how old were you?

**JB:**   That was probably . . . around '89 or so, which is not that long ago, but . . . I know a lot of people who, it turns out, have been doing this forever, you know, since stones were soft.

**Ethnographer:**   Did you know the people in your social group were involved until you got involved yourself?

**JB:**   Well, with the NYSFS crowd, no. There are a couple people there who I find are involved with the Eulenspiegel Society, the big, New York mainstream kinky people's group, who—I never knew it until . . . they showed up at an ASB party. However, looking back on it, having known these people for years, the only assumption is, they had to have been . . . I did not know it for those in NYSFS who I now know to be into it. For a large part of the greater Elbows cohort, yeah, I had a pretty good idea.

**Ethnographer:**   Then they didn't go out and recruit teenaged boys?

**JB:**   No, there was never anything like recruiting. . . . At the Lunacon party, they were going for photo IDs, for, you know, over eighteen, being very paranoid about that. There was a lot of paranoia about not getting in trouble for recruiting.

The New York fan group clearly took its responsibilities to the younger members of the community seriously, protecting JB and other minors from the complex sexual politics of the group. The effect that the presence in fandom of sadomasochism—as a social movement as well as sexual practice—may have on young fans during the formative years of sexual awareness is more problematic to determine for a number of reasons.

The ASB parties and social life seem to attract three distinct sets of participants. First are those who are interested in science fiction who also have a sexual orientation that involves role playing in sadomasochistic scenarios with some degree of real pain or captivity. For community members whose primary sexual formation includes a strong need for some sort of sadomasochistic pleasure, the opening up of discussion and community-based practice provides a haven where they can feel psychologically safe. In the context of parties in which strong safety rules are put in place and discussed in open debate, safety extends to sexual practice.

For another group of participants, those drawn by the sexual practice and the connection of the Internet, sex-play parties at science fiction conventions provide a convenient venue while disrupting the development of science fiction community life. For a number of years between 1991 and 1997, some nonfan members of the larger sadomasochistic community dominated parties at some convention venues, occasionally creating difficulties for the conventions and the hotels. This group have substantially abandoned the science fiction venue, according to Cecilia Tan, because they find science fiction fans too weird (note, this use of the term "weird" refers not to sexual practices but to community life in general, based as it is on fantastic literature).[15]

A third group could be considered sexual tourists, passing through for the excitement of having seen it, and the privilege of telling the story. This group represents the science fiction equivalent of the "trendoids":

**JB:**   It's fashionable, hip and trendy at this particularly time. *Spin* magazine . . . had a last page article on how S&M has become hot and fashionable and trendy.

While sadomasochistic sex play has been trendy since the early '90s, some sexual experimentation, including heterosexual polyamory, has been part of the fringes of science fiction culture since the '60s, when many sexually adventurous participants in the counterculture as well as in fandom were looking for alternative ways of constructing families and relationships in a freer sexual atmosphere. Interest in multiple-partner relationships continued in some sectors of the science fiction community while it went underground in the wider culture, which had grown more conservative through the '70s and '80s. In the late '90s, however, polyamory, a sort of compromise between the free love of the '60s—now considered dangerous due to HIV and other sexually transmitted diseases—and the rigid stricture of monogamy, has once again become a part of the popular consciousness of edge culture, as JB discussed in 1999:

> Polyamory, as it was dubbed three to five years ago, is an important part of my life, and has strong fannish linkage. There was an article in *Jane* four to six months ago, also an article in the *Boston Phoenix*, and an episode of MTV's *Sex in the 90's*. Almost anyone interviewed from the Boston area in any of those has some minor linkage, at least, to fandom, including yours truly.[16]

Whether engaging in sex based on the concepts of free love brought to the fore in the '60s, or in polyamorous or sadomasochistic or gay sex, for too long participants felt themselves to be protected from sexually transmitted diseases by virtue of their cultural integrity: as long as members engaged in sexual activity only with other members, diseases from outside the community could not penetrate the charmed circle.

> **Ethnographer:**   I can remember hearing a few years back, "We don't have to worry about it, because we stay within our group—and that kind of thinking—has that changed?
>
> **JB:**   Comme ci, comme ca. Half and half. It is still largely the case. I mean, I have heard . . . there is the presence of herpes—then again, what's the figure? . . . that's just endemic. It's almost impossible to avoid, no matter what you do, one form or the other. Umm, I have not heard of a single AIDs case, there may be some.
>
> **Ethnographer:**   Well, in gay fandom, they're dying.
>
> **JB:**   Yeah. One person who's very involved with New Jersey gay and lesbian rights—gay and lesbian and bisexual rights actually, since he's one of the most rabid bisexuals I've ever met—and various parties that he holds, or that he and his housemates hold, sometimes have been known to start with Safe(er) Sex workshops. People have a clue. People have a significant clue. I know, there are risks. There are risks to life.[17]

More recently, JB adds a note:

> Safe(r) sex remains more visible in fandom than in the general population, I think, though there are always stupid people and smart people doing stupid things. As well, most of my peers are older and more settled now and either (a) have settled down monogamously, (b) just don't have the time/energy to be as active as they were, (c) Hm. I'm not sure. There was a 3d option . . . [Polyamory][18]

## Conclusion

Sexual life in science fiction fandom, like sexual life outside it, is fraught with internal inconsistencies. Although the chair of the 1993 Gaylaxicon had recently died, leaving the community without a convention, without a beloved member, and although other members of that same community grappled with irrefutable presence of the disease in its midst, heterosexual participants in the sexually adventurous subcommunity continued with a stated position that disease could not penetrate their own groups. But we cannot overlook the significance of the growth of sadomasochistic sex play in the context of a growing fear, conscious or unconscious, of incurable diseases transmitted most often by genital sexual contact. When I first looked at science fiction culture, in the early 1980s, sexual experimentation in science fiction communities seemed to replicate those multipartner family chains represented in some of the fiction of the '60s, most notably Heinlein's *Stranger in a Strange Land*. By the '90s, sexual experimentation seemed to center around the growing ASB community conducted online and at ASB parties in homes and at conventions. While some of the more extreme practitioners might include genital or blood contact with people who were not their regular partner, most sadomasochistic play, particularly among the "trendoids" and "sexual tourists," may speak to the deeper issue in contemporary society both within and without the science fiction community: that of finding sexual satisfaction with a partner in an age when the more traditional forms of sexual contact have become potentially deadly to nonpaired sexually active adults. For many, sexual fantasy replaces sexual intimacy, and the violence represented by the play vents the very real frustration of thwarted drives. In this context, those who began the ASB movement in the science fiction community—participants for whom sadomasochistic sex play is part of their basic sexual makeup—have withdrawn into their own smaller groups, conducting their sex lives within their smaller community of science fiction fans with a serious interest in sadomasochism outside the convention scene, which has become, socially, a more volatile mix of proxy risk-taking that hides a real fear of sexual intimacy.

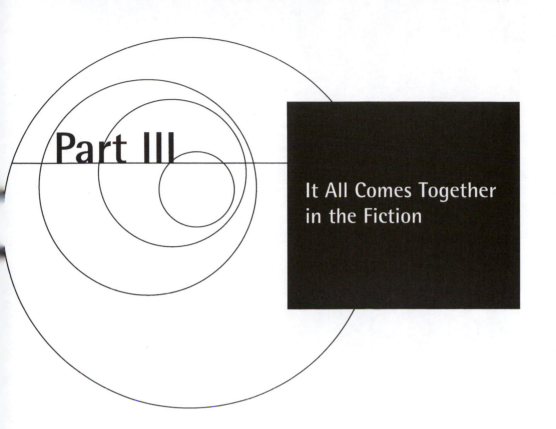

# Part III

## It All Comes Together in the Fiction

In the last issue of *Cheap Truth*, the underground criticism zine of the cyberpunks, author Bruce Sterling, writing as science fiction fan Vincent Omniaveritas, restated the ethos of the science fiction community about the role of criticism in the community: "The whole point of *Cheap Truth* was that anyone can do it. All you need is something to say, and a Xerox. You don't need a clique or a bankroll or PR flacks."[1] But there is more at stake here than just criticizing the cultural production of the industry; Omniaveritas and his happy band of pseudonymous rebels went *beyond* criticism in support of the aesthetic they approved. In their positions as novelists and short-story writers, they created the change they advocated in the field in which they worked. In doing so they found themselves laden with a brand name for their aesthetic—"cyberpunk"—and the credit/blame for moving the genre a notch up the literary scale through a macho revisioning of the computer nerd.[2]

It may seem a simpler thing to take the position of fan when one has already attained the position of writer than to take the position of industry-empowered author when one is a fan. But in the science fiction community, pretty much everyone starts out as a fan, and few relinquish the consumer position just to accept a new role in the field of cultural production. Sterling was a fan aspiring to be a professional writer before he made his reputation as one of the founders of cyberpunk, and he continues to be a fan today.

As we read through Parts I and II of this volume, we may become so enamored with the struggles of the diverse members of the fan community to bring together the reality of fandom that we can overlook the point of the exercise. In *Cheap Truth*, however, Bruce Sterling reminds us what it is all about: power in this community resides in the fiction. Some fans make for the community a conceptual geography, which they template on the landscape in the many science fiction conventions held around the world, and on the cyberscape of the Usenet, e-mail lists, and commercial online services where virtual life is played out not in the icons of cyberpunk, but in the words that were always the core of science fiction fandom. Their purpose, however, remains one of making a home for the creators as well as the appreciators of the genres of science fiction, fantasy, and horror, who are all drawn from the same group of people. Jim Baen, owner and publisher of Baen Books, described the quintessential writer of science fiction as the physicist who "read these stories as a hobby for about fifteen years, and sat back, and said . . . 'I can do better than that, and I have something to say.'"[3] Baen is talking about real scientist-writers like Gregory Benford, who wrote letters to the editors of fanzines as a teenager, long before he made his reputation as a prize-winning author or as a physicist.

When new groups enter into the community, they make themselves felt. They struggle for power—not only for a place on the geography of the fan community, but also for a place in the literature, just as Bruce Sterling and Gregory Benford and hundreds more authors and editors and critics did before them. And as we have seen in Chapter 6, and will see again, women and gays and a new generation of fans with their own tastes and preferences have taken their place not only in fandom, but in the industry. The changing fandoms demand their own voice in the genres, and their members take their places in the industry to provide the products their members want to see. So, in this final section, we examine this goal, this purpose of the community, to see how it works. The question we answer here is not "what does this have to do with fandom?" but "what is this fandom about?" It is about the production of a genre industry by and for the community of fans, which extends its influence well beyond this smaller community to influence the world at large. As we have said before, cyberspace existed as a technological goal decades before William Gibson popularized the term, but it was the fiction that provided the language by which cyberspace became a part of the world landscape. It was the publishing industry to which the first early fans flocked, it was an industry science fiction fans built, and it is an industry science fiction fans still dominate at the creative levels.

As we will see, however, it is also an industry long threatened by conglomeration practices that increasingly move the creative decisions into the hands of corporate executives with no connections to the genres either as fiction or as community. While small presses flourish in the community around the industry, they are ill equipped to do the job of the mass market in bringing the fiction of the possible and the impossible to the wider public.

And ultimately, as is proper, we come to the fiction. After decades of change on the inside of the community's shifting corporate identities, this is what it has all been for. The final chapter answers the question: out of all the struggling for power between outside forces and the community and the larger buying public that counts itself as fans, but not as members of the fan community in which it all began, what fiction wins in the marketplace and in the literary perception of the readers?

# From Fan to Pro: Getting Published 10

Sociologists Howard Becker and Pierre Bourdieu warn us that the traditional model of literary and art criticism that decontextualizes the artist and then examines the work as the creation of the individual genius is not, and has never been, valid. Rather, writers and artists work in social groups, which Becker calls "art worlds" and Bourdieu calls "fields of cultural production."[1] Becker demonstrates how the "artist" relies on the support structures of the art world, while Bourdieu argues that power arises through the struggle for position in relation to other positions within the power/production matrix. In the art worlds they describe, however, neither scholar visualizes the kind of merging of roles that takes place in the unique world of science fiction culture production.

Both Becker and Bourdieu describe art cultures formed primarily in adulthood through education and training. Within these art cultures one finds those trained as consumers and those trained in specific craft tasks that support the creation of the work, such as paint making or bookbinding, and those trained in the writing or the painting or other art form. Bourdieu claims that, in the struggle for position, the winner gains the power to define what tasks will be considered those of the writer or artist, but this theory seems quite similar to Becker's notion that the skills and tasks related to creation of a work of art may shift from categories of support to categories of art over time, based on the valuation consumers and critics place on specific tasks in their time. As Becker described, at one time artists made their own paints, and the value of the painting was primarily in the cost of the materials; now the value is primarily in the vision of the artist.

Both arguments can give us valuable insight into science fiction culture, and Bourdieu in particular makes overt the relationship between the struggle for position in the field and the power of the positioning as it arises in relation to other positions.[2] Each, however, seems to assume a division between the world of the consumer and the world that contributes to the production of the art. The production of science fiction, however, is marked by a blurring of all boundaries—those within the community and those that mark what Bourdieu calls the field of economic power. This blurring of boundaries occurs because the science fiction community includes both the field of production and a large segment of the field of consumption, and because participants in both fields—production and consumption—have a marked tendency to shift roles and take multiple positions that makes it difficult to determine where power lies within the community and what any part of the community's relationship to the field of power may be.

Writers in science fiction can move so fluidly through their various fields of production and power because they, like almost everyone at every level of science fiction production, start in the "field" of consumer, and do so at a very young age. Each passes through a period, usually in the early teens, of omnivorous reading.[3] With perhaps two exceptions, everyone interviewed for this book began reading science fiction avidly sometime between learning to read at four or five and nearing puberty around age thirteen. Let me make this clear: I do *not* mean that I selected from all the interviews those who started to read science fiction at an early age. I *do* mean that, with the exception of two or three people who began reading in college, all those interviewed for this book, including every industry worker, whether they appear in the book or not, were reading science fiction avidly by the time they were fourteen years of age.

The intensive training for the arts that other fields of cultural production initiate at the university level begins here in the teens and continues pretty much throughout the lifetime of the participant, who may choose to remain a fan or to enter the world of the professional at any level of the industry.

That is not to say that every fan who tries to write a book for publication or find a job with a science fiction publisher will succeed. Rather, those who do succeed will, in most cases, come out of the pool of hopefuls who established themselves as avid readers of the genre by their teens. For that reason, most industry hopefuls are encouraged to attend conventions, where they may make the social connections they will need to move into the business. For the same reason, science fiction publishing houses have continued the practice of reading unsolicited and unagented manuscripts received "over the transom." As Peter Heck, former editor at Ace Books and now author of three alternate history mysteries, explained, "In science fiction, one of the true facts is that every publisher in the business is reading the unsolicited manuscripts, because that's where the new talent comes from."[4] In that tradition, we will follow a book from transom to bedside table.

## Over the Transom and into Production[5]

Publishing in science fiction and fantasy has become increasingly difficult for a first-time author because so many fans—not only those involved in fandom but also those who read the books voraciously but do not engage in the community activities associated with fandom—act on their "I can do that" impulse and try to break into print. According to Heck, a book comes to a publisher as either an agented or an unagented submission. The agent has already made an evaluation and determined that the manuscript meets industry standards, so the agented book will receive faster attention from someone "a little bit higher up in the chain."[6] Not all agented submissions are handled equally, of course. A best-selling author shopping around for a new publisher will receive attention that a first-time author will not, and a friend of the publisher will likewise receive attention from fairly high in the editorial chain and with more speed than will an unknown.

Few agents are willing to accept a first-time writer as a client but, as Heck asserts, most publishers still review unagented manuscripts, called "slush" in the industry, looking for the rare jewel of a manuscript that will help to secure the next generation of science fiction/fantasy publishing. Some publishers farm out the "slush pile" to freelance readers, while others assign the reading of slush to the lowest members of the organization's editorial hierarchy. Josepha Sherman, a fantasy and science fiction author and freelance editor who has read slush and acquired new authors for various houses, describes a typical situation:

> **Josepha Sherman:** In a year we get about eight to ten thousand. They may be full manuscripts, they may be partials, they may be queries. We get a lot. Every house does. That's one of the reasons things get so backlogged.[7]

Clearly no company can afford to read so many questionable manuscripts; they would never have time to work on the books they publish. In fact, Sherman admitted that eliminating the worst of the lot takes very little time at all:

> Sometimes you don't have to read more than a paragraph. But the really bad ones are easy, because you know right off, the person can't write English, or is loony tunes. When it starts off as "imagine yourself as a sentient ice cream cone," you know you're not going to want it.

Like the really bad book, a really good book is easy to spot:

> **Ethnographer:** How long does it take to know when somebody has the spark?
>
> **Sherman:** Page one, sometimes . . . right from the first page I was grabbed. And that's happened a few times, but it's rare that it's that good.

The majority of submissions, books that appear to be mediocre in the first chapter, take longer to evoke a decisive response. According to Sherman, manuscripts targeted for rejection slips may receive only the most cursory of readings, sometimes as little as two chapters.

> When it's mediocre it's more difficult because you have to read more of it. It's not bad enough to reject out of hand, not good enough to rave about, and those takes the longest. . . . About 90 percent of what comes in is just plain mediocre. . . . People who just don't have the spark. . . . It just doesn't come to life. The characters are flat, the stories are hackneyed.

According to Sherman, the most common of the mediocre submissions are rewrites of role playing games and books based on *Star Trek*, but with the names changed.

During a group discussion with several editors at Tor Books, I asked whether they had a special formula for determining which books had the spark Sherman mentioned. At first the editors denied that they had any yardstick but experience and intuition, but then Patrick Nielsen Hayden suggested:

> I do a kind of internal transactional analysis. . . . If I am seriously
> considering something, it's gotten past the initial phases of "is this book
> written in complete sentences" and that sort of thing, . . . I have an internal
> dialogue with my sixteen-year-old self. How does it feel? What kind of time
> is my sixteen-year-old self having?
>
> Sixteen is not the median age of the science fiction readers anymore,
> but I think the sixteen-year-old self is nevertheless doing a lot of the reading
> that adults are doing. [Laughs] . . . When we are thirty years old and reading
> science fiction, it's our adolescent self doing it.[8]

Nielsen Hayden's wife and fellow-editor Teresa Nielsen Hayden, commenting on
that sixteen-year-old self, added, "It's a pretty embarrassing person to have inside of
you; it has no taste and no cool," but the capacity to tap into the "sixteen-year-old
self" while simultaneously reading as a critic seems to characterize most of the
successful editors in the genre.

Once the editor has decided he wants to acquire a book for his company, he
still has some roadblocks to overcome. I asked former Ace editor Peter Heck, "How
much freedom does the editor have to say, 'I'm going to run with this book'?"

> **Peter Heck:**    This depends on a number of things, one of the most important
> of which is the seniority of the editor in house. If someone has been there for
> a while, has been associated with a number of successful books, and has . . .
> established a reputation as 'here's somebody who can pick them,' then the
> publishers and the people on the next level up . . . will say, "So and so seems to
> have an eye for funny fantasy, and if she thinks that the fans will like this we'll
> go with it." . . . Somebody less senior, somebody who hasn't built up that kind
> of clout, has less opportunity. . . .
>
> Once an acquiring editor is convinced that this is a project you want to
> go with, then you've got to go to somebody a step up. At Ace it was the editor
> in chief, Susan Allison, who had, for all practical purposes, on books at a
> medium level, the final say: yes we're going to do this and are going to offer X
> thousand dollars for this.[9]

For a book with an asking price above a certain level, determined by the standards
of the house and the reputation of the editor, the editor in chief may have to approach the publisher, who may confirm or reject the editor's judgment on the offer,
or may suggest a lesser offer. For most first novels, however, the standard offering
price ranges between $2,000 and $6,000, depending on whether the book is a
media tie-in or an original novel, and the popularity the editor can hope to nurture
for the work of the new author. The "offer" refers to the advance on royalties, a
percentage of each book sold, that the author receives in advance. At this point,
many industry professionals suggest that the over-the-transom author engage an
agent familiar with the genre to negotiate the terms of the contract.

> **Heck:**    One of the things an agent does is serve as an interface between the
> editor and the author in this negotiating process, and to some extent defuse
> some of the rancor that might otherwise come if you were banging somebody
> down half a percentage point on the royalties or a couple of thousand dollars

on the advance. . . . Then it goes to contract, where all the things that you have negotiated are spelled out. The author has some opportunities to change things around at this point, although a new author has less clout in this than an established author.

At this point, the author will receive the first half of the advance agreed upon in the contract. Then:

> **Heck:** You decide when you are going to publish it. Typically you do this with the knowledge that it's something like a year from finished manuscript to final book, and a lot of the decisions made at this point depend on what state the manuscript you've got is in.[10] . . . You decide whether you can publish it pretty much as is, or whether you want some revisions. And, very often, a revisions letter is the way that's handled. You'll write anywhere from a three-to five page letter, sometimes longer than that . . . telling the author these are the kinds of things I think you should fix up in the plot. . . .
>
> [T]he editor may say, I think you should lose the stupid uncle in the third chapter, and the author may say, No, that character is really important, and here's why, and the author can win that argument. But this is the point of back and forth.[11]

The issue of editing manuscripts has become a contentious topic in the industry. In the past, industry lore has it, the job of an editor was to edit—to find a book with potential, work with the author to hone that book into the masterpiece it could be, and support the author through the process of publication. Now, however, each editor is responsible for so many tasks in the process, and for so many manuscripts to be reviewed, that the job of editing often takes place on the editor's own time rather than on the job per se. High-profile authors resist anyone else tampering with their prose, and new authors may not have the skill to turn the promising manuscript into the publishable book the editor anticipated. Above all, the quantity of available product that reaches at least the minimum standards of mediocrity is staggering. In this context, some publishers are making the decision that they will not edit:

> **Jim Baen:** It's been my experience that editors of that sort do as much harm as good. . . . It's also the most time-consuming thing we attempt to do. So in general, if the person were not sending a book I want to publish, I don't publish it. Occasionally [we will make suggestions, but] . . . we take a fairly strong position, that "thou shalt not edit. The author gets to publish the book she wrote.[12]

My own experience with Sheila Gilbert at DAW, who does edit the manuscripts she acquires, has been positive; however, I have also received comments from editors with whom I chose not to work that support Jim Baen's position that the process can do more harm than good. The issue, like many in the culture industry, rests on the specific perceptions of who holds what power and what constitutes a profitable use of that power. In an industry where approximately 90 percent of the product loses money, the "five-hundred-pound gorilla" best-selling author holds all the power, and none of the restrictions discussed in this chapter apply. The first time author with a manuscript that needs a lot of work may receive repeated rejections from editors who are unwilling to invest editing time without sufficient evidence that the results will prove financially worthwhile in the marketplace.

Between the two extremes fall the books received from the publisher's stable of authors under contract for a specified number of books or for a specific proposed book. How much editing a manuscript requires will depend on its condition when the editor receives the finished book. As Beth Meacham at Tor Books explained:

> You talk to a writer, or you read a proposal, and you . . . figure out what's right about it, what's wrong about it. . . . You work with the writer if it needs it at that stage to make the plot structure strong. And then some writers deliver their books a chapter at a time, other people send them in all at once, when they're done. Some writers send me their books first draft, other people wait until they're at fourth or fifth draft. You know, that's a very individualistic thing. Then I read. Then I read it again. Sometimes I read it a third time. And I make notes and think about it, and figure out what I like and what I don't like, if there are things that I don't like, and what's missing and what needs to be made stronger and what needs to be taken out.
>
> I spend a lot of time talking to my writers about what it is they really want to do with this book, because I like to know what they intend before I start giving suggestions for what they can do to fix it. Because I may be . . . telling them to do perfectly valid things but that will make it a totally different book from what they intended, and that's no good. That's not useful. . . . Then I usually will send the writer back the manuscript with notes on it, you know, marginal notes, little "rewrite this sentence," "change this," "you mean this word" stuff, and also a long letter detailing any greater structural problems or missing chapters or misdirected stuff, you know. The average editorial letter will run about seven to ten pages. And then they work from that. They will call me up and say, what did you mean by this, what did you mean by that. And they'll work from that to do a revised manuscript[13]

Tom Doherty, founder and publisher at Tor, explained the philosophy that guides this expenditure of editorial time that other publishers might see as excessive, or even oppressive:

**Tom Doherty:**    You just can't have something that is as good as what was published last year. You've got to have excellence. . . . But you've got a big problem with that. People don't [always] work at the same level. And yet, you also have the necessity to nourish authors. Not every book that Mark Twain wrote was at the level of *Huck Finn*. *Pudd'nhead Wilson* just isn't there, you know? Well, if you take the next step down from Mark Twain, you have authors who are deserving of important consideration, whose books you want to publish. And they give you a book that's not so good. What do you do with it? Do you say, "Hey, you worked all year. Tough luck, old buddy, we're not going to pay you anything this year. Go away, try again next year"? I don't think so. You publish the book. You publish it because of the body of the author's work, because he deserves this kind of consideration.

At Tor, the author has two standards to meet: his own and the excellence that Tom Doherty demands. Between the two stands the editor, because, according to Doherty,

> The problem with the so-so book is that it doesn't bring you more readers. People may put up with it, it doesn't build the field. . . . We understand that this is going to happen, . . . And this is the constant challenge. How do you publish certain books that you probably wouldn't publish if it weren't for the author? How do you publish the good books that the authors write? How do you find new wonderful things when you know first novels aren't read.

As we have seen, the wonderful first novel will find a home, and the well-constructed denizen of a niche may need little interference to prosper. But the books that need to be nurtured to reach their potential may rise or fall based on the editorial philosophy of the publisher as it is acted on by the editors. This same philosophy may extend to the next step of the process, the line edit that follows receipt of the revised manuscript.Early in my study line edits, the process whereby the line editor reviewed the manuscript sentence by sentence, revising for style and clarity, were considered a separate function and performed by a lower-level editorial staff member, but today responsibility for the line edit in some houses has pretty much disappeared into the copyedit phase. Where line editing continues as a separate function, it may be performed by the acquiring editor.

> **Beth Meacham:** I'll line-edit the revised manuscript, which again goes back to the writer for approval, because I don't pretend to know exactly what they meant at every time. . . . And then I'll get that back, as a final, finished manuscript, at which point it goes into production. And I'm done with it, pretty much, in terms of handling the actual text.

For the author, the most important step at this phase is the formal acceptance of the manuscript.

> **Peter Heck:** Eventually, the manuscript is in a finished form, and you get what's called the delivery and acceptance. There's often a payment to the author at that point . . . and in some cases, there's a payment on publication. Then the book goes out to a copyeditor.

## Even Copyeditors . . .

When a book reaches the copyedit stage, issues of content and structure have been negotiated and revised as agreed between the editor and the author. The copyedit should catch typographical errors, grammatical errors, and the details of proper name spelling and the occasional incomprehensible sentence. Some copyeditors, exerting the power of their own taste culture over the product, take a much broader approach to the job that comes closer to a line edit than a copyedit. Publishers usually farm out their copyediting, and often their proofreading, to a stable of freelancers working within the industry. With an hourly pay scale ranging between $10 and $18, copyediting and proofreading stand at the low end of the industry food chain—just above new authors. Freelancers generally fall into one of two categories: those breaking into the creative areas of editing and design, for whom freelance copyediting serves as entry level in the industry, and those with a love of the books who do not have the ambition or the talent for the more creative fields. While many of the top editors in the field had their beginning in copyediting, the skills required of a copyeditor often work against success in a less detail-conscious environment, and one often hears complaints about the "tin ear" of some copyeditors, as Peter Heck commented: "Copyeditors have the bad reputation of being humorless people who don't see the big picture and this is a slander, but it's not entirely untrue."

When I was looking for a copyeditor to interview for this book, many editors and even some authors referred me to Robert LeGault. Typically authors do not know who their copyeditor or proofreader is, but LeGault pointed out that authors with a preference could and do request a specific copyeditor, often from the small pool of freelancers known as fans of the genre within the science fiction/fantasy community. LeGault has been a science fiction reader since he was young and living in Washington, D.C. He attended his first Worldcon at the age of thirteen, but otherwise did not participate in the fan community until he met Teresa Nielsen Hayden in Seattle. Ultimately, both the Nielsen Haydens and LeGault ended up in New York, where LeGault worked in production for Tor Books and later for other science fiction and rock music publications. Currently, he prefers the freedom freelance work gives him, but occasionally he takes production jobs for specific projects.[14] He agrees with Heck's assessment of some copyeditors, and explains the importance to the book that the copyeditor or proofreader be a long-time reader of the genres:

> **Robert LeGault:**    Sometimes I'm tempted to say sf is fiction in which the author makes up funny compound words and contractions. That's a joke, but odd style is a very big part of a lot of science fiction writing, and some people just don't get it. And that's one reason that if I see a book by someone like Greg Bear, you know, that's doing a lot of experimental things with language, that I get what he's doing. . . .
>
> The best one I ever saw, somebody referred to a Moebius strip in some book, and the copyeditor wrote, "What's this, I don't understand," and I'm like, "That's not too obscure . . ." And so, if they don't understand that, a bad copyeditor can really mess up a book that way, by trying to standardize it. . . . this is what we call tin ear. They'll do it, but it'll like, be, "Well, the *Chicago Manual [of Style]* says that you shouldn't have a hyphen here." Or as we say, "The passive voice is to be avoided." . . .
>
> And some authors will say, "What the hell are you doing?" And others are really intimidated by it, and they'll go, "Oh, oh, I can't do that?" They don't understand that they can talk back to this stuff. So I've seen some bad examples of people that really, you know, were trying to do something a little

out there and original and they just sort of got stomped on by their copyeditor and didn't fight back.

According to Peter Heck, the editor is the first line of defense should a copyeditor prove to have a "tin ear."

> [The] book comes back from the copyeditor. . . . A good editor will read the copyedited manuscript when it comes in and will do a lot of erasing and a lot of pulling off of stickums, changes back the dumb things that the copyeditor did to the things that are right.

Some authors have the right to review and reject copyedits to their manuscript, but time constraints in the production process often make this impossible.

## Designing for the Marketplace

While the book is out for copyedit, the production design is worked out. The single most important aspect of design is the cover, which, for a good first book, may cost the publisher more than the book did, as Tom Doherty explained:

> Each book cover is a small billboard. After recommendation of friend or relative, the next 24 percent [of book buyers] buy it because of the package. They like what they see. If you put this small billboard in a hundred thousand supermarkets, you will sell a certain number of books. Now, you will get a lot of returns, but we're trying to build for the future. We try to put this small billboard, this cover, in front of hundreds of thousands of people knowing that for every hundred thousand we ship to the non-bookstore market we can expect to sell 40 percent. In the bookstores we do much better; we can expect to sell 65 percent. It's the heart of our market and deserves serious attention, but in a way it is like preaching to the choir. The supermarket, the airport, the hotel newsstand, and the drugstore are our outreach. They bring us new readers. If they are satisfied well enough, they become regular readers and often bookstore buyers.[15]

The new buyers brought to a particular book by an attractive cover, publishers hope, will like the book and spread word of mouth about it. The author's next effort will cycle through the process more quickly, selling to old buyers who buy based on the name, to new buyers influenced by the first group, and to new buyers influenced by the cover.

At Ace a committee decides what the book design will look like.

> **Peter Heck:** Decisions like that are made in the cover conference, which at Ace was sort of a joint meeting of the art department, the editorial department, and the copy department all at once, and ideas were sort of blue-skied among all three of these. . . . Sometimes the cover image is perfectly obvious. If the title of the book is *The Silver Horse*, let's get a silver horse on it. At other times, there is a lot of give and take, and sometimes you'll even say, have the artist do two or three sketches and let's see. . . . You decide what approach the copywriter who is going to write the blurb on the back of the book should take.[16]

After the decision to buy the book, the choice of cover is the most important. The billboard can only succeed if it advertises the product you are selling, and the wrong cover can prove disastrous as former chain-store buyer Stephen Pagel pointed out:

> I have actually discussed covers with publishers, and come back and said, "We caught it early enough, and we are going to make some changes in the cover." 'Cause, sometimes I think they accidentally mismarket the book. . . . I had a hard technical [sf] book come in. And I go, "You have a unicorn and some flowers on the cover of the book. It does not say technical novel to me." And then what happens is, the fantasy person says, "Unicorn and flowers," picks it up, flips the book over, and reads "bioengineering, and I have no idea what they are talking about," and they put the book down. Your technical person will never even pick up the book to begin with.[17]

This kind of expensive mistake happened with the paperback cover for Connie Willis's *Doomsday Book*,[18] a Bantam Spectra publication, which showed a knight on a horse and a lady with a jeweled fillet on her brow. The cover gave the erroneous impression that the book was an historical fantasy romance, but the book had its basis in science fiction time travel, not fantasy, and had no romance at all. As Pagel predicts, its intended readers never picked up the book, while those readers who did buy it passed negative, rather than positive, word of mouth. If *Doomsday Book* had been the first novel of a new author, the book would have gone down in the computer records as just another failure. But Connie Willis had a reputation and an audience and the book had already succeeded in hardcover. Most important, the company had a greater financial stake in the success of *Doomsday Book* than they have in the first book of most new authors. So they recalled the first printing and replaced the cover.[19]

Who chooses the cover art varies from publishing house to publishing house, but one rule of thumb seems to prevail: the more corporate the house, the less control the acquiring editor has in marketing decisions such as choice of cover art. Small independent houses like DAW or Baen Books don't use an art department; the publishers make the art decisions as the editor or in conjunction with the editor.[20] Tor has an art director, but its editors may choose art for their covers independently:

> **Meacham:**   One of the interesting things about Tor, one of the things that I've always loved about the house, is that it's the book's editor at Tor who figures out what goes on the cover, sometimes even commissions the cover art—I usually commission my own cover art. . . . It's one of the hardest parts of the job for me, because I am not by nature a visual artist. . . . We have an art director who's, she's brilliant. And she's always there to bounce ideas off of, or to take over if you come up a complete blank, which happens, but I get involved in every stage.[21]

In the late 1990s, the cover art for some genre books has been changing dramatically. Some bookstore buyers and in-store promotion staff have complained that covers that too literally identify the science fictional or fantastic elements of the genres make it difficult to cross a potential breakout book into general fiction, so some companies have taken to using less genre-specific art and even less recognizably figurative art on some of their covers. A more general cover art can backfire, however, and readers who might be drawn to the book as a genre offering may not identify it as such. In either case, artists, like everyone else involved in the production of science fiction culture, are chosen from a pool of talent working and showing in the community, and often participating in the convention culture and as members of ASFA, the Association of Science Fiction Artists.[22]

## Selling the Book

While the copyedited/decopyedited manuscript moves on to typesetting, the editor shifts attention to the sales force. At Berkley, according to long-time editor Ginjer Buchanan, "Marketing comes out of a synergy between sales and the promotion/advertising/publicity department,"[23] rather than out of a separate marketing department. Below, Peter Heck takes us through an fictitious example, *Planet of the Worm People*, by Joe Trufan:

> There will be several meetings in which the book is presented to the sales force. One is simply a very quick run-through: "Let's see, *Planet of the Worm People*. This is a new space adventure that we've gotten and we have very high hopes for this new author," and they move on to the next. And very often the sales people will say next to nothing at this point. They'll just note down the list and a brief description.
>
> There will be another meeting where you come in with a fuller, stronger description. You'll often have a preliminary cover at this point to show them. You'll say you have really high expectations for *Planet of the Worm People*, and we've got a really nifty cover, and this author is very well connected in the Minneapolis area so we think we can get a lot of books out there, which has a very strong community, and you start trying to market the book. The marketing process really starts to get intense, because the sales people are the first really nonfans and, in most cases, nonreaders that you are going to present the book to. And they are going to look at it basically in terms of the cover and the package. And your enthusiasm and your feeling for the book can make a big difference at this point.

The editor's enthusiasm can sometimes influence the print run, or number of books to be printed—the next make-or-break decision for a book—which is generally determined by the sales force based on prior experience with other books more often than a feel for the particular book under discussion. This is the one place where the reader/fan/industry link is most likely to break. The sales force, of course, is not always composed of nonreaders. Tom Doherty, founder of Tor Books, started in sales, and he recognizes the conflict that can arise between the creative side and the sales side:

> Mostly, editors have only a general idea of what's done to market books . . . the sales forces all think, "We're really great, we work so hard, and we're so good at marketing. If only the books were better we'd have all these best-

sellers." And editors all think, "We do these great books, if only we had a halfway decent marketing effort, we'd have all these best-sellers." Well, the truth is somewhere between. I used to make my editors sit with my sales people so they couldn't talk like this about each other. They were all mixed up. We didn't have a different floor for editorial, and a different floor for sales.

Miscalculations about the potential popularity of a given title can happen at any point in the process; often, however, errors occur when the nonreader enters the picture:

> **Heck:**   We just had a book, one of my books, which was a book that we had a very strong feeling for. We bought it because the people in the sales department had said buy more cyberpunk books. This stuff seems to be working.. . . . So, hey, we bought a cyberpunk book, and . . . the manuscript came in really clean and we thought that it was a great book. And we got what we thought was a really good cover on it. And we took it to the sales people. And they came back with what we thought was a ridiculously low print run . . . nobody likes the cover, nobody understands what this book is about. Well, really ridiculous print run goes out to the stores and sells out instantly. And we go back to print. And the sales chief comes down to the editor in chief and says, "Gee, this book . . . jumped out of the stores. I don't understand why this happened." And Susan [Allison] looked at him and said, "Well, you told us to buy more cyberpunks. That's a cyberpunk." He said, "Oh."

As Tom Doherty points out with typical bluntness, publishing is a crap shoot. Eighty percent of all new books by new authors are likely to fail, and even success is relative:

> You've got an industry paperback working with about a 40% sale, . . . producing ten books to sell four, I mean, that's with known authors. In a first novel, you can probably expect double the returns. . . . So now you've got to ship ten books to sell two, instead of ten to sell four. Well, you know, if four out of five books made are going to be scrap, it's hugely costly.

Some publishers have traditionally experienced a better sell-through, the percentage of books shipped that actually sell. Jim Baen claims a 70 percent sell-through by printing fewer copies of each title and distributing more selectively, a method that works well for a list of moderate sellers but makes it difficult to market a breakout book. Most publishers in the early 1990s took a line somewhere between the two extremes, calculating the number of copies required to provide maximum useful coverage of the markets with the maximum potential sales. The size of the print run would likewise signal to those markets the degree of confidence the publisher expressed for the title. A small print run would indicate little support for the book, but a large print run could cost the company more than it could afford to lose on a given title.

Once the major decisions about the book have been made—cover, target markets, release date—the sales force moves into action to get the book into the stores, a system that has changed dramatically twice since the 1960s. We can divide the outlets for science fiction books into three distinct markets: supermarket/

variety stores, such as drug stores and airport shops; independent specialty stores; and chain bookstores. Supermarket/variety stores receive their books through wholesale distributors, but the '90s have seen that system collapse from hundreds of distributors to just a handful. Given the growing number of competing books in all categories, and the decreasing number of wholesalers to supply this market, only the biggest sellers can hope to reach this impulse purchase market today.

Before the coming of the superchains, most bookstores were independently owned and shelves were stocked based on the decisions of the owner of the shop. The shop owner developed a feel for the taste of his customers, and made choices based on reasonable expectations of what that clientele would appreciate in new releases. In the 1960s, however, the chain stores began to exert competitive pressure on all the independents, many of whom survived by specializing in particular kinds of books. Today more and more independents are folding under the increased pressure from the superstores, which can often stock as many books in a given genre as an independent, but with the buying clout of the many stores in the chain. Ironically, the smaller mall chain stores are finding it difficult to compete with the ambiance and selection of their own superstores in most categories.

## Books in Chains

As the number of wholesale distributors and independent bookstores has declined, the success of a book depends more and more on bookstore chains and their superstores. While the buyer for the chain may read the genre and may even participate in the fan culture, the stockholders of the chain to which he answers have no stake in the success or failure of any given genre author. Editors have personal stories about buyers, as Kathryn Cramer and David Hartwell discussed:

> **Kathryn Cramer:** [One buyer for one of the two major chains] said that the books that he likes don't sell, so his own personal tastes do not enter into what books he promotes . . . his position was that personal taste was not an issue, because the things he liked never sold.

> **David Hartwell:** The buyer before him maintained for six years that he never read any fantasy or science fiction, that it would influence his judgment if he did that, that he wanted to make a purely marketing decision. It turns out that he was reading it, but this was his public position.

As with the publishing industry itself, buyers are making those judgment calls well in advance of the date that books actually appear on the shelves:

> **Stephen Pagel:** I mean, for me, today, which is the middle of February, I am reading the books that will be on the shelf in August and September. I am negotiating with the publishers what will be on the shelves in May and June. I am actually sitting at my computer ordering the books that will be hitting the store in April, and I am confirming the orders that are hitting in March, and I am watching the orders as they arrive in February to make sure that we have the correct stock. And [I am] having to do reorders of what's happened in January.[24]

During the early 1990s, most industry professionals considered Stephen Pagel, former buyer for Barnes and Noble, B. Dalton, and other chain bookstores, one of the most powerful people in science fiction publishing. Like most of the people in science fiction, Pagel had read the genre from early childhood:

> I was reading [Ray] Bradbury back in grade school. I was reading Tom Swift . . . and absolutely loved it. All through high school, [I] was able to negotiate with teachers . . .—if you will let me read science fiction or fantasy, I'll read two books for every one book everybody else is supposed to read. And I would write up great reports on those. All through college. I have six hours of English credit for studying Tolkien in two different classes. I took classes in sociology of science fiction, science fiction and psychology, I mean altogether I probably have about thirty hours of different [college] science fiction classes. I attended my first convention in '78. Ambercon, U. Kansas in '78.

Pagel is forty-three and an avid enthusiast for role playing games such as Dungeons and Dragons. In 1993 he moved to the sales department at White Wolf, a publishing company that produces role playing games such as Vampire as well as its own science fiction fantasy imprint, Borealis. But when we talked he still worked for the B. Dalton, Barnes and Noble corporation buying science fiction and fantasy for six chains of retail bookstores that represented about 1,000 stores. As buyer, Pagel moved science fiction into the top three categories financially for the company, sixth in terms of units sold, behind only general fiction, computers, children's, business, and psychology. This number had been lower before Pagel took on the job and dropped after he left it, demonstrating the power a buyer can have to influence the marketplace. I asked him how he had done it, and his answer demonstrated a mastery of the field and its production:

> I make a lot of choices. . . . Practically every month, I probably look at forty to forty-five new titles, twenty possible reissue titles, and depending upon the month, anywhere from . . . five up to thirty tie-ins due to sequels. . . . Within the month, I can be looking at a hundred titles. The larger stores will get all one hundred. The smaller stores will maybe get twenty or thirty titles. Size is the first thing, because that's how many linear feet they can develop. . . . Different chains have different philosophies. Right now, working with B. Dalton, I can buy anything for the store as the size permits. The Barnes and Nobles . . . prefer to stock your major titles, your fast selling-titles . . . your top ten best-seller. They don't have as much breadth, they have a lot of depth.

Each store has an employee responsible for maintaining inventory in an assigned category, and a good manager could work with the national buyer to tailor his section to regional taste:

> The managers can work a section . . . they can sit down there and see all the new stuff, order in special things. . . . I try and leave room for managers to be creative on their own.

While leaving room for managers' creativity and the general profile of the chain, the buyer has to look at the author:

Obviously when you've got your Terry Brooks, your David Eddings, Anne McCaffrey, Orson Scott Card . . . you can get huge numbers. Then you start looking at the midlist authors, then you look at your proprietary authors, or local authors, and then you look at brand new authors, and you've got to make decisions on each one of them. I mean, a rep can come in and we can easily spend anywhere from a half hour to an hour talking about four titles, how we're going to distribute them, what we're going to do, where I'm going to put them . . . do I think it is big enough that it can go in the front of the store, and there's just a lot of decisions to be made about every book. . . . Forty or fifty titles a month we do that for every month

Plus I'm watching current sales. I am watching the orders as they arrive in February to make sure that we have the correct stock and having to do reorders of what's happened in January.

While some buyers may make decisions based solely on past performance and a more or less assured bottom line, Pagel preferred working with the publishers' representatives to develop the presentation of new writers in the store where sales are made and the new name is ultimately made or broken:

If it's the new Terry Brooks or David Eddings, we don't have to spend a lot of time talking about that. It's going to sell. . . . We spend a lot of time discussing . . . the new authors. I don't like just throwing a new author out there. We throw it out on the shelf, who knows it's there. I want to work with the publishers . . . and we can do some things so people are aware what type of book it is . . . The newsletter I have, which is called *Sense of Wonder*, is in the stores, so I try to review new or less known authors.[25]

In an effort to support new authors, Pagel likewise extended the shelf life of newcomers, from the standard of eight weeks to three or even four months on the shelves. At best, however, a first- or even second-time author has only three months to build an audience before the book disappears. For booksellers as for publishers and writers, however, the fiscally conservative nature of the audience makes the process of introducing newcomers difficult:

**Pagel:**   Due to the economy today, the customer has some very financial choices to make. . . .

A lot of customers, they come in and they want a specific person. And it used to be, you know, we'd say we don't have the current Terry Brooks, but we've got a David Eddings, who writes fantasy like that. "Okay, let me try." Back when David Eddings's books were getting started you could do that. It's harder today to offer a customer someone new, because it's a financial risk. . . . And the only thing I can do is put the book out there. . . . It's between the individual stores across the nation, and the customers going in.

For any given title, the bookseller risks only the time and shelf space attributable to the sales that would have taken place if they'd shelved a better selling book in that space. Since the 1940s, the publishers have borne the burden of returns; unlike other retail businesses, bookstores receive full credit for books they do not sell. While hardcover books must be returned for this credit, mass market paperbacks are discarded; only the covers, stripped from the books, are returned.[26]

Even bookstores have to plan for the day when the current best-selling authors have died or otherwise ceased writing, however. Some buyers, like Pagel, have taken a certain pride in giving a break to the stars of the future, but most stores are unwilling to risk more on an unknown book than a brief stay in the shelf space allocated for product that may not sell.

## Technology and Sell-Through

A bookseller divides the book world into three consumer levels. Best-sellers, most important for the store or chain's survival, demand a great deal of floor space for a relatively short period, then may disappear or devolve into the small but steady seller. This second division, the midlist, may reflect long-term interest in a former best-seller, now in the backlist, but more often includes books that sell consistently but not spectacularly year after year. The midlist fills most of the back cases. And then there are the books like the one we have been looking at—that book slid over the transom, by an unknown author, who may someday develop into a major seller if given time to attract an audience. As we have seen above, even through the 1980s and the early '90s, bookstores made room for all three kinds of books. But already the genre midlist—those books selling consistently but in relatively small numbers that did not grow from book to book—was disappearing. At the World Science Fiction convention in September of 1992, I spoke briefly with Jacqueline Lichtenberg and Jean Lorrah, whose books had developed a loyal following of fans who bought every book in the Sime-Gen and Savage Empire series that the women wrote. Fans wrote their own stories in the fictional universe, subscribed to a newsletter, and gathered as a subgroup at conventions to discuss their interest in the series and in the esoteric systems that underlie the cultures constructed in the series. But after nearly a dozen books, neither author had increased her sales above about 17,000 copies, and each found herself cut from her publisher's list. While 17,000 copies had put them comfortably in the reliable midlist for many years, even the certainty that those 17,000 fans would buy the next book did not suffice to put another book in print. Peter Heck, an editor at Ace (but not of the authors above), explained why publishers are putting more pressure on the midlist to improve their sales:

> . . . you can't consistently put out 25K [25,000] copies of a book and sell through at even 80 percent, at which point you should be making money, unless you're paying advances that most authors would find it very difficult to live on. . . . For a first novelist, for somebody who's on their way up the ladder, 25K books a year, this is acceptable, this is something you can build on. For somebody that's more than two or three books into a career, and expects to get higher advances . . . numbers like that become increasingly deadly, because you can't pay somebody $10K and publish 25K copies of a paperback book and make money.

Of course, few books do sell through at 80 percent. Many do not earn sufficient royalties to cover their advance, and bookstores are wary of taking on a book that is not building an audience and does not sell consistently over time, but drops to zero after a short buying window in which the author's fans stock up. But until the late 1990s, an editor who believed in a new author could hope to invest in that author's future by buying the next, and even the book after that, as Jim Baen explained:

> If we publish one book by an author, their number two book gets . . . book-normed [averaged with the other books]. The second book is seldom as good as the first book. . . . So, by the third one, we are expecting it to be better, and by the fourth one, it's gotta be good, and much better executed. . . .

By the mid–'90s, however, factors in the "support" fields, such as shifts in bookstore economies and in distributorships, in print technologies, and even in the cost of ink and paper, undermined the economics of author development and made being a new writer more precarious than ever. Bookstore chains made the first major shift since the 1960s, away from the small mall stores to the "superstore" multilevel supermarket of books, music, and gift memorabilia. To many in publishing, the size of the new stores seemed like an opportunity to place more product for longer periods of time, enhancing the opportunities for new authors. But the bigger, more elegant stores cost more to run and therefore required a larger percentage of their stock to move quickly through their doors.

At the same time, chains bought more sophisticated computer inventory tracking systems, which became economically feasible—even necessary—with the larger stores. Computerized inventory tracking made it possible to measure the sales of each title on a day-by-day basis and to make decisions based on a much more narrowly focused reliance on track records of books by author and type. So, while the need to sell more books to hold a place on the shelves raised the bar for success, access to daily sales figures meant that few books would have the advantage of lag time between stocking the shelves and taking inventory, in which they might sell more books. And because the superstores had to sell more books to survive, few lagging titles could hold on to their shelf space past the next month's deliveries. The order for that author's next book would reflect not the order received the last time, but the number of books *sold* the last time-a practice called "ordering to the net," which can have devastating effects on even a significant seller, as multiple-award-winning author Mike Resnick explained:

> Here's an example of ordering to the net: The publisher prints 80,000 of your book. You sell 60,000—a 75 percent sell-through. Next book, the distributors only want 60,000 . . . the amount you sold. You sell 40,000—a 67 percent sell-through. Next book, they order 40,000, and you sell 25,000—a 63 percent sell-through.
>
> Next book, they order 25,000, you sell 15,000—a 60 percent sell-through . . . but your advances have gone through the floor, you have a reputation as an author whose last couple of books tanked, your publisher is making noises about dropping you from the list . . . and yet you've never sold less than 60 percent in an era where 50 percent is above average.[27]

The above figures are disastrous even for an established author, but, more to the point, they seem counterintuitive. One would think that, if you know you sold 60,000 copies, and you only ordered that many, the percentage of books sold would go up even if the number of books sold remained stable. But that doesn't happen for reasons both practical and psychological. Roughly 10 percent of those books will be damaged in processing and will never make it to the shelves. So you've lost 10 percent of your audience off the top. A few new readers will pick up the book and then be disappointed when they can't find the first one, and refuse to buy another. The readers who bought last time can't find the book because of the purchases of the first-time buyers, and will lose interest as well. And ironically (ironic because the bookseller knows that the reduced size of the order had nothing to do with reduced expectations for the book—I never said the business was logical!) the bookstore will allocate less shelf time and space to the book because of the reduced order. People can ask for special orders, but given the wealth of new product on the shelves, it seldom seems worthwhile for the overwhelmed customer to do so. And in only a vanishingly small number of cases will special orders trigger a reorder, because the person taking the special order may not know the book is science fiction or when it was issued and won't connect that special order with a need to buy more of that title.[28]

Most science fiction writers would be happy to sell 60,000 copies of a book at the best of times. Jim Baen calls the 40,000-copy seller the bread and butter of the genre; print runs of science fiction are usually half that of mysteries or romances, and laughable in general fiction, yet the overall sales in the genre can exceed those of the other genres with a knowledgeable buyer like Stephen Pagel.[29] But the superstores rely on big sales of fewer individual titles. So, when the number of books sold begins to drop, as they will if you drop the size of the print run, the time and shelf space a superstore can afford to allot to it likewise drops, in a hurtling downward spiral of the midlist.[30]

At other times this downsizing of book orders might have raised serious protest in the publishing industry, but two things were happening back at production that put the book producers solidly in line with the booksellers. The first was a short-term near disaster for the industry. Traditionally, booksellers have returned the covers of copies they do not sell in lieu of the paperback books, which, stripped of their covers, went to recycling or the dumpster. The low cost of pulp paper had fueled this strategy of unlimited returns for fifty years. Suddenly, in the space of about six months, the price of pulp paper doubled. This meant that books priced six months or a year ahead now cost significantly more to produce than expected. Printing ten copies to sell four, or two, ceased to be economically feasible.

Keep in mind here that science fiction/fantasy publishing may be one of the most conservative businesses in the marketplace. Marketing doesn't exist, for the most part, except in the hindsight of the sales department. While typesetting has been computerized for quite some time, few publishers accept manuscripts on disk. Laura Anne Gilman, editor in chief at Roc, talked about her struggle to have disks accepted from authors:

> I have been working with our production department to make sure that they will take disks. They have to be done in a very particular way, and you can't deviate. They don't have any flexibility. Which is insane, because I know the coders and the typesetters had the flexibility, but our production department

can't take the time to sort through everything and standardize it. And this is, again, it is across the board.[31]

Printing of the books likewise lagged behind available technology. With the increase in the price of paper, however, something had to change. Booksellers refused to give up their right to return unsold books for full credit, but their own inventory systems made it possible to order fewer copies of riskier books. Printing fewer copies in the print run could help, but it did drive up the production cost per copy, and printing fewer copies of a title left everyone in the lurch if a title unexpectedly took off, as Peter Heck's cyberpunk book did above.

Into the breach came technology. The basic production cost of a title had to be distributed over a smaller number of copies, but with the books on computer, printers did not need the long lead times to reprint, and the cost to set up for a reprint dropped. The savings in the cost of printing and shipping the unsold books made up for the increase in the per book price to print in smaller numbers. Which did not, of course, help the author:

> **Gilman:** On the plus side, again, plus and negative side, you have just–in–time publishing. Which means that you only print as many books as the stores need. And then when the stores need more, you can print them up immediately and ship them out. This is good because it means you can supply the demand. it's bad because you have smaller print runs initially, which means that each title is more expensive to produce, because it's a smaller quantity, which means, overall, the book doesn't perform as well. . . . If anything, it's going to get smaller and smaller so you can do it on a monthly basis. . . . So it's not a good time to be starting. And it's not even a good time to be an established author, because of these smaller print runs, which means that you can offer less up front. But I refuse to say that publishing is dead. I refuse to say that publishing is even dying. It's just changing its form. . . . Storytelling will go on. People will continue to buy stories . . . that interest them—whether that's mysteries or science fiction or romance or nonfiction. The trick is doing it [publishing] in the most fiscally responsible way.[32]

Just–in–time printing[33] has became more economically feasible as well as timely, but for the most part a method that may work well in general fiction or genres that depend on higher sales of fewer titles doesn't work as anticipated in the genres that have traditionally gone for more titles with moderate sales. As Gilman points out, it isn't a good time to be starting out, or even to be an established writer in science fiction, as a number of those established writers have discovered. Some authors have seen their print runs drop over the course of a couple of books from traditional print runs of up to 100,000 copies to a quarter of that number, eroding their position in the midlist. In fact, because most publishers based their success/failure decision on the sell-through—the percentage of the print run actually sold—rather than the number of copies sold, an author who starts out with 100,000 copies in print may be deemed a failure if he sells only 40,000 copies. By contrast, an author with a print run of 30,000 copies who sells 40,000 and requires a second print run will be considered a great success story. Although the number of units sold is the same, they are not exactly the same units, since those of the former author must carry the burden of the cost of unsold copies, but those of the latter do not. As the size of the print run drops into the lower ranges of the midlist, the author has reason to worry. Some publishers may have cut him from their lists already, and if his sales figures should drop below 25,000 units or so, he will be cut from the lists of most publishers.

Nor does a prestigious reputation in the field guarantee an author a slot on a publisher's list. In 1997, Norman Spinrad, controversial author and one of the founding lights of the New Wave of the 1960s, used the Internet to disseminate widely his complaint that, because industry publishers did not find the earnings on his most recent book acceptable, he could not sell his most recent novel at all. A number of counterclaims were made about Spinrad's problem: that Spinrad had written a general fiction book; that the fact that his protagonist wrote science fiction did not make the book a science fiction book; and that the book Spinrad was trying to sell was not up to his usual standards and did not merit publication. For whatever reasons, however, it had become clear to everyone in the field that a writer, even with the remarkable reputation of Norman Spinrad,[34] could not rely on his place in the history of the field to ensure a slot in the list of a genre publisher.

## The Pseudonym Solution[35]

As we have seen above, a history and reputation in the field will not guarantee that work today will receive a welcome at the major publishing houses, nor does it guarantee a living wage to those who have made there living in the field for twenty or thirty years.

For writers just starting out, the situation is, if possible, more dire. Readers, we have seen, can be extremely conservative, buying only those names that are familiar to them, and often they are wise to do so. It takes most people up to a decade to learn how to write a top-flight novel. First novels seldom have the polish of an author's later efforts, and most knowledgeable informants in the field agree that to bring a potential best-selling writer from the midlist to the "lease line"—in a bookstore, the most visible racks, usually near the entrance or next to the cash registers—takes about six to ten books.[36] Publishers know this. Jim Baen has explained above that a reasonable editor expects a "sophomore slump" with a second book that reverses itself in the third, after which the publisher reasonably expects sales to actually grow.

But because the bookstore chains buy to the net, the author really has to hit with the first book to get enough copies on the shelves for the second book to stay even. And if the author does suffer a slump in book two, the chains won't order enough of book three to warrant a fourth contract, although most publishers and editors know that if they can get it on the shelf, book four is likely to start the successful author on the sales upswing. The career ends, therefore, right at the point where it is about to start making everybody some money. In desperation, publisher have found a quick and easy way to fool the machines. Since the chain buyers make decisions about first novels based on the expectations of the publishers, but are bound by the computerized sales figures thereafter, the publisher's sales force simply presents book four as book one by a new author: the pseudonym is born.

The use of pseudonyms in fiction publishing certainly did not arise as a response to the tyranny of the computerized inventory system. Historically, the choice of pseudonym might signal an alignment with certain philosophical movements, or it might provide a clue to the writer's true identity, which, were it generally known, could generate a scandal based on class or gender or calling or political leaning. Writers of serious literature who occasionally write genre fiction, and writers whose first careers might be damaged if their reputation as a writer became known, have used pseudonyms. Prolific writers in multiple genres or subgenres have used pseudonyms to distinguish between their genres for their readers, particularly when the audiences for one genre may dislike the work in the other. In mystery, for example, the Barbara Michaels/Elizabeth Peters pseudonyms distinguish between "Michaels"'s contemporary suspense mysteries, which often have a supernatural element, and "Peters"'s mysteries, which do not have supernatural content. In Romance, Jayne Ann Krentz/Amanda Quick/Jayne Castle distinguish between the author's contemporary romances, her Regency period historicals, and her futuristic romances.

Some science fiction/fantasy/horror authors who write outside the genre complex may choose to use a pseudonym to distinguish between the genre-complex works and the works outside the complex (romance, perhaps, or thrillers). Robert Jordan, for example, seemed to take the book world by storm with his first Wheel of Time novel, *Eye of the World*, but in fact Jordan had written a number of books, including historical novels, under a number of pseudonyms. Most writers working within the three genres do not use different names as a genre/subgenre marker. C. J. Cherryh, for example, has successfully alternated between hard science fiction and fantasy since the mid-1970s, and Orson Scott Card, while best known for his science fiction, produces highly acclaimed and successful works of horror fiction.

Publishers realized that a pseudonym could fool the computers, who had no track records under the new names and therefore no net to buy to. Authors did lose the name identification they had built up with the readers their early books had attracted. In place of their questionable name value, the pseudonymous authors gain a second chance to hit big with their first book, another two or three books to learn the trade and write commercially successful novels, *good* novels, that a less efficient time would have given them under their own names.[37] A second chance under a new name doesn't always work, of course. A writer who fails under his or her own name may not learn the important lessons necessary to write successfully, or, once again, a readership turned on its head by bookstore practices may not stumble upon his books before they are gone again. But most publishers use the pseudonym solution judiciously, with successes like Kate Elliott, who has had a successful career with her Jaran novels, her Crown of Stars novels, and her collaboration with Melanie Rawn and Jennifer Roberson on *The Golden Key*, and Robin Hobb, who has found success with the Assassin trilogy.

Unlike the new writer trying to shape a career in perilous publishing times, established writers who find themselves trapped by the declining sales figures of their most recent books have more at stake when they move to a pseudonym. These writers risk not just the readership drawn to their names on the cover that they have established over long years of a mature career, but also the historical continuity of their names in the history of the literature. When that name has awards attached to it and a position as an innovator in the major movements of the genre, abandoning that history, and that history-making sensibility to pay the rent may be unthinkable and even impossible as a writer to do. With a readership increasingly shifting to the post–Neuromancer side of the great generational divide, the potential for sales by those on the far side decrease, while the new writer also suffers. In the next two chapters, we will look at the factors that determine best-seller status and what the field is doing about the rest of the genre.

# Best-Sellers, Short Fiction, and Niches

# 11

## Best-Sellers

While most writers spend their careers struggling to build a readership, the persistent are sometimes rewarded with "sudden" best-seller status; even more rarely, a first novel takes the world of science fiction or fantasy by storm. In the science fiction and fantasy genres, this means sales of about 200,000 copies, not in the same league as the megahits of Stephen King or most general fiction best-sellers, but enough to consider the book a major hit.[1] Most writers dream about writing the "King" sized best-seller that will secure their financial freedom to write, but the single most reliable indicator of a book's potential as a best-seller is the sales numbers of the author's previous book. If that was a best-seller, and the new book is similar and of consistent quality, then it will most likely be a best-seller as well. The writer striving to knock King off his throne doesn't want to hear this, of course, and hopes that the culture critics are correct, that best-sellers are made through the string-pulling of the publishing establishment, particularly if the publishing establishment is willing to put its promotion machine into action on her book's behalf. That position seems fairly defensible when you listen to Tom Doherty the salesman-turned-publisher:

> Publishing means basically to make public, and you've got to be commercial about it, or you won't have the resources to continuously make things public. . . . Get into [Barnes and Noble's] mailer; its an advertorial. You pay. To get in the front of the store, you pay. If you are on the lease line, you will sell many more copies than if you are somewhere hidden in the back of the store. We're constantly paying for positioning, we are constantly paying for display, for discounting, for promoting. It's very costly.[2]

Traditionally some authors have made it to the best-seller list in hardcover, but most science fiction sells in paperback. Few authors in the genres can expect to see their book in hardcover until they prove themselves as best-sellers.

**Laura Anne Gilman:**    It's rare for . . . a new book to start at the top of our list. Other publishing companies do it differently. They start off . . . [in] hard-cover. We tend to save our hardcovers and our trade books for people who have proven themselves, because it's asking a lot of a reader to spend twenty, twenty-five dollars on a brand new author. It's better to say, here's a new author, five, six dollars, and if you like it, then we'll see if there's enough market to support [a hardcover edition].[3]

The best-seller increases the return for the publisher on sales of the hardcover edition, and since much of the initial cost of editing and production is loaded into the hardcover cost, the publisher can expect a much higher return on the paperback edition as well. Some houses that specialize in mass-market, look to the hard-back publishers to acquire top titles while bringing in newer writers still in the paperback form with an eye to developing them into top selling names in hardback publication over time. According to Ginjer Buchanan, this is the method that works in the late 1990s for Ace:

Many of the top books are "fed" from the previous hardcover or trade pubs, but ultimately nearly everything winds up in mass-market [paperback]. A cursory look at the Forthcoming Books columns in *Locus* would substantiate that. As to the "how to break in" debate, some houses still won't do a first novel in hardcover (although if it's a certain kind of book, they'll try trade [paperback]). On the other hand, Tor had a program going for a couple of years specifically of first novels in hardcover.[4]

But for some companies hardcover books have become an important part of the marketing strategy in the making of a best-seller and in making their target sales of a title at all. In 1993, Beth Meacham explained Tor's approach:

We've found that as long as we can break even on publishing the book at hardcover . . . sell enough copies to pay for the production, pay for the advertising, earn out the half of the advance we assign to it, we end up generating a phenomenal amount of advance publication publicity for the paperback that we cannot get otherwise. We get the review attention, we get people talking about the book, and it's worthwhile to us to do that. If we were worrying about having to make phenomenal profits on our hardcovers as well as our paperbacks, we wouldn't be doing it.[5]

In the period covered by this book, roughly 1985 to 1998, the number of titles issued in science fiction/fantasy/horror has increased dramatically, while the re-view space devoted to the genres in the mainstream media has decreased to the point that the Science Fiction and Fantasy Writers of America (SFWA) has recently assigned a task force to study the problem.[6] Books released in hardcover may receive a thumbnail review in a major daily newspaper, but a new author in original paperback can expect even a thumbnail review in neither the mainstream press nor most genre-specific magazines, so the hardcover can be an important marketing tool. More importantly, with the collapse of the broad mass-market distribution system, companies such as Tor Books that relied heavily on that system have had to change their strategy. Tor has moved the hardback into the fore of their sales strategies:

> **Meacham:**   The publishing business has changed dramatically in the past five years. . . . There is no longer any viable "mass-market" for most genre books. We no longer expect to sell the majority of copies of any book in rack-size paperback. It's all hardcover/trade paperback publication these days, and for most books the hardcover is where the publisher and author make their money. This, of course, changes the way we acquire.[7]

Regardless of the quality of the book, it will never become a best-seller unless the publisher applies the full apparatus of hit-making to the production. While it may seem a simple formula—advertising budget=sales—it seldom works that easily. A book can't reach enough people to become a best-seller without heavy promotion, but promotion does not guarantee a best-seller. The buyer for the chains must also make decisions about which books he will allow on the lease line, based on a reasonable expectation of how many copies he can sell once he has exposed the audience to the product:

> **Tom Doherty:**   [The buyer's] going to judge how many copies can the book sell in the first eight weeks.. He'll take our word for it based on our batting average. So we've got to pick for him what we really think will work. Or next month, when we have something that will work, he won't buy enough.[8]

Stephen Pagel, however, credits the power to make or break a book to the buying public; promotion can bring the book to the attention of the audience, but it cannot make that audience buy:

> I always hear that the industry has power over the audience, [but]. . . . The customer is really the one who has the power, because the industry will publish what the customer wants. . . . Obviously not everybody sells like, we were talking about Eddings, McCaffrey, Card, some of those . . . but when you've got millions buying up here, and then the others, you've got just thousands buying down here, that's a huge gap.

Pagel believes that gap between the top sellers and the struggling performers provides opportunity for new writers to expand their audience, but that requires an amount of risk that few science fiction readers seem willing to take with their book dollars. But how did the Eddings and the McCaffreys, and the Robert Jordans, become the benchmarks for success? Tappan King, publishing executive who was with Lou Aronica at the start of Bantam's Spectra line, describes the process in terms of imprinting, much as pack creatures imprint with the pack leader:

> **Tappan King:**   One of the things that causes a book to become a best-seller is the readership imprinting on a particular writer at a certain point in their career, and that writer continuing to stay in print. . . . Because they are reasonably successful . . . the readers can continue to read them, and then that writer comes through with something quintessentially like *Them*, [about] which everybody goes, "This is the book we've all been waiting for."[9]

But Eddings himself failed to make successful sales figures when he tried to move away from the characters and universe he had created in his popular series, The Belgariad. As King points out, the book must convey the essential quality that drew the audience to that author in the first place, and do it better. If the writer tries to do something else, he may find an unforgiving public staying away in droves, as Jim Baen discovered when he published Newt Gingrich's alternate history, *1945*.[10] And, as Stephen Pagel tells us, while a popular author may seem like a more certain winner,

> publishers can only take so many risks. They can say, "Okay, we're going to put this author out there, we are going to back them, we're going to get good art to put on the book, we're going to do advertisement, we're going to do a tour." And you can do that a couple of times. And if it doesn't work, you've got to stop . . . because you can't publish what no one's going to buy. . . . There's been publishers out there that have said, "No, I'm publishing what I want to publish," and then they went out of business because people weren't buying it.[11]

The trick, then, is choosing a book with the potential to become a best-seller, and then promoting it until enough people buy it to land on *Publishers Weekly*'s best-seller list. Editors and publishers, engaged in the task of choosing the right book, speak of the best-seller in almost mystical terms. Everyone agreed that an editor faced further doom if she chose a book she did not like based on the expectation that others would like it, although in some cases that dislike might serve as a warped indicator of success. In spite of this anecdotal evidence, the editors agreed that, if they received a book they did not like but felt had potential, they would pass it on to "someone whose taste was more in sympathy with the book":

> **Teresa Nielsen Hayden:**   Never look at, say, a book . . . and say, "It really doesn't speak to me at all, you know; I don't see it as having any spark. But it looks just like all of those books that those other people over there like, and so surely of course they will like this one." Because that's a recipe for putting out stuff that's absolutely dead in the water. Either publish something else, or get out of handling that kind of book altogether if none of them ever speak to you. . . . You cannot make decisions on the basis of "somebody else will like this," because you don't know.

> **Patrick Nielsen Hayden:**   I agree entirely. I don't edit horror, for example. It does not speak to me. . . . I have no tooth for horror. And occasionally a horror book will slip through and I will like it anyway, and I don't know why that is, but I figure that I am really quite clueless on the whole subject so I should have no business editing it.

In addition to their united agreement that successful editors or publishers choose books they like, most of the professionals I spoke to in the editorial, production, and sales ends of the business seemed to share one aesthetic trait in common: *all* of those interviewed said that their favorite books did *not* become best-sellers. It seems that the variations and surprises in the form, which appeal to the editor or buyer who may spend ten hours a day reading the genre, work counter to the expectations and satisfaction of a mass audience that spends less time reading the material.

## The Rules

Confronted with the dual facts that 90 percent of all new books fail, and that expensive promotion can only save a few of them, success or failure as a publisher requires that someone pick the winners. Tor Books, consistently ranked at the top of the science fiction publishing industry, clearly does this better than most. Its reputation alone will draw submissions from the most talented and ambitious authors, but its editors, one would assume, must have some rules for making their decisions more successfully than others in their field. The reputations of specific star editors, like the late Terry Carr, of Ace Special Edition fame, who "discovered" Ursula Le Guin, would seem to support this assumption. When asked if they had a rule of thumb for choosing best-sellers, however, they all said there were no rules. And then, of course, they proceeded to recount those nonexistent, quasi-mystical rules they lived by:

> **Teresa Nielsen Hayden:** There's a very large element of chance in this. It all depends on whether everything comes together. Your cover comes together, your title comes together, your story comes together, the time—just the timing and zeitgeist comes together with your distribution to cause, suddenly, a very large number of people to read a certain book within a month. If that happens and if they like it, they'll tell their friends. And more people will buy the book. That book will sell a lot of copies. The *next* book will become a best-seller.

Chance certainly comes into the process. A good book with the wrong cover may fail, and, as we have seen, something as basic as producing an insufficient number of units can hinder the success of a potential best-seller. For the best editors, however, success relies on a combination of factors, including a tacit understanding of the forms of the genre; all the editors recognized for excellence by their peers have read widely in the best the genre has to offer, and they have internalized the criteria by which works have historically been classified as "best." Editors likewise require a knowledge of the needs of the consumers of the moment, and most of the editors in science fiction/fantasy publishing keep tabs on the societal mood of the moment by attending at least some conventions. But catching the zeitgeist and targeting books to that market is always a risky thing, because the zeitgeist changes. As Tappan King argues,

> [Samuel R. Delany's] *Dhalgren* could not sell a million point three copies today. It'll work. I mean, such a book could come out today, even given the paradox of there having been *Dhalgren*, but it wouldn't speak to the same number of people.

Since the 1980s, Delany has had trouble with the market for his work, for which there remains a select readership, but nothing like the mass appeal his complex, dense work enjoyed at the height of the New Wave during the '60s. In the high-risk business of science fiction publishing, therefore, analytic minds will pursue the mystic variable of the zeitgeist in flux, as Stephen Pagel does when he looked to the outside world for trends in sales in science fiction:

> Science fiction goes more for the mind, fantasy goes more for the heart. If there are layoffs, we sell more fantasy, because people don't want to come home and think. When you read science fiction you think; they want to come home and escape. They're going to read a fantasy. Little things like that—you just catch the flow of what is going on. What I think is absolutely wonderful, is we happen to have a president who reads. And is not ashamed to say he reads. You know, . . . Reagan used to ship the books back in unopened boxes that the publishers sent because he said, why do I want these books. A big difference.

Pagel's analysis appears flawed in the late 1990s, with low unemployment and high sales in fantasy, which seems to bring us back to where we started, looking for the mystical answer to a pragmatic question: what propels a quarter of a million buyers to choose one particular title from the hundreds on the shelves, while only a few thousand customers will pick up each of the others:

**Patrick Nielsen Hayden:**   I kinda know something has a certain amount of commercial "zots" when I see it, and sometimes I'm wrong.

**Beth Meacham:**   Whether it punches buttons in other people. Whether it appeals to a very, very large number of people on some level. And it is very hard to quantify that.

Literary quality will not guarantee success, although there seems to be consensus that commercial work with good literary values will sell better than its less intelligent counterpart. The quality of the writing alone can't make a success if the book doesn't punch any buttons, however, and those buttons don't seem to be the ones that most people think of when they are discussing science fiction. I asked the editors if science fiction's hot buttons were the intellectual buttons of having a bright idea, and the editors agreed the intellectual pleasure of the idea did not make a science fiction best-seller:

**Beth Meacham:**   No, no. . . . It's a book that makes you feel good.

**Ethnographer:**   What is it about a book that will make you feel good? Does it have to be a happy book?

**Teresa Nielsen Hayden:**   No. Depends. It varies from person to person, time to time, subject to subject, zeitgeist to zeitgeist.

**Beth Meacham:**   There's no way to quantify that. I just know. . . . The books that become huge rating successes in some way make the readership feel good.

**Teresa Nielsen Hayden:**   Sometimes that is really good handling of a unique excitement—

**Beth Meacham:** The Stephen Hawking book[12] did it, that way.

**Tappan King:** I think in some sense, what you're getting is the combination of a kind of literary craft with an empathy of the writer with the reader's psychological needs. That's about the best I've been able to figure out. If the writer understands how the reader feels, whoever the reader might be—you know, a feminist, or a troubled adolescent with power fantasies, which they traditionally say it is—If the author empathizes with those needs, the needs to have that experience, and is a good craftsperson, that book gets to be success-ful. That's about all I've been able to figure out.

This explains why a book like *Dhalgren*, not a happy book in any sense of the word, could sell more a million copies during the decade of the New Wave, and why it may be experiencing a bit of a revival among late-adolescent literati today. What it says about the impending zeitgeist should, perhaps, give us pause. As the most successful science fiction publisher in the industry, however, Tom Doherty must be more in touch with that zeitgeist than anyone in the business, and not surprisingly, he concurs that the best-seller must make the reader feel good, and further pins down what that means today:

**Doherty:** I think that people will much better relate and much more will-ingly buy a book [set] in the future which they would find interesting to live in. . . . I don't think dystopias work commercially. Now, are there exceptions? Of course. Are there many dystopias that have been major works? Of course. [But] I think it has to be written several levels above *Star Wars*, your classic bright young people winning against terrible odds. *Star Wars* is your standard, absolute classic space opera, and I think that kind of thing will always sell best.

*Star Wars*, of course, is more than the classic space opera; it recapitulates the arche-typal battle between good and evil in a coming-of-age story in which the wise elder, in the form of Obi-Wan Kenobi, passes on his knowledge and experience to the young man, Luke Skywalker. Age dies and the young man fulfills his quest, his destiny, saves the universe, and takes his place as the adult of power. In the Lucas version, of course, youth must undergo his rite of passage three times, and in each more and more of the symbolism is stripped away until youth confronts his Oedipal struggle head-on and overcomes to take the place of the father, but in greater wisdom. That story has made people feel good for thousands of years, and Lucas had the craftsmanship to pull it off in a way that many authors of quest fiction long to do, frequently while scorning the films that did it so well.

In his quest, Luke Skywalker's mentors guided him along the path of adult-hood while cautioning him away from the dark side of adult power. To Jim Baen, who publishes mostly military science fiction and quest fantasy, this moral struc-ture—good wins, evil is defeated—underlies the pleasure of the book:

Baen books tend to have a moral substrate to them. . . . That I regard as a deep proprietorial secret: books without a moral substrate won't sell. . . . It's one of the things . . . I have to like in a book that I publish. It is very convenient that it is a virtual necessity [for success]. Sometimes, there will be exceptions to this rule. Gibson's *Neuromancer*, as far as I can tell has no [moral substrate] But it was fascinating and, done one time, was really interesting.

Success, today and in the future, would seem to depend on recognizing that well-crafted book that connects with the needs of its buying public. And that means the flexibility to know when the zeitgeist has moved away from utopic rites and to follow it wherever the public sensibility has gone. As Stephen Pagel warned us at the beginning of our quest for the best-seller, the audience that buys or ignores the book demands of its culture producers those products that support the worldview they hold. Publishers who try to shape that audience with their products, like Jim Baen's efforts to further his political views with the publication and big-book promotion of Newt Gingrich's *1945*, find their audience abandoning them and must scramble to make up the credibility they may have lost with their buyers.[13]

## Short Fiction: Anthologies and Magazines

The full-length novel form clearly accounts for almost all the best-selling science fiction/fantasy/horror in today's market,[14] but, according to editor and writer Gardner Dozois,

> The work that's being done at the top of the book best-seller list is generally speaking not work that's going to have a big influence on the evolution of the field and the direction that science fiction is going to take in the future. It's usually the work that's being done in the science fiction magazines, usually at short fiction length, that really shows you where science fiction is going to go in the next couple of decades.[15]

Award-winning novelist Michael Swanwick frequently returns to short fiction to exercise his own skills on the evolution of the field:

> I write short fiction in order to experiment, to discover new possibilities, to learn, and to keep myself in practice between novels. And to keep myself honest. It's possible to put on airs about being a writer, but not when you're actually writing. The written page humbles you.[16]

Many writers use short fiction to develop their careers: they begin with a short story, sometimes in a semiprofessional magazine, and move up to one of the handful of established genre magazines. Once a writer has established a name in the short fiction market, the next step is a novel, an expanded form of one of the short stories or novellas that appeared in the short fiction press or cobbled together out of a number of stories that appeared there. Nancy Kress's *Beggars in Spain* started as an award-winning novella, which became the three-volume Beggars series. Lucius Shepard's *Life During Wartime* began as a series of stories, including the powerful "R and R," in *Asimov's Science Fiction Magazine*. In some cases, the strategist starts with a novel in mind and publishes bits of it as short stories to draw the reader into that world before bringing out the novel. Logically, this approach erodes the buyer's resistance to new authors because the author is not new to the reader.

A writer known for both long and short forms has the freedom to move back and forth between them, letting each inspire the other. Ellen Datlow, coeditor of *The Year's Best Fantasy and Horror*, former fiction editor of *Omni Magazine*, and current editor of *Event Horizon*, gives an example:

> [William] Gibson's novel *Virtual Light* grew out of the short story "Skinner's Room," which was commissioned for an architecture exhibit in California. I picked up the story for *Omni*. And Gibson says that he enjoyed writing the story so much . . . that he decided to do a novel afterward.[17]

Few writers can move back and forth from short to long fiction with the grace and clarity of the authors mentioned above, and some, like Nancy Kress, leave the short fiction arena poorer when they move to novels. Those who do continue to write short fiction do it for the love rather than the financial gain, as Michael Swanwick explained:

> Why write short stories? God knows, it's not the money. Last year I was between novels and went on a short story binge—I averaged a new story every five weeks . . . and sold them all. My total income for the year, counting reprints, was seven thousand dollars. If it weren't for what I earn from novels, I wouldn't have a career, I'd have a profitable hobby.

While the novels pay the grocery bills, however, it seems the short stories feed the soul:

> **Swanwick:**   A short story, however can be held in the mind all in one piece. It's less like a building than a fiendish device. Every bit of it must be cunningly made and crafted to fit together perfectly and without waste so it can perform its task with absolute precision. That purpose might be to move the reader to tears or wonder, to awaken the conscience, to console, to gladden, or to enlighten. But each short story has one chief purpose, and every sentence, phrase, and word is crafted to achieve that end. The ideal short story is like a knife—strongly made, well balanced, and with an absolute minimum of moving parts.[18]

Jane Yolen explained her affinity to the short form as closer to poetry:

> I began my writing life as a poet, and I still find the short form the most intriguing and comfortable to write. My mind can wrap itself around a short story in a way it cannot around a novel. In fact, when I write my novels, they tend to read like discrete stories or story-pieces linked together rather than that grand sweeping arch of a true novel[19]

Very rarely, and only Martha Soukup comes immediately to mind in the generation of writers coming of age in the 1980s, short-story writers will remain true to the form and not shift to the novel:

> **Martha Soukup:**   I'm born out of my time, I guess. If this were the '50s, I could have a career and I could support myself. But it's the '90s and you don't make money on short stories anymore. Now, I have many concerned friends

all trying to figure out some way to convince me that I want to write a novel. But nobody's managed it yet.[20]

By the 1980s, however, the mass reading public seemed to have lost its taste for short fiction. While part of the decline in interest in short fiction (or the failure of short fiction to increase its readership as the novel has) can be attributed to the breakdown of the traditional magazine distribution systems, this same period also saw the average length of a science fiction or fantasy novel increase and the disappearance of the "double," two short novels published between one set of covers.[21] In spite of the down market, however, the short form that started the genre and provided an economically feasible place to experiment with change continues to see publication in anthologies, in general interest magazines like *Playboy*, and more regularly in specialty genre magazines such as *Analog* and *Asimov's* and the small press and semiprofessional magazines.

## Specialty Magazines: The *Asimov's* Example

In 1998, the Hugo Award for best short story, for best novella, and for best novelette went to stories published in *Asimov's Science Fiction Magazine*. At the same time, *Asimov's* editor, Gardner Dozois, picked up his tenth Hugo award for best editor since taking on the magazine in 1985. As with most of the influential names in the genre, Dozois began reading science fiction early, and by the 1960s he was an avid reader of the magazines, especially those edited by Cele Goldsmith, the first woman to win a professional Hugo. Dozois saw in the short fiction Goldsmith presented the potential for new authors to bring new ideas into the field. Precisely because short fiction paid so badly, a magazine could afford to take a chance on a new idea or new author, and, as short fiction writer Martha Soukup pointed out, that author could expect a much greater number of readers for a short story in a magazine than she could as an unknown in a first novel: "I do remind myself . . . I think *Science Fiction Age*'s circulation is well over 100,000 now. And it hit me, suddenly . . . that at any given moment 100,000 people could be reading my story."

Of course, short fiction in the magazines is usually ephemeral, as Soukup also realizes: "And then, five months from now, nobody will be reading my story, and a year from now, if anybody wants to find my story, they won't be able to track it down. But at that month, people were reading my story."

Short fiction changes the genre not in the way one book, such as *Lord of the Rings*,[22] changes the genre, but by exerting influence over time:

> **Gardner Dozois:**   The work that's going to change the direction of the field, by influencing strongly the writers who are going to be writing the stuff and also by influencing the taste of the readers who are going to be reading the next generation of stuff, is usually still done at short-fiction length. It's usually done by unknown or newish writers. . . . In spite of the fact that it's on the bottom of every pay scale, and not much attention is paid to short fiction writing anymore by the critics, it's really still short fiction that drives the field.[23]

Different editors have different visions for their magazines, of course, and not all editors establish their goal as hosting the fiction that moves the genre. Stanley

Schmidt, edits *Analog* a magazine devoted to the continuance of hard science fiction, while *The Magazine of Fantasy and Science Fiction* has passed through several editors in the 1990s, each with their own vision of the magazine. But short fiction published in *Asimov's* tend to stand apart as the cream, winning more of the prizes in the field than any other short-fiction publication. Writers such as Bruce Sterling who have published in *Asimov's* have gone on to change the field, and writers like Ursula Le Guin, who have changed the field in the past, come back to publish their short fiction in the magazine.

Like most people in the field, I wanted to know how Dozois managed this feat of producing the most prestigious regularly published genre magazine year in, year out, for so many years. Part of the answer was technical, and part of the answer was aesthetic.

## A Day in the Life of an *Asimov's* Submission

*Asimov's* receives about one thousand submissions a month. Before Dozois can make an aesthetic judgment about submissions, he must read them, an overwhelming task, but one an editor must handle with dispatch, and each submission must be tracked and accounted for:

> **Dozois:** An unsolicited manuscript will come in to the magazine address, it'll be opened by an assistant, taken out of the envelope, and a Post-it with the date it arrived will be put on it and that will be put on a pile on a shelf of a big bookcase. . . . And I sort them into three piles. There's the professional pile, which is fairly self-evident.

For someone who has been a part of the business as long as Dozois, the process of determining the professional credentials of a writer are fairly simple:

> Whether I know the name is the most general criterion, whether it's a professionally agented manuscript is another criterion, what kind of professional credentials are listed in the cover letter is another criterion, but . . . big-name professionals, I will be familiar with their work. People who have some hint of professional credentials but are not really professional writers will go in the semiprofessional pile . . . if you've been to Clarion [writers' workshop], or you have semiprofessional sales . . . credentials from outside the field . . . the semiprofessional pile may buy you a couple extra minutes of attention, but that's it.
>
> By far the largest proportion of the manuscripts, is what we ungraciously call the slush pile. . . . I just read about 500 [slush] manuscripts yesterday when I was in New York. I like to think that if I start hitting something that's good in the slush I actually will recognize it . . . and in fact my track record is pretty good on being able to spot the few gems that are in the slush, and they turn up every once in a while . . . which is why you have to pay attention. You usually can tell whether a manuscript is worth bothering with within the first, oh, thirty seconds or so.

Most stories will receive one of two form rejection letters, or a third, slightly more personal standard-format letter signed by the editor. Stories that are closer to what the magazine can use, but still need some work, will receive a personalized letter:

I explain what's wrong with the story, and after that's the level where I say, well, this is what's wrong with the story but if you fix it, we'd be interested in seeing it again. And then you are into the professional level, where you are dealing on a fully professional level.

Once a story has been accepted, or rewritten and then accepted, it goes to contracts. *Asimov's* does not accept electronic submissions, but when the magazine purchases a story Dozois asks for a disk copy. Unlike the book publishing business, magazines rely heavily on desktop publishing to streamline the process and keep the costs in line.

## Aesthetic Choices

The magazine editor must make two kinds of aesthetic decisions: form and content.

> **Dozois:**   I spend a lot of time worrying about the aesthetic balance of the issues. . . . Are there too many long stories or too many short stories? Is there enough hard science fiction? Is there too much fantasy? Are there too many downbeat stories, or too many funny stories? All of this sort of thing. . . . My theory is that there should be a wide eclectic spread of material in each issue. . . . No matter what your taste in fiction is, you've got a chance of opening the issue and being able to find something that you like in it.

Balancing the magazine's content proves the more difficult challenge. Its sister magazine, *Analog*, appeals specifically to a hard science fiction audience, but *Asimov's* must try to please a wide variety of tastes within the limitations of the quality fiction he receives:

> **Dozois:**   We need good stories. . . . We get fewer good hard science or fewer good alien worlds type of adventure stories than I'd like to see, . . . science fiction stories set on alien worlds and alien societies, like the stuff that Jack Vance or Poul Anderson used to write. We don't see much of that. . . . We don't publish many pure sword and sorcery stories. We don't print much hardcore horror, but there's no rule that doesn't have an exception to it.
>
>      As far as what actually makes an *Asimov's* story . . . I go by instinct basically. If a story engrosses me, if it's a story with color and sweep and action and good realistic characters, these are the sort of things I am looking for. The perfect *Asimov's* story is the story that I start reading and I forget that I am reading this story to evaluate it. And I forget about whether we need more hard science stories for the April issue, and I forget all about those factors and . . . an hour later I wake up out of this daze with a shiver and realize that I finished the story and an hour has gone by. . . . I figure if I like a story, the chance is that the reader is going to like it to.

One of the most difficult tasks for an editor is finding the right kind of stories for his audience in a market where most of the writers are targeting an audience that the magazines can't reach.

> **Dozois:**   I'll tell you this. Every magazine editor, and every book editor I've talked to in the last ten years, has complained that they get too much fantasy,

too much horror, and too many near future dystopia stories. But it doesn't seem to reduce the number of them coming in. The reason is that they're easier to write than it is to write the other kind.

As a writer in the disparaged genres myself, I found this an unlikely answer, and I reminded Dozois that the book market for fantasy currently outsells that for science fiction. Since *Asimov's* does publish some fantasy, I didn't understand why those editors over the past ten years hadn't shifted their formats to appeal to the audience buying the books. Dozois's answer proved surprising:

> Part of the reason [that the magazines don't shift to the fantasy/soft horror format] is that every fantasy anthology series that has been started in the last ten years has failed miserably. There seems to be a big fantasy audience out there, but they won't buy fantasy short fiction. . . . *Realms of Fantasy*, . . . is a modest success at this point. . . . I don't think a horror magazine would work at the moment unless they could work out a deal with Stephen King. Now *Stephen King's Horror Magazine* would sell. But I know for a fact that King has been approached four or five times at least to set up *Stephen King's Horror Magazine* and has refused on every occasion, so this isn't going to work.

Dozois admitted that the failure of short fantasy in the marketplace surprised him, but concluded:

> I think that many fantasy fans are only comfortable with big fat books or, even better, trilogies or open-ended series with lots of sequels. . . . Fantasy reading is a comfort literature to some extent. People want to sit down with a big fat thousand-page fantasy novel, and they want to immerse themselves in that secondary world and they want to settle down comfortably in it as they would into a tub of warm water, and they want to soak there. They don't want a fast read. . . . This has made it more difficult to establish a fantasy magazine.

Of the genre-specific magazines, *Analog*, founded as *Astounding Science Fiction Magazine* in 1930, remains the longest running one that has at least a partial interest in fantasy. *Weird Tales*, a title that goes back to 1923, specializes in fantasy and horror but has had limited success and long gaps in its publishing history.[24] *Realms of Fantasy* and *Marion Zimmer Bradley's Fantasy Magazine* likewise appeal to niche audiences, but none of the regularly published magazines seem to tap the vast number of fantasy readers who have kept Robert Jordan on the best-seller list through most of the 1990s.

## Anthologies

Short fiction appears in book form either as a collection or as an anthology. Collections, or groups of short stories written by one author, appear far less frequently in science fiction/fantasy/horror than they do in the mainstream, and most of them come from small press niche publishers. Anthologies appear in two basic varieties: the original and the reprint anthology. At one time, original anthologies were a mainstay of the field, but they have become an increasingly hard sell since the 1970s. Few original anthology series survive for more than a handful of books. Jane

Yolen's *Xanadu* fantasy anthology series proved unsuccessful in the marketplace in spite of the high quality of its fiction and the market value of many of the names who published in it. Bantam Spectra's *Full Spectrum* has enjoyed five editions since 1989, and in 1998 Tor's *Starlight* came out for the second time, but the effort to produce diverse, high-quality short fiction for a book-reading public in the 1990s has for the most part failed.

To succeed, an anthology must overcome resistance from buyers on two fronts. The first, of course, is the length of the fiction. Most readers of book-length genre fiction need to be coaxed to try short fiction. The second is the bane of all publishing: many readers resist buying even anthologies unless there is a familiar name on the cover. Anthologies that succeed, therefore, must have as writer/editor a well-known author who acts as a brand name, identifying the style and type of short fiction, and sets on the anthology the imprimatur of the star. Theme anthologies, based on a particular conceit and usually stocked with stories gathered from friends of a star editing author, are therefore more common, and more commonly successful, than the anthologies with more innovative work by new authors. Recent theme anthologies have included Esther Friesner's *Chicks in Chainmail* series of humorous stories written primarily by women poking fun at the early heroic fantasy icon of busty women warriors in brass bras. Alternate histories also abound in the anthology format, of which Mike Resnick's *Alternate Presidents* is an example.

Reprint anthologies gather together previously published stories based on a theme, such as vampire or ghost stories, or based in a specific time period, such as the "year's best" anthologies. St. Martin's Press publishes the two most prestigious the "year's best" anthologies, *The Year's Best Fantasy and Horror*, edited by Ellen Datlow and Terri Windling, and *The Year's Best Science Fiction*, edited by Gardner Dozois. David Hartwell's *Year's Best SF*, for HarperPrism, a more recent competitor in the marketplace, likewise receives critical attention. But the effect of the limited original short fiction market affects all of the "year's best" anthologies. Both Dozois and Hartwell have been criticized for selecting too many of their stories from their own writers, Dozois from *Asimov's* and Hartwell from among his novelists. Datlow and Windling draw from a wider base often by leaving genre fiction publications behind and looking for fantasylike fiction in the mainstream.

## The Aesthetics of Length

When we look at Gardner Dozois, Ellen Datlow, Martha Soukup, and Jane Yolen, interviewed about short fiction for this book, we find that, however much their taste in terms of content may differ, they all share a certain aesthetic of preferred length in a story.

Talking with editors Ellen Datlow and Ginjer Buchanan, and writer Kathe Koja,[25] we find a sharp contrast between the aesthetics of space and time for short versus long fiction.

> **Ellen Datlow:**    Once in a while I'll get a story with potential . . . but it's too short, it needs more development on certain themes that the author's brought up, and certain interesting things that I feel he or she hasn't covered. . . .

That's very unusual. It's much more likely that we'll get somebody to cut something. . . .

**Ginjer Buchanan:** there's a difference in pacing to a novel than a short story. I mean, I will get things submitted . . . you know, unagented, that are novel-las.[26] And people don't realize that they're not long enough to be published as novels. And they might be perfectly fine novellas, in which case I suggest that they try to sell them to magazines, but I think that it's very rare that I would get something that would, that I would say, you know, if you took 200,000 words out of this it would be a short story.

Martha Soukup, who writes at the shorter end of the short fiction spectrum, referred to Neil Gaiman's explanation when trying to define her aesthetic of short fiction: "Neil Gaiman called me a miniaturist . . . I want to paint something that is small and evocative and suggests a large canvas but isn't. It's not a piece of a large canvas." Soukup added, "It's how much you are trying to make the story do, that's what takes the time, not how many words the story is."[27]

But to make a short story work on more than one level, that "how much you are trying to make the story do" that Soukup talks about, each word has to count:

**Datlow:** In short stories it's almost like every word has to mean something. . . . You don't have the time to be leisurely. . . . I hate to use the word hook, . . . but you have to have something: an event, a really effective image, an interesting character or voice, something in the first paragraph that make the reader continue reading and bring her into the story pretty quickly. . . . Lucius Shepard, I don't know if he made up this phrase, but when we were teaching Clarion, he said, "You have to kill your children when you write." You can't be so tied to any of your words that they are there just because they are gorgeous. You have to kill them. You have to make it work for the story or the novel.

Gardner Dozois makes the same point more specifically: "Every word, every sentence drives the plot, establishes character, sets tone, or shouldn't be there." Not sparse, he insists; a story can be lyrical, but the author should not confuse lyricism or necessary description with bloat. And Jane Yolen talks about the emotional impact of the short fiction as well as the compactness of its message:

I adore writing short fiction, prefer the short form, because of its compression and its attention to a single unified emotional punch. I get lost—both as a writer and a reader—in the wanderings/meanderings of novels. Even good novelists lose sight of characters, context, subtext, etc. Even the best of them.

Datlow compares this aesthetic of concision to that of the long fiction marketplace:

**Datlow:** [But] I think most books should be shorter . . . you can cut almost anything to some extent and make it better. There's a lot of sloppiness, especially with the advent of the word processor; almost anything, novel or short story, could be tightened up.

Again, Dozois echoes this sentiment that most novels would improve if they were cut by a third. Novels are too padded, he says, and admits he is more likely to turn a 600-page novel into a 20-page story than the reverse. Gordon Van Gelder, horror editor at St. Martin's Press who has taken on the editorship of *The Magazine of Fantasy and Science Fiction* (*F&SF*), disagrees with Dozois and Datlow, but admits that his recent experience with short fiction has modified his position somewhat:

> **Gordon Van Gelder:**   When I was primarily editing novels, I used to discuss various novels with Gardner [Dozois] and he'd say he thought it was too long, and I'd say I wish the author had written a longer book. I like novels where you can take off your hat and coat, walk around for a while, live inside the covers.
>
> Since I started editing *F&SF*, I've definitely grown more impatient as a reader, and I understand better Gardner's desire for shorter books. A lot of writers these days do abuse the word processor; they go on too long. But holding up a novel to the criteria of a short story is wrong; it's like telling a marathon runner she should pace herself for the 880. They're different forms.

The problem with shorter novels, of course, returns to buyer resistance, as author Kathe Koja pointed out:

> A paperback has to feel a certain way, which is why, in a book like *The Cipher*, let's say, Dell used that flash-card size print to make it look like a real book because it was a little skinny book.[28]

In later correspondence, Gordon Van Gelder explained that Koja's experience with *The Cipher* was not an uncommon example:

> *The Cipher* isn't the only book to get bulked up because the publisher thought it looked too short. Nowadays, slimmer books get lost on the shelves and booksellers don't like the lower prices.
>
> **Datlow:**   . . . Gordon [Van Gelder] says, well, he's a novel editor and he can't stand reading short stories because he feels they should be longer. I haven't talked to Gordon about this since he was made editor of *Fantasy and Science Fiction*, but it must be weird working in both forms at the same time, and I wonder if he feels differently now about the short story.

Van Gelder does note a change in his attitude, but continues to mark a serious reservation not about the short story as a form, but about the execution of that form by many writers:

> I wouldn't say that I hate short stories, but I have noticed that my tastes tend to run towards the longer stories—but that may just be because so many of the shorter ones (especially short-shorts) are executed poorly. A good short-short takes as much thought as a good novel (as Terry Bisson has said), and instead most writers treat short-shorts like first drafts or like what Ellen Kushner years ago called "jerk-off stories"—the writer sits down, fiddles with his pen for a few minutes until something comes out, and then he's done and feels better.

Lawrence Watt-Evans finds little difference between long and short fiction per se, but notes instead, "The greatest pleasure in writing *anything* is creating a thing of beauty that conveys what you want it to convey, and length simply doesn't come into that. Why should it?"[29] The deciding factor is not how long the work is, but how well it has done what it set out to do, part of which requires the selection of the length appropriate for the purpose of the piece.

Short fiction that fails seem to suffer from two publishing conundrums falling simultaneously on some writers, which would make it impossible for success. First, authors who aspire to success as novelists are encouraged to build an audience first with short fiction in the magazines and anthologies. Since the author's personal aesthetic prefers the longer form, the "short story" she submits often represents a summary or chapter that will become a novel, and is aesthetically closer to the norms of the long form. And since the short story takes less time to write than a novel, many authors look to magazine or anthology publication to supplement their income while writing the longer work. Since the short form pays just a fraction of the amount an author can receive for a novel, and since income from the short fiction is seen as a stopgap measure while the novelist does the "real" work of the novel elsewhere, writers are less likely to put as much work into polishing and perfecting the short story as they do in their longer work. The author himself places less value on the short form, and that devaluation shows in the finished product.

The best authors, of course, can extract the individual story our of the sequence of stories that may make up a novel, but all agree that simply handing over a first chapter does not a short story make:

> **Michael Swanwick:** So novels contain stories. These stories can sometimes be extracted and published alone. Oftentimes, but not always, they will need to be reworked if they're to be successful. You're right when you say that it's almost always done as "a cynical strategy for maximizing profit," but that's only another way of saying "an attempt to make enough money to keep writing." And like so many spit-and-bailing-wire literary makeshifts, the results can sometimes rise up into art.

Clearly there are aesthetic differences between short fiction and the novel at the millennium that revolve around economy of expression, but those limits of expression also define what it is possible for a short story to do. Authors who identify themselves primarily with novels may not have the aesthetic sensibility of the short form, which, according to Ellen Datlow, can be expressed as: "writing deep, not wide." A short story is a work of art that combines thoughtfulness and economy of expression with an opening that pulls the reader in from the first word. Martha Soukup describes the heart of the story in miniature that she paints with those spare words:

> I write the classic kind of short stories—it is the short story that is about the *crystallizing event* in somebody's life. You know, I'm not writing about characters who go on to have adventure after adventure. I'm writing about people in like the crisis of their life. . . . Anything else would be anticlimactic. It's something small and personal, but extremely difficult for that person.

Geoffrey Landis's Hugo-winning short story "A Walk in the Sun"[30] proves that it is possible to write the hardest science fiction about the crystallizing experience in a person's life. In "A Walk in the Sun," an astronaut is stranded on the moon, alone after a crash landing. To keep the solar cells on her spacesuit charged she must stay in direct sunlight until help can arrive, but this means that she must walk for all the hours she waits for help, because the terminator, the line between day and night, continues to move as the moon rotates. The solitary and seemingly hopeless walk in the sun becomes a walk through her memories of her dead sister, who gradually seems to take on more reality. In the story we see the coming together of a scientifically driven life-or-death crisis that becomes the vehicle for a character to strengthen her relationship with her past. And, as Soukup points out about her own work, to take this character beyond her rescue would be anticlimactic.

## Niche Publishing

To this point, we have talked about mass-market publishing, and its requirements to successfully fill the science fiction/fantasy/horror niche. Some of the companies we have talked about, such as Baen Publishing Enterprises and DAW Books, have found their niche in the mass-market and function there with limited staff and a series of contractual arrangements with larger publishing firms to bring production and distribution costs under control. But within the structure of the genres from readership through publisher, there remain smaller niches that cannot support the attention of an industry that survives on figures of 40,000 to 100,000 or more units of a given title. While too small for major industry attention, these smaller niche markets still represent important taste cultures within the structure of the community of consumers and producers. Not surprisingly, some of these taste cultures have significance precisely because of their esoteric nature. They exist for the insiders who have the need for something beyond mass taste, whose experience within the community gives them access to the niches where small numbers do not mean instant death to a title.

### Orb

Fortunately for the genre cluster, the community of insiders recognizes the need for niche publishing to support those titles of high literary or social value to the genre, that may not have the mass appeal to support them in the mass-market. Tom Doherty, of Tor Books, has made an effort to establish a niche within his publishing firm to allow good books with low sales to live on for future generations of science fiction fans:

> **Tom Doherty:**   We're really bothered by the fact that there are books that sell 200 a month that you can't keep in print in mass-market. Mass-market, our base price is fifty thousand. We take penalties down to fifteen thousand, and below fifteen thousand it's extraordinarily costly [to print a title]. So . . . you tend to print three years' worth. Well if you're selling two hundred a month, you're talking 2,400 a year, that's 7,500. Number 1, it's costly, and number 2, by the end of the third year it's yellow.[31] We thought people who wanted

these books that badly would probably be willing to pay more if you could find a way to give value received. So we decided we would keep a number of books in print. . . . Do a better binding, do an acid free paper, and do bigger type. We'd have to charge twice as much for single volumes, but we've got double books and omnibuses with three books in them.

The basic idea is, we can run the small printings on these slower trade presses. And if we run them on a good paper, with a decent cover, we think value is received and people will be pleased that we can keep books like [Pat Murphy's] *Falling Woman*, where we're selling two hundred a month. And this is the kind of thing to put into Orb. And that's just what it is: a device to keep things in print.

For a company like Tor to take a chance and keep a book like *Falling Woman* in print they need to know that they will have those 200 sales a month, something that a niche publisher may not have with an original book. So Orb releases previously published works that developed a following.

In the case of *Falling Woman*, a novel of psychological depth and seriousness about the relationship between a divorced, noncustodial mother and her grown daughter, Tor already owned the publishing rights and could shift the title to the imprint for quality reprints with little trouble. Tor picks up other titles, like Storm Constantine's Wraeththu series, published in an Orb omnibus edition, when their original publisher lets the printing lapse and the rights revert to the author. But Orb is an imprint of Tor books, which is in turn owned by St. Martin's Press, which gives them access to editorial staff and production arrangements. Small presses without these advantages actually provide most niche publishing in the field.

## Small Presses

According to Albert N. Greco, in 1987 the Bureau of the Census listed 2,298 book publishers, a far lower number than the 18,000 to 20,000 publishers tracked by R. R. Bowker, publisher of *Books in Print*.[32] The difference in the numbers reflects the dissimilar emphases of the two sources: the Department of Commerce stresses the *business* of publishing: tax numbers, employees, and so forth, while Bowker focuses on the *publishing* of books. That means there are ten times as many small presses generating published books than there are companies involved in publishing primarily as a business with paid employees.

In science fiction niche publishing, firms arise to fill a number of perceived needs, such as the Donald M. Grant Company, which has produced

specialty books in the fantasy genre for over 45 years. . . . placing an emphasis on time-honored book design and an abundance of full color and black and white illustrations. Indeed, the company's forte is the production of fine editions designed for the book collector and for the book lover. Particular concern is always shown in the use of quality bindings, paper, typography and reproduction of artworks.[33]

In a marketplace dominated by throwaway books made of disintegrating paper, Grant fulfills the need for fine collectors' editions of well-known fantasy and horror writers, including Stephen King, Robert E. Howard, and H. P. Lovecraft, with illustrations by equally respected artists such as Tom Canty, Don Maitz, Jon J. Muth, and Alicia Austin.[34]

While some small presses specialize in production of special editions of writers with some degree of mass appeal, others provide for the varied tastes that gravitate to the science fiction/fantasy/horror genre community but that are not satisfied by the same fare that lifts a book into the sales levels that support publication by a major mass-market house.

### The Little Houses That Horror Built

Horror may be the most problematic of the genres, not least because it is so difficult to define. For the purpose of the mass-marketplace, horror is pretty much synonymous with three names—Stephen King, Anne Rice, and Dean Koontz—and a franchise—V. C. Andrews. Although a few more names occasionally break the surface of mass audience recognition, few have had the staying power of these four. In the late 1990s, therefore, horror is carried on for the most part under cover of the term "dark fantasy" in the science fiction and fantasy categories or in the small presses, including Tom Monteleone's Borderlands Press and Marc A. Michaud's Necronomicon Press. In an interview conducted at Necon, a convention for horror professionals, Tom Monteleone explained his involvement in horror fiction:

> My dad was into it. He use to get me to watch a lot of the old movies from the '30s and '40s. . . . I was reading DC comics[35] . . . tales of the uncanny, the unseen, terror tales, it was just endless variations. [Then] the super hero stuff came and I drifted away from the comics and really started reading the anthologies. . . . Ballantine Books was a paperback line. In the '60s they reissued a lot of these wonderful short stories and collections and anthologies. . . . [And] all the old '50s monster movies. They all fit into the whole.

Monteleone broke into the profession writing science fiction and fantasy. When Stephen King's success in the 1970s suggested that horror might have a life as a genre like science fiction or mysteries, Monteleone switched back to his first love. That led him into publishing and Borderland Press:

> **Tom Monteleone:**   [Small press publisher] Charlie Grant was doing. . . . *Shadows* . . . an original anthology series, . . . whoever wanted to submit something could. He did *Shadow* anthologies . . . for ten years . . . [and] he just couldn't deal with it anymore.
>
>      I just felt like with *Shadows* gone there was no real forum for the vanguard. So I took it upon myself to give it a shot, and I did an anthology called *Borderland* in homage to the William Hope Hodgson novel from the '50s, *The House on the Borderland*. And the title is suppose to mean this is the outer edge of what's being done . . . we don't want any vampires or zombies, or werewolves or mummies or serial killers, you know, none of that bullshit.
>
>      And the first volume received such critical acclaim. And I was getting reviews like "This is the best anthology of the decade ever," weird shit like

that. I had no idea that I had uncovered some cultural/social need here so I was trapped into continuing to do it.

Creating an anthology publication to highlight the cutting edge of creative work in the genre was Monteleone's first step in the process of legitimizing horror fiction. But *Borderland* needed something more to set it apart from the myriad theme anthologies about vampires, werewolves, and category motifs that go bump in the night.[36] Monteleone wanted to give the best of horror the same publishing values of the best of literature:

> I did shop the paperback [to a mass-market company]. I just wanted to do a prestige hard cover. . . . I just tried to create my own legitimacy. We named the company after the anthology. The anthology already had this high profile and I figured that the anthology would legitimize the company, people would already recognize it.[37]

Monteleone's approach, first to contract the anthology to a mass-market paperback publisher and then to offer a prestige edition from his own publishing company, served his niche in several ways. Although he eschewed the easy tropes that sold most theme anthologies on the bookshelves, Monteleone's name value among the core of horror readers and in the industry bought him the attention he needed to approach the marketplace with his cutting-edge anthology. The mass-market paperback brought the anthology itself to the attention of the cream of the horror reading and writing audience and removed any stigma that might attach to a self-published original. Then, with the imprimatur of the mass-market publisher already affixed, Monteleone could bring the second part of his agenda into play: moving horror back out of the throwaway book category and into the collectible arena of H. P. Lovecraft and Shirley Jackson. At the same time, that first *Borderland* set the level for those that would follow:

> **Monteleone:**   I say I want a *Borderland* story, they know what I'm looking for, so they don't send me the tired old crap and the traditional icons that I just don't want to deal with. I want new directions for this field.

Monteleone the writer has created *Borderland*, the anthology and the press, not to get rich or even to make money; in fact, volumes of the anthology have on occasion been delayed while he amassed the funds he needed to pay for the print run. Rather, this niche publisher sees his press as a service to his community:

> I feel that I've gotten into it now and I can't get out because I kind of fill a niche. I would feel that I was betraying a whole new generation of writers.[38]

For Tom Monteleone, a fiction writer first and a publisher only by necessity, a sense of duty to his genre has kept his company going. Like other publishers of prestige editions, Monteleone looks to name authors like Harlan Ellison and Peter Straub as well as the *Borderland* anthology to support the company's quest for a more literate brand of terror.

But horror has many niches, and Marc Michaud's Necronomicon Press fills a very different one, for works of the classic "weird fiction" author H. P. Lovecraft and others of his generation, including Clark Ashton Smith and sword and sorcery author Robert Howard:

> **Marc Michaud:**    I was sixteen [when] I started publishing. . . . We found a whole bunch of articles by Lovecraft, they were astronomy articles he had written for a small Rhode Island paper that happened to be published in my hometown . . . [so] I transcribed all the articles for myself and showed them around to people at the first World Fantasy Convention in Providence.

While Stephen King had begun to create an identifiable niche for horror, and heroic fantasy was beginning to offer serious competition in the marketplace, prizes and conventions still focused on science fiction, particularly on hard, nuts and bolts science fiction. The Hugo Award, for example, has always gone to science fiction titles regardless of the quality of fantasy titles available for votes in a given year. World Fantasy gave professionals in fantasy and horror a place to gather and develop a sense of solidarity, and it gave the genres a venue for presenting their own award, the World Fantasy Award, to compete with the Hugo. Michaud's own first convention, the first World Fantasy Convention, held in Lovecraft's hometown, proved the perfect place to find an audience for Lovecraft's early newspaper pieces:

> **Michaud:**    It was such a wonderful convention, we even published a book about five years later on the convention. That was like the starting point for a lot of people. . . . 1975, King was just getting big in the field. And people said, "This [transcription of Lovecraft's early articles] is great stuff. You should find somebody to publish these." . . . We wrote around a little bit and finally we had written to James Turner who suggested, "Oh, you have to find a small press, that's not commercial enough for us." So we said, "Let's try doing it ourselves." My brother was helping me out. . . . He was eleven years older than I am.
>
> So we started off that one book and started digging deeper and going over to the library and found a wealth of material that never had been reprinted. . . . To someone who is not familiar with Lovecraft or is not a Lovecraft fanatic, a lot of this stuff is pretty dry or uninteresting. But to the hard-core Lovecraftian, it's really fascinating and they really love to get their hands on it.

Lovecraft's early work had fallen into the public domain, so the Michaud brothers did not have to ask or pay for the rights to publish.

> Anything that he has published in an uncopyrighted periodical, such as the small press publication . . . or a newspaper that has not been copyrighted, was automatically in the pubic domain under the old copyright law. . . . A lot of that material is essays, poems, or work that was published in the small press. He was very active in the small press himself when he was growing up . . . in his twenties to imitate Dunsany.[39]

In 1976, Marc Michaud and his brother Paul began Necronomicon Press with a print run of 500 copies of that first book. It took several years to sell the run via word of mouth. Paul left the business, but Marc continued, adding friends and editors who specialized in weird fiction as well as family members who hand-collated and stapled the publications. Necronomicon Press specializes primarily in reprints of classic weird fiction—a subset of horror characterized by exotic mythologies and monsters and a sense of creeping evil popular before the codes of decency cleaned up genre fiction and comics in the '50s—and in writings about the major names of the weird fiction movement, most particularly Lovecraft himself. Necronomicon Press is perhaps as well known for its reviews of horror fiction published in the newsletter Michaud started in 1990, *Necrofile*:

> We publish a few magazines, *Necrofile*, the review of horror, we publish four issues of that a year. We publish *Crypt of Cthulhu*, that's usually about three issues a year. We publish two issues of *Lovecraft Studies* a year, and then we have some other journal-type publications . . . and those are on regular schedules. And then we just do a lot of individual booklets, whether be it fiction or essays, or poetry, whatever strikes me at the moment.

In 1991, Michaud added a series of small books and chapbooks of high-quality horror fiction by contemporary authors to the Necronomicon Press catalogue:

> We received an unsolicited submission from Brian Stableford, who sent us "The Innsmouth Heritage." . . . I liked that story so much that it convinced me that it would be a great way to kick off a new series. . . . Getting that Fred Chappell story, "The Lodger," was a major coup for us. . . . And we just came out with a story collection by Joyce Carol Oates, which I was thrilled to be able to do.[40]

Michaud's Necronomicon Press has won a number of World Fantasy Awards, including Chappell's award for "The Lodger" and awards for *Necrofile*. Ellen Datlow includes the press's chapbooks in her review of horror fiction for *The Year's Best Fantasy and Horror*, and the press's chapbooks have received reviews in the major newspapers, including the *New York Times* and the *Washington Post*. But the company still operates out of Michaud's living room:

> Now I use computers for everything, but back then. . . . I would do an actual layout, demo-ready layout, to bring to the printer . . . and then with myself and my family, which I should comment on also is a very important aspect of small-press publishing, we basically do all the binding work and come out with catalogues and go forth.

Michaud believes that the small press offers him options he would not have in a larger operation, and he values the flexibility a small press gives him to take chances that major publishers can not afford:

> The serious people in the field aren't all that interested in reading the Anne Rice novels, the Stephen King novels anymore. They're looking more to innovation, something a little different, a little unique, you're not going to get that from a Bantam [Books] . . . a professional publisher could not afford to give this kind of material, they would lose money on it.
>
> The other benefit of a small press is that I can be struck with an idea, like *Necrofile* was conceived over lunch one day with Stefan Dziemianowicz and then in a month and a half our first issue came out. . . . So we can move very quickly, and it also affords me control over everything that comes up.

For Marc Michaud and Tom Monteleone, and for the many other small press publishers of books and magazines in science fiction/fantasy/horror, the value of their work can be summed up in three basic tenets:

1. Keeping the history of the genre alive.

2. Developing the genre in new cutting-edge directions that the mass-market cannot afford to do.

3. Providing the materials of legitimation for the genre, including critical materials and quality collector's editions.

The existence of these structures within the community of the genre itself clearly marks it as an art world with a complex interactive set of fields of cultural production and legitimation, as described by Pierre Bourdieu, not a simple consumer marketplace. Books, even books of horror, are not the same as boxes of soap powder, even if the institutions of critique of mass production would have us think so.

## Sex and Science Fiction: The Niche Beyond

As we have seen in earlier chapters, science fiction has grown up over the past seventy years. As community standards of decency have changed, so have the limitations and requirements of science fiction/fantasy/horror publishing. Not all works in the genre complex contain scenes of extreme violence or graphic sexuality, but today few editors or their publishers would reject or modify a manuscript because it contained material generally considered "mature."[41] Beyond the limitations of community standards, however, mass-market publishers in science fiction give way to small presses in yet another niche in the community.

Without specifically intending to do so, Cecilia Tan's Circlet Press, which she runs with longtime companion Corwin, has filled the niche for high-quality erotic literature in the arenas of the genres under discussion in this book. As we saw in Chapter 8, Tan discovered through the Internet that she was not alone in writing and reading erotic science fiction and fantasy. But Net fiction was free, and of widely varying quality. Tan wanted something more for her fiction, and Circlet Press was it:

> **Cecilia Tan:**  People who were interested in publishing good science fiction literature usually aren't interested in seeing something so explicit. . . . So really my only outlet left for those stories was to publish them myself.[42] . . . And I knew that there were people out there who liked to read it, I just didn't know if people would part with money for it. . . . So, my first print run was a hundred copies. I went to one convention, and I sold them out. . . . I figured all my friends would buy one, . . . and people who were total strangers were running up to me and saying, "Are you the person who wrote that book? I have to have a copy." And I'd be like, "Well, here, $3." . . . I priced it low because I figured then maybe people would take a chance and buy it, and. . . . I could have made it a bigger book and charged more for it and people would have still gone for it. But, . . . I figured people wouldn't mind taking a risk of $2.95 for that book.

With Circlet Press off the drawing board, Tan realized that she needed to know more about the business of publishing. At the same time, she needed a change from her day job. A master's degree in writing and publishing seemed like the ideal way to go about putting the press on a sound footing:

> What I am getting is actually a professional degree. That is, the sort of thing people who haven't worked in publishing before get this degree [to] build a portfolio that they'll be able to show to a prospective employer. You know, this is my partly finished novel with a prospective for an agent. . . . Some people for their projects have done things like have started their own magazine . . . and they have gotten thesis credit for it. I figure, I already started this publishing company.[43]

When we initially discussed the program in 1992, Tan had not yet spoken to her academic adviser about using the press as her degree work. She has since completed her master's, for which she did use Circlet Press as her thesis project.[44]

In its early stages, Circlet Press focused on science fiction rather than fantasy or horror. Always, however, Circlet Press strives to blend the genre aspect of the story and the depictions of sexuality in high-quality erotica:

> First of all, I am looking for good writing. And if the writing is good, then I am looking for some sort of fresh idea. If [the story] takes place in . . . just a carbon copy of someone else's universe, or a role playing game universe or something like that, then it starts to dull my interest very quickly. And then the erotic element has to be in some way integral to the plot of the story. It can't just be two characters go off and have an adventure and on the way they have some sex.

In fact, fantasy titles have proven to sell somewhat better than the science fiction for Circlet Press, which is consistent with the trends in the wider genre publishing community.

Ironically, the broadening of community standards that has enabled Circlet Press to reach a wider audience has worked against it in acquiring a wider range of works:

> **Tan:** I would like to publish things that are even not as explicit . . . but I haven't seen much material. I think mostly because the first two books have been sort of sadomasochistically oriented that a lot of the manuscripts I have been receiving have been from people who think, "Oh, that's what they like and so I'll send that."

> **Corwin:** And also, a lot of stuff that is less explicit is a lot easier to get published somewhere bigger.

> **Tan:** That's true. Somewhere that may pay better.

While starting the press seemed like a risk at the time, in retrospect, the fan audience had already shown that the interest already existed to support sexually explicit literature:

**Tan:**   I am surprised no one ever did this before. First of all, you know all about slash fiction.[45] . . . There's so many people walking around at cons wearing chain mail bikinis and stuff and you know they don't wear it home. But there's a certain acceptance in the fan community of people expressing themselves and so forth, and . . . I think we're bringing to the surface a tradition that had always sort of been there, and there's never been a specialty publisher for it. It needs someone to stand up and say, we're really proud of this.

In the years since Tan and Corwin started Circlet Press, they have widened their product placement in the bookstores and developed a reputation for high-quality erotica in the marketplace. As we have seen with all of our small-press publishers, however, Circlet Press remains a shoestring operation, filling its niche only with the dedication of those who believe that literature should meet the needs not only of the mass audience but of the select subgroups with more esoteric tastes. While the small presses mentioned in this chapter have come into their own primarily in the '80s and '90s, we must also remember that they thrive in a literature community with a long tradition of the small press both as a medium for special interests and as a starting place for the great names in the genre.

The small press, of course, represents an important part of publishing throughout the world of letters. What may be more surprising about the small press in science fiction is the degree to which it turns its back on the wider world of small press to present itself as a service in the continuum of fields and position taking in the science fiction community.

### Follow the Money

I use the term "continuum" advisedly above, for, as we have seen, the various forms of publishing blur at the boundaries to the point that we can make few hard and fast distinctions. Our small presses operate out of the homes of their owners, but so does mass-market publisher Baen Publishing Enterprises. Baen also shares the distinction of private ownership with the small presses, but so does DAW Books, which shares offices with Penguin/NAL and now Putnam Berkley in New York City. To the Department of Commerce size matters; Baen and DAW, with paid employees, tax numbers, and a sole purpose of doing business in publishing, would make the Census cut while Circlet Press and Necronomicon Press in all likelihood would not. For the purposes of this study, however, Baen and DAW share with the small presses two important criteria that distinguish their operations from the corporate lines.

The first is control of the income the company produces, which falls completely within the power of publisher-owners who are long-term readers of the genres. For corporately owned imprints, the financial outcome of success leaves the community for owners and shareholders with no interest in the genres and often no interest in books at all. Increasingly, those owners and shareholders reside and hold citizenship outside the country, so the profits of successful science fiction publishing, like the profits from most other publishing including newspapers and magazines, also leave the country. While the fact that the money leaves the country for stockholders and private ownership abroad is a serious concern to writers, who feel that advances and promotion of their books have suffered as publishers try to turn operating expenses into profit statements, a more insidious concern may prove more problematic over the long term.

The second criterion that distinguishes small presses and a handful of privately owned mass-market publishing companies is control of the product. The ultimate decision of what a press will publish falls to the owners. For small presses, and for our privately owned mass-market publishers Baen and DAW, control of the product and its content falls within the authority of long-term members of the science fiction and fantasy community, and of the wider community of American letters. Editors at the imprints of the major corporate publishing houses aver that they have freedom to select the works their companies will publish, but each, ultimately, must answer to the authority of corporate ownership held abroad.

In itself, this is nothing new. Since the 1960s major corporations have been swallowing up the privately owned publishers of science fiction and fantasy as well as mainstream literature and the other genres. In *Enterprising Women* I discussed a corporate entertainment mega-corporation so convoluted that one of its member companies actually brought a copyright infringement case against another, completely unaware that it was, in effect, suing itself. This trend to conglomeration has continued, but in the 1980s and '90s it has done so in a way that consolidates most of the corporate publishing in science fiction/fantasy/horror in the hands of two companies, one in Great Britain and one in Germany, with a second tier of somewhat less controlling interests in the genres in two other foreign entities, one Australian and the other German.

## Bertelsmann AG

In 1998, the German publishing/entertainment conglomerate Bertelsmann AG tried to buy Random House, largest publisher in the United States and home of science fiction/fantasy imprint Del Rey Books (named after Lester Del Rey, who ran the imprint with his wife Judy-Lynn Del Rey until his death; she continued it until her own death in 1986). When it appeared that the U.S. Federal Trade Commission would require an investigation of Bertelsmann before permitting the acquisition, Bertelsmann shifted its strategy, merging Random House with its already acquired Bantam Doubleday Dell (BDD). An investigation was required only of the two U.S.-based assets, and the sale was allowed to go through. Bertelsmann now owned Del Rey as well as Bantam Spectra, publisher of some science fiction and the defunct Dell Abyss horror line, and Doubleday Books, owner of the Science Fiction Book Club.

The long range effect of this merger on publishing in the genre remains unclear, but it is known that in recent bidding wars outside the genre Bertelsmann made the final decision about which company in the conglomerate would have the right to make the high bid. Much bidding for potential and known best-sellers may thus become a pro forma decision based on Bertelsmann's overall strategy, reducing the amount of real competition.[47]

This has already happened in the science fiction field. In 1998 Bantam Spectra lost licensing rights to *Star Wars* tie-in books to Del Rey (both by now owned by

Bertelsmann). Bantam had recently changed its *Star Wars* payment policy from an advance plus continuing royalties (standard arrangement for an original book) to a larger advance but no continuing royalties (standard for work made for hire). The Science Fiction Writers of America (SFWA) had worked to change the payment rules for licensed books (which can pay very small set fees for tie-ins to less known or less popular source products). The *Star Wars* contracts themselves paid very well, but SFWA was in a heated debate over action to protect royalty payments as a general rule. When the licensing contract changed hands, discussion about action against Bantam was dropped. But Bertelsmann still held the contracts because it owned both Bantam and Del Rey.

In early 1999 Bertelsmann petitioned the FTC for permission to purchase Ingrams, the largest wholesale book distributor to libraries and independent book-stores and the one many publishers rely on to reach these stores. The purchase would have meant that the distributor would be owned by a company in competi-tion with both with the publishers and, through its interest in Barnes and Noble Online, with the booksellers. Writers' groups and booksellers counter-petitioned the Justice Department to stop the sale, and Bertelsmann ultimately withdrew its petition.

### Pearson PLC

In July 1998, I telephoned editor Ginjer Buchanan at her Berkley Ace office to do some fact-checking for this chapter. A voicemail message told me not to leave any message but to call again on Monday, when Putnam Berkley would have completed its move to the Hudson Street location of Penguin Books. The move completed the consolidation of Pearson's acquisition of Putnam Berkley from Seagram, conglom-erate owner of MCA, Inc.[48] Penguin had purchased the New American Library in the 1980s; Putnam Berkley added the science fiction/fantasy imprint Ace[49] and the media licensing imprint Boulevard to its existing genre imprint Roc. Buchanan assured me that Ace and Boulevard would be back to business as usual as soon as the boxes were unpacked. But Roc over ten years has cut back dramatically on new releases and reduced its editorial staff from four editors to one editor and an edi-torial assistant, both of whom work on other genres too.[50]

### Holtzbrinck and Murdoch

Though not as significant in terms of the number of entities it controls in science fiction and fantasy, the German Georg Von Holtzbrinck deserves our attention because as parent company of St. Martin's Press it owns Tor Books, the most prestigious science fiction publisher for the past decade. Looking at Tor, we can see two reasons for its success. The publisher, Tom Doherty, applies standards of excel-lence to middlebrow space opera and fantasy as high as those for his literary titles. Von Holtzbrinck has avoided the wave of mergers and acquisitions that have unset-tled much U.S. publishing; more to the point, it has left in place the agreement between St. Martin's and Tom Doherty that allows Doherty an extraordinary degree of autonomy in running his company.

Australian Rupert Murdoch's HarperCollins publishes some science fiction under both HarperCollins and HarperPrism. Murdoch adopted U.S. citizenship to let him expand in the electronic media market. In July 1999, his company, News

Corp., completed purchase of Hearst Book Group, which includes Morrow and Avon. His stake in science fiction publishing still seems small compared to Pearson's or Bertelsmann's, but he exemplifies the international businessman to whom national boundaries and citizenship become simply obstacles in the quest for profits and controlling interest.

## Implications

Corporate America has sold control of the production of culture in publishing to closely held interests that are not our own, with national interests that likewise do not always coincide with our own and are for the most part under the complete control of one dominating personality—the seventy-eight-year-old scion of the Bertelsmann empire and the rapaciously entrepreneurial Murdoch of News Corp. The degree to which these mergers will control the books we see, or don't ever get to see, may be determined by efforts to influence or direct American Culture. It is more likely that corporations will exert their influence by accident, as the unconscious cultural assumptions of the corporate owners conflict with equally unconscious but considerably more diverse American world views.

How much this should worry you depends on who you are. If you are a major writer, you may have some concern. Shrinking competition in the corporate marketplace could reduce the number of potential bidders and lower all-around bids for your long-term multi-book contract. But you will not go away hungry as long as audiences continue to buy your books in vast numbers.

If you are a writer who sells marginally in the marketplace, you may have a problem. The industry is coming to the uncomfortable realization that more titles are produced than the market can support, and some retrenchment must be expected under any circumstances. In the past, some writers could hope to receive contracts in spite of flagging sales. Some names weighed heavily in the science fiction/fantasy/horror community, which, though making up only 10 percent of the buying audience, usually included the industry professionals making the decisions. Or a writer might produce works that, while not attracting a widespread audience, did engage personal preferences of decision makers. An author a bit ahead of the curve might continue to receive contracts while the "zeitgeist" caught up and made the works best-sellers. In multinational corporate publishing, none of these authors are likely to receive a contract. Increasingly, authors receive attention only to the extent that they can answer the question, "What have you done for me lately?" in terms of mass-market sales.

If you are a bookseller, you are probably part of a chain, and you are already in synch with the new system, grateful that the publishers will now send you only tried and true sellers so that all your space will make money for you. If you are not part of a chain, you may mourn the homogenization of the genre, and it will become increasingly difficult for you to make a living next to the mega-selling all-purpose chains. You may, however, retool to accommodate the small presses, which may become an increasingly important part of the marketplace. It has already been reported that "generation X" spends a larger percentage of their discretionary income than any other demographic group on books, but that they are buying mostly small press, and mostly poetry and books about rock,[51] which means that—

If you are a small press, you can expect to do well by picking up the niches the megacorporations let fall by the wayside in their search for megabucks. If you are an independent mass-market press, you can do a better job than the megacorporation at targeting the zeitgeist, while filling specific niches for your bread and butter. Growth, of course, could be dangerous.

If you are the audience, you have as much control over the product as you are willing to take. Jim Baen's experience with New Gingrich's *1945* shows clearly that an audience will not buy a book simply because it is set before them, so a publishing corporation cannot influence public or culture by forcefeeding the audience books they don't want or agree with. But it will take work to overcome a more subtle influence that keeps many books from reaching the shelves at all. The new generation of readers have already learned this lesson, and they spend their money at the small presses, where the books for smaller, more select audiences appear. Ten years ago, most audiences had no idea that a whole world of small presses existed in an underground network of pocket communities. Today, with Internet technology, anyone can find a niche and buy its literature.

In the past, society was divided into two groups: the literate and the illiterate. Now society has switched to the assumption of some degree of literacy in all its citizens, and remakes its distinctions in terms of literacy levels and tastes. Mass-market publishing by the megacorporations now targets the lowest forms of narrative literacy while electronic media and the small presses service the high-end literacy market as another niche.

Ultimately, we can take a simple lesson from this. As Sony discovered when it tried to make American movies,[52] audiences do not blindly follow where money and advertising lead, but choose based on their own selection criteria. Successful genre publishers recognize the fact that readers, even of lowest common denominator fiction, do reject materials cynically produced to take their money and do have a very good idea what they want, even if the editor doesn't quite know what that is. So, rather than worry that the publishing megacorporations will take control of American culture, we might do well to wonder whether they will survive in American mass-market publishing at all. Most industry professionals agree that Bertelsmann and its ilk will succeed best by keeping hands off and letting community insiders surf the zeitgeist, but optimism that this will happen seems increasingly forced.

# Laboring in the Fields of Cultural Production

# 12

As we discussed in Chapter 10, Pierre Bourdieu describes the art world as "the space of literary or artistic position-taking,"[1] which he further defines as a struggle for position in the hierarchy of power that includes both economic and symbolic power. The ultimate prize in the struggle is the authority, the power, to define what a writer is. At one end of the struggle he describes the symbolic capital of the autonomous artist who produces for a culture defined as his peers who are trained through the same processes to read the same symbols and to likewise create art using them. This level, in Bourdieu's analysis, often finds the artist or writer rich in symbolic capital and the critical praise of his or her peers, but poor in economic capital and aligned with the class struggle of the field of power in which the field of cultural production exists. The heteronomous artist, by contrast, finds that his field of cultural production meets the field of consumer taste in such a way that he may experience little symbolic capital attached to his work, but may conversely enjoy greater economic capital.[2]

To put it another way, some artists and writers, usually in the avant-garde, produce only for others who, like themselves, have tastes shaped at the most extreme esoteric position of their genre. They generally stay poor, but are appreciated by their friends. Others, who write for the bourgeois taste, may experience wealth if their production meets the approval of the consumer field and becomes a popular book. The autonomous author may have the will but not the power to shape the culture, while the heteronomous author seems to have the power but not the will to shape the culture. In fact, of course, the heteronomous author only remains so as long as he does not choose to exert the power to change the consumer culture. While that culture seems open to change at the level of fact, where journalism and technology and even some science fiction reside, people are much more resistant to cultural change at the level of structure where most fiction acts.

Genre fiction—romance, science fiction, fantasy, mystery, thriller, western—would seem by definition to fit into the category of heteronomy. As we have seen throughout this book, however, the science fiction/fantasy genres have a much more complex relationship to both symbolic and economic power. And, unlike much genre fiction, science fiction can claim empirical evidence of its impact on the field of power in which the literary field is contained.

In this chapter we will look at the genre complex at its most literary, autonomous end and at its more bourgeois, popular end. We will examine the conflicts that arise within the small, self-contained community of industry professionals and their core readers in which both ends of the spectrum vie for "respectability." And more important, perhaps, we will watch the complex dance of position-taking among producers vying for a voice, an affecting presence, and an income in the field of genre production in the postmodern age.

## Fantasy: Fat (Epic) Fantasy and Contemporary Fantasy

As most readers of the genre know, fantasy, especially epic or quest fantasy, developed into a marketing genre out of a popular demand for more books like J. R. R. Tolkien's *Lord of the Rings*, which appeared in a controversial paperback edition in the 1960s. This simplistic understanding fails to take two distinct early developments into consideration. First, fantasy literature predates science fiction by many centuries. While the collection of folk and fairy tales as written entertainments for bourgeois consumption experienced a boom in the eighteenth and nineteenth centuries, we can trace the oral narrative, the tales themselves, and fables and heroic romance, back through many centuries to the Greece of Homer and across national and even continental boundaries, to the Japan of *The Tale of Genji* and the China of Cinderella. In literary fiction, we find that Luculus wrote it in ancient Greece. Spenser wrote fantasy, as did Shakespeare, in early modern England. Hawthorne wrote it, and so did Edgar Allan Poe, in nineteenth-century America. And, in the ghetto of twentieth-century science fiction and fantasy, Edgar Rice Burroughs wrote it, and so did Robert Howard and H. P. Lovecraft and C. L. Moore and Fritz Leiber and a host of others, writing contemporary fantasy and mythological horror fiction and sword and sorcery.

Between the age of Hawthorne and the coming of Tolkien, few critics outside the narrow confines of its enthusiasts looked at or appreciated the fiction of the fantasy ghetto. Still, the genre thrived in the critical eye of children's and young adult literature, from authors like L. Frank Baum and Edith Nesbit and, later, C. S. Lewis.[3]

Twentieth-century fantasy has proven difficult for literary critics to understand, in part because most critics examine works based on arbitrary divisions such as time period (nineteenth century, Early Modern, . . . ) and literary genre (poetry, the novel, . . . ) that do not work for fantasy. If we look beyond these distinctions of convenience, we find that the history of fantasy exists as a dialectic about the significance of the romantic in society and as a representation of social commentary since the Reformation. Briefly, the two sides of this dialectic can be seen thus:

1. The lore of the peasant, the folk, the exotic from other lands, has some significance as amusement for children, and may be important for the development of certain ideas of social order and values in children, who cannot comprehend the world as it really is. The bowdlerizers of fairy tales fit into this schema, as do some writers for children. In its North American manifestation, we see the stories of

Pecos Bill and other tales of the westward expansion, and the works of, for example, L. Frank Baum.

2. Striving for the transcendental, the numinous, is the most profound and satisfying need in mankind, and only the ancient lore can connect us to the spiritual side of human existence that has been driven underground by the forces of a dead rationalism that is destroying us as a nation (whatever that nation may be). Here we find the other side of romanticism, the side of Mary Shelley and, later, William Morris and the pre-Raphaelites, in whose direct descent we can see the work of Lewis and Charles Williams Wilson and the father of postmodern fantasy, J. R. R. Tolkien.

North America, too, had its answer to the dialectic of the infantile, but its growth, through Lovecraft, out of a darker, more Protestant, Tradition did not offer the hope of redemption that the romanticism driven by Catholicism from England did. Between the two extremes of the fantastic lay their reconciliation, in writers like Lewis and like Tolkien himself, who saw the value of the childlike in the adult who strives to live life through the numinous.

## The British Invasion and the Dialectic of Progress

Because *The Lord of the Rings* appeared in England in 1955, we sometimes make the mistake of marking its influence from that date, which gives us serious problems trying to establish its link to the cultural context of its time. In fact, though an unauthorized version of the book did appear slightly earlier in the United States, Tolkien's influence on, and place in, American culture dates from the immense popularity it achieved in its Ballantine Books edition of 1965. Soon after, in 1968, Ursula Le Guin's *A Wizard of Earthsea* appeared. Le Guin's tale of Ged the wizard stood at the reconciliation point between children's literature—the book and its sequels, grounded in philosophical Taoism, are categorized as Young Adult—and the adult literature of the transcendentalist fantasists.

On the face of it, no time in the history of the United States seems less likely to mark the rise of an obsession with the Celtic Twilight of heroic fantasy. The United States was on a straight course to the moon. In spite of thousands of Thalidomide babies in Europe we had not yet discovered the ecological price we would pay for our technology. Vietnam was still an advisory action, and forward progress of the modern seemed to have proven itself as the one true faith that brought command of the planet under the enlightened rationalism of science.[4] In fact, however, like the citizens of Omelas,[5] we had access to wealth and stability only as long as we were willing to sacrifice the unseen among us—in this case, to keep the women on Valium and to remain prepared for nuclear bombs to incinerate us with little or no notice.

Given the contradictions of the time, the straightforward trajectory of technological excess represented by the modern seemed less appealing to women who didn't want to spend their lives tranquilized and to men and women both who didn't want to be incinerated by bombs. The postmodern rejection of that linear trajectory brought us to a new dialectic in which the fantastic took a greater role in art, music, literature, and the lives of the "flower power" generation, with the debate waging in cultural manifestations of the choice Americans had to make: to move forward in linear pursuit of the Manifest Destiny of technological advancement; to create a new, more humanistic Manifest Destiny through appropriate use of space-faring and other technology, particularly pharmaceutical chemistry and sexuality;[6] or to reject utterly the siren call of the technological future for the mythic past. Tolkien led the way to the mythic past of literature, drawing his readers back to folk tales; the musical form of this backward-looking rejection of the technological present found itself in the lyrics of some acid-rock bands, but more particularly in the resurgence of the interest in folk music, including songs of the WPA (Works Progress Administration) period and the Child Ballads. It was during this resurgence of backward-seeking romanticism that MacEdward Leach founded the Department of Folklore and Folklife at the University of Pennsylvania and Herbert Halpert founded the department at Memorial University of Newfoundland. The period also marked a resurgence of interest both scholarly and popular in the medieval period, which led to the founding of the Society for Creative Anachronism as well as to the growing popularity of the subgenre of fantastic fiction marked by the free interpretation into contemporary prose of works of medieval literature as rewritten in the pre-Raphaelite sensibility of William Morris's poetic translations of Germanic sagas and Alfred Tennyson's *Idylls of the King*.

### The Hot Button of Sha-na-na

While the fairy tale grew in importance as a literary source for adult metaphorizing in the British invasion of Mervyn Peake and the considerably more popular J. R. R. Tolkien, voices in the New Wave, in particular Michael Moorcock with his Elric Saga, made use of the tropes of the medievalist forms to comment on the form in a more conventionally postmodern sort of anti-sword-and-sorcery fiction. While the New Wave took on both the Modern and the retro-Celtic Twilight movements in England, Americans such as Marion Zimmer Bradley and Anne McCaffrey took this side of the Atlantic into the realm of science-fantasy, quasi-medieval cultures with the rationale of lost colonies in the dark age of a space-faring culture. In Darkover and Pern, Bradley and McCaffrey created multibook universes that fans would return to again and again. Like Tolkien, both women had created worlds without the ironic reflexivity of the New Wave postmodernism that destroys the suspension of disbelief. Fans came to live on Darkover or Pern, and unlike Middle Earth, both worlds allowed their temporary citizens of twentieth-century readers to bring their space-faring, forward-trajectory modernism with them.

The success of both series, their positioning in the field of consumer taste/economic power, can be traced precisely to that characteristic that makes them uncomfortable for critics to look at: they allow the living, contradictory reader to inhabit simultaneously and without undue cognitive dissonance both the backward-seeking Twilight of the pre-Raphaelite forebears and the forward-seeking optimism of American space culture. And on Darkover and Pern women found female characters in whom they could locate their own struggle for acknowledgment in a culture that treated them as second-class citizens.

But in the wake of Vietnam and a loss of goal-centeredness in the space program after the successful moon landing, the industry needed something that catered to a taste that was increasingly turning its back on science. Publishers and their consumers longed for the purity of fantasy form and content of *The Lord of the Rings*, to such an extent that consumers willingly became amateur providers under the tutelage of the rule books and dice of Dungeons and Dragons and the role-playing games that followed it. And then, in 1977, Terry Brooks's *The Sword of Shannara* hit the bookstores with enough similarity in content to *The Lord of the Rings* to satisfy both the publisher and millions of fans.

*The Sword of Shannara*, of course, shared little that critics would find of value in Tolkien's work, having more in common with a game of Dungeons and Dragons. But Brooks had extracted and schematized the single key archetype that would motivate fans to lay down money for "fat fantasy" for the next two decades. He set a company, like Tolkien's company, on a quest, like Tolkien's quest. But Tolkien's quest offered a complex study of the heart of duty and the purity of purpose to be found in the determination of the simplest folk when confronted by evil. And he located that evil in the avarice of industrialization and its craving to dominate the landscape and the people in it. Brooks's quest fell right out of the fairy tales of romanticism: a young man in search of his manhood. Brooks became a best-selling phenomenon, and his Shannara series, referred to disparagingly as Sha-na-na, after a campy band that mocked '50s-style delinquent rock, became the model for the phenomenon of the Fat Fantasy.

## Fat Fantasy and the Neverending Trilogy

*The Lord of the Rings* heralded not only the age of the created world quest fantasy, but also its most popular form: the fat fantasy. In mass-market publishing, a novel is defined not by its form but by its length, 60,000 words or less for some line paperbacks primarily in romance (Harlequin Romances, for example), or 80,000 to 100,000 words in a standard volume of science fiction or fantasy. Like mystery, science fiction/fantasy/horror had a tradition of setting a variety of stories, both novel length and short form, in the same created universe. Asimov's famed *Foundation* series began as a sequence of short stories published in the pulps of the early 1940s and earlier; many of H. P. Lovecraft's stories took place in his Cthulhu Mythos. But each story was complete in itself, sharing primarily a setting and characters rather than plot. *The Lord of the Rings*, though generally issued in three volumes (thus heralding the coming of the fantasy trilogy in marketing), is in fact one unbroken story separated into three volumes primarily in consideration of the weight of a single volume at that length and the stress that weight would place on the binding. Presenting the massive novel as a trilogy gave the publishing house the benefit of several separate sales over which to collect revenues for one work of fiction, and it allowed subsequent authors of "trilogies" time to finish the book while the first and then second third of the whole went to press and began to accumulate revenues for publisher and writer.

But the writer, freed from the constraints of bookbinding considerations, then had more incentive to extend the story over yet more volumes. With Terry Brooks's Shannara series and, soon after, David Eddings's Belgariad, we begin to see the truly never-ending story, "trilogies" that could extend to seven, eight, or ten volumes, none of which fit the formal definition of a novel. Most of the volumes give the reader only middles of stories, endless braiding with a structure more like the contemporary soap opera than the novel. Unlike the soap opera, however, these series did not follow the story of a family over generations. They followed a young man's unending quest for manhood through a sequence of magical feats and the attainment of magical talismans, generally ending in his becoming king of the land he had traversed as a poor adventurer.

By 1988, when DAW Books published Melanie Rawn's *Dragon Prince*, however, audiences were up in arms about the cost of paperback books, which was moving to $4 from a price of about $.50 in 1965. One answer was to give the buyer more book for the buck, as Raymond E. Feist did, and Robert Silverberg, in the first of his Majipoor books, *Lord Valentine's Castle*. Readers discovered what the Victorians had known before them: the longer book allowed the reader to inhabit the world the author creates, to learn its customs and manners, and to extend the fantasy over longer periods of time than the shorter novels.

## The Girl-Prejudice and Fat Fantasy

Up until this point, we have male writers providing coming of age tales about young men, the target audience for science fiction and fantasy publishers. But women buy more books overall, if not in science fiction, and they had already made the science fantasies of Bradley and McCaffrey a success. In 1988 DAW Books, owned by women with the passing of founder Donald A. Wollheim, published Rawn's *Dragon Prince*. Even under Wollheim himself, DAW had been notable for publishing women, including C. J. Cherryh and Marion Zimmer Bradley, in science fiction and fantasy. But Rawn had several strikes against her from the community's point of view. She came out of media fandom, during the period of the most intense backlash against women's fiction. Although *Dragon Prince*, like other fat/seriated fantasies, examined a young man's coming of age, the book itself, while very long, had complete internal structures, with a beginning, middle, and an end. The young Prince Rohan becomes king early in the book; by the end of the first novel he has become a man, married, fought a war to assert his right of kingship, and had a child.

Rawn and DAW broke several rules here. The book, at about 575 pages, could have been cut into two or three pieces and sold under separate covers. Many people in the business still felt that fans would associate the length with the Victorian novels they were required to read at school and turn away from the large volumes. But they didn't. Rawn's hero fell in love, married, and suffered to protect his family during war and against treachery, a clear formula for romance, and Sioned, the woman Prince Rohan marries, appears in the book as a strong force for action in her own right, rather than as a set piece as reward for the young man achieving his majority.

Worst of all, Rawn was successful, and DAW began to attract more women who wrote fat fantasy, including C. S. Friedman and Mickey Zucker Reichert, as well as men, including their own Tad Williams, who found the longer form hospitable. Fat fantasy got longer, and today a DAW fat fantasy can run to as many as 900 pages under one set of covers. In the late 1990s, when it became not-quite-correct to scorn all women's science fiction and fantasy, women's fat fantasy novels seem to have acted as the lightning rod for anti-women sentiment in the community, and its writers are scorned for writing romances, for the undisciplined sprawl of their work, and, most vociferously, because the scribbling women are taking up the shelf space and driving the serious men of hard science fiction out of business. DAW, which had come to be known in the '90s as a women's publisher both because the company was owned by women and because it published work by many women in both fantasy and science fiction, took the hit for feminizing the shelves of the manly genres.

The claim is spurious on the face of it. Tad Williams is the best selling of DAW's fat fantasy authors, and he is a man, as are Ray Feist, Robert Silverberg, and the two names that have fairly dominated the fat fantasy market of the '90s, Terry Goodkind and Robert Jordan, both published by Tor Books, not DAW. In 1998, Tor invested heavily in Jordan, who has written historical novels under a different name. Jordan's *Wheel of Time* fat fantasy series has taken the story of the young man coming of age to new lengths, literally, and his popularity seems to be matched only by Stephen King. In the Philadelphia area I surveyed during July 1998, seven of his titles filled the entire display at the end of the science fiction shelves at several mall bookstores, including a B. Dalton, a Waldenbooks, and a Barnes and Noble super-store. As Dougherty told us in Chapter 11, a publisher can buy positioning, but a quick search for Jordan's name on the Yahoo web search engine reveals fifty-five websites created by fans and devoted to Jordan's work. This is more than twice as many websites than the same search turned up for any other fat fantasy writer of the '90s.

Sales indicators likewise show Jordan ahead of his competition. Five of Jordan's titles since 1993 have reached *Publishers Weekly* hardcover general best-seller list and remained on it for at least five weeks.[7] Ingram's list of the fifty most ordered books in the fantasy genre show eight Jordan titles. The number is more striking when you look at the top ten of the Ingram list, where we find four Jordan titles, two by Tolkien, and two by Goodkind. Anne McCaffrey is the only woman in the top ten, with a new release, *Acorna the Unicorn Girl*.

Clearly men are financially more successful than women overall in the fat fantasy field, and clearly fat fantasy is the sales winner in the field of fantasy overall. The question we might ask then is why only Tor and DAW engage in extensive sales and marketing of fat fantasy. One might think the answer lies in the conflict between the artists' wish for a shorter, cleaner product and the publishers' wish for the fat fantasy that draws the audience, but one hears more often editors bemoaning authors who turn in manuscripts half again as long as promised. So why don't these other publishers want the fat fantasies?

To a great extent it is the risk. As we have seen, a few names dominate the list of best-selling fantasy authors, and while a publisher must produce a certain number of titles in a given month, the Ingram list of books in demand from the distributor seems remarkably impervious to dramatic shifts. The July 20, 1998 list shows eight Jordan books in the top twenty-five, with four in the top ten; the August 17, 1998 list again shows eight Jordan books in the top twenty-five, with four in the top ten. All the multiple title authors on the list are well-known long-time best-sellers, most of whom have been mentioned in this chapter, and the few newer authors come onto and off the lower end of the list fairly quickly.[8]

If an editor is lucky enough to find an author who pushes the same archetypal buttons, she must still convince the reading public to pick up the book. And while she is taking the gamble on the book, she must be aware that the cost to produce a big book is considerably greater than for one with a standard 300 or so pages, and that she must find a way to market the book in order to draw the fat fantasy reader to the new work. The book must be Tolkien-ish enough that it will draw the quest fantasy reader; it must be different enough so that the reader does not feel cheated with an old book in a new cover. And the cover must draw precisely the right audience, which means another extraordinary expense, because the fat fantasy cover illustrators are expensive. Most publishers choose to remain with the standard length for science fiction/fantasy, between 80,000 and 100,000 words, with a less expensive cover artist, balancing losses against potential gain and coming up on the side of minimizing risk under the assumption that the need for fat fantasy is already being met. More deeply, perhaps, most editors choose the shorter book because fantasy and science fiction as genres, growing out of the short-story pulps, have a tradition of shorter lengths, which many participants in the community who have now become professionals accept as the "correct" length for fiction in the genres.

### Contemporary Fantasy

Unlike otherworld fantasy, in which the author creates a fairy-tale-like context of kings and queens and magical swords for his hero to pass through the quest to manhood, contemporary fantasy belongs to the Gothic tradition of Bram Stoker's *Dracula* and Poe's "Fall of the House of Usher," of legend rather than fairy tale. For those who come new to the genre, it may seem that contemporary fantasy began with Anne Rice's *Interview with the Vampire*, and truly Rice did revive the interest for the vampire legend while surfacing the erotic component of the character of the vampire.[9] *Interview with the Vampire* begins with a vampire living in contemporary America of the 1970s telling the story of his long past to a young reporter, thus giving a contemporary background to the historical narrative of Lestat's early years. In fact, however, contemporary fantasy has been a part of the genre since its beginning. Lovecraft wrote stories contemporary to his time, and Fritz Lieber's 1943 *The Conjure Wife* appeared as recently as 1991, in a Tor Double with Leiber's 1978 short contemporary fantasy, *Our Lady of Darkness*.

By the 1960s, contemporary fiction had fallen on hard times as the literary science fiction of the New Wave and the Celtic Twilight coming-of-age quests supplanted the more traditionally popular forms in the marketplace. Vampires, as Nina Auerbach points out, became the early exception to this rule, led in the genre by Rice and Chelsea Quinn Yarbro's historical vampire novels. But fantasy authors like the Scribblies, Steven Brust, Emma Bull, Pamela Dean, Will Shetterly, and Kara Dalkey, or the Canadian fantasist Charles De Lint, had not forgotten the history of contemporary fantasy in the genre's past, and they waited only for the publishers to give them free rein to bring the genre back to life.

Editor Terri Windling took the first move in 1986, when she devised the Borderland shared fantasy universe, a contemporary urban landscape where Faerie met humankind at its borders. In 1987, with illustrator Tom Canty, Windling devised the Fairy Tale Series for Ace Books; they later moved it to Tor. Windling chose from the best fantasists in the genre to create contemporary fantasy novels based on traditional fairy tales. Charles De Lint's *Jack, the Giant Killer*, which is dedicated to Katherine Briggs, "brings the old tales of *Jack the Giant Killer* and *Jack and the Beanstalk*, as well as other bits of fairy lore, to modern day Canada."[10]

By 1991 the interest in contemporary fiction had improved dramatically, fueled in part by Windling and Canty's efforts, and by writers like Tanya Huff and Mercedes Lackey, who won their audience with otherworld fantasy before adding contemporary fantasy to their bibliography.[11] 1991 saw the publication of high quality works by Megan Lindholm, Charles De Lint, Pamela Dean, Emma Bull, Jane Yolen, and others. Unlike the fat fantasy quest books, contemporary fantasy in the '90s does seem to have a preponderance of women writers. In part this movement seems to be a reaction to the exclusive boys' club of cyberpunk, substituting folk-rock for punk in the sex–drugs–rock-and-roll equation and a more poetic sensibility in place of hyperactive "information density." In part, particularly among Windling's writers, it also seems fueled by the need for fantasy as a genre to offer a literary counterargument to the economic power of the fat fantasy quest series. Not surprisingly, while winning greater esteem in the core community of an inner "culture defined by their peers" as described above, the contemporary fantasies do not experience the same economic success as the fat fantasy quest fiction.

## Literary Fantasy: Not Just for Kids

Literary fantasy seems to arise from three distinct branches of the fantasy tree, all of whom derive much of their source material from the fairy tales and mythologies collected and translated in the eighteenth and nineteenth centuries. The first group are the fabulists, including Jane Yolen, Patricia McKillip, and Ursula Le Guin. The fabulists seem to follow a line of artistic influence in children's literature, and the three writers mentioned here have all written for children and young adults as well as for adults. McKillip, for example, does a young man coming of age in the Riddlemaster trilogy and a young woman coming of age in *The Forgotten Beasts of Eld*, for which she won a World Fantasy award for best novel in 1975, both in the young adult category.[12] *Song for the Basilisk*, by contrast, gives us glimmers of the tragedy of Rook Caladrias and his realization, in his late thirties, that he can no longer hide from his own identity.[13] These authors seem to share a deeply symbolic and poetic use of story in which folklore and mythology play an important part. Stylistically they may seem to the untrained eye simple and transparent, but it is the flow of the words, rather than the words themselves, which usually carry the poetry.

A second group, writers of contemporary and otherworld fantasy, we have discussed above. While not all the writers of contemporary fantasy attain the high standard of literary quality of some of their fellows, those influenced by editor Terri Windling and her passion for the pre-Raphaelites make a stand for the romantic adventure stories of writers like Alexandre Dumas and the Baroness D'Orczy, and, in the more recent past C. S. Forester's Hornblower series and the works of Rafael Sabatini.[14] Windling began her crusade for the return of powerful fairy stories and adventure fantasy at Ace Books, but later moved the series to Tor. Her authors followed.

To the adventure romance they add the tropes of fantasy: elves, vampires, gypsy curses. Steven Brust's *The Phoenix Guard* gleefully recapitulates the style of Dumas's *Three Musketeers*, while Pamela Dean's *Tam Lin* offers a story of the coming of the fairies in a small college town.[15] While some of the books in this category, like *The Phoenix Guard*, use a postmodern reflexivity to cast an ironic light on the romance, others rely on the juxtaposition of the contemporary setting with the traditional fairy tale elements for their deconstructive disjuncture.[16] It is important to note here that we are talking about postmodern writing not as criticism, but as a joyful rejection of the seriousness of modernism for a style that both enlightens and, more particularly, entertains. First, there must be pleasure in the written word and the play of tropes.

The third form of literary fantasy, and the only one that seems to draw the critical attention of the academy, is that which approaches the haunting incidentality of South American magical realism. As Brian Attebery points out, two particularly interesting pieces in this mode are John Crowley's *Little, Big* and Mark Helprin's *Winter's Tale*. Attebery does an excellent job not only comparing the literary merits of the two, but also exploring the reasons why the less satisfying *Winter's Tale* has enjoyed greater acclaim. Both books move the reader from past to present, introducing elements of the magical and the impossible into the lives of characters who the reader perceives as strange, but with a strangeness of which the characters seem unaware. In essence, Attebery explains, Crowley has been the victim of his origins within the science fiction/fantasy ghetto and his publication under a science fiction/fantasy imprint, which literary critics generally ignore, while Helprin's more identifiably mainstream earlier works and his publication in the mainstream press drew gave him access to the mainstream critical machine. For the discussion in depth, I shall simply refer the reader to Attebery's chapter, "Fantasy and Postmodernism."[17]

Increasingly, however, it seems that under the dual influences of the contemporary fantasy of the Celtic Twilightists and the South American Magical Realists, an increasing number of writers with their roots in non-Western cultures are drawing on their own magical traditions for a new form of political writing about women and otherness one does not find in either of the two postmodern forms that encourage them. Chitra Banerjee Divakaruni's *The Mistress of Spices*[18] was a favorite among readers of literary fantasy in 1998. The mistress of spices is a young woman consecrated to the demanding magic of the spices in the shop she runs in the Indian section of Berkeley. Clad in the body of a crone and forbidden to leave her shop, Tilo must cope with the problems of her immigrant Indian customers and the internal conflict between her duty to the magic of the spices and her own willfulness and desires. But *The Mistress of Spices* is sold as a mainstream literary work, not as fantasy. In the world of fantastic postmodern literature, it becomes difficult to distinguish when a work is created in the spirit of fantasy given permission through the postmodern aesthetic of pastiche to steal from its past to comment on the present in a playful manner, when the postmodern is stealing from the tropes of fantasy to critique the very pastiche it has created in its critique, or when the apparently postmodern pastiche of the fantastical is actually an artistic rendering of the contemporary belief culture of the writer.

## The Growth of the Literary in Science Fiction

Historians of the field set the beginning of literary science fiction either in the romantic period of Mary Shelley or in the 1950s of Alfred Bester and Ray Bradbury. In the former case, of course, genre specialization in fiction had not yet divided the critical world or the marketplace. In the latter case, the few exceptions of literary excellence seemed to fade into the morass of technology-enabled adventure fiction, the authors of which prided themselves on the transparency of their technique.[19] While the various factions in the field disagree on its long-term effect on the genre, the New Wave in the 1960s, led by J. G. Ballard, John Brunner, and Michael Moorcock in England and Harlan Ellison, Thomas Disch, Samuel R. Delany, and Roger Zelazny,[20] among others, in the United States, did spread the influence of science fiction with literary aspirations. Even old-line genre writers including Isaac Asimov and Arthur C. Clarke broke their own molds, with *The Gods Themselves* and *Childhood's End* respectively.

Critics have likewise ascribed to science fiction periods of literary doldrums that in fact have seen hardy sub-specializations of literary fiction flourish, including the rise of feminist science fiction in the 1970s and cyberpunk in the '80s. In the '90s, the pattern of borrowing from literary movements of the past and the mainstream continues. Cyberpunk blends well with postmodernism, the density of stylistic pastiche set increasingly in a near-time future that contrasts starkly with the space opera of more populist science fiction. Ironically, however, many writers who aspired to literary science fiction preceived cyberpunk as socially regressive. Women writers like Melissa Scott appropriated the tropes of the boys' club and, in true science fiction tradition, made comment on them. Scott's books for Tor, including *Burning Bright* and *Trouble and Her Friends*,[21] challenged the boys' club with lesbian feminist politics, while Shariann Lewitt introduced the computer-as-trope to the cybergoth experience.[22]

### Against Cyberpunk

Cyberpunk, with its in-group/out-group cliquishness, did not attract all competitors in the literary science fiction arena. Insiders point to the work of Greg Bear, and particularly his novel of biological transcendence, *Blood Music*,[23] in which an experiment in cellular technology runs amok, devouring all organic life as separate entities and converting it into the stuff of its own massive intelligence. *Blood Music* seemed to herald a new age of "hard sf" based on the metaphoric nuts and bolts of cellular and genetic technology rather than the real rivets of spaceships or the plugged-in sex-drugs-rock-and-roll of cyberpunk. But few could give to cellular biology the transcendence that rocket ships had given to technological destiny.

Some writers continue to use biology as their science of choice, offering warnings about the relationship between civilization and the environment. In *Slow*

*River*, multiple Lambda Award-winner Nicola Griffith sets a cautionary tale of corporate greed and personal loyalty against the technology of organic sewage treatment. Lewitt weds concerns about the urban environment to cyberpunk in *Memento Mori*,[24] in which a computer created to control the regulation of the planetary services—everything from the trains and sewers to communication with the outside universe—plays chess with the protagonist while the population dies of a mysterious disease. Unlike the case for cyberpunk, where the environment is a pernicious obstacle course, the conquest of which proves manhood, authors like Griffith and Lewitt present the urban landscape as precarious at best, one that requires cooperation, not conquest, for survival not only of the protagonist but of the species.

Kim Stanley Robinson has perhaps been most successful in creating literary fiction about the nuts and bolts of space exploration. He does this first by proving with his Orange County Trilogy, often referred to as the Three Californias, that he can win in any sandbox in which the postmoderns choose to play.[25] Orange County is not a trilogy, of course, except that it does comprise three books, something that few "trilogies" can say in the '90s. Each book takes a look at a possible near-future for Orange County. *The Wild Shore* postulates a post-apocalyptic future where the shattered remains of the United States are kept in a state of technological development below the level of the steam engine. *The Gold Coast* proves that Robinson can be as information-dense and as hiply paranoid as the next cyberpunk in an accelerated world of black projects and military contracts. This is the corporate side of cyberpunk, run by its own brand of cowboys and bandits. *Pacific Edge*, the last of the three, offers a future of vastly reduced population in which the remaining civilization in Orange County has learned to live within the limitations of its environment. *Pacific Edge* ignores the cybertrope described above to offer a parable about better living through knowing your groundwater and your softball.

We can see each book in the Orange County trilogy as an exercise in utopia or dystopia. Each moves at a literary pace appropriate for the approach the author takes to the future, proving that Robinson can do what the cutting-edge boys are doing in any of their subgenres. So, when he returns to the traditional science fiction of near-future space exploration in the Mars trilogy—*Red Mars, Green Mars, Blue Mars*—we know he does so out of personal choice, not limitations of skill. The Mars Trilogy, which explores the development of the planet Mars in near time, confronts again the conflicting strategies for surviving an inhospitable environment. *Green Mars* won the Hugo Award for best novel in 1994. I must admit, however, that I read only the first, *Red Mars*. While I expect the occasional mathematical formula for verisimilitude in science fiction, I found the inclusion of Greimas diagrams of structural linguistics, which were used to explain one character's perception of his experience, more offputting as overkill in terms of signs of literary competence.[26]

## The Postcyberpunk Postmodern Male

While women's science fiction has for all its history embraced issues of gender and/or generativity, increasingly we find the fiction of the postmodern male writer dissecting the meaning of masculinity. Of course, the writing of men has always carried the unexamined assumption that adventures were something men had, and books about adventures were therefore books about men. But, today, thirty years after the New Wave proved you could write about sex as well as mythology in literary science fiction, men are choosing to write about being a man, in all its uncertainty, in a thoughtful, literary way. Three things seem to have made this change in the writing of some men in science fiction possible. The first, the New Wave, expanded the reach of science fiction into the mainstream, but it also expanded the mainstream, with its soul-searching novels of masculine identity crisis, into the world of science fiction. Few science fiction authors would hang up their spaceships for the introspection of a Philip Roth, but the presence of Roth and John Cheever made the possibility thinkable. The second, the women's movement, brought gender issues into the mix of science fiction itself, and masculinity, as a model of gendered behavior, did not fare well in the fiction of authors such as Joanna Russ or Suzy McKee Charnas. Some response clearly seemed necessary; the immediately available one, shutting up the women, worked for a period of years in the backlash '80s, but could not stifle the voices who were selling books in the wilderness.

But for science fiction writers with literary aspirations and a manly image to uphold, cyberpunk once again provided an interface with the mainstream that offered a key to the representation of masculinity: postmodern irony. In the ironic mode, one could admit to the truth about struggling to win love or social position, to maintain the manly facade in the face of uncertainty. This secret knowledge men share about their own weakness and struggle is too painful to lay on the table in passion; the distance of irony gives the protection of superior cool to writer and reader both.

In *Count Geiger's Blues*,[27] Michael Bishop takes on comic book popular culture, superheroes, and skatepunks to explore masculine culture. Xavier Thaxton, our protagonist, works as an fine arts editor for the *Salonika Urbanite* in Georgia, where he has taken on the guardianship of his fifteen-year-old nephew, a skatepunk who refers to himself as "the Mick." The book begins with a farcical attack on all things popular cultural, including a '50s-comix approach to nuclear waste, which gives Thaxton superpowers that transform him from the icon of weakness to the epitome of popular masculinity, rescuing the weak and making love with the rich and glamorous Bari Carlisle. Gradually the book deconstructs each icon it has set up for ridicule. Bari and the Mick teach Thaxton how to appreciate the worthier forms of popular culture, but even as Thaxton moves toward the perfection of manliness, Bishop strips away the false assumptions on which that transformation has been based. After all, contamination with nuclear waste has never given anyone superpowers. It has, however, killed and sickened. We are left with our assumptions about masculinity and popular culture sorely tested.

Jonathan Letham's first science fiction book, *Gun, with Occasional Music*, offers Conrad Metcalf as an ironically Chandler-esque hard-boiled (masculine) detective, and a near-future that includes animals genetically altered for humanlike intelligence. These altered animals can be just as venal and criminal as their human counterparts, and they seem to exist solely to give the story a surreal edge. Metcalf, *Gun*'s hero, steps in the Day-Glo footprints of Sam Spade as he follows a dame who can't be trusted into a nest of intrigue involving the highest levels of middle-class perversion and the lowest cellars of the criminal underworld.

In *As She Climbed Across the Table*, however, Lethem makes use of the world of academia to challenge the issue of masculine and feminine in a love story between an anthropologist, Phillippe Engstrand, a physicist, Alice Coombs, and the object of Alice's study, a hole in the universe created in the physics lab. The characters reverse social roles: he chooses limited projects of study and is home to cook dinner most nights, and she works late and obsessively on her project at the forefront of hard science. While they are able to perform tasks culturally assigned to the other, however, Letham leaves the culturally imbued engendering of emotion fairly well intact. Engstrand must contend not only with his "lesser" status in the family unit, but with his lesser status in the academic world he inhabits with his scientist–lover. The absurdist touches give the narrative its ironic distance, while the story itself explores the emotional life of competing for love with the inanimate and with the whole interior love of the goal in a work-driven member of the relationship. But Tor published *Gun, with Occasional Music*, and Vintage books, a Random House imprint that does not specialize in science fiction, published *As She Climbed Across the Table*. And here we see the problem of the postmodern for science fiction, and the dilemma for its writers. Science fiction receives very little literary attention, whereas postmodern literature is the darling of the academy and the new "generation X" of readers. So writers, given the choice, may wisely choose the label under which they will receive better cash rewards and greater recognition, while leaving science fiction more impoverished because of the defection of its most innovative producers.

## The Gender Wars, Redux

As we have seen in earlier chapters, gender issues in the science fiction/fantasy/horror genre complex cannot be summarized quickly or easily. In fact, the only "fact" we may take for obvious truth is this: whatever assumptions the reader has made about gender distinctions in the literature are probably wrong. The most common false assumption contains within it most of the others: *Women can't write hard science fiction*, with *It is too complicated for their fluffy little brains, which do much better with elves and fairies* left unsaid, but frequently not unthought.

When we look at the evidence, however, we find that women have won the lifetime achievement award in fantasy/horror only three times since the award was founded in 1977. Honored in this way have been Ursula Le Guin, in 1997, Evangeline Walton in 1989, and C. L. Moore in 1981.[28] Women fantasists who have *not* received such recognition include Joyce Carol Oates, Patricia McKillip, Jane Yolen, Andre Norton, Marion Zimmer Bradley, Anne McCaffrey, and Tanith Lee,[29] to name just a few who certainly meet the criteria of longevity and contribution to the field of winners like Harlan Ellison, Manly Wade Wellman, and L. Sprague de Camp. Women have fared little better in the annual World Fantasy Awards for individual works. Ellen Datlow and Terri Winding consistently win as best editors for their *Year's Best Fantasy and Horror*, but between 1977 and 1995 only three women won for best fantasy/horror novel, and only nine received recognition in all short forms of fantasy/horror combined, out of a total of about 100 possible awards during the time frame.[30]

It isn't difficult to prove the dominance of white men in most cultural forums in the United States, as I just did above with fantasy fiction. Convincing people against their prejudices that women write science fiction and not just fantasy presents a greater challenge, especially to the women like Lois McMaster Bujold and C. J. Cherryh. The two have won more Hugo awards for their hard science fiction than any other women to date,[31] but Carolyn Cherryh publishes under initials, and I have heard fans praise the work of "Louis" McMaster Bujold. We may adduce, therefore, that women are more likely to have their science fiction accepted if the prejudiced reader can persuade himself or herself that the work is written by a man.

In spite of their documentable popularity, many critics have complained that the science fiction of Bujold and Cherryh has no science in it. *Barrayar*, Bujold's 1992 Hugo winner, and *Cyteen*, Cherryh's 1989 winner, have both received such criticism because their critics, professional and conversational, did not consider in vitro reproductive technology "real science."

The works of new authors such as physicist Catherine Asaro herald a new twist in the gender debate. Asaro's science is indisputably "hard": she is the only science fiction writer I know who continues to include complex technical descriptions of how the propulsion systems on her space ships work. Though genetic manipulation does appear in her books, her characters are more notable for the step-past-cyberpunk bioware-enhanced integration with the artificial intelligences that control their biosystems and their ships. But Asaro's stories are romances; the story drivers in each of her first three books have involved characters with enhanced empathetic abilities finding a mate whose similar abilities complement their own. The fact that her *Primary Inversion* gives us *Romeo and Juliet* in space and that *The Last Hawk* gives us a role-reversal of *The Sheik* does not change the basic ingenuity of the context she supplies around these basic themes. Asaro's romantic science fiction offers harder science than do those who created the subgenre, and she moves the romance even more to the forefront of her books.

When we look at work as diverse as that of Marion Zimmer Bradley, C. J. Cherryh, and Catherine Asaro, we can still find similarities that distinguish women's science fiction and that lead to discomfort in some of the audience. The masculine form, long accepted as the standard, examines social change wrought by technological change. The "idea," or speculative science, is the key to the work, the plot works out the social outcome of the idea, and the characters develop in relation to the scientific idea and the plot. While Kim Stanley Robinson's Mars trilogy certainly offers interesting characters and relationships, the books are clearly about the science and the scientific arguments involved in terraforming the planet Mars, a classic theme in science fiction.

The feminine form also has a scientific idea, but that idea is secondary in the story to the working out of interpersonal relationships between characters. The plot may operate as a vehicle to put the characters in a situation in which they can interact with each other through the science. In *Barrayar*, for example, the plot of political intrigue serves to explain how Miles Vorkosigan, hero of Hugo winning books *The Vor Game*, came to have his fragile and stunted physique. The scientific idea, in vitro gestation using a device called a replicator, drives the relationships and the plot as hostile forces capture the replicator in which Miles is growing, and as Miles's mother, Cordelia Naismith Vorkosigan, battles for the safe return of her growing fetus. Asaro's *Primary Inversion* uses the science of genetic engineering and quantum physics to put two unlikely characters in a situation that is both untenable and unavoidable. Asaro's universe establishes three interstellar powers: The neutral Allieds; the Imperialates, led by a family of superempaths; and the Eubans, with an aristocracy arising from genetic experiment gone wrong. To receive sexual satisfaction, the pleasure center in the brains of the Euban aristocracy must receive stimulation from empaths in pain. The romance plays out in opposition to this status quo, which the plot uses primarily to set impossible obstacles in the way of true love.

### Milking the Cash Cow: The New Midlist

The most common complaint one hears among science fiction authors in the late '90s is that that midlist is dying. Publishing companies deny this and claim the midlist is as strong as ever, but that it was never as strong as the "good old days" complainers describe it. In fact, each faction describes the situation truthfully as they see it. The evidence seems fairly incontrovertible that authors who sold a steady 15,000–20,000 units of each new title once seemed assured of at least a minimal contract for their new books, and that now the same authors find themselves without publishers and trying a second and even third pseudonym to return to print.

Today, the midlist seems reserved for new authors the publishers hope to build. Authors who do build an audience over two or three books continue to receive contracts as their books grow in popularity, but lose their contracts if their popularity declines. And publishers have raised the bar, in terms of units sold, that authors must clear before they are assured of continuing contracts. Authors, of course, point out that new authors were always coming into the field, and that today the increasing number of such authors is a cynical response to demands by more experienced authors for a living wage. In science fiction, there truly is someone beating down the door for the $5,000 contract, and it is cheaper for the publisher to keep turning over new writers hoping for a hit than to support a stable of low but steady performers. It is an industry, and in the 1990s, even the arts are downsizing for maximum efficiency.

At the turn of the millennium, the midlist does not reside in even the moderate sellers of original science fiction, but in shared world lines under the name of a best-selling author, in novels based on role playing games played with dice, cards, or computers, and in the media tie-ins. In that sense, the midlist is more robust than ever.

### The Many Faces of Collaboration

Science fiction may differ from other genres in the variety of ways in which and the extent to which writers work together. In some cases, writers collaborate as equals. William Barton and Michael Capobianco regularly write together as well as separately. Debra Doyle and Jim McDonald likewise write both space adventure and young adult fiction together.

Some shared universes, including the Thieves' World and Wild Cards and the Borderland, establish a shared context in which a group of friends will write short stories or even complete novels, each starring the particular character created by the author of the story and published under the heading of the shared universe. For the friends who participate, the stories become a kind of game that the knowledgeable reader may participate in vicariously by reading the stories. The reader who lacks this inside knowledge of the relationships of the writers still has the added depth of the shared context into which to place the individual stories he reads. Since many readers resist short fiction in the genres because they prefer to read in a comfortably familiar landscape, shared world fiction offers a valid compromise between the desire of the writer to write short stories and the desire of the reader to read long books.

Collaborations between equals stand or fall on the reputations of the equals who participate in them. But equals who sell as well as the old masters—Asimov, Heinlein, Clarke, Bradley, Norton, are few and far between. The old guard is aging, many have already passed away, but the readers still clamor for work by writers who cannot produce enough—or, in the case of the dead, at all—to satisfy the need. Into this vacuum publishers are feeding the unequal collaboration.

## Sharecropping[32] in the Fields of the Masters

How does a publisher supply his market's demand for new books by his most popular writer when that writer is dead, or aging and no longer able to write with the speed and security that once fed the demand? The first choice of all the publishers and the editors who have talked to me has been the same: they would develop new writers to take the place of the Old Guard and transfer the affection of the audience from the passing generation to the new. As we have read time and time again, however, science fiction audiences cling to the names they know, admitting new members to the pantheon very slowly.

To circumvent this reticence, publishers enter into arrangements with pack-agers to produce unequal "collaborations" or shared-universe fiction. Packagers are go-betweens who make the arrangements for a book and then sell the package: license for use of copyrighted materials and names, including the name of the famous author, contract with the writer who will actually do the work, and even in some cases the cover art and other services.[33] The cover of the book will foreground the famous author's name, and the actual author's name will appear in considerably smaller print. Of the advance and royalty, the packager receives from a third to a half, and the name author and writing author split the difference in some ratio as agreed in the contract. In some cases the brand-name author has received up to 40 percent of the total payment for the book, leaving as little as 10 percent for the actual writer, while in other cases the balance is divided equally between the two.

Packagers put together a variety of shared-universe projects. In cases where the name author is still alive, the cover may give the names of the creator of the universe—such as Andre Norton or Anne McCaffrey—and the name of the new author as co-writers. Often the name author will have some input into the novel, providing an idea or an outline, or reviewing the completed manuscript, but in no case have I heard of the kind of sharing of tasks that usually accompanies a collab-oration between equals.

In some cases the shared universe will constitute a framework created by the name author, either in his or her fiction, as with Isaac Asimov's Robot universe, or as a construct specific to the shared world. Jerry Pournelle's War World seems to be this kind of universe, although Pournelle has himself written in it. In the case of the shared world, the name author often has little or no input into the writing, except that in some cases he or she may exert veto power when the name author feels that the "sharecropping" author is moving the product away from a direction consistent with the name author's stated positions.

It seems clear why publishers would take this route: if readers want more Asimov and Asimov is dead, hire someone else to be Asimov. As a publishing ploy it goes back well into the industry's history to include the many Carolyn Keenes[34] and continues to include the V. C. Andrews tradename today. Because science fiction as a genre integrates its core readers and writers so thoroughly, publishers cannot pass off a dead author as one who still actively writes, but they can offer something in the world of that dead author. The less savvy reader, however, won't notice that the name in large print on the cover is not the name of the author. So the publisher continues to bring in the money. It seems less clear why an author trying to establish his or her own reputation would take on a writing task in which most of the income and credit go to someone else.

The answers are as varied as the writers who give them, but consistently, no writer sharecrops for just one of those reasons. One reason, of course, is money. Roger MacBride Allen had several well-received science fiction novels of his own when he took up the challenge to do three novels in Asimov's Robot universe. He admitted that he received only 25 percent of the advance and royalty for his contribution—the book—but pointed out that even 25 percent of the royalty on a project with Asimov's name on it was a great deal more than he had ever earned for his own books. But, like most of the people in the industry, Allen is also a fan, and he found the opportunity to play with Asimov's Robots irresistible.

Susan Shwartz, an author of a number of books in her own right, has co-authored with Andre Norton, and she has participated in the braided novels of Jerry Pournelle's War World shared universe. For Shwartz, who also holds down a high-pressure job on Wall Street, the lure was less the money and more the communality. Andre Norton had taken an interest at the beginning of her career, and Shwartz considered it a privilege to write from Norton's outline. But Shwartz is well known in the community for her interest in military science fiction, which is epitomized by the work of Jerry Pournelle. Working with a number of her friends in Pournelle's War World universe gives her the pleasure of collaborating with her equals the way the shared worlds created by equals do, in a world she enjoys as a reader.

For some writers, working in a better-known author's field can provide a variety of positive returns, but for others the format can exploit both the writer and the consumer. In some cases new writers will take work in a shared world or as the "other writer" under a major author's name in the hope that the cachet of the best-selling author will somehow rub off on their own name, but this does not, in fact, happen. Readers recognize the universe that the best-seller created and they equate the book with those familiar elements, paying little attention to the style or creative plotting or character development of the less recognized co-writer. Some hopefuls, who would not otherwise receive a contract at all, seize on the opportunity to get into print, to become a professional, and find when they have done so that neither the fame of the name author nor the respect of his or her position in the community attaches to the person who writes with their name. Many such authors find themselves hurt and surprised when their peers scorn their efforts, and further find themselves crushed when their own careers do not take off.

For publishers, this approach seems to be wearing out its welcome, and the shared world or best-seller/sharecropper titles no longer mean an automatic best-seller. Writers continue to do them, however, and the best of them continue to push their name author onto the best-seller lists while winning for themselves an opportunity to play in the worlds they enjoy as fans.

## The Games People Read

Shared worlds in science fiction are the logical outgrowth of a trait that has always set the genres apart from others. That is, writers and artists regularly steal from each other in an interlocking web of proprietary invention that creates a variable set of ground rules for the suspension of disbelief in certain mileux. For example, Isaac Asimov invented the Three Rules of Robotics in his early short stories collected in the volume *I Robot*. Historians of the field generally locate the development of the concept of the robot itself from the 1921 Czech novel *R.U.R.* by Karel Capek. In 1998, Joe Straczynski tossed the Rules of Robotics into the pot with mind control conducted by psicops, a concept that appears in the 1950s work of Alfred Bester, whose name Straczyinski borrows for the leader of his own psicops. In another long-running dialogue, Joe Haldeman's *Forever War* borrows self-contained battle-suits from Robert Heinlein in order to comment on that author's *Starship Troopers*. Borrowing bits of worlds would seem to be just a step away from borrowing an entire world.

Core audiences could follow these dialogues through time, but even more immediately they could participate themselves in the creation of their own adventure narratives using the worlds of gaming. Computer games like Doom and Tomb Raider and role playing dice games like Dungeons and Dragons and card games like *Magic* represent just the tip of the iceberg in an increasingly complex variety of games in which the player identifies with a character and participates in the creation of an extended acted-out group narrative based on the ground rules of the game. Gaming conventions have sprung up around the country since the early 1980s, and Dragon Con, the convention for youth culture fans, devotes an entire hotel to the playing out of extended fantasy games.

Books became a logical extension of the role playing game milieu, and some mass-market publishers negotiated license arrangements with game producers to issue game-related books. Game companies TSR,[35] White Wolf, and Wizards of the Coast all fielded series of books based on their own games and written as work for hire at nominal fees, sometimes as low as $2,000, with no royalty or subsequent payment. While a few more successful writers in the subgenre have managed to negotiate more favorable conditions, for the most part authors in this arena relinquish all rights to their work when they accept a contract to write in the game universes. While most of the Dragonlance, Ravenloft, and other TSR books are extremely basic, some books based on more recent and more sophisticated games, such as Myst, are written at a more challenging level. Each, however, provides a second delivery system for the game producer's product. In a few cases, authors such as Margaret Weis and Tracy Hicks, and R. A. Salvatore, may develop a following beyond the confines of the gaming community. When these authors break out into the original science fiction or fantasy marketplace, unlike most media and second-name collaborators, they can bring their reader base with them.

### Star Trek, Star Wars, and Their Cousins: Media Tie-ins

In the science fiction community, writers who don't do media tie-ins usually dismiss them with a scornful sniff. Tie-ins are poorly written, poorly paid, and cynically passed off on a duped public that doesn't know the difference between the real thing and snake oil. The publishing companies get rich on the backs of the hacks churning out books from the desert of originality—television and film—while good, decent science fiction writers go hungry because the ignorant public tramples their efforts as it storms the shelves in search of the newest retelling of the same old story; tie-in writers don't even bother to change the setting and names of the characters so that it *looks* new.

Unfortunately for those who would like to defend the tie-ins and their neighborhood of the industry, a quick look through the available offerings in the media section of the bookstore will immediately show up examples of bad writing, bad storytelling, and condescension to the readers. Some writers do have genuine horror stories of receiving a mere $2,000 on a work made for hire contract[36] for a book that went on to sell more than 100,000 copies, with no revision of the contract or additional payment, while the company continued to reap profits on the book for many years. But the record for media tie-ins is more complex than the objections make it appear, and they certainly don't address the big question: why do millions of people who won't pick up any other science fiction today buy these books?

In fact, one cannot talk simply about "media tie-ins" at all. The subgenre breaks easily into two sections, each of which must be reviewed separately: tie-ins related to *Star Trek* or *Star Wars*, and everybody else.

### Media Tie-in Stars

*Star Trek* remains a mystifying phenomenon that, even after writing a book as dense as this one on its fans, I cannot claim to fully understand. As everyone must know by now, *Star Trek* started as what its creator referred to as "Wagon Train in Space" but can more clearly be understood as "The Navy in Space." A ship out on patrol, with a crew of characters sketched out in broad archetypal outline, searched out problems that needed to be resolved quickly, preferably without blowing anything up, as special effects were expensive, but with resources on which to call as required. Whatever the audiences of the '80s and '90s saw in this premise, the audience of the '60s did not, and the original series died after three seasons, where it lay moribund until the groundswell of fan interest convinced producers to go back to the studio in the '70s and '80s for a series of movies and four more televised series, of which all but the first, a cartoon version of the original characters, exceeded the lifespan of their progenitor. Since that groundswell woke up trademark holders to the value of their product, we have seen, in addition to television and movies, games, comic books, and memorabilia from the sublime to the absurd.[37]

And, of course, there are books. Books written about *Star Trek* for an academic audience and books exhorting the avid viewer to find everything from science to religion to chicken-soup comfort in its images vie for space on the shelves with oversized volumes of concordances, blueprints, episode guides, and guides to behind the scenes. But in most of the shelf space, more space than some stores reserve for all the rest of science fiction combined, one finds the novels. Novels for children and young adults and a novel for a general readership in each of the two main incarnations of the universe appear every month, and a novel in each of the two more recent televised versions is published most months as well. A quick scan of online superstores shows more than 1,400 print items available with *Star Trek* as the subject, more than double that of *Star Wars*, its closest competitor. On the Internet, whole sites exist just to catalogue and link readers to the many sites on which they can find amateur *Star Trek* fiction online, and fanzines still find a ready audience. Editors for both products and many agents have complained that they are inundated with submissions in the universes, and in fact neither license holder accepts or even opens unsolicited manuscripts. Established professional writers with a style or interests that seems consistent with the needs of the publisher are invited to participate and provided with a bible that sets down the context and characters and also the guidelines for the universe, the most important of which is that, by the end of the book, the characters must return to the state in which the television timeline left them. Only a select handful of writers have been able to make even slight changes that they could carry on to subsequent books.

### Not all *Star Trek* (or *Star Wars*) Is Created Equal

The name *Star Trek* or *Star Wars* acts to a certain extent like a brand name on a box of soap, but unlike soap, which is the same in every box, the content of each book does differ, and fans of the subgenre have learned over time to make distinctions among the authors even when the author's name appears in fine print. In *Star Wars*, Kevin Anderson seems to have sold slightly better than the few others who have written trilogies in the adult series. The *Star Trek* franchise, which puts out many more books in a single fictional universe than any other, has a stable of writers who regularly sell at the top of the field, including the leader, Peter David, whose romance between *Next Generation* characters Troi and Riker made it one of the most popular of the series, and writers Ann Crispin and Diane Duane, among others.

What the best of the *Star Trek* and *Star Wars* novels give their audiences is a story with an adventure plot acted by characters the reader already knows in a setting familiar enough to feel comfortable in but still strange enough to provide the estrangement effect readers of science fiction crave. The science in the books, as in the series, is minimal and frequently laughable. It does, however, give enough of a sense of nuts and bolts to satisfy the reader that this fictional future, which she has already seen on television, is possible. Most important, however, the characters in the books are known to the readers as fully realized people they have watched grow for years on television. The good writers reflect in their books the complexity

of characterization the actors have developed and catch the "voice" of those characters. The best writers can develop the less well drawn characters into more
complex people.

## And All the Rest

Given the success of *Star Trek* and *Star Wars* and *Doctor Who* (which had a good run
through the 1980s but has been in decline through the '90s), it is inevitable that
publishers would jump on the bandwagon with more tie-ins. Ace Books even
developed an imprint specifically to deal with tie-ins, many of which come to the
publisher through packagers like Byron Priess, who puts together the Marvel
Comics tie-ins. Publishers have released tie-in series for *X-Files*, *Quantum Leap*,
*Highlander*, *Xena*, *Hercules*, *Lois and Clark*, *Forever Knight*, and *Babylon 5*, to name a
few. None of these sell in the same league as the "*Stars*", and none pay more than a
fraction of what the *Star Trek* and *Star Wars* writers receive. Nor are all tie-in series
equally popular. Ashley McConnell wrote the first *Quantum Leap* books, which
have sold very well, but others in the list have not proved so successful. *Xena* sells
well, but *Hercules* does not. *Highlander* seems to be a hit among tie-in series, although the show's ratings never approached those of *The Legendary Adventures of
Hercules*, on which that less successful tie-in line is based. *Babylon 5* has been
hampered by Straczyinski's limitations on what the books can explore until the full
five-year cycle of his initial plot line has run on television.

When we look at the current successes, however, we can see several characteristics of the successful series that seem to set them apart from the others. First, the
writers seem, for the most part, to avidly love the characters they write and the
settings they write in. One gets the sense that they would write this stuff even if
they didn't get paid to do it, and in some cases they do just that.[38] Because so many
professional writers have an actively fannish interest in some of the characters they
choose to write, and because there are so many fan writers available to professional
publishers through the Net, the publishers have a wider selection of writers with
proven track records to choose from.

But loving the character doesn't mean that a writer has the knack of picking
up someone else's creation and running with it. And sometimes, no matter how
well the books are done, the audience simply choose not to accept the literary version of their favorite show. *The Legendary Adventures of Hercules*, for example, is one
of the top-rated syndicated shows on television, but it does poorly in the tie-in
market, I suspect, because the television show has stripped the character of the
complexity he has enjoyed through the millennia. The character in the television
show is witty, and the show laughs at itself in sly and campy ways as the hero under-
takes his many adventures. But this very campiness destroys the real conflict that the
character suffers in the legends. There is no struggle within the self here, no
question whether the hero will win. In place of tension, one receives jokes. *Xena*,
by contrast, offers campy humor as a defense against the dark issues that trouble the
heroine. Like Duncan McLeod of *The Highlander*, she must struggle with her own
past as it shapes her responses to the adventure that makes up the center of the book.
We are always reminded of the characters' *connections* to their own history, to the
worlds they travel in now and have traveled before, and to other people who fall

within their orbit as they solve the puzzle of the plot. Like all good fiction, the best of the tie-ins are about people we feel we know. Because tie-in writers have a leg-up—we really *do* know these people from watching them week after week on television—they don't need the skill of a William Faulkner to attach our interest in the characters. But the good writers do know that the characters are what we come for.

## Conclusion

In this book we have seen the culmination of twenty years of conflict and contest, of striving and growing in all the tangled and complex aspects of the science fiction culture. We've seen writers and editors and publishers who created universes with their fiction. We have seen readers who built a community around the industry in which they argued and bragged and demanded their say, raised children, and passed back and forth among the positions of reader and organizer and critic and writer and editor, sometimes walking away in disgust, sometimes clinging to the world they've created with mixed pride and embarrassment. Most of all, we have watched change come to this culture, not peacefully, but with all the rancor one might find when any social group feels threatened by change. In their struggles we can see the changes that have overtaken us all, played out in a laboratory of created rules and self-selected participation.

And ultimately, they handed us the fiction. Because, first and foremost, this has been a book about how popular culture happens: how the books arrive on the shelves and why it's these particular books; how the genre moves to television and the movies and the sewing machine and the home video camera and the fanzine; how we realize a life around the cultural products we are handed; and how we enter into the process of negotiation and creation to shape the products we are given. Power, as I was reminded time and time again through the years of working on this book (and on my own less than best-selling forays into the field of cultural production!), rests first and always in the hands of the individual buyer with his six or twelve or twenty dollars in hand, making choices about what he will or will not buy. On that decision rests the fate of writer and publisher, editor and bookseller. The industry meets with its readers because it is desperate to predict what that audience will want *next*.

The industry is not powerless, of course. The readers who make up the science fiction community, through face-to-face interaction, and the millions more who make their opinions known through computer-mediated communication, know that they can only get the products they want if they are willing to work for them—by speaking up at conventions, or participating in write-in campaigns for favorite television shows, or sending letters to publishers and favorite authors, or making special requests at bookstores. The perfect blending of supply with demand happens when the reader becomes the writer, tells her story, and sells it to a publisher. When that story resonates with the wider audience of readers, the audience has exerted its greatest power, not by resisting the industry or by being coopted by it, but rather by coopting the industry.

Warnings against being coopted by the cause of commerce are common, but I end this study with a warning of a very different kind. In today's computer-speeded marketplace, the numbers are the harshest taskmaster in the short run as well as the long run, and they show a troubling trend. The science fiction industry seems to have split into two strongly marked divisions: Lowest Common Denominator (LCD) fiction, which provides the financial fuel but has become increasingly limited by formula, and a more sophisticated but inward turning literary fiction that does not pass beyond the small market for more thought-provoking fiction in the genre readership. While this basic structure is not new, two things mark it in the late 1990s that bode ill for the long term survival of science fiction or fantasy as a "literary" genre. First, in the pursuit of short term gain, LCD fiction adheres with increasing tenacity to a narrowing set of formulaic conventions. Since a book's success or failure can be measured in weeks rather than the year or more of the past, readers no longer have the luxury of the several books it takes to accustom themselves to changes in the formula. Without constant, if slight, changes to the formula, even LCD fiction stagnates, and most will fall by the wayside while the genre fails to thrive.

The second disturbing trend appears in the less formulaic fiction intended for a more demanding audience. In the past, great works of science fiction might cross over to receive attention in the mainstream market. Ursula Le Guin, Samuel Delaney, William Gibson are a few examples. In the present, fiction that aspires to a more complex reading finds it increasingly difficult to break out of its niche. As a result, science fiction writers who want a mainstream audience are bypassing the genre marketplace altogether and selling their work as "magical realism" or other catch-phrases of the mainstream. While this is good for the individual writers, it weakens the genre community, which finds itself writing fiction for the tiny "quality" market within the confines of its known readership, while at the same time narrowing its constraints on LCD fiction. Taken together, the two traits reflect a turning inward that may lead to the shrinking of the genre to insignificance.

It cannot be stressed too much here that the return to smaller numbers of readers, and therefore sales figures, does not mean a return to the golden age when genres were small and the writers were hungry and proud of it. The market and interest core of the cultural context in which science fiction takes place has changed dramatically, and on one thing the industry in which Science Fiction resides as a poor cousin will remain adamant. If the genre doesn't make money, by today's standards, not those of 1950, it will die as a mass-market phenomenon. While the community and its literature can limp along in small press and self-published forms, the books will be more expensive and the ability to attract new audiences will vanish.

The readers are in control now, as always, but they lose control over how the genres will *change* if they don't exercise that control quickly enough. The Science Fiction publishing establishment are not helpless either. They must learn to market their best to the mainstream literary establishment, so that their brightest stars will come home to the genre. And they have to make room for the new in LCD fiction as well, to keep that market healthy over time. Like the publishing establishment, the chain bookstores must make a firmer commitment to their future as well, by persevering with books that may bring new ideas to the LCD market. By the time the market tires of the tenth volume of *Lord Somebody's Quest*, leaving ten thousand copies collecting dust on the sales floor of each Superstore, it is too late to wish there was something new to take its place.

# Appendix: Bulletin Boards, E-Mail, and Usenet

Anyone with a telephone, a modem, and a PC with basic communications software could host a bulletin board. One specialized science fiction BBS located in Philadelphia during the mid-1980s operated out of a bedroom in the small apartment the host, a Drexel University student, shared with four other students. All the roommates shared an interest in science fiction and related games and comix, and not an inch of wall space showed around the posters of anime and science fiction characters. Here, amid the debris of the techno-fan, the bulletin board perked along with contributors connecting to the host machine during those periods of the day when the roommates relinquished the phone line.

E-mail lists, by contrast, require an internet account. The account holder subscribes to the list at the listholder's server, to which all messages are sent. Listserv or Majordomo software then distributes the messages as e-mail to all the subscribers. Science fiction fans already had a model for the e-mail list in APA (amateur press association) publications. APA members send to the editor as many hardcopies of their contributions as the APA has subscribers. The editor collates the contributions and sends out a mailing that includes one copy of each contribution to each member. APAs still continue to circulate on paper, but many more members of the community participate in e-mail lists than ever belonged to APAs. And unlike the APA, which requires fairly deep insider knowledge for participation, e-lists attract participants who have never participated in communal activities around science fiction at all.

An e-mail list functions much as an APA does, except that, with software to do the work of collating and mailing, the e-mail list did not suffer the APA's limitations on size. Some e-mail lists today have as few as dozens of members, while others, like the *Babylon 5* list, have thousands. At the end of the 1970s, however, the growth of e-mail lists was limited by the number of people who had mail accounts on Internet machines, for the most part educational and research institutions.

Howard Rheingold discusses at some length the creation of the Usenet by two students at the University of North Carolina,[1] so there is no need to recreate his work here. Suffice it to say that Usenet came into existence as a byproduct of the search for a way for computing centers that were not connected via the Internet to talk to each other. Such computing centers were often the hub of a local area net that included students and faculty at institutions that did not have Internet connection. Though information might pass from one computing center to another through long distance telephone lines, much as a bulletin board passes information, the information so passed would become accessible to members of the local area net through terminal connections to the UNIX hub. Individual topics on Usenet function much like local bulletin boards. Because they are housed, by agreement, on multiple servers throughout the world, participants with access to one of those servers likewise have access to as many topics of the worldwide Usenet as their server agrees to carry.

# Notes

## Introduction

1. For the critical base of theory on the postmodern, the reader is referred to the usual suspects: Guy Debord, *Society of the Spectacle*; just about anything by Jean Baudrillard, but *Selected Writings* is a good place to start; Hal Foster, ed., *The Anti-Aesthetic: Essays on Postmodern Culture*; and Arthur Kroker and David Cook, *The Postmodern Scene: Excremental Culture and Hyper-Aesthetic*. Larry McCaffery and Bruce Sterling are probably best known for developing the relationship between the postmodern and science fiction literature.

2. The "field of cultural production" is Pierre Bourdieu's term (see *The Field of Cultural Production: Essays on Art and Literature* for the imaginary space in which audiences and producers of cultural products, like novels or poetry, have an impact on each other).

3. The idea that artistic creation takes place within a social matrix is hardly new. Howard Becker describes the world of artists, critic, and galleries in his book *Art Worlds*. Bourdieu takes this a step farther, and propounds a field of cultural production in which position taking is related to power—social capital—within the social matrix of possible positions. Neither the world Becker describes nor that of Bourdieu is specifically postmodern. But when compared to Edward Said's critique of the modernist construction of literature (*The World, the Text, and the Critic*), it seems clear that neither Becker's nor Bourdieu's social model of production reflects a particularly modern sensibility either. The unique and solitary figure is dead; the artist-hero is a worker in the fields of culture under the sharp-eyed supervision of the critic and subject to the vagaries of consumer taste and the patronage of strangers. Our theoretical perceptions of artistic creation now look backward to a time when the social had more value than the uniquely individual and appends that valorization to the hypermodern arena of the marketplace—a postmodern act, if not a postmodern theory!

4. Bourdieu, *Field of Cultural Production*, 30.

5. Gary Alan Fine, *Shared Fantasy: Role-Playing Games as Social Worlds*.

6. Camille Bacon-Smith, *Enterprising Women: Television Fandom and the Creation of Popular Myth*.

7. *Enterprising Women*, 298–305.

## Part I. Introduction

1. David G. Hartwell, *Age of Wonders: Exploring the World of Science Fiction*, 23.

2. Romantic literature in the context of this discussion was primarily adventure romance such as that produced by Edgar Rice Burroughs and Rafael Sabatini, whose fiction of pirates and privateers still fuels the imaginative landscape of some writers in the science fiction and fantasy fields today. It has become a common conceit of the genre for authors to write in the mode of their favorite writers of adventure romance; these efforts can vary as widely as Steven Brust's bow to Alexandre Dumas (*The Phoenix Guards*) and Dave Wolverton's revisiting of H. G. Wells's *War of the Worlds* in the setting and style of Jack London's "After a Long Winter" (in *War of the Worlds: Global Dispatches*).

3. See Alfred Korzybski, *The Manhood of Humanity*. Although Korzybski developed his theories in response to the devastation of World War I, they found a ready following during the Great Depression of the 1930s, when he published *Science and Sanity: An Introduction to Non-Aristotelian Systems and General Semantics*. I don't know whether Gernsback had read Korzybski, but it is quite clear that John W. Campbell, Jr., editor of *Astounding*, had. His writers included A. E. Van Vogt, who based his science fiction on Korzybski's concept of non-Aristotelian logic, and L. Ron Hubbard, who went on to found Scientology. At its height, followers of Korzybski's cult of the engineer, including philosophers, mathematicians, and social scientists, believed that the worlds ills—war, hunger, injustice—could be solved if engineers took positions of power at all levels of the government and judiciary.

4. Damon Knight, *The Futurians*.

## Chapter 2. The Secret Masters of Fandom

1. Damon Knight, *The Futurians*.

2. Walt Willis and Bob Shaw, "The Enchanted Duplicator: The Tale of Jophan's Epic Odyssey from Mundane to the Tower of Trufandom," in *Warhoon 28*. My thanks to Patrick Nielson Hayden for lending me this fascinating compilation of Walt Willis's fannish works.

3. Willis and Shaw, 259.

4. There are a number of insider reports about the early days of fandom, including Damon Knight's *The Futurians*, Brian Aldiss's (with David Wingrove) *Trillion Year Spree: The History of Science Fiction*, and David Hartwell's *Age of Wonders: Exploring the World of Science Fiction*.

5. *Amra* 49, August 1968.

6. Paper fanzines still exist today; some recent award-winning titles include *Lan's Lantern* and *Mimosa*. Fanzine writers like Dave Langford of England, however, have made the leap to the new technology by offering their fanzines on the Net as well as by paper subscription.

7. Knight, *The Futurians*.

8. Ben Yalow, interview, Bronx, New York, August 1993.

9. Sarah Goodman, interview, San Francisco, September 1993.

10. The Chicago area does have its own conventions now, of course, the most notable of which is the annual Windycon.

11. Yalow interviews, March and August 1993.

12. Teresa Patterson, interview, Orlando, Florida, 1992.

13. Lunacon had trouble with its growing and diverse membership before Boskone; Balticon and Disclave have had meltdowns as well, as has Fourth Street in the Midwest.

14. Monty Wells, interview, Boston, February 1993. (Monty Wells died on April 15, 1998, after a long illness.)

15. The information for this section was gathered serendipitously during a coffee break at Boskone, in February 1993. It does not contain direct quotes because I had run out of tape and therefore had to rely on notes. This section was reviewed and corrected for accurate reporting of the conversation by Elisabeth Carey, who has my gratitude for her patience and assistance.

16. Arisia had also moved out of the city in the late 1990s, but it was held at the Westin at Copley Place in 1999.

17. Laurie Mann, e-mail comments, June 7, 1998.

18. Elisabeth Carey, e-mail discussion, September 1998. (By e-mail convention, asterisks around words indicate boldface.)

19. For my understanding of the issues presented in this section I am deeply indebted to Elisabeth Carey and Monty Wells for their conversation at Boskone, February 1993, and to the impassioned input of a young, unidentified fan who asked me not to record her comments.

20. Carey, e-mail discussion, September 1998.

21. Disclave, the Washington, D.C. convention, currently finds itself blackballed by its local hotel establishment because of extensive damage caused to the hotel property during the 1997 event. Organizers assert that the participants who caused the damage were not, in fact, part of Disclave, but members of a separate group that used the name Disclave when dealing with the hotel. The 1998 and 1999 Disclaves were canceled, however, because the group could not find a hotel in the local area to book the convention.

22. I am speaking of the science fiction convention as here described, with a wide variety of events focused on the practice of science fiction. Larger expositions, such as the Comics Exposition in San Diego, also draw many science fiction fans and organizers, and large corporate shows likewise may draw a larger audience for a single event, like an appearance of a major *Star Trek* star, but those events do not fall within the purview of this work.

23. Ed Kramer, telephone interview, November 1994. At the time of the original interview, Dragon Con had forty-six area directors. Updating his interview in December 1998, Kramer indicated an increase of eight area directors in the intervening four years.

24. Ben Yalow, interview, 1993.

25. Ben Yalow, interview, 1993. Only repetitions have been omitted from this quote.

26. Peggy Rae Pavlat, e-mail interview, October 1994.

27. This group discussion was conducted at a crowded and very noisy fast-food restaurant in Cockeysville, Maryland in 1985. The identities of many of speakers were lost in the noise; however, the "Marty" referred to here is Marty Gear.

28. Jeudi told a part of this story when she accepted her Big Heart award, and repeated it in more detail in her interview. I have included it in both places because it puts the accomplishments she describes here in the context of the hopelessness that she had to overcome.

29. NASFiC is the North American Science Fiction Convention, held in the continental United States when the Worldcon moves abroad. The 1985 NASFIC, here called by its nickname Chilicon, is officially LoneStar Con I.

30. For a variety of reasons the write-in bid remains a sore spot for many convention planners in the community, and at their request I have protected the identity of my sources for this information.

31. Clint Biggelstone, interview, San Francisco, September 1993.

32. Boston and Los Angeles respectively, although Laurie Mann points out that in Boston MCFI, not NESFA, runs Worldcons (personal e-mail correspondence, June 7, 1998). According to the MCFI website, "Massachusetts Convention Fandom, Inc. (MCFI), was created in 1974 by the people who ran Noreascon (1971) under the auspices of NESFA. Its purpose was to bid for a Boston Worldcon in 1980. It ran Noreascon Two (1980) and Noreascon Three (1989)." ⟨http://world.std.com/~sbarsky/mcfi/⟩.

33. Worldcons held outside the continental United States tend to be smaller, less well attended, and often more geographically dispersed than domestic conventions.

34. Yalow, interview, 1993.

35. Ed Kramer, telephone interview, November 1, 1994.

### Chapter 3. Worldcon: Mobile Geography in Real Time

1. Frances Yates, *Art of Memory*.

2. J. Steven York, interview, San Francisco, 1993.

3. Chris York, interviewed with J. Steven York, ConFrancisco, San Francisco, 1993.

4. Erving Goffman, *The Presentation of Self in Everyday Life*.

5. In this section I rely heavily on the work of Goffman, particularly *Presentation of Self in Everyday Life*.

6. Damon Knight, in *The Futurians*, discusses some of the earliest rivalries in New York. Fan writer Walt Willis humorously describes his encounter with fan feuds and friendships in "The Harp Stateside, Or Over There with Grunch and Eggplant," *Warhoon 28*.

7. In discussing science fiction fashion, I found the concepts in Roland Barthes's *The Fashion System* extremely generative.

8. Camille Bacon-Smith, *Enterprising Women*, chapter 2.

9. For a more detailed discussion of buttons, shirts, and accessories, see Bacon-Smith, *Enterprising Women*, or Stephanie Hall, "Reality Is a Crutch for People Who Can't Deal with Science Fiction: Slogan Buttons Among Science Fiction Fans."

10. Maureen McHugh, ethnographic topic conversation, GEnie, March, 1994. Note also Goffman, *Presentation of Self In Everyday Life* for discussion of uniforms.

11. Martha Soukup, March 1994.

12. Steven Brust, personal communication via Genie, March 1994.

13. When I began this study almost fifteen years ago, the genre classifications here described seemed well articulated in the fan aesthetic but had not been formally codified. Since the growth of the Costumers' Guild (described later in this chapter), however, this and a great deal more that will be discussed here have become codified. Thom Boswell's *The Costume-Maker's Art: Cloaks of Fantasy, Masks of Revelation* is an excellent photographic source for costume. Divided generically as described in this section, Boswell's book contains photos

and comments from costume artists who participate in the science fiction community and those who do not, but who meet in the Costumers' Guild.

14. Stephanie Hall, "Monsters and Clowns: A Deaf American Halloween."

15. Erving Goffman, *Frame Analysis: An Essay on the Organization of Experience*.

16. Dragoncon, held in Atlanta in July, seems to be one of these venues. It regularly attracts more than twice as many fans as a Worldcon, but many traditional fans shun the event because it emphasizes comic books and science fiction and fantasy gaming for its own sake, not just as an adjunct to the print literature.

17. At this convention participants learned that the 1993 Chicago Gaylaxicon committee had canceled the convention because the committee chairman had died of AIDS.

18. MagiCon Pocket Program, September 3–7, Orlando, Florida, pp. 4–5.

19. Most Worldcons do give participants at least two weeks' advance notice to set schedules and contact one another about the panel. In practice, however, most panel members discuss their topic together only ten minutes before they are scheduled to appear.

20. In a progress report mailing, 1993 ConFrancisco did give specific dating advice, which included things like showering every day, brushing teeth, and striking up a conversation. This advice particularly targeted young men in the community who may choose to be unkempt as a form of social rebellion and then not understand why the young women do not want to date them.

21. Mary Kay Kare, interview, September 1992.

22. If the convention covers expenses with a sufficient surplus to do so, some months later the committee will refund all or part of the entry fee. This is a marked contrast to most media conventions, where the convention pays the expenses of guests and where many onscreen guests can command hefty appearance fees.

23. Karen Anderson, San Francisco, Worldcon, 1993. Stephen Hawking is, of course, the noted physicist and theorist of black holes.

24. I spoke to the Sandses again at Philcon in November 1996, when Leo Sands said they were planning to sell their business. By 1998, when I next saw them, they had done so, although they continued to attend key conventions as hucksters with an increasing emphasis on media tie-in books and New Age and neo-Celtic music. I did not see the family at the usual conventions in 1999.

25. Sands family, Rye, New York, Lunacon, breakfast, March 21, 1993.

26. When I last saw Matt, at Philcon with his family in 1996, he was a teenager, almost as tall as his father, and helping to set up the family business in the huckster room before leaving to join his friends in the gaming area.

27. *Lunacon '94 Progress Report*, New York Science Fiction Society, Lunarians, Inc., 1993.

28. Interview, Boston, February 20, 1993.

29. Howard Gardner, *The Unschooled Mind: How Children Think and How Schools Should Teach*, 244–48.

30. Interview, February 1993.

31. JB, interview, Maryland, April 10, 1993 (updated January 1999).

32. The 1982 Philcon was not actually held until January 1983, so was officially dubbed '82.1, using the computer software parlance of an issue number and an update on that issue.

33. In one of those small-world synchronicities, JB has since moved to Boston, where this roommate and fellow fan is now his supervisor at his current job (e-mail discussion, January 1999).

34. Richard (JB) Segal, e-mail discussion, January 1999.

35. Confrancisco deliberately dubbed the committee responsible for these events the "Grand Guignol Division." In addition to the Hugos and the masquerade, the Grand Guignol Division also organized opening and closing ceremonies, dances, and other "spectacular" events.

36. See Victor Turner, "Liminal to Liminoid in Play, Flow, and Ritual: An Essay in Comparative Symbology" for basic discussion of the application of concept of communitas to nonreligious events.

37. Ray Bradbury, guest of honor speech, ConFederation, Atlanta, September 1986.

38. See Dell Hymes, "Narrative Form as a 'Grammar' of Experience: Native Americans and a Glimpse of English."

39. Sally Fink, costume panel, Philadelphia, 1985.

40. Susan Shwartz, private e-mail, March 15, 1993. (By e-mail convention, lines around words indicate underlining or italic.)

41. Names are references to characters in Gordon R. Dickson's Dorsai series of books about a planet of honorable mercenary soldiers.

42. With the usual multiple referent layers, David Chalker, the young boy who opens the books on the "Heroes" presentation, is the son of well-known science fiction writer Jack Chalker.

43. This would seem to be the classic fulfillment of the postmodern warning. The commodity, mass-market genre fiction, is not the book but the multiple images the books create of a past or future, which images (not real history, or a real future) become the organizing principle around which the falsely constituted sense of community is constructed. The model fails in two important points, however: (1) the science fiction community has constituted itself in this "postmodern" way since 1926; and (2) all cultures create themselves out of a combination of functional needs, organizing structures, and images given meaning to the extent they fulfill the desires of the people for explanations of a direct or metaphoric kind.

44. Media fanzines most often contain fiction based on television or movie characters. Science fiction fanzines generally contain commentary, news, and chat about fandom itself, with an occasional book review column.

45. The first Hugos were awarded in 1953 to Alfred Bester's *The Demolished Man*, to *Galaxy* and to *Astounding* in a tie for best Professional magazine, to Willy Ley for Excellence in Fact Articles, to Ed Emshwiller and Hannes Bok in a tie for best cover artist, to Virgil Finlay for best interior artist, to Philip José Farmer for best new SF author or artist, and to Forrest J. Ackerman as Number 1 Fan (ConFrancisco program book, San Francisco, 1993). The awards have since grown to include many more categories.

46. The Nebulas are the peer awards in science fiction, voted by the membership of the Science Fiction and Fantasy Writers of America (SFWA).

47. Florida Association for Nucleation and Conventions, Inc. (FANAC), *MagiCon Progress Report 6*, Orlando, Florida, 1992, pull-out ballot.

48. Personal communication, David Bratman, ConFrancisco Hugo Awards Committee, February 1994.

49. All fans who have purchased a membership for the current Worldcon may vote on the Hugos for the publishing year that precedes the Worldcon (MagiCon, e.g., held in September 1992, awarded Hugos for materials published in 1991). Fans who participated in the preceding Worldcon may also participate in voting for the final nominees from which the final vote will be taken. In fact, however, out of the thousands of potential voters, only a few hundred choose to vote in any given year.

50. The one exception to this rule continues to be involvement in media fandom, which is often scorned by both fans and professionals in the literary community. Issues of copyright infringement and licensing agreements do come into play in the commercial publishing field, but core fandom, like most communities, is very conservative and guards its traditions jealously. The disdain seems to reflect an old resistance to women in fandom, a continuing difficulty with young fans, and a sense of confusion about the changes both groups bring.

51. *Isaac Asimov's Science Fiction Magazine*, April 1991.

52. Ellipses here represent several very brief slips in the tape.

53. Nancy Kress, acceptance speech, Orlando, 1992, for the novella "Beggars in Spain" (later included as a part of the novel *Beggars in Spain* and the trilogy published by Avon Books, 1993–96).

## Chapter 4. The Cyberscape: GEnie and the Rise of the Internet

1. Sherry Turkle, *Life on the Screen: Identity in the Age of the Internet* and *The Second Self: Computers and the Human Spirit*.

2. Clifford Stoll, *Silicon Snake Oil: Second Thoughts on the Information Highway*.

3. Andrew Ross, *Strange Weather: Culture, Science, and Technology in the Age of Limits*.

4. Douglas Rushkoff, *Cyberia: Life in the Trenches of Cyberspace* and Mark Dery, *Escape Velocity: Cyberculture at the End of the Century*.

5. Eric Raymond, ed., *The New Hacker's Dictionary*, 414–16.

6. Howard Rheingold, *Virtual Community: Homesteading on the Electronic Frontier*, 77. See Katie Hafner and Matthew Lyon, *Where Wizards Stay Up Late: The Origins of the Internet* for discussion of the development of ARPANET and its expansion into the Internet.

7. Saul Jaffe, described on SF-Lovers webpage.

8. Rheingold, 120.

9. According to AOL's online company profile, the company was formed in 1985 ("About the Company, America Online, 1998," http://www.aol.com/corp/profile). In fact, the product did not make an appearance in science fiction culture until late 1994. At the time, David Axler was promoting AOL at science fiction conventions on the East Coast, much to the derision of GEnie-ites at the time. AOL did go on to become the leading commercial

online service provider in the world, and many science fiction fans and professionals use its e-mail and Internet services. But AOL, which offers an easy-to-use graphical interface to its services, proved unsatisfactory as a locus of community precisely because that ease of use made it impossible to establish communal boundaries against the casual browser. To some extent, user-unfriendly interfaces kept the conversation limited to adults and technologically sophisticated younger subscribers serious enough about the subject to seek it out and cope with the recondite conversations. The latter, of course, had always been the target audience for science fiction, which had the cultural mechanisms already in place to assimilate them.

10. Jim Macdonald, telephone interview, October 1992.

11. Macdonald, e-mail correspondence, January 1999.

12. Shared Worlds are fictional settings in which more than one author creates characters and narratives. Shared Worlds may be owned by one author or by a group creating together. Works produced in the shared world may be collaborations or the product of an individual author. The Thieves World and Wild Cards are two of the better-known shared worlds.

13. Susan Shwartz, interview, November 1992.

14. Macdonald, telephone interview, October 1992. The reference to the Public Forum, a Genie discussion area outside the SFRT, demonstrates the fans on the SFRT ranged beyond their own home ground for information but came back to the SFRT to discuss it.

15. Macdonald, interview, September 1993.

16. Macdonald, e-mail, January 1999.

17. Shwartz, e-mail discussion, 1993.

18. Shwartz, interview, November 1992. I have changed "Mary" 's name to preserve privacy for her friends and relatives.

19. Rheingold, *Virtual Community*, 34.

20. Damon Knight, *The Futurians*.

21. Mitch Wagner, GEnie Online History Topic, May 31, 1993.

22. Patrick Nielsen Hayden, GEnie Online History Topic, May 31, 1993.

23. Mitch Wagner, e-mail correspondence, January 5, 1999.

24. John Bunnell (Djonn), GEnie History Topic, June 4, 1993. Note that Bunnell uses one of the online norms for titles, all initial caps, in this Topic entry.

25. At this point, Youvelle bought the service. While keeping the basic name, it reduced the capitalized second letter to lower case to indicate that Genie was no longer a product of General Electric.

26. Public Access Networks Corporation, New York. Description at http://www.panix.com.

27. Like myself, many participants keep a separate, older model computer for use with Genie, while conducting their serious Net business on a faster, smarter machine. Participants drop off the service as their older machines die.

28. Perhaps not surprisingly, this virtual participation has not resulted in a significant growth in attendance at the traditional science fiction convention venues. But there has

been an explosion of new venues, both fannish, like Dragon Con, and commercial, like the many studio-connected conventions for action shows like *Xena* and *Highlander*. The growth of Net fandom, rather than reducing face-to-face interaction, seems to have refined it, so that even obscure syndicated television shows can attract enough paying participants for a specialty convention focused on their product.

29. Penguin-Putnam, for example, has a newsletter for its romance lines, Berkley/Jove, Topaz, and Signet Regency Plus, and one for each of the science fiction lines it owns or contracts services for, including Roc, Ace/Boulevard, and DAW, to all of which fans may subscribe on the Penguin-Putnam Website, http://www.penguinputnam.com. The newsletter arrives in the subscriber's e-mail on a monthly or semimonthly basis.

30. *The Zocalo*, #148-A, May 18, 1998.

31. The Listserv receives messages from anyone subscribed to the list and distributes the messages to everyone subscribed to the list. When servers are offline for repair, when electronic mailboxes are full, or when participants change addresses or temporarily lose service, their messages are returned to the list manager, who must isolate the problem and correct it. On a small list or a newsletter, the amount of time devoted to this task can be minimal. On a large and active list, however, more subscribers have trouble with more messages, and the tasks of solving the problems take an increasing amount of the manager's time.

32. Why there are no supporting excerpts from the discussion list in this section: I originally joined the list just for fun, after friends had goaded me into watching the syndicated contemporary action-fantasy program. Members of the list did not want to be studied, and I agreed not to do so. When I took on the list as its manager, I explained that I wanted to learn how discussion lists operated. We agreed on a compromise, that I would study the list for general information and that I would not use list members' names or discussions. I have honored this promise to the best of my understanding of it, which includes removing the name of the program from the following discussion.

33. ACTION-F is a pseudonym, as is *Action*; neither refers to any list or media product by that name in existence now or that may exist in the future.

34. Discussion lists vary in their gender distribution, but ACTION-F consistently maintained a membership that was well over 50 percent women, with women providing at least 90 percent of the posts. Most of the organizers and participants at the conventions for the product were also women, although most of the activities at the conventions cutomarily attract a more even distribution by gender.

35. Camille Bacon-Smith, *Enterprising Women*, 22–37.

36. Bacon-Smith, *Enterprising Women*, 31–37.

37. Fan efforts to save *Alien Nation* on Fox had failed, and efforts to rescue favorite characters on the same network's *War of the Worlds* had likewise met with contempt.

38. *Babylon 5*, which will be discussed below, received a number of reprieves, thanks directly and indirectly, in part, to fan involvement.

39. CERN European Laboratory for Particle Physics, Geneva, the home of the WWW and its creator, Tim Berners-Fee. Lee, who had been working with hyperlinks in a single system since 1980, expanded the idea of a universal open network in which links could reach across machines and even continents. The development of the WWW required, first, a standard transfer protocol (HTTP, via TCP/IP); second, a standard translation protocol (HTML);

and third, a standard locator protocol (URI); all of which had to cross operating system platforms and hardware distinctions. The World Wide Web, with its protocol standards, became publicly available in 1993 ("A Short History of Internet Protocols at CERN," Ben Segal / CERN PDP-NS, April, 1995, http://nicewww.cern.ch/~pintopc/www/divers/HistWebCern.html).

40. NCSA, the National Center for Supercomputing Applications, University of Illinois at Urbana-Champaign. Netscape's corporate backgrounder has this to say about Marc Andreessen, creator of Mosaic and, later, of Netscape:

> As an undergraduate at the University of Illinois in Champaign, Andreessen created the NCSA Mosaic browser prototype for the Internet with a team of students and staff at the university's National Center for Supercomputing Applications (NCSA). With a friendly, point-and-click method for navigating the Internet and free distribution to network users, NCSA Mosaic gained an estimated two million users worldwide in just over one year. Andreessen earned his bachelor of science degree in computer science at the University of Illinois in 1993.

While it seems clear from the backgrounder that Andreessen was part of a team developing Mosaic at Urbana-Champaign, it also seems clear that when the smoke lifted Andreessen had the software, Jim Clark had the venture capital, and Jim Barksdale had the executive skills not just to put the Web on the map, but to create the map for the developing ranks of Web enthusiasts.

41. Even today some websites show the continued influence of early advice: use text, not graphics, because the latter take too long to load.

42. Yahoo: According to "The History of Yahoo 1994–1997" ⟨http://www.yahoo.com⟩,

> The name Yahoo! is supposed to stand for "Yet Another Hierarchical Officious Oracle," but Filo and Yang insist they selected the name because they considered themselves yahoos.

Filo and Yang, according to the website, are David Filo and Jerry Yang. While studying toward their Ph.D.s in electrical engineering at Stanford University in the early 1990s, the duo compiled their list of favorite sites, and later developed the list into a hierarchical search tool that makes the Web manageable for many users. While other search engines pride themselves on the number of site references they can produce, Yahoo has a hierarchical system much like Gopher's hierarchy trees and offers a more focused search. Of course, in 1994, when Filo and Yang turned their hobby into a business, there weren't any significant competitors in the search engine field at all. (Their website does not indicate whether Filo and Yang ever received their doctorates in engineering.)

43. The increase in machine speed that helped the Web-based shift to graphics also put America Online, with its user-friendly graphical interface, at the forefront of online services. IDT purchased Genie through its subsidiary Youvelle in 1996, but has yet to produce a viable graphical interface. With the purchase of Compuserve by America Online, the two original leaders in the field of online service have essentially disappeared.

44. *Plug* Ace/Boulevard can be found at http://www.penguinputnam.com/clubppi/news/ace; Penguinputnam.com also hosts the Online Newsletters for DAW Books and the Roc imprint http://www.penguinputnam.com/clubppi/index.htm. Baen Books maintains a CGI bulletin board at http://www.baen.com/bar/.

45. Saul Jaffe, SF-Lovers Digest Website, http://sflovers.rutgers.edu/.

46. When a website can expect more traffic than the server can handle, the site owner may take advantage of offers by other sites to mirror, or store and present, a copy of the mirrored site. So, you can find the Science Fiction Resource Guide hosted not only by SF-Lovers but also by Geocities, the Internet Group, and sites in Germany, Spain, Turkey, and others (Baden, SFRg, http://sflovers.rutgers.edu/).

47. Joe Siclari, FanHistory Project Chairman, F.A.N.A.C., Inc., "FanHistory: What We Are Doing" at http://www.fanac.org.

48. Joe Siclari, at http://www.fanac.org.

49. See http://www.scifi.com.

50. "If STAR TREK was 'Wagon Train to the Stars,' then BABYLON 5 is Casablanca in space." J. Michael Straczynski, Genie, December 2, 1991.

51. J. Michael Straczynski, Genie, February 4, 1992. Straczynski's Genie posts, as well as his Internet communications, are collected at http://www.midwinter.com/lurk.

52. *Zocalo*, issue 147, at http://www.highfiber.com/~katana.

53. Websites are at:

> TNT: http://tnt.turner.com/babylon5/
> Warner Brothers: http://www.babylon5.com/cmp/
> Fan Club: http://www.thestation.com/
> Lurker's Guide: http://www.midwinter.com/lurk/.

54. *The Lurker's Guide to Babylon 5* is designed and maintained by Steve Grimm, a fan of the show. According to Steve, he receives no payment from anyone connected with the series for his work on the website.

55. It should be noted here that the fantasy action series *The Highlander* has likewise spun off a second television series and a new *Highlander* movie. Like *Babylon 5*, *Highlander* made good use of a highly computer literate fan base. Unlike the case of *Babylon 5*, however, *The Highlander's* production company involved itself in the organization of its own specialty conventions where stars of the series helped to promote *Highlander* tie-in merchandising paraphernalia. It is possible that the profits from merchandising tipped the scales in favor of an extended run for the series and its forthcoming sequel.

**Part II. Introduction**

1. Alfred Bester, *The Demolished Man*.

2. C. M. Kornbluth, "The Marching Morons."

3. Damon Knight, *Why Do Birds*.

**Chapter 5. The Women Were Always Here: The Obligatory History Lesson**

1. David Kyle, speaking at the Hugo Awards ceremony, MagiCon, Orlando, Florida, September 1992.

2. I have begun my look at the early women in fandom with the 1950s rather than before because my current informants, still active in fandom today, report the '50s at the earliest as the start of their fan activity. Women wrote and participated before then, but their stories are for the histories and for those who have the opportunity to speak to them today.

3. Anthologists have made available some of the material written by women writers of the Golden Age through the feminist revolution. *Women of Wonder: The Classic Years: Science*

*Fiction by Women from the 1940s to the 1970s,* based on a three-volume anthology compiled in the 1970s by Pamela Sargent, is once again available in a trade-paperback format. *Women of Wonder* includes women science fiction writers from the 1940s (C. L. Moore and Judith Merrill) to the 1970s, but even in this anthology there are almost as many stories from the '70s (ten) as there are from all the other decades covered in the book (eleven stories, spanning three decades). Women's work in fantasy and horror seems to have suffered "disappearance" from the record to an even greater extent than their science fiction, but the reader might wish to take a look at Jessica Amanda Salmonson's *What Did Miss Darrington See? An Anthology of Feminist Supernatural Fiction,* an anthology of speculative fiction from Feminist Press.

4. To some extent, contemporary feminist critics are beginning to correct this omission. Sarah Lefanu, for example, does discuss Marion Zimmer Bradley in *Feminism and Science Fiction.* While Lefanu criticizes the message that supports the status quo she sees in Bradley's fiction, she does recognize the importance of the author in the genre.

5. Robin Roberts, *A New Species: Gender and Science in Science Fiction,* 45. My own work includes interviews with science fiction writers and with fans conducted over the last decade and a half.

6. Personal correspondence from Joanna Russ, May 10, 1994, in response to my question of April 26, 1994.

7. Damon Knight, *The Futurians.* The interpretation is my own.

8. Here it is important to make a distinction between science fiction fanzines and the media fanzines discussed in *Enterprising Women,* which are often elaborately produced collections (or single-work publications) of fiction based on source products from within the entertainment industry. Science fiction fanzines are generally smaller productions that offer primarily nonfiction writing: letters from readers and responses thereto, convention reports, and essays of daily life that fans share with one another. Sometimes the fanzines will mention science fiction or include reviews, but this is not necessary. To be a science fiction fanzine, the publication need only arise from and circulate within the community as a form of dispersed interpersonal communication.

9. Connie Willis, "The Women SF Doesn't See."

10. According to a later communication from Anderson, she did find the Coles at the 1993 Worldcon, where this interview was conducted.

11. Karen Anderson, interview, San Francisco, September 1993.

12. Jacqueline Lichtenberg, Sondra Marshak, and Joan Winston, *Star Trek Lives!.*

13. Walt Willis, "The Harp in Oopsla," Installment 13.

14. Although Norton wrote under a man's name, the readers I spoke with always seemed to have been aware that she was a woman writer.

15. Sarah Goodman, e-mail correspondence, July 1993.

16. Joanna Russ, *The Female Man,* 35.

17. Russ, *Female Man,* 151.

18. For obvious reasons I cannot publish the name of the fanzine or the writer in this public forum. However, the material came to me through Temple University's Special Collection fanzine holdings, where they remain and can be found. Lest the reader wonder whether this

was one of the many identity scams rumored about fandom at the time, I should mention that the writer was a well-known figure with many connections in the fan community, not an apocryphal name appended to an article or column.

19. "The List of Worldcons," *Bucconeer Souvenir Book* (Baltimore: Baltimore Worldcon 1998, Inc., 1998), 70–74.

20. This is an important distinction. Doris Lessing was writer guest of honor at the 1987 Worldcon held in Brighton, England. In the United States her status as a science fiction author is held in serious doubt by many, although it appears often in the feminist scholarship in women's science fiction.

21. Ben Yalow, interview, September 1993.

22. "The Hugo Award Winners," *Confrancisco: The Souvenir Book* (San Francisco: San Francisco Science Fiction Conventions, Inc., 1993).

23. "The Hugo Award Winners," 1993.

24. Brian Aldiss devotes several pages (260–64) of *Trillion Year Spree* to Tolkien and his influence, as does David Hartwell in *Age of Wonders*, 21–22. I will not repeat what they say, but instead refer the reader to the sources.

25. Joan Winston, *The Making of the Trek Conventions*.

26. While I formulated the above from a variety of observations and sources, I am also indebted to Joanna Russ, who mentioned in her correspondence of 1994 many of the same effects from her own experience, providing additional confirmation and support.

27. Camille Bacon-Smith, *Enterprising Women*.

28. It is important to note that not all the New Wave writers were men. Pamela Zoline's "Heat Death of the Universe," for example, first appeared in *New Worlds*, the highly experimental British magazine that stands as the essential New Wave publication. And even at the time Ursula Le Guin's work seemed to bridge some virtual divide between the two camps.

29. Roger Zelazny, *Lord of Light*.

30. Samuel R. Delany, *Dhalgren*.

31. Russ, *The Female Man*, 151.

32. See, for example, Sarah Lefanu, *Feminism and Science Fiction*.

33. Roberts, 45.

34. Theodora Kroeber's works include *Ishi in Two Worlds: A Biography of the Last Wild Indian in North America* and *Alfred Kroeber: A Personal Configuration*.

35. Since this is an ethnography I will only detail the effects the book has had on the community; I will not comment on it critically. Literary criticism abounds on the subject, so much so that contemporary feminist critics such as Marleen Barr (*Lost in Space: Probing Feminist Science Fiction and Beyond*), Sarah Lefanu (*Feminism and Science Fiction*), and Susan Bassnett (in *Where No Man Has Gone Before*, ed. Lucie Armitt) use the book more as a standard against which to compare and trace the evolution of newer works than as a source of new interpretations.

36. Much as I would like to claim that my own persuasive powers and the weight of my scholarly authority swayed this vote, I should point out that such was not the case. As editors and writers in the genre, all the participants in this discussion felt that their positions as

members of the creative community of science fiction and fantasy literature gave their evaluations more validity than my own as a mere scholar. The only question was the date, which, when confirmed, shifted the vote to Le Guin.

37. Samuel R. Delany's *Ballad of Beta-2*, published in 1965, likewise explored the significance of folklore to understanding a culture. In *Ballad*, an anthropology student does space-based fieldwork to uncover the missing words from a ballad picked up by an unmanned probe. The student discovers during his fieldwork that the song is not the meaningless recombination of archaic phrases former scholars had believed. Rather, the words and phrases have gained new meanings, and the song tells the history of the space culture.

38. For this purpose, I have used versions of both articles as published in Ursula Le Guin's *The Language of the Night: Essays on Fantasy and Science Fiction*.

39. The source for this material is Ursula Le Guin, introduction to the Women's Press edition of *The Language of the Night*, but as republished in *New York Review of Science Fiction*, October 1988.

40. Le Guin, 1988, 3.

41. Two of the five times, women have been guests at Worldcons held in Boston.

42. Joanna Russ, personal correspondence, May 1994. As with Le Guin, I leave the detailed criticism of Russ's work in the hands of those who have dealt with it admirably already. I recommend in particular Sarah Lefanu, *Feminism and Science Fiction*, both for her discussion of feminist utopia (53–70) and for the chapter that focuses on Russ, "The Reader as Subject" (173–98). And, of course, Russ has discussed both the issues of women's writing (*How to Suppress Women's Writing*) and feminist utopias ("Amor Vincit Foeminam: The Battle of the Sexes in Science Fiction," *Science Fiction Studies* 7 (1980): 2–15, and "Recent Feminist Utopias," in *Future Females: A Critical Anthology*, 71–85. Both Russ articles can now be found in her *To Write like a Woman*.

43. Russ, *How to Suppress Women's Writing*. I have recorded this segment in its entirety because little seems to have changed in college writing classes in the intervening years. Women still reject their own experience, or worry that they are not "serious" writers when they produce it. Men still bring outrageous stories constructed out of Jack Kerouac and William Burroughs and expect praise for their daring misogyny.

44. Actually, some degree of this segregation by genre has occurred in Britain in the '90s. But the long tradition of inclusion does seem to permit writers of "literary" works to both write in the science fiction genre and receive acceptance by science fiction fans for their genre work. While a small but growing number of writers in North America, particularly feminists and postmodernists, have moved into using science fiction tropes in their fiction, those writers do not meet the same kind of acceptance that their British counterparts, such as Doris Lessing, have done in that country.

45. Joanna Russ, personal correspondence, May 10, 1994.

46. *Enterprising Women*.

47. Joanna Russ, April 21, 1994.

48. Suzy McKee Charnas, e-mail correspondence, May 1998.

49. Joanna Russ, April 21 1994.

## Chapter 6. Women in Science Fiction: The Backlash and Beyond

1. Joanna Russ, *Extra(Ordinary) People*, 59.

2. Lewis Shiner, "Inside the Movement: Past, Present, Future," in *Fiction 2000*, ed. George Slusser and Tom Shippey.

3. This description comes from my own observations and from the complaints of women writers whose opportunities to speak were denied them on convention panels to which they were assigned during conventions.

4. Lois McMaster Bujold, interview, World Fantasy Convention, Minneapolis, October 30, 1993.

5. Kathy Sands, interview with the Sands family, Rye, New York, March 1993. The Sandses have since sold their store and do not travel to conventions as hucksters to the extent they did when their children were young.

6. Suzy McKee Charnas, e-mail correspondence, May 28, 1998.

7. My own work, of course, may contribute to this impression, along with Henry Jenkins III's *Textual Poachers: Television Fans and Participating Culture* and articles by Constance Penley and Joanna Russ, among others.

8. The term "model building" does not quite convey the extent or magnitude of the activity in fan life. Models may be constructed from kits, but more often they are constructed out of materials selected by the builder, and may range in size from the miniature to the full-size reproduction of bridge and shuttle sets such as those regularly on display at the annual Toronto Trek convention.

9. Joanna Russ, letter, May 10, 1994.

10. Joanna Russ, letter, January 15, 1993.

11. Robert Silverberg, interview, Philadelphia, November 15, 1987.

12. Material in this section updated May 28, 1998 with the assistance of Elisabeth Waters, secretary to Marion Zimmer Bradley.

13. Jean Krevor, computer bulletin board communication, GEnie, June 22, 1996.

14. Camille Bacon-Smith, *Enterprising Women*, 203–5.

15. The comment in parentheses is a 1999 addendum to the original interview which was conducted in June 1993.

16. The irony of this claim is striking when we look at the winners of the prize for best fantasy/horror novel awarded at the World Fantasy Convention. Of the best novel prizes awarded since 1975, only two have been awarded to women alone, and only three have been awarded to women at all—Patricia McKillip received the honor in 1975 for *The Forgotten Beasts of Eld*, and Elizabeth Lynn received it in 1980 for *Watchtower*. Ellen Kushner's *Thomas the Rhymer* won in 1991, along with James Morrow's *Only Begotten Daughter*. Again, of course, we can see the pattern of the backlash laid over the granting of prizes in fantasy. More to this point, men have received the award for the fiction attributed to women in far greater numbers than women have done.

17. Connie Willis has also won a number of Hugo Awards for her short fiction, includ-

ing one for her short story, "Even the Queen," in 1993, the year she also won the best novel award.

18. "Spock Among the Women," *New York Times*, November 1984.

19. For example, the most feared man in Barrayar's secret service fears Miles's stay-at-home mom. This might seem an affectation, except that on several occasions, particularly in *Shards of Honor* and *Barrayar*, we see Cordelia in action, so we can understand the poor man's feelings exactly.

20. Lois McMaster Bujold, interview, October 30, 1993.

21. This growing parity does not extend to the short-story magazine market, where, despite a growing number of women in positions to select their work, women account for no more than 25 percent of the story market, and almost none of the feature article/column/review market. (I estimated calculations based on periodic review of tables of contents of major science fiction magazines available in local bookstores.) There is however, one exception to this situation: Marion Zimmer Bradley's *Fantasy Magazine*. Women likewise hold a more nearly equal place in the theme anthologies that have recently mushroomed on the bookstands. While a growing number of women are breaking into the horror category, this field seems to remain dominated not by men per se, but by two specific men, Stephen King and Dean Koontz.

22. Beth Meachum, interview, Boston, February 1993.

23. Minor revisions to text of interview were made by Laura Anne Gilman, December 21, 1998.

24. Follow-up telephone interview, July 23, 1996. Betsy Wollheim here refers to the children's book about the engine that succeeds against impossible odds.

25. Damon Knight, *The Futurians*.

26. At the death of Elsie Wollheim in 1996, members of the GEnie online service left messages of remembrance and condolence on the bulletin board devoted to the publishing house. Participants of the bulletin board wanted to send the messages to DAW as a demonstration of their feelings for Elsie, but were stymied when some subscribers to the service used the death of Wollheim's wife and business partner to vent their feud against Wollheim, who had died in 1990 (personal observation of interaction 1996).

27. Betsy Wollheim, telephone interview, July 23, 1998.

28. Betsey Wollheim and Sheila Gilbert, interview, San Francisco, September 1993.

### Chapter 7. Gay and Lesbian Presence in Science Fiction

1. John Clute and Peter Nichols, *The Encyclopedia of Science Fiction*, 1176.

2. ConFrancisco World Science Fiction Convention Program Book, September 1993. According to the *Encyclopedia of Science Fiction*, 417, "The Lovers" was first published in 1952 in *Startling Stories*.

3. See in particular Samuel R. Delany, *The Motion of Light in Water: Sex and Science Fiction Writing in the East Village, 1957–1965*.

4. For material on the postwar period in the history of the struggle for equal rights see John D'Emilio, *Sexual Politics, Sexual Communities: The Making of a Homosexual Minority in the*

*United States, 1940–1970.* See also articles by D'Emilio, Allan Berube, and Leila J. Rapp in *Hidden from History: Reclaiming the Gay and Lesbian Past*, ed. Martin Duberman et al.

5.  Naomi Basner and Brian Hurley, interview, Rye, New York, March 1993. Brian passed away recently, and is missed.

6.  New York: Baen Books, 1990. The title comes from the name of a well-known filksong by Leslie Fish, who also contributed a story to the volume.

7.  Don Sakers, interview, Rockville, Maryland, July 1994.

8.  Although the fan in question is no longer living, I feel it would be inappropriate to name him when the informant has asked for anonymity. I did, however, feel it important to explain to the extent possible the "scandal" of which Sakers spoke.

9.  Clute and Nichols, *Encyclopedia of Science Fiction*, 3.

10.  Forrest J Ackerman, *Gaylaxicon V Program Book*, Rockville, Maryland, 1994. As scholars of the postwar rights movement will know, the Daughters of Bilitis were not founded under that name until 1955. Reading D'Emilio's *Sexual Politics, Sexual Communities*, 102, or *Hidden from History*, ed. Duberman et al., in fact, one would assume that the group came about somewhat spontaneously at that time. It seems equally clear in reading D'Emilio, however, that he is somewhat dismissive of the women's postwar activity in bringing lesbian interests to a public forum. While not known by the name Daughters of Bilitis in 1947, the group clearly existed in some form. Ackerman refers to it by the name by which it later became known.

11.  Forrest J Ackerman, internet publication, http://www.best.com/~4forry/lesbian. htm. No date given.

12.  Joanna Russ, letter, May 10, 1994.

13.  My copy was published by Ace Books in 1967.

14.  Stephen Pagel, interview, February 1993.

15.  Titles like Heinlein's *Stranger in a Strange Land* or Herbert's *Dune* transcended their genre categories; they appealed to a large college audience drawn to their explorations of alternative lifestyles they extrapolated from the sexual revolution and drug culture of the contemporary psychedelic age.

16.  Clute and Nicholls, *Encyclopedia of Science Fiction*, 315–18. Please note that the descriptor "impenetrable" is my own. There is no indication in the *Encyclopedia* that either of its editors would endorse that adjective.

17.  This editor has asked to remain anonymous on the subject of this information, but is personally known to me as an editor working in that publishing house during the period in question.

18.  Naomi Basner, interview, Rye New York, March 1993.

19.  Melissa Scott, interview, Washington D.C., June 27, 1993.

20.  Basner, 1993.

21.  Lambda Sci-Fi: D.C. Area Gayalaxians recommended reading list at http:// members. aol.com/lambdasf/booklist.html offers this summary:

One of Ms. Bradley's "Darkover" novels, set on a lost Earth-settled planet, where humans have interbred with an indigenous, telepathic race and where the dominant culture is feudal, yet psychically advanced. This is the story of Regis Hastur, a member of Darkover's telepathic aristocracy who is awakening to his psychic powers and his gayness, and his youthful love affair with one of his subjects. (This novel also includes a gay villain.)

Bibliographies of Marion Zimmer Bradley's work are available from a variety of venues online, including http://www.mzbfm.com/mzbworks.htm

22. Slash fiction is that subgenre of media fiction devoted to sexual relationships between characters of the media source product. In most cases of slash, the sexual partners are both men: however, the pair can be any romantic combination drawn from the media source products. The name specifically means that the orthographic character "/" is used to separate the names of the partners from a television or movie product when there is a sexual relationship in the story. The ampersand is used for a friendship relationship. See *Enterprising Women* for a detailed discussion of slash fiction.

23. Ellen Kushner, *Swordspoint*.

24. Numerous sources, including Convention Book, Gaylaxicon V, Lambda Sci-Fi, 1994, 2

25. Mercedes Lackey, *Magic's Pawn*.

26. Basner, interview, 1993. Basner was a member, though not a founder, of the Network. She left the organization shortly after this interview.

27. Carl Cipra, interview, Rockville, Maryland, July 1994.

28. WisCon 21: The Gathering of the Feminist Science Fiction Community, Madison, Wisconsin (http://www.sf3.org/wiscon/, June 1997). Diversicon 5: Greater Than the Sum of Its Parts, by SF Minnesota. Diversicon's guests of honor for 1997 include Tanya Huff and Maureen McHugh, both known for their depiction of gay characters.

## Chapter 8. Youth Culture

1. In fact, my invitation to be a guest speaker at the 1996 Philadelphia Science Fiction Conference offered these two apparently contradictory panel options: "Where Did All the Young Fans Go?" which asked the question "Have we lost a generation somewhere?" and "X—the New Generation Gap" with the question "Do younger readers and writers see sf differently?"

2. To the best of my knowledge, the rise of goth culture and the concomitant breakdown of old structures seems to have been a phenomenon of the Northeast more than other parts of the country. There are other specific conventions in areas with goth populations that have accommodated the change more easily, and yet other parts of the country where concentrations of goth culture do not appear at conventions. Most of my experience, however, has been with the convention scene in the Northeast.

3. JB, interview, Baltimore, April 10, 1993

4. Valerie Steele, *Fetish: Fashion, Sex, and Power* 55.

5. The gothic/cyberpunk fans interviewed in this book maintained a tradition of naming their houses. The name then becomes a tribal identification as well. So Hollowpoint (which started out at a different house, with a somewhat different mix of people, as Cambodia) is the name not only of the house, but of the group that lives in the house.

6. Forrest Black and Amelia G. report that since this interview they have moved to California, where they write for a wide variety of publications (e-mail, January 1999).

7. See n. 5, and the discussion of Cambodia that follows.

8. Shariann (S. N.) Lewitt, correspondence, November 5, 1992.

9. Ed Kramer, update to conversation, December 1998.

10. This number, supplied in 1998, is more than double the size of the Dragon Con database in 1994, which tracks the growth of the convention. Worldcons, by contrast, seem to have shrunk to a stable figure of 5,000 over the same period.

11. Ed Kramer, taped telephone interview, November 1, 1994.

12. Figures on length of convention reflect updates to 1994 Kramer interview provided by e-mail, December 1998.

## Chapter 9. Other Sexual Identities and Fandom

1. Mark Dery, *Escape Velocity*, 183–225; Sherry Turkle, *Life on the Screen*, 210–32.

2. Howard Rheingold, *The Virtual Community*, 1–22.

3. I don't think anyone is surprised to find a footnote-bow to Donna J. Haraway here. If you haven't read "The Cyborg Manifesto," do so right now, and then go back and read the middle of this book again.

4. The work of authors such as Philip José Farmer and Theodore Sturgeon.

5. Marleen Barr, "Permissive, Unspectacular, a Little Baffling: Sex and the Single Feminist Utopian Quasi-Tribesperson," in *Erotic Universes: Sexuality and Fantastic Literature*, ed. Donald Palumbo. Ironically for a book with the word "erotic" in its title, only one or two of the articles discuss works of science fiction or fantasy with specifically erotic content. The lesbian feminists were by no means alone in putting sexual politics above sex.

6. Cecilia Tan, interview, November 1992, updated via e-mail, January 1999.

7. Cecilia Tan, *Black Feathers: Erotic Dreams*.

8. Interview at Hollowpoint, 1993. I attended the panel discussion in question, and can confirm that the report of it in this interview is substantially correct. To protect the identities of the speakers, however, I will refrain from identifying the convention other than placing it in the Northeast convention circuit during the 1992–93 convention season.

9. Cecilia Tan and Corwin, interview, Philadelphia, October 1992.

10. Cecilia Tan, e-mail, January 1999.

11. Cecilia Tan, personal communication, December 1997.

12. Cecilia Tan, interview, Philadelphia, October 1992

13. Cecilia Tan, December 1997

14. Cecilia Tan and Corwin, October 1992.

15. This group did not abandon East Coast science fiction venues until after causing major destruction in one D.C. area hotel in 1997 (Disclave '97 Official Statement of the Washington Science Fiction Association, Tuesday, May 27, 1997). The convention has been unable to find a hotel since, and has suspended convention organizing activities for the present.

16. JB, e-mail correspondence, January 1999.

17. JB, interview, April 10, 1993.

18. JB, January 1999.

### Part III. Introduction

1. Bruce Sterling, *Cheap Truth* (Austin, Texas, not copyrighted, but dated November 1986). ⟨http://www.csdl.tamu.edu/~erich/cheaptruth/⟩

2. One wonders whether Bourdieu (*The Field of Cultural Production*, 56–64) watched the rise of the cyberpunks, who did create manifestos in their polemic fanzine and in the introduction of *Mirrorshades*, edited by Bruce Sterling and who demonstrated a knowledge of the history of the field both in their fanzine, in critical articles published in the various science fiction magazines, and perhaps most eloquently, in William Gibson's "The Gernsback Continuum," a short story in *Mirrorshades*.

3. Jim Baen, interview, Riverdale, New York, December 1992.

### Chapter 10. From Fan to Pro: Getting Published

1. Howard S. Becker, *Art Worlds*, and Pierre Bourdieu, "Fields of Cultural Production," in *Fields of Cultural Production*. Bourdieu recognizes Becker's work, but claims that Becker fails to recognize the dynamic struggle for position that takes place within the field or "art world."

2. A publisher, for example, is powerful because he controls the access a writer has to the consumer field, but access gives power only because the writer has written something that requires an audience and an audience exists that is willing to pay money for the writing. A publisher who lacks writers has no product. If he has no audience, he has no money. In either case, he goes out of business and loses his power.

3. David Hartwell describes this omnivorous, undiscriminating stage of reading in *Age of Wonders* 3–17.

4. Peter Heck, interview, Orlando, September 1992. As of 1998, and under pressure from corporate owners, a few publishing houses have curtailed their reading of unsolicited manuscripts, a move that is under attack by science fiction professionals who, like Heck, fear the loss of the new talent traditionally found in the bottom of the slush pile.

5. For those who would like a more general background about publishing in which to situate this discussion, I recommend Albert N. Greco's *The Book Publishing Industry* for the "nuts and bolts" approach—very statistical—or Herbert S. Bailey, Jr.'s kinder, gentler *The Art and Science of Book Publishing*. Bailey's book is also fairly laden with diagrams and statistics, but has a more personal, wry feel to it.

6. Peter Heck, September 1992.

7. Josepha Sherman, interview, New York, December 1992.

8. Patrick Nielsen Hayden, Teressa Nielsen Hayden, Tappan King, Madeleine Robbins, and Beth Meacham, group interview, Massachusetts, February 1993.

9. Peter Heck, 1992.

10. At this point Heck also discussed the criteria for scheduling a book purchased on the basis of sample chapters and an outline. I know of no one presently making offers based on a partial manuscript over the transom—a first book by an author with no track record (pub-

lishing record in short fiction or in a related genre). A particularly promising partial may receive encouragement and a verbal promise to put the manuscript ahead of new submissions when it is finished, but I haven't seen anything more concrete in terms of an offer for a first-time partial manuscript.

11. Peter Heck, 1992. In the case of my own three novels for DAW Books, the editor did not send letters for revisions but called, and we discussed the questions and the possible solutions over the telephone. I looked at my computer file while she looked at the hardcopy manuscript, and we compromised and found specific places in the manuscript where particular fixes would fit. The choice to go with a letter or with a phone call may depend on company policy (a letter in the file gives evidence of the changes the editor wanted), how extensive the revisions are to be (mine were not extensive; more thorough revisions might be too complex to discuss on the telephone), and the particular needs of the author.

12. Jim Baen, interview, December, 1992.

13. Beth Meacham, interview, Boskone, 1993.

14. Robert LeGault, interview, Boston, 1993.

15. Tom Doherty, interview, Framingham, Massachusetts, February 1993; updated with comments April 1999.

16. Peter Heck, 1992.

17. Stephen Pagel, interview, Framingham, Massachusetts, 1993.

18. Connie Willis, *Doomsday Book* (New York: Bantam Books, 1992). (The cover referred to appeared on the September 1993 paperback edition.)

19. Ironically, Bantam is the only house, among those whose staffs I interviewed, with an official marketing department.

20. During my interview at Baen Books I observed a cover conference with the editor and publisher, both of whom assured me, with some humor, that they did not have an art department tucked in the attic with the editor and the accountant. Information from DAW comes from personal experience; Sheila Gilbert, my editor, has chosen the art for my three novels, and in casual conversation has occasionally discussed the selection of cover artists for the company's best-sellers.

21. Beth Meacham, 1993.

22. At this point, the reader may expect a section in which I discuss the work of particular authors with interviews about their work. The specifics of the art of science fiction, however, like the specifics of such forms as filksinging, fanzining, and gaming, fall too far outside my own personal experience to handle them with any kind of expertise in this book. I do hope, however, that ethnographers who follow will look at these gaps in this work as opportunities rather than flaws.

23. Ginjer Buchanan, interview, Rhode Island, 1993.

24. Stephen Pagel, 1993. Pagel works for White Wolf, the game publisher, and serves as editor for the small press Meisha Merlin Publishing, which offers titles by authors such as Storm Constantine, Tanya Huff, and co-authors Sharon Lee and Steve Miller.

25. While using the newsletter to draw attention to the lesser-known authors, Pagel also includes interviews with the best-selling writers, which will be discussed in Chapter 11.

26. Albert N. Greco gives a functional answer to this traditional return policy (pp. 27–30).

Most industry professionals I spoke to, however, refer back to a six-month promotional offer that Macmillan ran in 1949. According to these professionals, the return offer gave Macmillan such an advantage in the marketplace that other publishers had to follow with similar promotions, and no one publishing company has felt that it had sufficient clout to unilaterally modify their return policy. Some are suggesting that, with the Bertelsmann purchase of Random House, the parent company may have enough share of the market to force the needed reforms on the return policy.

27. Mike Resnick, responding to my question on the e-mail discussion list sf-lit@loc.gov, July 8, 1998.

28. This is not the case for specialty bookstores, of course, but such stores represent a very small percentage of the number of sales required to keep an author in print.

29. While Pagel claims for his tenure at B. Dalton/Barnes and Noble sales figures that exceeded the other genre fictions, *USA Today*'s list of best-selling forms of fiction put science fiction dead last, with only 6 percent of the fiction market (December 24, 1996, p.8D, as reported in *Market Share Reporter* (1998), ed. Robert S. Lazick). The figures for the report, however, take into consideration only major sellers, and not the many books with small sales that represent the majority of science fiction/fantasy sales overall. While the Science Fiction and Fantasy Writers of America struggles to find a way to introduce the smaller books into the published statistics, the superstore chains already have the information in their computers and are buying accordingly.

30. The Science Fiction Book Club, one of the Doubleday book clubs, provides an alternative to bookstores for sales. Since the book club prints its own edition and pays only a small licensing fee for the rights to print and sell the title, sales through the book club do not improve the author's position or sales figures with the publisher. For many authors (and their audiences), however, the book club is the only opportunity they have of seeing their book in a hardback edition.

31. Laura Anne Gilman, interview, Philadelphia, November 15, 1997.

32. Laura Anne Gilman, 1997; minor revisions by Gilman, 1998.

33. Just-in-time printing should not be confused with printing on demand. In the former, the publisher is simply decreasing the number of books in each print run and increasing the number of those runs. Printing-on-demand allows a third party to reprint the book and pay a fee to the publisher. Printing-on-demand books are generated one at a time and may have small variations in the print quality when compared to the publisher's print run, although the content remains the same and the on-demand copy may cost a bit more. On-demand printing should not, as a rule, affect the printing history of mass-market. publications. I believe printing on demand *will* be useful primarily in supplying difficult to find out-of-print books to a very small and select buying market. It may prove useful to small-press publishers, but that remains to be seen.

34. Spinrad is best known for his New Wave novel *Bug Jack Barron*, and for his somewhat incendiary critical essays.

35. The topic of pseudonyms in the pursuit of extended shelf life is highly sensitive both for the authors who have resorted to a pseudonym and for the publishers who directed them onto this path. Therefore I will not be quoting specific figures in the field, but will speak more generally, to preserve anonymity where it seems required. As a compromise to the needs of the readers for some examples to help document the section, I will name a few

pseudonyms, though without drawing attention to the name under which the author originally published.

36. This is consistent with Howard Gardner's assessment that it takes about ten years for any creating genius in a field to grasp a command of the domain in which he or she works. Howard Gardner, *Creating Minds: An Anatomy of Creativity*, 32: "No matter how potent such an intoxication [of the crystallizing experience], at least ten years of steady work at a discipline or craft seem required before that metier has been mastered."

37. Discussing pseudonyms in the genres, the science fiction manager of a local B. Dalton bookstore mentioned that he had recently tracked down the name under which a current hit author had published. He had ordered her earlier books because he personally liked the new ones so much, but then admitted he'd had to return the books, since they were not of a quality he felt he could sell. He took away from the experience a heightened admiration for the author because she had made such a complete transition in her work.

## Chapter 11. Best-Sellers, Short Fiction, and Niches

1. Tappan King, group discussion, February 1993. In this chapter, general best-sellers are categorized based on the *Publishers Weekly* fiction lists, hardcover or mass market paperback as indicated by the book's publication format, which represents sales figures in hundreds of thousands for hardback books and usually no less than a quarter of a million units for mass market paper. As the astute reader will gather from the earlier chapters of this book, however, those figures reflect book orders, not actual sales, which will not be computed until the return period has passed. Trade paperback lists are not discussed here. For specialized genre best-sellers, I referred to the *Locus* list of best-selling science fiction and fantasy based on polling of specialty bookstores nationwide. Best-seller status on the Locus list represents far fewer sales per title—as few as 50,000 units.

2. Tom Doherty, personal interview, Framingham, Massachusetts, 1993.

3. Laura Anne Gilman, interview, Minneapolis, November 1993, updated with minor revisions by Gilman, December 21, 1998.

4. Ginjer Buchanan, e-mail addressing the author's question about the "collapse of mass-market," December 1998.

5. Beth Meacham, interview, Framingham, Massachusetts, 1993.

6. The explosion in science fiction publishing occurred in the 1980s, and has been experiencing some cutbacks at some companies. Roc, for example, has reduced its science fiction/fantasy editorial staff by about 60 percent and now releases one or two new titles a month (Laura Anne Gilman, interview, Philadelphia, 1997). Tor Books had expanded its reach in original science fiction, and the number of licensed media tie-ins have increased to such an extent that an actual decrease in titles overall does not seem to have changed since the period of rapid industry growth in the mid-'80s.

7. Beth Meacham, e-mail, December 1998.

8. Tom Doherty, interview, 1993.

9. Tappan King, group discussion, 1993.

10. Newt Gingrich and William R. Forstchen, *1945* (Riverdale, N. Y.: Baen Books, 1995). Baen, who is a staunch supporter of Gingrich, published the conservative Republican's alternate history of World War II in hardcover with a full promotional push, but the book

itself received scathingly negative reviews and had a catastrophic quantity of returns. In its August 23, 1996 issue, Jim Baen told *Time* that he had a disastrous 97,341 copies of the title sitting in the warehouse.

11. Stephen Pagel, interview, Framingham, Massachusetts, February 1993.

12. Stephen W. Hawking, *A Brief History of Time: From the Big Bang to Black Holes*.

13. Many culture critics have claimed that culture producers create products that consciously or unconsciously promote the hegemonic agenda, which the consuming public then absorbs without discrimination or thought. It becomes clear here, however, that even when the culture producer does support the hegemony (which is in no way universal among publishers) and even when that hegemony seems popular, as the conservative vote in 1994 would have led one to believe, the culture producer still cannot make the consumer buy the product. Consumers may live within a culture while rejecting some of its forms, as they did with Gingrich's *1945*.

14. In August 1998 Tor Books released the major anthology hardback *Legends*, edited by Robert Silverberg and with shorter works set in the fictional worlds of epic fantasists such as Robert Jordan and Anne McCaffrey. While this anthology reached best-seller status at least within the genre category, it draws its target audience not from readers of short fiction but from readers of the wildly popular multivolume fantasy epics.

15. Gardner Dozois, interview, Philadelphia, September 1998.

16. Michael Swanwick, e-mail conversation, January 1999.

17. Ellen Datlow, interview, Rhode Island, 1993, with minor updates to text version, January 5, 1999.

18. Michael Swanwick, e-mail correspondence, January 1999.

19. Jane Yolen, e-mail correspondence, January 1999.

20. Martha Soukup, interview, San Francisco, September 1993. As of 1998, Martha continues to write short stories rather than novels. She has one collection, *The Arbitrary Placement of Walls*, published by DreamHaven Books in 1997.

21. The Ace Doubles of the 1960s are the best known, although I have a double from a Belmont Press published in 1958 on my shelves (James Blish's *Giants in the Earth* and Robert Silverberg's *We, the Marauders*). Tor books tried to bring back the double in the early 1990s with minimal success.

22. From a literary standpoint, *Lord of the Rings* is constructed as one novel in six parts. Because of its length, however, the work is generally published in three volumes of two parts each.

23. Gardner Dozois, September 1998.

24. In the late 1990s, under the editorships of George Scithers, founding editor of *Asimov's*, and Darrell Schweitzer, *Weird Tales* is making another comeback attempt.

25. Ellen Datlow is the former fiction editor of *Omni Magazine* and current editor of *Event Horizon*; Ginjer Buchanan is senior executive editor at Ace Books. The interview was conducted at NeCon horror convention, Rhode Island, July 1993.

26. Fiction in the short category comes in four basic lengths: the short-short story, usually

under 2,000 words; the short story, 7,500 words or less; the novelette, between 7,500 and 17,500 words; and the novella, between 17,500 and 40,000 words.

27. Martha Soukup, September 1993.

28. Kathe Koja, group interivew with Ellen Datlow and Ginjer Buchanan, Rhode Island, July 1993.

29. Lawrence Watt-Evans, e-mail correspondence, January 1999.

30. Geoffrey Landis, "A Walk in the Sun," *Asimov's Science Fiction Magazine*, October 1991.

31. The high acid content of pulp paper used in mass-market paperbacks, and in some trade paperbacks as well, causes the paper to yellow and crumble.

32. Albert N. Greco, *The Book Publishing Industry* 2.

33. Donald M. Grant publisher, June 1998 (http://www.grantbooks.com).

34. Donald M. Grant, 1998.

35. During the period Monteleone is discussing, DC Comics was well known for its gory horror comic books, which eventually led to the code of decency that cleaned up comic books in the 1950s.

36. According to Ginjer Buchanan, category horror is: "Haunted houses, haunted children, whatever. That's category horror, like there's category romance and there's category western, adult and straightforward, like there's category science fiction" (group discussion, Rhode Island, 1993).

37. Tom Monteleone, interview, NeCon, Rhode Island, July 1993.

38. Tom Monteleone, 1993.

39. Marc Michaud, interview, Rhode Island, 1993.

40. Bob Morrish, "Spotlight on Publishing—Bob Morrish Interviews Necronomicon Press," *Cemetery Dance*, Spring 1996 (http://www.necropress.com/texts/interview/htm).

41. The question of why sexual material or graphic violence should be considered "mature" while sophisticated scientific extrapolation is not is worth considering, but it does fall outside the examination we are currently conducting and must await a further study.

42. Again, to draw the distinction between self-publishing and the vanity presses, it is important to note that Tan has published widely in the erotic press; her work has appeared in several editions of *Herotica*, published by Plume Books, and she has a short story collection, *Black Feathers: Erotic Dreams* published by HarperCollins.

43. Cecilia Tan, interview, 1992, updated January, 1999.

44. Cecilia Tan, personal discussion (untaped), October 1997.

45. Slash is fiction about a sexual relationship between two media characters, such as *Star Trek*'s Kirk and Spock. The term "slash" refers to the orthographic character between the last-name initial of the two characters (K/S is erotic fiction about Kirk, "K" and Spock, "S"). While the slash can be used to identify a heterosexual pairing of media characters in an sexual relationship, it has most often been used to designate a same-sex sexual pair. See "Homoerotic Romance" in Camille Bacon-Smith's *Enterprising Women*, 228–54.

46. "Boldly Going Where Others Are Bailing Out," *Business Week* 46, April 6, 1998 (Responsive Database Services, Inc., Beachwood, Ohio, 1998); "Bertelsmann Hits a Snag in Acquisition;" *New York Times* (National Edition) 167 (51,144), B1, May 2, 1998 (Responsive Database Services, Inc.); "FTC Clears Merger Path for Publishers," *New York Times* (National Edition), 167 (51,173), B1, May 30, 1998 (Responsive Database Services, Inc.); John Marks, "A New Microsoft of American Publishing," *U.S. News & World Report* (124,13), 55.

47. Judy Quinn, "Hot Deals in a Brave New Bertelsmann World," News Bytes, *Publishers Weekly Online*, July 27, 1998

48. Sarah Lyall, "Penguin Is Buying MCA's Putnam Berkley for $336 Million," *New York Times* Late Edition, D1, November 27, 1996; Jim Milliot, "Penguin, Putnam Consolidate Sales Management," *Publishers Weekly*, Feb. 10, 1997.

49. Buchanan reminded me, during our brief discussion, that consolidations and mergers are nothing new. Ace Books itself had been an independent company before its acquisition by Berkley.

50. Laura Anne Gilman, interview, 1997.

51. Jim Emerson, "Despite the Development of New Media, Book Sales Continue to Increase and Are Projected to Reach $33 Bil/Yr by 2001," *Direct* 10(7) (May 18, 1998), 97.

52. After purchasing Columbia Pictures in 1989, Sony consistently failed to break even on the movies it produced. In 1994, it lost $3 billion dollars before contracting investment banking firm C. S. First Boston to find them a buyer for the company, now named Sony Pictures Entertainment. Casey Wian, "Sony to Walk Off Movie Set?" *Cable News Network*, November 12, 1996; "Sony Pictures on the Block," *Cable News Network*, November 12, 1996.

## Chapter 12.

1. Pierre Bourdieu, *The Field of Cultural Production*, 30.

2. Bourdieu, 29–60.

3. Brian Attebery's *Strategies of Fantasy* provides a brief description of this past in its introduction, as well as a useful bibliography of other scholary examinations of fantasy, including his own *The Fantasy Tradition in American Literature: From Irving to Le Guin*. The fact that the works in this bibliography are, for the most part, now out of print says much about the low regard in which the academy views contemporary American fantasy fiction.

4. With this description it must be clear that I am not talking about modernist literature, which is actually antimodernist literature—a critique of the very linearity of modern time. Modern literature critiques modern culture using literary techniques that are new and therefore classified as "modern" themselves. With the fantasists, however, we have the modern likewise being critiqued, but with the tools of romanticism, glossed through the pre-Raphaelites, that preceded the modern. While Attebery defines the fantasists' literature as asynchronic and therefore postmodern, those who cling to temporal delimitation of literary movements may find it more comfortable to refer to fantasy as antimodern romanticism, thus bypassing the issue of positioning the postmodern within the modern.

5. Ursula Le Guin, "The Ones Who Walk Away from Omelas," *The Wind's Twelve Quarters* (New York, Harper and Row, 1975) 224–231. (First appeared in *Dimensions 3*, 1973.)

6. In science fiction, Heinlein's 1961 book, *Stranger in a Strange Land*, which I recall as being

popular in the later '60s, and Herbert's *Dune*, a 1965 Berkley Book, were the most popular, and best-selling, of the representations of this direction.

7. ⟨http://www.bookwire.com⟩ is the combined website for *Publishers Weekly* and a variety of other serious providers of publishing information to professional audiences.

8. The Ingram list is the record of books ordered from the largest general distributor in the country, but does not take into account books ordered by the chains which have their own ordering and distribution systems ⟨http://www.writerswrite.com⟩.

9. Nina Auerbach discusses the erotic attraction, particularly for women, of vampire characters in *Our Vampires, Ourselves.*

10. Introduction to Charles De Lint's *Jack, the Giant Killer* (New York: Ace Books, 1987). The Introduction does not have an attribution, but is most likely by Terri Windling.

11. Mercedes Lackey's *Jinx High* offers the reader a young woman neopagan witch as hero/detective in a Diana Tregarde story. Tanya Huff's *Blood Price* was the first of Huff's Blood series, in which detective Vicki Nelson meets and forms a romantic and working partnership with romance writer and vampire Henry Fitzroy.

12. Patricia McKillip, *The Riddle-Master of Hed, Heir of Sea and Fire*, and *Harpist in the Wind*, now published in one volume as *The Riddle-Master; The Forgotten Beast of Eld*. Information about award, Baltimore Gun Club, LLC, *Program Book, 21st annual World Fantasy Convention*, Baltimore, 1995.

13. Patricia McKillip, *Song for the Basilisk.*

14. Contemporary authors who fall outside the science fiction/fantasy genres but who are nevertheless read avidly by practitioners of the adventure romance style within the community include Patrick O'Brian and George MacDonald Fraser, both of whom write in the style of the period in which their adventure romances are set.

15. Steven Brust, *Five Hundred Years After*; Pamela Dean, *Tam Lin* (New York: Tor Books, 1991).

16. Personal interview with the Scribblies writers' group—Steven Brust, Emma Bull, Pamela Dean, and Will Shetterly (Kara Dalkey was not present)—founders, with, among others, Jane Yolen, of the pointed ironic literary jest, the Pre-Joycean Fellowship, which aligns them with the pre-Raphaelite movement updated to their own time.

17. Attebery, *Strategies of Fantasy*, 36–50.

18. Chitra Banerjee Divakaruni, *The Mistress of Spices.*

19. Sources for the historical summary of this section include David Hartwell, *Age of Wonders*, and Brian Aldiss, *Trillion Year Spree.*

20. Here I rely on the above, and also on John Clute's and Peter Nichols's *Encyclopedia of Science Fiction* and on personal memory and my own library dating from the period of the New Wave. The reader who notices that the names mentioned here are all of men should be aware that the New Wave was primarily a male phenomenon, with a few women, such as Pamela Zoline, who earn a footnote in the movement. Like cyberpunk, this may be a function of a semiconscious exclusion of women. Ursula Le Guin, writing at the same time and with a social science sensibility, seems to have worked outside the purview of the New Wave. The New Wave did, however, open up an acceptance of literary science fiction that the women's movement of the 1970s could exploit for its own purposes.

21. Melissa Scott, *Burning Bright* (1993) and *Trouble and Her Friends* (1994).

22. Shariann Lewitt, *Memento Mori*.

23. Greg Bear, *Blood Music*.

24. Lewitt, *Memento Mori*.

25. Kim Stanley Robinson, *The Wild Shore* (1985), *The Gold Coast* (1988), and *Pacific Edge* (1990). Tor Books has more recently reissued the entire series in trade paperback through its reprint series, Orb.

26. Kim Stanley Robinson, *Red Mars* 196–98.

27. Michael Bishop, *Count Geiger's Blues* (New York: Orb, 1994; Tor, 1992).

28. *Program Book, 21st Annual World Fantasy Convention*.

29. To be consistent with the award itself, I have included only living fantasists who have contributed to the world of fantasy for at least twenty years. Thus, fantasists like Angela Carter would now be disallowed, and Isabel Allende would be considered too new to receive a lifetime award.

30. *Program Book, 21st Annual World Fantasy Convention*, 6–10.

31. Both Ursula Le Guin and Connie Willis have won more Hugos, but not in hard science fiction. Willis has won more Hugos than any other woman in the history of the award, all but one in short fiction, including the 1997 award for her short story "The Soul Selects her Own Society . . . " Willis was co-winner for best novel for *Doomsday Book*, tying for the honor in 1993 with Vernor Vinge for his *A Fire upon the Deep*.

32. Sharecropping is the term generally used in the industry to denote an author of lesser status making money for a publisher by working with someone else's ideas or creations rather than with original ones of his own. The term is reserved for building on the works of other writers of science fiction literature, and does not carry over to describe writers of media tie-ins.

33. The situation is not as bad in fantasy, which had its explosive growth after the golden age of most of the science fiction Old Guard. There is only one Tolkien, of course, and his estate has been parsimonious in granting licenses to use the Tolkien name, so fans must satisfy themselves with books marked "in the style of" rather than "in the Rings Universe by J. R. R. Tolkien."

34. The name used for writers of the Nancy Drew mystery stories from the 1930s to the present.

35. As of 1998, TSR Books is no longer owned by TSR, the company that brought out the original Dungeons and Dragons, but has been purchased by Wizards of the Coast.

36. "Work made for hire" contracts stipulate that the amount paid up front constitutes full payment for all rights to the work created under the contract. The author of the work retains no rights to any of the work, including any of the characters he or she may have created in the course of producing the work.

37. As I write this chapter in late 1998, Leroy Dubeck, chess grand master and former president of the United States Chess Federation, has been asked by the Franklin Mint to create a completely revised set of rules for playing three-dimensional *Star Trek* chess, to accompany the games the memorabilia company sells under a licensing agreement with

Paramount. I have not, as yet, concluded whether this constitutes the sublime or the ridiculous, but I suspect it may baffle science by taking up both ends of the spectrum at the same time.

38. A number of industry professionals of my acquaintance write *X-Files* fan fiction under pseudonyms on the net and even, occasionally, in the fanzines. I have myself participated in a round robin story with about a dozen other writers, many professionals, that was subsequently published in a fanzine under a single pseudonym.

### Appendix

1. Howard Rheingold, *The Virtual Community*, 117–21.

# Bibliography

Abrahams, Roger. "Play in the Face of Death: Transgression and Inversion in a West Indian Wake." In *The Many Faces of Play*, ed. Kendall Blanchard. Association for the Anthropological Study of Play. Champaign, Ill.: Human Kinetics Publishers, 1986.

Agar, Michael H. *The Professional Stranger: An Informal Introduction to Ethnography.* Orlando, Fla.: Academic Press, 1980.

Aldiss, Brian W. with David Wingrove. *Trillion Year Spree: The History of Science Fiction.* New York: Avon Books, 1986.

Apter, Emily and William Pietz, eds. *Fetishism as Cultural Discourse.* Ithaca, N.Y.: Cornell University Press, 1993.

Armitt, Lucie, ed. *Where No Man Has Gone Before: Women and Science Fiction.* London-New York: Routledge, 1991.

Attebery, Brian. *The Fantasy Tradition in American Literature: From Irving to Le Guin.* Bloomington: Indiana University Press, 1980.

———. *Strategies of Fantasy.* Bloomington: Indiana University Press, 1992.

Auerbach, Nina. *Our Vampires, Ourselves.* Chicago: University of Chicago Press, 1995.

Bacon-Smith, Camille. "Batman: The Ethnography." In *The Many Lives of the Batman: Critical Approaches to a Superhero and His Media*, ed. Roberta E. Pearson and William Uricchio. New York: Routledge, 1991.

———. "Breaking the Frame: Intrusion on a Costume Event." Annual Meeting of the American Folklore Society, Cincinnati, Ohio, 1985.

———. *Enterprising Women: Television Fandom and the Creation of Popular Myth.* Philadelphia: University of Pennsylvania Press, 1992.

———. "Spock Among the Women." *New York Times Book Review*, November 16, 1986.

Bailey, Herbert S., Jr. *The Art and Science of Book Publishing.* 3rd ed. Athens: Ohio University Press, 1990.

Bainbridge, William Sims. *Dimensions of Science Fiction.* Cambridge, Mass.: Harvard University Press, 1986.

Bakhtin, Mikhail M. *Rabelais and His World*. Trans. Hélène Iswolsky. Bloomington: Indiana University Press, 1984 (1968).

Barr, Marleen S. *Lost in Space: Probing Feminist Science Fiction and Beyond*. Chapel Hill: University of North Carolina Press, 1993.

——. "Permissive, Unspectacular, a Little Baffling: Sex and the Single Feminist Utopian Quasi-Tribesperson." In *Erotic Universe: Sexuality and Fantastic Literature*, ed. Donald Palumbo. Westport, Conn.: Greenwood Press, 1986.

Barthes, Roland. *The Fashion System*. Trans. Matthew Ward and Richard Howard. Berkeley: University of California Press, 1990 (1967).

——. *Mythologies*. Trans. Annette Lavers. New York: Hill and Wang, 1972 (1957).

——. *S/Z*. Trans. Richard Miller. New York: Hill and Wang, 1974 (1970).

——. *Writing Degree Zero*. Trans. Annette Lavers and Colin Smith. New York: Hill and Wang, 1968 (1953).

Bascom, William. "The Forms of Folklore: Prose Narrative." *Journal of American Folklore* 78 (1965): 3–20.

Baudrillard, Jean. *Fatal Strategies*. Trans. Philip Beitchman and W. G. J. Niesluchowski. New York: Semiotexte, 1990 (1983).

——. *Selected Writings*. Ed. Mark Poster. Stanford, Calif.: Stanford University Press, 1988.

Bear, Greg. *Blood Music*. New York: Ace Books, 1985.

Becker, Howard S. *Art Worlds*. Berkeley: University of California Press, 1982.

Bellman, Beryl Larry and Bennetta Jules-Rosette. "Perception as Lived Experience: Do They See It Differently?" In Bellman and Jules-Rosette, *A Paradigm for Looking: Cross-Cultural Research with Visual Media*. Norwood, N.J.: Ablex, 1977.

Ben-Amos, Dan. "Analytic Categories and Ethnic Genres." *Genre* 2, 3 (1969): 275–301.

——. "Toward a Definition of Folklore in Context." *Journal of American Folklore* 84 (1971): 3–15.

Benedikt, Michael, ed. *Cyberspace: First Steps*. Cambridge, Mass.: MIT Press, 1991.

Benjamin, Walter. *Illuminations*. Ed. Hannah Arendt, trans. Harry Zohn. New York: Schocken Books, 1969 (1923–50, posthumous).

Bennett, Tony. *Outside Literature*. New York: Routledge, 1990.

Berger, John. *Ways of Seeing*. New York: Viking Press, 1973 (1972).

Bester, Alfred. *The Demolished Man*. New York: Timescape/Pocket Books, 1978 (1953).

Birdwhistell, Ray L. *Kinesics and Context: Essays on Body Motion Communication*. Philadelphia: University of Pennsylvania Press, 1970.

Bishop, Michael. *Count Geiger's Blues*. New York: Orb, 1994 (Tor, 1992).

Bourdieu, Pierre. *The Field of Cultural Production: Essays on Art and Literature*. Ed. Randal Johnson. New York: Columbia University Press. 1993.

——. *In Other Words: Essays Toward a Reflexive Sociology*. Trans. Matthew Adamson. Stanford, Calif.: Stanford University Press, 1990.

——. *Language and Symbolic Power.* Ed. John B. Thompson, trans. Gino Raymond and Matthew Adamson. Cambridge, Mass.: Harvard University Press, 1994.

Boswell, Thom. *The Costume-Maker's Art: Cloaks of Fantasy, Masks of Revelation.* Asheville, N.C.: Lark Books, 1992.

Brooke-Rose, Christine. *A Rhetoric of the Unreal: Studies in Narrative and Structure, Especially of the Fantastic.* Cambridge: Cambridge University Press, 1981.

Browning, Frank. *The Culture of Desire: Paradox and Perversity in Gay Lives Today.* New York: Crown, 1993.

Brust, Steven. *Five Hundred Years After.* New York: Tor Books, 1994.

——. *The Phoenix Guards.* New York: Tor Books, 1992.

Caillois, Roger. *Man, Play, and Games.* Trans. Meyer Barash. New York: Schocken Books, 1979.

Castle, Terry. *Masquerade and Civilization: The Carnivalesque in Eighteenth-Century English Culture and Fiction.* Stanford, Calif.: Stanford University Press, 1986.

Caughey, John L. "Imaginary Social Relationships in Modern American." *American Quarterly* 30, 1 (Spring 1978): 70–89.

——. *Imaginary Social Worlds: A Cultural Approach.* Lincoln: University of Nebraska Press, 1984.

Cawalti, J. "The Concept of Formula in the Study of Popular Literature." *Journal of Popular Culture* 3 (1969): 381–403.

Chambers, Iain. *Popular Culture: The Metropolitan Experience.* London and New York: Methuen, 1986.

Chapman, Antony J. and Hugh C. Foot. *Humour and Laughter: Theory, Research, and Applications.* London and New York: John Wiley, 1976.

Chodorow, Nancy. *The Reproduction of Mothering: Psychoanalysis and the Sociology of Gender.* Berkeley: University of California Press, 1978.

Clareson, Thomas D., ed. *SF: The Other Side of Realism, Essays on Modern Fantasy and Science Fiction.* Bowling Green, Ohio: Bowling Green University Popular Press, 1971.

Clute, John and Peter Nicholls. *The Encyclopedia of Science Fiction.* New York: St. Martin's Press, 1995 (1993).

Constitution of the World Science Fiction Society. Article II, Section 2 and 3, published in the Program Book of ConStellation, the 41st World Science Fiction Convention. Baltimore, June 1983.

Culler, Jonathan. *Structuralist Poetics: Structuralism, Linguistics, and the Study of Literature.* Ithaca, N.Y.: Cornell University Press, 1975.

Czikszentmihalyi, Mihaly. *Beyond Boredom and Anxiety.* San Francisco: Jossey-Bass, 1975.

Davis, Fred. *Fashion, Culture, and Identity.* Chicago: University of Chicago Press, 1992.

Dean, Pamela. *Tam Lin.* New York: Tor Books, 1991.

Debord, Guy. *Society of the Spectacle.* New York: Zone Books, 1994.

Delany, Samuel R. *Ballad of Beta-2.* New York: Ace Books, 1965.

——. *Dhalgren*. Hanover, N.H.: Wesleyan University Press, 1996.

——. *The Einstein Intersection*. New York: Ace Books, 1967.

——. *The Motion of Light in Water: Sex and Science Fiction Writing in the East Village, 1957– 1965*. New York: Arbor House / W. Morrow, 1988.

De Lint, Charles. *Jack, the Giant Killer*. New York: Ace Books, 1987.

D'Emilio, John. *Sexual Politics, Sexual Communities: The Making of a Homosexual Minority in the United States, 1940–1970*. Chicago: University of Chicago Press, 1983.

Derrida, Jacques. *Writing and Difference*. Trans. Alan Bass. Chicago: University of Chicago Press, 1978.

Dery, Mark. *Escape Velocity: Cyberculture at the End of the Century*. New York: Grove Atlantic, 1996.

——, ed. *Flame Wars: The Discourse of Cyberculture*. Durham, N.C.: Duke University Press, 1993. Special issue of *South Atlantic Quarterly* (Fall 1993).

de Saussure, Ferdinand. *Course in General Linguistics*. Ed. Charles Bally and Albert Sechehaye with Albert Reidlinger, trans. Wade Baskin. New York: McGraw Hill, 1959 (1915).

Divakaruni, Chitra Banerjee. *The Mistress of Spices*. New York: Anchor Books, 1997.

Duberman, Martin Bauml, Martha Vicinus, and George Chauncey, Jr., eds. *Hidden from History: Reclaiming the Gay and Lesbian Past*. New York: Meridian Books, 1989.

DuPlessis, Rachel Blau. *The Pink Guitar: Writing as Feminist Practice*. New York: Routledge, 1990.

Eco, Umberto. *Semiotics and the Philosophy of Language*. Bloomington: Indiana University Press, 1986.

Fiedler, Leslie A. *Love and Death in the American Novel*. New York: Scarborough Books, 1966 (1960).

Farb, Peter. *Word Play: What Happens When People Talk*. New York: Knopf, 1974.

Fine, Gary Alan. *Shared Fantasy: Role-Playing Games as Social Worlds*. Chicago: University of Chicago Press, 1983.

——. "Legendary Creatures and Small Group Culture: Medieval Lore in a Contemporary Role-Playing Game." *Keystone Folklore* 24, 1 (1984).

Firth, Raymond. *Symbols: Public and Private*. Ithaca, N.Y.: Cornell University Press, 1973.

Foster, Hal, ed. *The Anti-Aesthetic: Essays on Postmodern Culture*. Port Townsend, Wash.: Bay Press, 1983.

Fox, Steven. "Theoretical Implications for the Study of Interrelationships Between Ritual and Play." In *Play and Culture: 1978 Proceedings of the Association for the Anthropological Study of Play*, ed. Helen B. Schwartzman. West Point, N.Y.: Leisure Press, 1980.

Friedrich, Paul. *The Meaning of Aphrodite*. Chicago: University of Chicago Press, 1978.

Gaines, Jane. "Women and Representation: Can We Enjoy Alternative Pleasure?" In *American Media and Mass Culture: Left Perspectives*, ed. Donald Lazere. Berkeley: University of California Press, 1987.

Gardner, Howard. *Creating Minds: An Anatomy of Creativity Seen Through the Lives of Freud, Einstein, Picasso, Stravinsky, Eliot, Graham, and Gandhi.* New York: Basic Books, 1993.

——. *The Unschooled Mind: How Children Think and How Schools Should Teach.* New York: Basic Books, 1991.

Geertz, Clifford. *The Interpretation of Cultures: Selected Essays.* New York: Basic Books, 1973.

Gennep, Arnold van. *Rites of Passage.* Trans. Monika B. Vizedom and Gabrielle Caffee. Chicago: University of Chicago Press, 1960 (1909).

Georges, Robert A. and Michael O. Jones. *People Studying People: The Human Element in Fieldwork.* Berkeley: University of California Press, 1980.

Gibson, William. "The Gernsback Continuum." In *Mirrorshades: The Cyberpunk Anthology*, ed. Bruce Sterling. New York: Arbor House, 1986.

Gilligan, Carol. *In a Different Voice: Psychological Theory and Women's Development.* Cambridge, Mass.: Harvard University Press, 1982.

Goffman, Erving. *Frame Analysis: An Essay on the Organization of Experience.* New York: Harper Colophon Books, 1974.

——. *The Presentation of Self in Everyday Life.* Garden City, N.Y.: Doubleday Anchor Books, 1959.

——. *Relations in Public: Microstudies of the Public Order.* New York: Harper Colophon Books, 1971.

Goldstein, Kenneth S. *A Guide for Fieldworkers in Folklore.* Hatboro, Pa.: Folklore Associates, 1964.

Gombrich, E. H. "The Use of Art for the Study of Symbols." In *Psychology and the Visual Arts: Selected Readings*, ed. James Hogg. Baltimore: Penguin, 1969.

——. "Visual Discovery Through Art." In *Psychology and the Visual Arts: Selected Readings*, ed. James Hogg. Baltimore: Penguin, 1969.

Gossen, Gary H. "Verbal Dueling in Chamula." In *Speech Play*, ed. Barbara Kirshenblatt-Gimblett. Philadelphia: University of Pennsylvania Press, 1976. pp. 121–46.

Grahn, Judy. *Another Mother Tongue: Gay Words, Gay Worlds.* Boston: Beacon Press, 1984.

Greco, Albert N. *The Book Publishing Industry.* Boston: Allyn and Bacon, 1997.

Green, Rayna. "Magnolias Grow in Dirt: The Bawdy Lore of Women." *Southern Exposure* 4, 4 (1977).

Gross, Larry. "Life Vs. Art: The Interpretation of Visual Narratives." Paper prepared for the U.S.-Hungarian Conference on Social Perception and Interpretation of Interaction in Literature, Budapest, 1983.

Grossberg, Lawrence, Cary Nelson, and Paula A. Treichler, eds. *Culture Studies.* New York: Routledge, 1992.

Gubar, Susan. "Representing Pornography: Feminism, Criticism, and Depictions of Female Violation." *Critical Inquiry* 13 (1987): 712–41.

Gumperz, John J., ed. *Language and Social Identity.* Cambridge: Cambridge University Press, 1982.

Hafner, Katie and Matthew Lyon. *Where Wizards Stay Up Late: The Origins of the Internet.* New York: Touchstone, 1996.

Hall, Edward T. *The Dance of Life: The Other Dimension of Time.* Garden City, N.Y.: Anchor Books, 1983.

——. *The Hidden Dimension.* Garden City, N.Y.: Anchor Books, 1990 (1966).

——. "Proxemics." *Current Anthropology* 9 (1968): 93–95.

——. *The Silent Language.* Garden City, N.Y.: Anchor Books, 1981 (1959).

Hall, Stephanie. "Monsters and Clowns: A Deaf American Halloween." *Folklife Annual* 90, ed. James Hardin. Washington, D.C.: American Folklife Center at the Library of Congress, 1991. pp. 122–31.

——. "Reality Is a Crutch for People Who Can't Deal with Science Fiction: Slogan-Buttons Among Science Fiction Fans." *Keystone Folklore* 34 (1989): 19–31.

Hall, Stuart. "Culture, the Media, and the Ideological Effect." In *Mass Communication and Society*, ed. James Curran, Michael Gurevitch, and Janet Woollacott. London: Edward Arnold, 1977.

——. "Subcultures, Cultures, and Class: A Theoretical Overview." In *Resistance Through Rituals: Youth Subcultures in Post-War Britain*, ed. Stuart Hall and Tony Jefferson. London: Hutchinson, 1976.

Haraway, Donna J. "The Cyborg Manifesto." In Haraway, *Simians, Cyborgs, and Women: The Reinvention of Nature.* New York: Routledge, 1991.

Hartwell, David G. *Age of Wonders: Exploring the World of Science Fiction.* New York: McGraw-Hill, 1985.

Hawking, Stephen W. *A Brief History of Time: From the Big Bang to Black Holes.* New York: Bantam Books, 1998.

Hebdige, Dick. *Subculture: The Meaning of Style.* London: Methuen, 1979.

Heilbrun, Carolyn G. *Reinventing Womanhood.* New York: Norton, 1979.

Heim, Michael. "The Erotic Ontology of Cyberspace." In *Cyberspace: First Steps*, ed. Michael Benedikt. Cambridge, Mass.: MIT Press, 1991.

Heinlein, Robert A. *Stranger in a Strange Land.* New York: Putnam, 1961.

Herbert, Frank. *Dune.* New York: Berkeley, 1965.

Herdt, Gilbert, ed. *Gay Culture in America: Essays from the Field.* Boston: Beacon Press, 1992.

Hesbois, Laure. *Les jeux de langage.* Ottawa: Editions de l'Université d'Ottawa, 1986.

Holland, Dorothy and Naomi Quinn, eds. *Cultural Models in Language and Thought.* Cambridge: Cambridge University Press, 1987.

Horney, Karen. *Feminine Psychology.* Ed. Harold Kelman. New York: Norton, 1967.

Huff, Tanya. *Blood Price.* New York DAW Books, 1991.

Huizinga, Johan. *Homo Ludens: A Study of the Play Element in Culture.* Boston: Beacon Press, 1967 (1950).

Hymes, Dell. *"In vain I tried to tell you": Essays in Native American Ethnopoetics.* Philadelphia: University of Pennsylvania Press, 1981.

———. *Foundations in Sociolinguistics: An Ethnographic Approach.* Philadelphia: University of Pennsylvania Press, 1974.

———. *Language in Culture and Society: A Reader in Linguistics and Anthropology.* New York: Harper and Row, 1964.

———. "Narrative Form as a 'Grammar of Experience'." *Journal of Education* 164, 2 (1982): 121–42.

———, ed. *Reinventing Anthropology.* New York: Pantheon, 1972.

Jenkins, Henry III. "*Star Trek* Rerun, Reread, Rewritten: Fan Writing as Textual Poaching." *Critical Studies in Mass Communication* 5, 2 (1988): 85–107.

———. *Textual Poachers: Television Fans and Participatory Culture.* New York: Routledge, 1992.

Jones, Diana Wynne. *The Tough Guide to Fantasyland.* New York: DAW Books, 1996.

Jones, Steven. "A Sense of Space: Virtual Reality, Authenticity, and the Oral." *Critical Studies in Mass Communication* 10, 3 (September 1993).

Kadushin, Charles. "Networks and Circles in the Production of Culture." In *The Production of Culture*, ed. Richard A. Peterson. Beverly Hills, Calif.: Sage Publications, 1976. pp. 107–22.

Kalčik, Susan J. " . . . 'like Ann's gynecologist or the time I was almost raped': Personal Narratives in Women's Rap Groups." In *Women and Folklore: Images and Genres*, ed. Claire R. Farrer. Austin: University of Texas Press, 1975. pp. 3–11.

Kaplan, E. Ann. *Women and Film: Both Sides of the Camera.* New York: Methuen, 1983.

Kirshenblatt-Gimblett, Barbara. "Speech Play and Verbal Art." In *Play and Learning*, ed. Brian Sutton-Smith. New York: Gardner Press, 1979. pp. 219–37.

———, ed. *Speech Play: Research and Resources for the Study of Linguistic Creativity.* Philadelphia: University of Pennsylvania Press, 1976.

Knight, Damon. *The Futurians.* New York: John Day, 1977.

———. *Why Do Birds.* New York: Tor Books, 1992.

Kornbluth, C. M. "The Marching Morons." *Omni* (October 1980).

Korzybski, Alfred. *The Manhood of Humanity.* Lakeville, Conn.: International Non-Aristotelian Library Publishing Company, 1950 (1921).

———. *Science and Sanity: An Introduction to Non-Aristotelian Systems and General Semantics.* Lakeville, Conn.: International Non-Aristotelian Library Publishing Company, 1958 (1933).

Kramarae, Cheris, ed. *Technology and Women's Voices: Keeping in Touch.* New York: Routledge and Kegan Paul, 1988.

Kress, Nancy. *Beggars in Spain.* New York: William Morrow, 1993.

Kroeber, Theodora. *Alfred Kroeber: A Personal Configuration.* Berkeley: University of California Press, 1970.

——. *Ishi in Two Worlds: A Biography of the Last Wild Indian in North America*. Berkeley: University of California Press, 1961.

Kroker, Arthur and David Cook. *The Postmodern Scene: Excremental Culture and Hyper-Aesthetics*. New York: St. Martin's Press, 1986.

Kuhn, Thomas. *The Structure of Scientific Revolutions*. Chicago: University of Chicago Press, 1970 (1962).

Kushner, Ellen. *Swordspoint*. New York" Arbor House, 1987.

——. *Thomas the Rhymer*. New York: Morrow, 1990.

Lackey, Mercedes. *Jinx High*. New York: Tor Books, 1991.

——. *Magic's Pawn*. New York: DAW Books, 1989.

Lakoff, George and Mark Johnson. *Metaphors We Live By*. Chicago: University of Chicago Press, 1980.

Lamb, Patricia Frazer. "Romance, Eroticism, and/or Hurt-Comfort: What's Really Going On Here?" Paper delivered at the 1986 National Women's Studies Conference, Urbana, Ill.

Lamb, Patricia Frazer and Diana Veith. "Romantic Myth, Transcendence and Star Trek Zines." In *Erotic Universe: Sexuality and Fantastic Literature*, ed. Donald Palumbo. Westport, Conn.: Greenwood Press, 1986. pp. 235–89.

Lefanu, Sarah. *Feminism and Science Fiction*. Bloomington: Indiana University Press, 1989.

Le Guin, Ursula K. *Dancing at the Edge of the World*. New York: Grove Press, 1989.

——. *The Dispossessed*. New York: Avon Books, 1975.

——. *The Language of the Night: Essays on Fantasy and Science Fiction*. Ed. Susan Wood. New York: Perigee Books, 1979.

——. *The Left Hand of Darkness*. New York: Ace Books, 1969.

——. "The Ones Who Walk Away from Omelas." *Dimensions 3* (1973). Reprinted in *The Wind's Twelve Quarters*, 224–31. New York: Harper and Row, 1975.

Lévi-Strauss, Claude. *The Savage Mind*. Chicago: University of Chicago Press, 1973 (1962).

Lewitt, Shariann. *Memento Mori*. New York: Tor Books, 1995.

Lichtenberg, Jacqueline, Sondra Marshak, and Joan Winston. *Star Trek Lives!* New York: Bantam Books, 1975.

Lüthi, Max. *The European Folktale: Form and Nature*. Trans. John D. Niles. Philadelphia: Institute for the Study of Human Issues, 1982 (1947).

Lynn, Elizabeth A. *Watchtower*. New York: Berkley, 1979.

Lyotard, Jean-François. *The Postmodern Condition: A Report on Knowledge*. Trans. Geoff Bennington and Brian Massumi. Minneapolis: University of Minnesota Press, 1989.

Malzberg, Barry N. *The Engines of the Night: Science Fiction in the Eighties*. Garden City, N.Y.: Doubleday, 1982.

Marks, Elaine and Isabelle de Courtivon, eds. *New French Feminisms: An Anthology*. New York: Schocken Books, 1980.

McCaffery, Larry, ed. *Storming the Reality Studio: A Casebook of Cyberpunk and Postmodern Science Fiction*. Durham, N.C.: Duke University Press, 1991.

——. *Across the Wounded Galaxies: Interviews with Contemporary American Science Fiction Writers*. Urbana: University of Illinois Press, 1990.

McCaffrey, Anne and Mercedes Lackey. *The Ship Who Searched*. New York: Baen Books, 1992.

McKillip, Patricia A. *The Forgotten Beast of Eld*. New York: Athenaeum, 1974.

——. *The Riddle-Master*. New York: Ace Books, 1999.

——. *Song for the Basilisk*. New York: Ace Books, 1998.

Miller, Nancy K., ed. *Poetics of Gender*. New York: Columbia University Press, 1986.

Modleski, Tania. *Loving with a Vengeance: Mass Produced Fantasies for Women*. Hamden, Conn.: Archon Books, 1982.

——, ed. *Studies in Entertainment: Critical Approaches to Mass Culture*. Bloomington: Indiana University Press, 1986.

Morgan, David. "Culture Work and Friendship Work: The Case of 'Bloomsbury.' " *Media, Culture, and Society* 4 (1982): 19–32.

Morrow, James. *Only Begotten Daughter*. San Diego: Harcourt Brace, 1996.

Moskowitz, Sam. *Seekers of Tomorrow: Masters of Modern Science Fiction*. Cleveland: World Publishing Company, 1966.

Mukarovskỳ, Jan. *Structure, Sign, and Function: Selected Essays*. Trans. John Burbank and Peter Steiner. New Haven, Conn.: Yale University Press, 1978.

Mulvey, Laura. "Visual Pleasure and Narrative Cinema." *Screen* 16, 3 (1975): 6–18.

Mussell, Kay. *Fantasy and Reconciliation: Contemporary Formulas of Women's Romance Fiction*. Westport, Conn.: Greenwood Press, 1984.

Nichols, Bill. *Ideology and the Image: Social Representation in the Cinema and Other Media*. Bloomington: Indiana University Press, 1981.

Ortner, Sherry B. and Harriet Whitehead, eds. *Sexual Meanings: The Cultural Construction of Gender and Sexuality*. Cambridge: Cambridge University Press, 1981.

Palumbo, Donald, ed. *Erotic Universe: Sexuality and Fantastic Literature*. Westport, Conn.: Greenwood Press, 1986.

Parrinder, Patrick. *Science Fiction: Its Criticism and Teaching*. London: Methuen, 1980.

Paulson, Ronald. *The Fictions of Satire*. Baltimore: Johns Hopkins University Press, 1967.

Pike, Kenneth L. "Towards a Theory of the Structure of Human Behavior." In *Language in Culture and Society: A Reader in Linguistics and Anthropology*, ed. Dell Hymes. New York: Harper and Row, 1964.

Powell, Chris and George E. C. Paton, eds. *Humour in Society: Resistance and Control*. New York: St. Martin's Press, 1988.

Pratt, Annis. *Archetypal Patterns in Women's Fiction*. Bloomington: Indiana University Press, 1981.

Propp, Vladimir. *Morphology of the Folktale*. Trans. Laurence Scott. Austin: University of Texas Press, 1968 (1928).

Radway, Janice. "Interpretive Communities and Variable Literacies: The Function of Romance Reading." *Anticipations, Proceedings of the American Academy of Arts and Sciences* 113, 3 (1984): 49–73.

——. *Reading the Romance*. Chapel Hill: University of North Carolina Press, 1984.

Raymond, Eric, ed. *The New Hacker's Dictionary*. Cambridge, Mass.: MIT Press, 1991.

Redfern, Walter. *Puns*. Oxford: Basil Blackwell, 1984.

Rheingold, Howard. *The Virtual Community: Homesteading on the Electronic Frontier*. Reading, Mass.: Addison-Wesley, 1993.

Rimmon-Kenan, Shlomith. *Narrative Fiction: Contemporary Poetics*. London: Methuen, 1983.

Roberts, Robin. *A New Species: Gender and Science in Science Fiction*. Urbana: University of Illinois Press, 1993.

Robinson, Kim Stanley. *The Gold Coast*. New York: Tor Books, 1988.

——. *Pacific Edge*. New York: Tor Books, 1990.

——. *Red Mars*. New York: Bantam Spectra, 1993.

——. *The Wild Shore*. New York: Ace Books, 1985.

Ross, Andrew. *Strange Weather: Culture, Science, and Technology in the Age of Limits*. London: Verso, 1991.

Rushkoff, Douglas. *Cyberia: Life in the Trenches of Cyberspace*. San Francisco: HarperSanFrancisco, 1994.

Russ, Joanna. "Amor Vincit Foeminam: The Battle of the Sexes in Science Fiction." *Science Fiction Studies* 7 (1980): 2–15.

——. *Extra(Ordinary) People*. New York: St. Martin's Press, 1984.

——. *The Female Man*. Boston: Beacon Press, 1986 (1975).

——. *How to Suppress Women's Writing*. Austin: University of Texas Press, 1983.

——. *Picnic on Paradise*. New York: Ace Books, 1968.

——. *To Write like a Woman: Essays in Feminism and Science Fiction*. Bloomington: Indiana University Press, 1995.

——. *The Zanzibar Cat*. New York: Baen Books, 1984.

Russell, W. M. S. "Folktales and Science Fiction." Presidential Address. *Folklore* 93 (1982).

——. "More About Folktales and Literature." Second Presidential Address. *Folklore* 94 (1983).

Sahlins, Marshall. *Culture and Practical Reason*. Chicago: University of Chicago Press, 1976.

Said, Edward W. *The World, the Text, and the Critic*. Cambridge, Mass.: Harvard University Press, 1983.

Sakers, Don, ed. *Carmen Miranda's Ghost Is Haunting Space Station Three*. New York: Baen Books, 1990.

Salmond, Anne. "Theoretical Landscapes: On Cross-Cultural Conceptions of Knowledge." In *Semantic Anthropology*, ed. David Parkin. New York: Academic Press, 1982.

Salmonson, Jessica Amanda. *What Did Miss Darrington See? An Anthology of Feminist Supernatural Fiction*. New York: Feminist Press of the City of New York, 1989.

Sapir, Edward. *Language: An Introduction to the Study of Speech*. New York: Harcourt Brace Jovanovich, 1921.

Sargent, Pamela, ed. *Women of Wonder: The Classic Years: Science Fiction by Women from the 1940s to the 1970s*. San Diego: Harcourt Brace and Co., 1995.

Schwartzman, Helen B., ed. *Play and Culture: 1978 Proceedings of the Association for the Anthropological Study of Play*. West Point, N.Y.: Leisure Press, 1980.

——. "Sociocultural Context of Play." In *Play and Learning*, ed. Brian Sutton-Smith. New York: Gardner Press, 1979.

Scott, Melissa. *Burning Bright*. New York: Tor Books, 1993.

——. *Trouble and Her Friends*. New York: Tor Books, 1995.

Sedgwick, Eva Kosofsky. *Between Men: English Literature and Male Homosocial Desire*. New York: Columbia University Press, 1985.

Shiner, Lewis. "Inside the Movement: Past, Present, Future." In *Fiction 2000: Cyberpunk and the Future of Narrative*, ed. George Slusser and Tom Shippey. Athens: University of Georgia Press, 1992.

Showalter, Elaine, ed. *The New Feminist Criticism: Essays on Women, Literature, and Theory*. New York: Pantheon Books, 1985.

——. "Piecing and Writing." In *The Poetics of Gender*, ed. Nancy K. Miller. New York: Columbia University Press, 1986. pp. 222–47.

Singer, Jerome and Dorothy Singer. "The Value of the Imagination." In *Play and Learning*, ed. Brian Sutton-Smith. New York: Gardner Press, 1979.

Slusser, George and Tom Shippey, eds. *Fiction 2000: Cyberpunk and the Future of Narrative*. Athens: University of Georgia Press, 1992.

Smith-Rosenberg, Carroll. "The Female World of Love and Ritual: Relations Between Women in Nineteenth-Century America." *Signs* 1 (Autumn 1975): 1–29.

Spacks, Patricia Ann Meyer. *The Adolescent Idea: Myths of Youth and the Adult Imagination*. New York: Basic Books, 1981.

——. *The Female Imagination*. New York: Knopf, 1975.

——. *Gossip*. New York: Knopf, 1985.

Spinrad, Norman. *Bug Jack Barron*. New York: Walker, 1969.

Spradley, James P. *Participant Observation*. New York: Holt, Rinehart and Winston, 1980.

Staicar, Tom. *The Feminine Eye: Science Fiction and the Women Who Write It*. New York: Frederick Ungar, 1982.

Stallybrass, Peter and Allon White. *The Politics and Poetics of Transgression*. Ithaca, N.Y.: Cornell University Press, 1986.

Steele, Valerie. *Fetish: Fashion, Sex, and Power*. New York: Oxford University Press, 1996.

Stenger, Nicole. "Mind Is a Leaking Rainbow." In *Cyberspace: First Steps*, ed. Michael Benedikt. Cambridge, Mass.: MIT Press, 1991.

Sterling, Bruce, ed. *Mirrorshades: The Cyberpunk Anthology.* New York: Arbor House, 1986.

Stern, Leslie. "The Body as Evidence: A Critical Review of the Pornography Problematic." *Screen* 23, 5 (1982): 39–62.

Stewart, Susan. *Crimes of Writing: Problems in the Containment of Representation.* New York: Oxford University Press, 1991.

——. *On Longing: Narratives of the Miniature, the Gigantic, the Souvenir, the Collection.* Durham, N.C.: Duke University Press, 1993 (1984).

Stoll, Clifford. *The Cuckoo's Egg: Tracking a Spy Through the Maze of Computer Espionage.* New York: Doubleday, 1989.

——. *Silicon Snake Oil: Second Thoughts on the Information Highway.* New York: Doubleday, 1995.

Stone, Allucquère Rosanne. " 'Will the Real Body Please Stand Up?' Boundary Stories About Virtual Cultures." In *Cyberspace: First Steps*, ed. Michael Benedikt. Cambridge, Mass.: MIT Press, 1991.

Stone, Kay F. "The Misuses of Enchantment: Controversies in the Significance of Fairy Tales." In *Women's Folklore, Women's Culture*, ed. Rosan A. Jordan and Susan J. Kalčik. Philadelphia: University of Pennsylvania Press, 1985. pp. 125–45.

——. "Things Walt Disney Never Told Us." In *Women and Folklore: Images and Genres*, ed. Claire Farrer. Austin: University of Texas Press, 1975. pp. 42–50.

Sutton-Smith, Brian. "Creativity and the Vicissitudes of Play." *Adolescent Psychiatry* 15 (1988): 307–18.

——. "Games of Order and Disorder." Paper presented at the annual meeting of the American Anthropological Association, 1972.

——. "In Search of the Imagination." In *Imagination and Education*, ed. Kieran Egan and Dan Nadaner. New York: Teachers College Press, 1987.

——. "The Metaphor of Games in Social Science Research." In *Play, Play Therapy, Play Research*, ed. Rimmert van der Kooij and Joop Hellendoorn. International Symposium, Amsterdam, 1995. Berwyn, Pa.: Swets North America, 1986. pp. 35–65.

——, ed. *Play and Learning.* New York: Gardner Press, 1979.

——. "Reversible Childhood." *Play and Culture* 2 (1989): 52–63.

Sutton-Smith, Brian and Diana Kelly-Byrne, eds. *The Masks of Play.* New York: Leisure Press, 1984.

Tan, Cecilia. *Black Feathers: Erotic Dreams.* New York: HarperPerennial, 1998.

Tedlock, Dennis. *The Spoken Word and the Work of Interpretation.* Philadelphia: University of Pennsylvania Press, 1983.

Thomas, Sari, ed. *Film / Culture: Explorations of Cinema in Its Social Context.* Metuchen, N.J.: Scarecrow Press, 1982.

Thompson, Bill. *Sadomasochism: Painful Perversion or Pleasurable Play?* London: Cassell, 1994.

Toelken, Barre. "Folklore, Worldview and Communication." In *Folklore: Performance and Communication*, ed. Dan Ben-Amos and Kenneth S. Goldstein. The Hague: Mouton, 1975.

Tomas, David. "Old Rituals for New Space: Rites de Passage and William Gibson's Cultural Model of Cyberspace." In *Cyberspace: First Steps*, ed. Michael Benedikt. Cambridge, Mass.: MIT Press, 1991.

Turkle, Sherry. *Life on the Screen: Identity in the Age of the Internet*. New York: Touchstone Books, 1995.

——. *The Second Self: Computers and the Human Spirit*. New York: Simon and Schuster, 1984.

Turnbull, Colin. "Learning Non-Aggression." In *Learning Non-Aggression*, ed. Ashley Montague. New York: Oxford University Press, 1978. pp. 161–221.

Turner, Victor. *Dramas, Fields, and Metaphors: Symbolic Action in Human Society*. Ithaca, N.Y.: Cornell University Press, 1974.

——. *The Drums of Affliction*. Oxford: Clarendon Press, 1968.

——. *The Forest of Symbols*. Ithaca, N.Y.: Cornell University Press, 1967.

——. "Liminal to Liminoid in Play, Flow, and Ritual: An Essay in Comparative Symbology." In *The Anthropological Study of Human Play*, ed. Edward Norbeck. Rice University Studies 60, 3. Houston, Tex.: Rice University, 1974. pp. 53–92.

——. *Revelation and Divination in Ndembu Ritual*. Ithaca, N.Y.: Cornell University Press, 1975.

——. *The Ritual Process: Structure and Anti-Structure*. Ithaca, N.Y.: Cornell University Press, 1969.

Turner, Victor and Edith L. B. Turner. *Image and Pilgrimage in Christian Culture: Anthropological Perspectives*. New York: Columbia University Press, 1978.

Vance, Carole S., ed. *Pleasure and Danger: Exploring Female Sexuality*. Boston: Routledge and Kegan Paul, 1984.

Vinge, Vernor. *A Fire upon the Deep*. New York: Tor Books, 1992.

West, Alan, Colin Martindale, and Brian Sutton-Smith. "Age Trends in the Content of Children's Spontaneous Fantasy Narratives." *Genetic, Social, and Psychological Monographs* 111 (1984): 389–405.

Whorf, Benjamin Lee. *Language, Thought, and Reality: Selective Writings of Benjamin Lee Whorf*. Ed. John B. Carroll. Cambridge, Mass.: MIT Press, 1954.

Williams, Raymond. *Television: Technology, and Cultural Form*. New York: Schocken Books, 1975.

Williamson, Judith. *Consuming Passions: The Politics and Images of Popular Culture*. New York: Marion Boyars, 1986.

Willis, Connie. *Doomsday Book*. New York: Bantam Books, 1992.

——. "The Women SF Doesn't See." *Isaac Asimov's Science Fiction Magazine*, October 1992.

Willis, Walt. "The Harp in Oopsla." Installment 13, *Oopsla* 12 (March/April 1954). Reprinted in *Warhoon 28*, ed. Redd Boggs. New York, 1978.

Willis, Walt. "The Harp Stateside, or Over There with Grunch and Eggplant." In *Warhoon 28*, ed. Redd Boggs, 145–224. New York, 1978.

Willis, Walt and Bob Shaw. "The Enchanted Duplicator: The Tale of Jophan's Epic Odyssey from Mundane to the Tower of Trufandom. 1954. Reprinted in *Warhoon 28*, ed. Redd Boggs. New York, 1970.

Worth, Sol, ed. *Studying Visual Communication*. Ed. Larry Gross. Philadelphia: University of Pennsylvania Press, 1981.

Worth, Sol and John Adair. *Through Navajo Eyes: An Exploration in Film Communication and Anthropology*. Bloomington: Indiana University Press, 1972.

Wright, Will. *Six Guns and Society: A Structural Study of the Western*. Berkeley: University of California Press, 1975.

Zelazny, Roger. *Lord of Light*. New York: Avon, 1967.

Zoline, Pamela. "The Heat Death of the Universe." *New Worlds*. Reprinted in *The Heat Death of the Universe and Other Stories*. Kingston, N.Y.: McPherson, 1988.

# Index

Thompson, Becky, 23
Tocqueville, Alexis de, 54
Tolkien, J. R. R., 101, 115, 203, 244–47, 249
Tor Books, 35, 85, 93, 125, 127, 193, 196, 198, 201, 214, 217, 230–31, 240, 248
Tortelluci, Phil, 61
Trimble, Bjo, 82, 97–98, 111
Turkle, Sherry, 63
Turner, Jim, 66–68

Usenet, 64–65, 77–78, 82, 84–85, 89–90, 181–82

Van Gelder, Gordon, 227–28
Veal, Tom, 23
Vess, Charles, 168
Vinge, Joan D., 109
Von Holtzbrinck, Georg, 240

Wagner, Karl Edwards, 49
Wagner, Mitch, 74–75
Watt-Evans, Lawrence, 78, 228
Wells, Monty, 17–18
Whalen, Michael, 58
Wilhelm, Kate, 100, 106, 109
Williams, Charles, 245
Williams, Tad, 131, 248
Willis, Connie, 120, 200

Willis, Walter, 11, 98
Windling, Terri, 226, 250–51
Wollheim, Betsy, 42, 128–34
Wollheim, Donald, 9, 75, 124, 128–34
Wollheim, Elsie, 128–29
World Science Fiction Convention (Worldcon), 3, 11–12, 15, 17–19, 22–23, 25–59, 31–34, 38, 41–42, 44, 56–62, 65, 87, 96, 97, 100–102, 104, 109, 127, 131, 135, 139–41, 148–49, 153, 166–68
World Wide Web, 2, 77, 84–85, 87–88, 142, 144; web browser, 84; website, webpage, 29, 64, 79, 84–86, 89–90, 137, 176; websurfing, 85–88. *See also* Internet
Wrede, Patricia, 121–22
Wynn, A. A., 128

*X-Files*, 262

Yalow, Ben, 12–19, 22, 26–29, 56, 100, 111–12
York, Chris, 32, 33
York, J. Steven, 32, 33

Zelazny, Roger, 49, 102–3, 115, 158, 252
Zetterberg, Julie, 59
zine. *See* fanzine
Zone, The (game), 157, 161, 165, 174

# Acknowledgments

It would be impossible to mention all the people who contributed to this book, but I'd like to make a special thank you to JB and the gothic community at Hollowpoint for their willingness to share their lives. Ben Yalow, who probably knows more about hotels and science fiction conventions than anyone else on the planet, shared his knowledge with me over the space of two years. Susan Shwartz and the Genie crew helped me through all the years I spent there, learning about online community in its early stages and its maturity.

From the publishing industry I received more cooperation than I would have believed possible. My special thanks go to Daw and Tor, to the folks at Ace and Roc, and to Gardner at *Asimov's* for never failing to answer my questions or set me straight when I had it completely wrong!

Thank you all for your support, your insight, and your kind permission to share your words with the readers of this book. Special thanks to Barb Wright, for reading and proofing and shoring me up when it looked like the book would never end, and to Leroy Dubeck, who kept us both fed at Susanna Foo. And a special dedication to Dave, who has put up with an author and an academic for a mother with humor and support for most of his life.

Interviews, e-mail conversations, and discussions are quoted with the permission of the participants.